PROCEEDINGS

OF THE

WORKSHOP ON THE POLITICAL ECONOMY OF CONFEDERATION

Institute of Intergovernmental Relations

and

Economic Council of Canada

The findings of the papers and the discussants' comments
are the personal responsibility of the authors and, as
such, have not been endorsed by Members of the Economic
Council of Canada, or the Institute of Intergovernmental
Relations.

Donald Gordon Centre for Continuing Education
Queen's University, Kingston, Ontario
November 8 - 10, 1978

Catalogue No. EC22-66/1979   Canada: $6.50
ISBN 0-660-10201-3   Other countries: $7.80

CONTENTS

iv

FOREWORD

It is now over two years since the election of the Parti
Québécois government. At that time a referendum was thought to
be coming in two years' time, and it looked as though one of the
most momentous decision points in our history was almost upon us.
Many individuals and organizations felt an urgent need to communicate to the Quebec public, and to the Canadian public at large, and
say what they thought it was important to know before Quebecers
voted one way or the other. After a few months' lag there was a
flurry of conferences; a National Unity Task Force was commissioned;
work began within the Quebec government analysing forms of
sovereignty-association and their implications; inside the federal
government, in the Federal-Provincial Relations Office, the
"Co-ordination" group was formed to develop a federal position;
the C.D. Howe Research Institute started an ambitious program of
about a dozen studies to be published *seriatim* over the coming
months; Canada West Foundation set up a work program, as did many
other individuals and groups around the country. Political scientists
re-emphasized their already strong commitment to study of the political structure and dynamics of the federation.

The members of the Economic Council also felt that they wanted
to contribute. It was obvious that the Council could not give a
rounded view on the issues as a whole, since so many of the relevant
questions in the national unity debate were outside of economics.
But the Council felt that it could contribute some economic information, or economic intelligence, to help put the economics part of
the debate on as good a factual basis as was possible in the nature
of the case. A set of Confederation papers were prepared under the
direction of Dr. Neal Swan.

Resources of finance and personnel, however, were limited, and
it was not possible to attempt coverage of all the important economic
aspects of Confederation in the time thought to be available. For
this and other reasons the Council decided not to try to produce a
publication of its own -- a "consensus" document. Instead, it decided
that a workshop to discuss the findings of a number of research
efforts would be a useful way for results to be made available. In
this fashion each study could be seen in context and relation to
others, and critical on-the-spot review could be given by other
professionals working in the area.

After discussion with the Institute of Intergovernmental
Relations at Queen's University it was decided that the format should
be a joint workshop with them, to be held at Queen's University.
This joint venture made it possible to take a broader perspective

on the questions relative to the debate on Confederation, by including
a mixture of economic, historical and political science papers.

It should be emphasized that the choice of this method of
dissemination of the research results was made at some risk that
the individual researchers would draw conclusions from their analysis
with which Council members of the Economic Council and the Institute
of Intergovernmental Relations, or any other person for that matter,
might legitimately disagree. Thus, the Council and the Institute
do not necessarily subscribe to the findings of any of the papers in
these proceedings, but present them in the interest of informing the
general public of some of the issues at stake.

INTRODUCTION

This introduction has two purposes. One is to provide a background to the economics papers, since these tend to be rather more technical than the others, with a view to helping in understanding them and in assessing their relevance to the current debate on the future of Confederation in Canada. We consider matters such as: the appropriate selection of hypothetical future "scenarios"; reservations that could be made to the analyses because of their relative neglect of dynamic factors; the distinction between what is knowable about the economic future with greater or lesser clarity and certainty; the role and significance of assumptions in economic analysis for those who are not closely familiar with the methods that practising economists adopt; and the relative importance of economic versus non-economic factors. This part of the introduction draws heavily upon the address given by Dr. Ostry, Chairman of the Economic Council of Canada, in opening the workshop.

The second purpose is to provide some indication of the objectives of each of the papers individually, of the main conclusions reached, and occasionally of the path from the one to the other. Such a quasi-summarizing exercise should make it easier to capture the main messages of the workshop as a whole and will permit those who would prefer to study in depth only a limited number of the papers to make an appropriate selection among them.

Seven of the twelve papers in this volume are on economic questions. As stated in the foreword, these were intended by the Economic Council to provide economic information or "economic intelligence," in order to help put the economics part of the debate on an improved factual basis. It may be, however, that an assured factual basis is not possible for a broad range of economic issues because of the complexity of the forces in play, the imperfections of data, and the incomplete state of the science of economics. This is particularly so for large structural changes in economic arrangements for which comparative economic history provides some guidance, but only some.

An extremely important purpose of such economic intelligence work is presumably to inform voters in a Quebec referendum of relevant economic facts, as well as citizens in the rest of the country to the extent that their readiness to accept change in federalism might influence the relative attractiveness of the alternatives facing Quebec voters. The ideal technique is fairly clear. It would involve contrasting the expected economic performance of federalism with the expected performance of a fractured country, however each of these is defined. How do the alternatives look for Quebec? For

viii

other parts of the country? A second purpose, mentioned in the
Chairman's opening address as having been stressed by the Economic
Council in commissioning its part of the work, was to analyse
possible changes in those aspects of the Canadian economic system
whose alleged malfunctioning might have been influential in bringing
on the present crisis.

The first, "information providing," task requires some attempt
to define relevant alternatives or scenarios. Two alternatives are
federalism and separation. On the latter, fractured country
alternative, the papers do not give extensive consideration to
sovereignty <u>with</u> association. The reasons for this, given by Ostry
in her opening address, were, first, that the economics research
itself soon showed that "Rump Canada," in Clarence Barber's superbly
inelegant phrase, would have little to gain over the long haul from
association, so that the possibility of it's happening seemed vanishingly
small; and, second, that the nature of the association concept was
very difficult to pin down, especially during the first half of the
P.Q. government's term, the time when the research was being done.
Nevertheless, it should be emphasized that it is possible for those
who wish to do so to make some applications of the analysis in the
papers to the sovereignty-association alternative. Equally, Ostry
added, the possibility of a *fédéralisme* that was radically *renouvelé*
was considered most unlikely. But that did not mean that improvements
were impossible in the economic sphere -- far from it. Nor did the
improbability of sovereignty-association mean that no economic links
whatsoever could exist. Indeed, one of the most important features
of Canadian economic institutions and policies, particularly in
federal-provincial roles and relations, has been their change over
time in response to changing priorities and circumstances.

In considering alternative scenarios it was considered less
useful to contrast alternatives for the system as a whole than to
contrast alternatives for control over each of four economic variables
that largely define how much economic "sovereignty," or "independence,"
a province or a nation has. Moreover, sovereignty in the economic
sphere is not only multidimensional, it is also continuously variable,
rather than being there or not there, in the four economic dimensions.
These dimensions are the tax and expenditure system, the external
trade system, the monetary system, and the conventions regarding
factor mobility. The principal analysis is done for these four
dimensions, but some analysis is also provided regarding the exercise
of such other important kinds of policy as regulation, expenditure
structure and non-tariff foreign trade policy. On the tax and expenditure system: the present federal arrangement gives Quebec a partial
say on taxes and expenditure in Quebec and a partial say on taxes

and expenditure outside Quebec; independence, with or without association, would give Quebec full say within Quebec and no say outside; and a Swiss style confederation would fall in between. On external trade: Quebecers at present share power with others in Canada to decide upon a common external tariff and commercial policy; with independence, Quebec might gain zero extra sovereignty in this area (a Common Market agreement), or some extra sovereignty (a free trade area), or full extra sovereignty (no trade association at all). On the monetary system: the shared jurisdiction of Quebecers with other Canadians might be left as it is with no gain in sovereignty (monetary union), or there could be a partial increase in sovereignty by means of a separate currency but a fixed exchange rate, or a bigger increase by means of a separate and floating currency. On factor mobility: the Quebec government exercises no present control over movement of people and capital into Quebec from Canada, although the Quebec people share control with other Canadians over immigration from abroad. Independence could go with varying degrees of sovereignty here, depending on whether Quebec control on foreign immigration of people was supplemented by control over immigration from the rest of Canada or control over capital movements or both.

Thus, in doing research on a particular issue concerning change in constitutional arrangements it is only necessary to take into account those changes in each of the four dimensions of economic sovereignty that are relevant to the issue at hand. The papers need to be read with this is mind. For example, in studying the implications of changes in control over the tax and expenditure system for taxes paid by Quebecers it is not very important what one assumes about monetary union. But for trade flows a wider spectrum of changes in the economic components defining independence needs to be examined. Consequently the scenarios in the papers often vary according to the topic being looked at.

A *caveat* concerning all the papers given, and particularly stressed by Ostry in her opening address, is that some of the relevant economic facts cannot be uncovered by the current tools of economic analysis, powerful though they be. If these particular facts are important, in that they could seriously influence living standards and unemployment in Quebec or elsewhere, they would dwarf into insignificance the conventional facts in either this volume or the work of others such as the C.D. Howe Institute, the Parti Québécois and the federal government.

The Economic Council Chairman was referring to what Maynard Keynes called "the animal spirits" of entrepreneurs and to the unpredictability of human reactions in crisis. These could play a key, albeit a questionably predictable role in the event of separation. If capital was withdrawn in large amounts from Quebec by businessmen and others, the impact on employment and income in Quebec -- and indeed in the rest of Canada -- could be more significant than any economic factor analysed at the workshop. Equally, if independence liberated a spirit of dynamic co-operation within Quebec, as some péquistes have argued, that could also be of dominating importance. Ostry's point was that there are dynamic factors whose impact is both potentially large and in practice unknowable. How does one allow for such dynamic uncertainties? She did not know, but felt a serious uneasiness about not being able to do so. Consequently, it is important to keep firmly in mind that the analyses presented in this volume are not the whole story. It is possible that they are less significant than the "undoable" analysis.

The inability to allow for dynamic factors, stressed by Ostry, is not the only caveat concerning the analyses at the workshop. In most of the economics papers the reader will observe that a number of assumptions are made, under which the analysis is carried on. They vary widely in plausibility. Does that mean that none of the results can be trusted?

It does not, but it does mean that proper interpretation of them needs great care, if one is not to be misled. Some examples will il-lustrate. In Glynn's paper, "The Net Provincial Expenditures Asso-ciated with Federal Government Expenditures, and Fiscal Autonomy," certain calculations are made about the increase in the taxes necessary to sustain an unchanged level of government services in an independent Quebec. Glynn assumes, for purposes of this calculation, that the unemployment rate would not be changed by separation from that ruling in the year to which his data relate. That seems to be an important assumption, because if separation brought a higher unemployment rate the consequent fall in tax collections and rise in unemployment insurance payments would mean an increased tax burden in Quebec greater than Glynn calculates, and conversely if separation brought a lower unemployment rate. What Glynn is doing is deliberately ignoring the influence on tax levels of the unemployment rate variable, despite the fact that he knows it to be important. He does this so that the effect of changes in the variable he is chiefly interested in -- the degree of control by the provincial government over the tax and expenditure system -- can be isolated for "inspection," as it were. This practice, of isolating the effect of one variable by assuming the other variables to be constant (the procedure of ceteris paribus in the jargon), is standard in economics work, and is a substitute for what some natural scientists do in physically controlling the conditions under which they do their experiments. The conclusion that a lead ball and a goose feather accelerate under gravity at the same rate in a perfect vacuum is not made less useful by the fact that air resistance is "assumed to be zero," and Glynn's conclusions about tax levels are not made less useful by the fact that changes in the unemployment rate are "assumed to be zero."

Glynn also assumes that the tobacco tax is paid by consumers of tobacco. What that means is that any new extra tax on a pack of cigarettes, say of ten cents, would raise the price by the full amount of that tax, i.e., ten cents. It need not be so: tobacco producers might absorb some of the increase, either by not raising the price as much as ten cents, or by foregoing all or part of a price increase that they had been planning to implement in the absence of the new tax. This is a different kind of assumption from the previous one, since Glynn would undoubtedly have preferred to use an accurate estimate about how much an extra tax raises the price, rather than an assumption about it. Here is a second role for assumptions, to provide information about numbers whose size is unknown because the necessary research has not been done. Where different values for such unknown numbers ("parameter values," in the jargon) might make a big difference to the final answer, more than one assumption may be tried, as Glynn does for the number describing how much of the corporation tax is passed on in higher prices. This "information role" for assumptions need not always be numerical. In calculating changes in trade flows it makes a difference whether producers compete mainly on price or mainly on quality and brand. Empirical evidence exists on this, but it is not conclusive. Hazledine, in his paper "The Costs and Benefits of the Canadian Customs Union," makes different assumptions in this respect from those made by Auer and Mills in their paper "Confederation and Some Regional Implications of the Tariffs on Manufactures." This makes for differences in their results even when they study comparable separation scenarios.

Perhaps the most common general assumption in economic analysis, made in all the economic papers presented at the workshop and usually accepted without question in other contexts, is that of individualistic self-seeking behaviour by economic agents ("maximizing of profit and utility" in the jargon). Such behaviour is often equated by economists with "economic rationality." In the context of economic analysis of the possible separation of Quebec this may be a riskier assumption than usual. A particular example is the role of this assumption in the paper by Hazledine, and in

the main body of the analysis in the paper of Auer and Mills. In
both cases it is supposed that separation would not be followed by
a complete cessation of trade (a trade embargo) between Quebec and
the rest of Canada. The implicit basis for this assumption is that
a trade embargo would not be in the self-interest of either producers
or consumers. With this assumption, the calculated employment
changes are quite small. Without it, employment losses could be
very much larger, as Auer and Mills show in a brief analysis of the
trade embargo case. Analysts who implicitly or explicitly drop the
assumption of self-seeking economic rationality will arrive at very
different results for the impact of separation from those presented
in this volume.

A final point, of surpassing importance, is testified to by the
inclusion in this volume of six papers by historians and political
scientists. The study of economic questions alone cannot give a
rounded view of the issues in the debate on confederation. Many of
the relevant issues are not economic, but lie in the realms of
language, culture, political structure, and philosophical cleavage
on whether the ideal country should coincide with a nation, or whether
more than one nation can and perhaps should co-exist within a single
country. The non-economic papers in the volume offer some perspective
on these wider issues and an introduction to a number of key points
related to them. Indeed, a careful reading of these proceedings as
a whole may lead some to conclude that it would be better, on both
theoretical and practical grounds, to switch the emphasis in the
debate from economic to non-economic matters.

* * * * *

Dr. Hazledine, a staff member of the Economic Council of Canada,
began the workshop with his paper: "The Costs and Benefits of the
Canadian Customs Union." In retrospect, a title like "Certain Costs
and Benefits of the Canadian Customs Union" rather than "The Costs..."
would have conveyed the contents more accurately. Hazledine's basic
purpose is to find out whether the fiscal independence and changes
in tariff arrangements accompanying a departure of Quebec from Canada
would significantly affect living standards there. He is not concerned
with the effects on living standards of other changes that might
accompany separation, e.g. any alterations in the flows of investment
funds in and out of Quebec whose effects would have to be added to,
or subtracted from, those estimated in the paper. He also poses the
same questions regarding fiscal and tariff changes for each of four
other regions. If Ontario left, and all the rest, including Quebec,
stayed, how would Ontario living standards change? What if the
Atlantic region left? the Prairie provinces? British Columbia?

The effect of the fiscal and tariff changes on living standards depends on the details of the scenario examined. Under Option 1, the scenario Hazledine treats most fully, a separate Quebec would impose the Canadian level of tariffs on imports from the rest of Canada, as would the rest of Canada on Quebec; a new Quebec currency would exist and would be devalued or revalued as necessary to achieve an acceptable balance of payments; Quebec would gain access to all federal tax sources but correspondingly lose all present federal expenditures; and government policies or market forces would be used to achieve some small degree of adjustment of wage levels in Quebec relative to post-separation Canada. An important "informational" type assumption is made by Hazledine; that companies typically sell in markets where competition is on the basis not just of price but also of product quality characteristics. These are not the only characteristics and assumptions of Hazledine's option 1, but they are probably the ones that are most important for determining the size of the living standard effects he finds. Those who feel, for example, that monetary union rather than devaluation of a new currency should be an element in a future scenario will find the results less interesting than those who believe that separation would involve a new currency.

Option 1 shows changes in living standards that are large by conventional standards in economics, though perhaps smaller than popular opinion might have suspected. Quebec's "real absorption" -- the total available economic pie -- drops by $1.5 billion, or about 5 per cent of gross domestic product. Option 1 for other regions gives respectively: in British Columbia a $0.7 billion loss, in the Prairies a $0.7 billion gain, in Ontario a $2.4 billion gain, and in Atlantic Region a $1.6 billion loss.

Hazledine also considers two other options in his work but presents only partial results (initial balance of payments and employment effects). One of these options is unilateral free trade; the other, done for Quebec alone, is a separation scenario in which Quebec and the rest of Canada maintain a free trade area, but Quebec keeps the present tariff levels on other countries, and the rest of Canada goes to free trade.

Robin Boadway, a discussant for Hazledine's paper, finds the results of this study "much as one would expect," given the existing trade flows among the regions. He comments on the sensitivity of the results to the particular formulation of the model and considers alternative techniques for modelling the problem.

Dr. Auer and Miss Mills (A and M) are interested in certain

xiv

aspects of the question: who are the gainers and losers from the present Canadian tariff? In posing such a question one has to specify the alternative state of the world against which the effects of the present tariff are to be measured. A and M choose four such alternatives. The first occupies the bulk of the paper and relates to a Canada that remains united. Once the general techniques have been established by analysis of this case, three other alternatives, all of which deal with variants of Quebec separation, are quickly dealt with.

A and M's first alternative is a Canada in which tariffs have been removed, and in which sufficient time has elapsed for companies affected by the resulting fall in selling prices to reduce their output (occasionally to the point of going out of business) and lay off workers, and for selling prices in the stores to have come down as a result of the lower customs duties. It is also assumed that the time period is too short for displaced workers to have found alternative jobs, and too short for devaluation or any other policy measures to be able to affect employment or price levels. A and M comment that defining their alternative in this way serves the useful function, ancillary to that of identifying gainers and losers from the present tariff, of highlighting the size of the adjustment problem in manufacturing, if free trade were to come.

In A and M's free trade world some people have lost their jobs for a while, but all people are paying lower prices for what they buy. The lower prices occur disproportionately, however, on food and clothing, tariffs on these being higher than average. That means that the poor, who spend a higher-than-average proportion of their income on food and clothing, are disproportionately benefited by tariff removal. In fact, one widely-used definition of the number of individuals in poverty is to count those who spend more than 70 per cent of their income on food, clothing and shelter. A and M show that the number of people in poverty, defined this way, declines considerably after tariff removal. Thus, tariff removal puts some people out of work but at the same time raises some people out of poverty; it is the comparison of these two effects that constitutes the heart of the paper.

The key results are in Table 10. It shows that free trade would raise more Canadians out of poverty than it would put out of work, and that this is true for eight of the ten provinces, including Quebec. The variation by province is such that the implicit "poverty cost" of the tariff relative to the temporary employment losses avoided is much lower in Ontario, Manitoba and Price Edward Island than in the other provinces.

A and M next examine three separation scenarios, giving numerical results in Table 11 for employment losses, but not for consumer gains. The hostile trade boycott scenario, a possible but perhaps unlikely eventuality, shows severe employment losses. What A and M call a "tit-for-tat" scenario is comparable to Hazledine's scenario 1 as regards the assumed tariff changes, though not in certain other respects. Here Quebec and Canada both impose the present Canadian tariffs not just on the rest of the world, but also on each other. A short-run job loss of 41,000 results in Quebec, and 23,000 in the rest of Canada. Under either of these two scenarios no consumer benefits would appear. The remaining scenario, the "mixed" policy, has Quebec putting tariffs on Canadian goods, as well as on those from the rest of the world, but Canada opting for complete free trade. Quebec suffers the same short-run employment loss of 41,000 as under "tit-for-tat," while Canada loses many more jobs, 165,000, but will now have substantial consumer gains as well.

Victor Corbo, the discussant for this paper, comments on certain methodological aspects of A and M's analysis. He feels it is dangerous to use the nominal tariff as an indicator of effective tariff protection to the provinces and, generally, questions Dr. Auer's attempt to extrapolate from Canadian to provincial data.

The third workshop paper, by Mr. Glynn, takes up an important consequence of separation that has received surprisingly little attention in the debate in recent months. In a separate Quebec, with or without association, either tax levels or the availability of government services, or both, would have to change. The same would be true for any other province that left the confederation. The neglected question is just how big such tax or expenditure changes would have to be. Since, as mentioned, they will occur even with association, they should be of great interest to both parties to the debate.

No one can answer this kind of question exactly, or for the long term. But one can get a reasonably good approximation for the short term, say during the first year or so after a separation.

Mr. Glynn attempts to calculate, in effect, by how much a finance minister in a newly independent Quebec, or any other newly independent province, would have to change taxes or expenditures in the first budget after independence. He also attempts to convey the meaning of the necessary changes by pointing out how they would affect tax dollars paid by families at different income levels.

The methods used are standard and fairly uncontroversial in the sense that, though reasonable men can make different assumptions at many points in the analysis, much the same broad quantitative results come out. Glynn's baseline for comparison is an independence scenario in which the objective is to retain all government services that were available before independence. These services include, for example, old age pensions, unemployment insurance benefits, defence, the post office, agricultural subsidies, and so forth. In a province like Quebec a major part of the post-independence bill for providing these services could be met from the province's newly acquired access to previously federal taxes. But since the share of federal taxes collected in Quebec is less than Quebec's share of the value of federal services received, maintaining those services would require tax increases. Similarly, an independent Ontario could reduce taxes. Glynn works out the size of these tax changes.

An important result for Quebec is that total taxes would need to rise by about $2 billion a year (Table 6), or about a $1,000 rise in yearly taxes paid per family. Table 8 shows that total tax collections from three major sources, income tax plus general sales tax plus corporation taxes, come to about $4,000 per family in Quebec, so that the $1,000 increase is very substantial relative to current tax levels. Figures for what would happen if other provinces became independent are also given.

The distributional implications of the $1,000 tax change are shown in Table 8. Financing the increase in Quebec through the income tax leaves poor families with less than $6,000 a year not much affected, but the upper middle group, $15,000 - $20,000, would pay $1,650 more, and the over $20,000's over $4,340 more. Since these increases, as Glynn puts it, "far exceed what has normally been the practice of Ministers of Finance to adopt on their budgets," he closes by exploring a scenario for Quebec in which expenditures are cut substantially in order to keep tax increases within bounds. The results (in Table 11) show that this can be done, but that the result is a very marked increase in the regressivity of the tax/expenditure system as a whole, with the poor now bearing a much greater proportion of the adjustment burden.

David Perry, in discussing this paper, focusses his remarks on the technical aspects of Glynn's approach and argues that the distribution of federal revenues and expenditures was performed at a level of aggregation too high to yield precise results. He emphasises that these results, based upon information from a single year, will reflect the presence of certain institutional factors of a transitional

nature. He expresses his worry that the results, as presented, will
be accepted by many readers as being completely accurate predictions.

* * * * *

A survey of the attitudes and opinions of 51 influential persons
in Nova Scotia, conducted by two Queen's professors, G. Rawlik and
G. Perlin, shows that these leaders are staunch Canadians and enthu-
siastic Maritimers. 80 per cent regard themselves as Canadians
first, but as one respondent remarks, "this is accompanied by a very
strong provincial identity."

Sixty-nine per cent of the group surveyed believes that
Confederation has benefitted the provinces, citing in explanation
the advantages Nova Scotia derives from being part of a country
"as large, powerful and wealthy as Canada." In contrast, only 16
per cent feel that Confederation has a detrimental effect.

Belief in Confederation, however, does not prevent Nova Scotians
from criticising national economic policies seen to be inappropriate
for the Atlantic Region. A grievance commonly expressed is that
Ottawa has not been energetic enough in fighting regional disparity,
and that Federal economic policy continues to discriminate against
the Atlantic Region. Many stress that more sensitive national policies
in transportation, taxation, tariff rates and marketing are needed as
a precondition for economic recovery in the Maritimes.

Indeed, 55 per cent of those questioned believe that the federal
government actually understands the province's problems. Many of the
respondents perceive the federal government as "a huge, very complicated
and quite inaccessible machine." The provincial government, on the
other hand, is regarded as "more accessible, much less complex and
more humane." Over 70 per cent feel that the provincial government
does a creditable job of communicating the province's problems to
Ottawa, although frequently without success.

Many of the Nova Scotians surveyed are concerned by the Atlantic
Provinces' dependence on federal equalization and transfer payments.
They assert that this dependency "has to stop," and maintain that
"the provincial economy is far too concentrated in the service sector,
far too dependent on government money and not sufficiently productive."
What Nova Scotians lack, in the eyes of those who form the province's
elite, "is qualified and adventuresome entrepreneurs to accept the
challenge" of making the province self-sufficient.

The sample group that participated in the Queen's survey was

also questioned on various possible reforms. The answers here again
prove to be interesting. For example, a slight majority, 51 per cent,
state that they are in favour of some regionalization of administrative
services, but 59 per cent are opposed to decentralization of jurisdictions. Almost half feel the provinces should take an active role
in the establishment of monetary policies, and 57 per cent support
provincial policy and the federal budget. However, Perlin and Rawlik
stress that "at no time did respondents give the impression that they
sought the aggrandizement of provincial powers at the expense of the
federal sphere."

When dealing with Quebec and the possibility of separation,
the Nova Scotia leaders reveal a strong desire to avoid the partition
of Canada. Eighty-eight point two per cent of the group fear that
Quebec's separation will have a somewhat or very harmful effect on
Nova Scotia. In the eventuality of an independent Quebec, 89 per cent
of those surveyed are of the opinion that their province will have no
choice other than to remain within Confederation.

Peter Gunther, discussant for the above paper, emphasises the
coexistence of a strong national allegiance among Maritimers along
with a definite sense of regionalism, of what is Maritime. These two
characteristics of the Maritime population, reflected in the response
of a selected sample to the P & R survey, constitutes for Gunther
"the Canadian irony."

*   *   *   *   *

It is often argued that important savings can be made in the
cost of providing government services when two or more countries
merge to form one. The resulting single department of external affairs,
for example, may be less costly than the previous two or more; an
amalgamated defence force may not be as expensive as the sum of the
two or more pre-existing forces. Similarly, the break-up of a country
is often argued to lead to important additional costs in providing
government services. In the fifth paper, Mr. MacDonald investigates
these arguments, asking: if Quebec separated, what would be the change
in the cost of providing the present level of government services?

The problem turns out to be far more difficult than one would
have thought. In tackling it, Mr. MacDonald finds it helpful to make
a fourfold classification of federally provided public services, and
an understanding of this classification is the key to following his
treatment of some very complex issues.

First, the need for expenditure on some services can be shown
to increase in a fairly regular way with the number of individuals
served, whereas this is not so for other services. MacDonald calls

the first group the "regionalized" services, since they are very often characterized by considerable expenditures at the regional level and they account for the great bulk of federal service expenditures. An example is the processing and administering of unemployment insurance claims for which expenditures are larger, the larger the number of claimants served. Within the regionalized services it is important for analytical purposes to treat separately expenditures at "head office" and expenditures "in the field." MacDonald calls the second, minority group of services "unregionalized." An example is the National Research Council where the need for expenditures is only dimly related to whatever population one considers to be served, whether or not the ability to provide the services is so linked.

The fourfold classification is obtained by dividing each of the regionalized and unregionalized services into two groups, according to whether Quebec already spends more than a token amount on providing provincial services of a similar type (but never identical; outright duplication is assumed not to exist, though the implications if it did are briefly discussed), or whether it does not. An example of the former is agriculture, of the latter, Statistics Canada.

For the regionalized services MacDonald estimates the impact on unit costs of the amount of service provided. The work is done separately for head office and field costs, and it is found that unit costs generally decline in both cases as output rises, though not at a rapid rate. For a service where Quebec already has a head office and field operations providing services similar to the federal ones, the increased scale attainable after the takeover of federal services following separation means that unit costs can be lowered, and money saved. There is a corresponding but smaller increase in costs at the federal level as the scale of operation there is reduced. But for a service where Quebec has no existing similar service, the need to provide an inefficiently small head office to replace functions formerly available from a federal head office raises costs in Quebec; there is also a cost increase in the rest of Canada.

For unregionalized services, most have Quebec equivalents, no change in cost would be expected after a hypothetical separation. The unregionalized services that do not presently exist in Quebec have to be analysed one by one for technical reasons. What would happen to Quebec's spending on this minority group of services turns out to be very much a judgment call in each case. MacDonald examines in detail two fairly large types of service in this group, related to external affairs and to research respectively, and leaves the others for future research.

MacDonald's final estimates of the cost saving implied by having the federal government provide services, as compared with a situation where these services would have to be provided independently by a separate Quebec, appear in Table 6-2. The savings are very small and could even be negative under certain assumptions. His middle-of-the-road estimate is a saving of about $180 per capita per annum. He notes that gains under the federal system from avoiding negative externalities (spillovers) or losses from outright duplication of services might easily be much larger.

In discussing this paper, Dan Usher compares MacDonald's attempt to construct his cost functions - a technical problem in measuring scale economies - with the endeavor to "build bricks without straw," given the poor numbers available to work with. He feels that MacDonald makes untenable assumptions in order to circumvent this 'numbers' problem, although the nature of the task at hand may have weighed against any better alternative approach.

*   *   *   *   *

What are the roots of discontent as a political scientist sees them? Evenson and Simeon (E and S) answer that our political institutions are presently unable to successfully harmonise the aspirations of three groups of people, "nation-builders," "province builders," and "Quebec-nation builders." The solution to the crisis, if there is one, lies in re-engineering our political institutions so that they can come closer to achieving what each of these three groups wants.

E and S believe that the fundamental social and economic order of Canadian society is not in question in the present crisis which is rather a problem of the relation of governments to one another in the federal system. Regional and national interests, as expressed through provincial and federal governments, are in constant conflict, and the present informal arrangements for resolving disagreements are failing at the task. Three conventional theories of why conflicts arise exist. One focuses on cultural differences among Canadian provinces. A second stresses competition between federal and provincial political and bureaucratic leaders. A third sees the development of Canadian resources as leading to a pattern of regional disparities that produces interregional frictions. E and S's approach, with its concept of the three forces, nation-building, province-building, and Quebec nation-building, cuts across these theories, and gives a new perspective on the present crisis. In E and S's terminology, the crisis can be described as a weakening of the first force relative to the other two.

Country-building began with the BNA Act and was continued
with the transcontinental railway system and industrialization
behind the tariff. Between World War II and the late 1960s it
took the form of developing through federal leadership a pan-Canadian
system for security against poverty and sickness, of widening access
to higher education, and of attempting to apply Keynesian economic
policies to keep unemployment low. Since 1968 federal concern has
turned to direct regulation and the centralization of power. Country-
builders have always seen the federal government and national
institutions as the chief architects of national development.

Weaknesses of country-building have appeared, with a national
view of economic policy proving too narrow in such a regionally
diversified economy. Federal political institutions, such as the
party caucuses, the electoral system, the cabinet, and party discipline,
permit neither adequate representation of provinces and regions, nor
integration of their diverse views. The representative function has
been undertaken by provincial governments, and the integrative one
by the federal-provincial conference. Any country-building strategy
for reform would have to allow a greater regional voice in the internal processes of federal policymaking.

Province-building forces stem from a sense of regional community
strengthened by the growing responsibility and fiscal clout of the
provinces. Ironically, federal institutional policy has led to
resource-fueled growth in provincial power and to north-south links
that weaken provincial ties to Central Canada. Furthermore, the
power of the provinces has been enhanced by virtue of the fact that
they have constitutional responsibility for the fastest recent growth
areas in government -- health, education, and social welfare. At
the same time, the federal government has lost legitimacy from its
failure to cope with regional disparities, notably unemployment,
and from its inability, given the difficulty of achieving constitutional change, to implement even popularly demanded centralization
measures. The politicians and civil servants who most strongly
expound the cause of province-building have also argued that there
is popular regional discontent with federal policies that affect the
regions in areas such as transportation, resources, agriculture and
fisheries, and that provincial influence on federal decisions in
these areas is weak or non-existent.

What province-builders want is more of the taxpayers' money
distributed to provincial governments, less federal interference in
provincial affairs, and more provincial say in federal actions that
affect provinces. At the limit, they see the national interest as
the sum of provincial interests and come very close to espousing the
concept of a con-federal state.

     The third force at work is Quebec nation-building. This force
poses a much more fundamental challenge to the federal system than
either the weakening of country-building or the strengthening of
province-building. The election of a separatist government in Quebec
is its latest manifestation, radically transforming the debate, but
every Quebec government since 1960 has pressed for fundamental
changes in the federal system. The federal response has been to give
more powers to the provinces generally, to implement changes such as
the Official Languages Act to accommodate French Canadians, and to
accept various forms of special status to accommodate the Quebec
provincial government.

     The grievances of French Canadians have been economic, in that
francophones in Quebec have had lower average incomes than anglophones
inside and outside Quebec and considerably higher unemployment, and
in that economic power in Quebec has been concentrated in the hands
of the anglophone minority. The grievances have been cultural, in
that francophones inside and outside Quebec feel the danger of being
assimilated to the English majority and culture, and those outside
Quebec have often been denied French language services. And finally,
the grievances have been political. Despite the fact that Quebec has
had a fairly strong voice in Ottawa (though with good cabinet posts
only recently, and with the problem that this advantage is closely
tied to the fortunes of the Liberal party), Quebec nation-builders
argue that past federal policy has been unrepresentative of francophones, in conflict with French aspirations and values, infringing
on Quebec autonomy, and operating to the disadvantage of the Quebec
economy. The recent strengthening of francophone representation in
the bureaucracy may help to reduce these problems, but it has resulted
in considerable friction with anglophones.

     Quebec nation-builders have come to feel that the cultural,
economic and political problems can best be tackled through the
creation of a politically independent Quebec nation-state. Paralleling
this feeling is the trend since 1960 for more power to accrue to the
Quebec government, rather than more rights for French Canadians
everywhere. The new middle class in Quebec, both the creator and
the creature of this development, increasingly sees the Quebec state
as the instrument for preserving Quebec culture and controlling the
economic destiny of Quebecers.

     Only a minority of Quebecers, at this point, are Quebec nation-
builders. Committed federalists distrust ethnically based nationalism,
emphasize individual rights, and feel that federalism can best preserve
humanist values including the rights of French Canadians outside
Quebec. Third option federalists put less emphasis on the federal
system's ability to preserve rights and more on its expediency and

profitability. They stress that Canada is "two nations" and they require special status for the Quebec nation. The péquistes go further and believe that separation would benefit both French and English Canada, although they expect economic association to continue. Despite these varying views, support for Quebec nation-building within Quebec is strong enough, argue E and S, that any successful modification of federalism will need to take account of it.

E and S summarize their argument by saying that the "political crisis of Canadian federalism thus comes down to a clash between rival governments, each tending to speak for one of the three drives we have surveyed: for national leadership, for greater provincial control, or for a special role for Quebec as the political expression of a distinct national community." Moving on to remedies, they note that the rival drives lead to much overlapping of federal and provincial responsibilities. Little political integration of the two levels exists, policy reconciliation, such as it is, occurring in a fashion similar to that whereby disputes are resolved in international relations, with literally hundreds of joint meetings and conferences. Intergovernmental meetings, however, are very unsatisfactory as conflict reconciling mechanisms; they tend to be secretive; action comes slowly and sometimes not at all; responsibility is divided and public accountability difficult to achieve.

E and S conclude that the urgent need is for the kind of changes to the Canadian constitution that would permit the country to handle intergovernmental relations better and more formally. The changes should incorporate machinery for making intergovernmental agreements easier to arrive at and arrangements that would increase public accountability for decisions taken. The federal government needs to be made more representative and mediative of regional differences and, more important, ways must be found to improve the relationship between it and the provincial governments.

In discussing this paper, Stanley Roberts agrees that the current crisis is political in nature, that "the roots of discontent" lie deep within the Canadian federal system. He provides many fascinating insights into the Western point of view and suggests that federal structures should be reformed to give the West more effective regional representation.

*   *   *   *   *

Many westerners feel that they are disadvantaged by the tariff, by resource taxation and by the structure of railway freight rates. Professor Norrie's paper aims to see if this feeling is justified.

The essence of the complaints that westerners make, according to
Norrie, is that federal policies in these three areas keep incomes
in the region below their potential and prevent industrialization.

He argues that western grievances will be justified if serious
problems of unrealized income and industrialization do exist and if
they are attributable to federal policies that distort and interfere
with market forces, changing the geographical distribution of income
and industry in Canada from what it would be in a more neutral policy
environment. He would regard as unjustified a complaint that the
federal government had failed to adopt policies deliberately designed
to overcome natural economic disadvantages, such as decreasing effective distance from markets by subsidization of transportation. The
main focus of the paper is a report on an empirical investigation of
allegations of discrimination in railway freight rates, though Norrie
deals briefly with the tariff and resource issues. The main effect
of the tariff is to create more industrial jobs in central Canada,
to raise living costs for all Canadians, and to lower the value of
natural resources. It can be argued that these effects discriminate
against westerners, because unlike central Canadians they have to
move to take advantage of tariff-created jobs, and because westerners'
wealth is more concentrated in natural resources. Other tariff-created
problems are dealt with briefly and then the paper moves on to
resources. The main issues here are the federal export tax on crude
oil, the 1974 disallowance of royalty payments as a deduction for
federal company tax, and federal challenges to Saskatchewan oil and
potash policies. After briefly reviewing the literature on what
level of government ought to control resources (an issue somewhat
independent of who has the legal right to do so under the BNA Act),
Norrie concludes that "the issue of resource taxation does seem to
be a legitimate area for federal-provincial concern."

In investigating whether there is freight rate discrimination
against the west, Norrie enumerates five complaints: that the railways charge less per ton mile for raw materials moving out of the
west than for processed goods, thereby destroying otherwise natural
industries for the west; that decentralization of production within
the west is inhibited by not having zone rates like those in the east;
that living costs are raised because the railways' charges for products shipped from central Canada are higher to the Prairie provinces
than to Vancouver; that manufactured goods move west more cheaply
than they move east, making competition for western manufacturers
tougher than it need be; and that the recent practice of increasing
rates by a constant percentage for all products exacerbates the latter
problem. The general solution proposed by the west is to price
railway services more in line with their costs.

Norrie argues on theoretical grounds that the first, fourth and fifth complaints are strange, because it seems likely that the railway would make more profit by pricing in just the opposite way to that suggested. And the third complaint, valid enough, is evidence that the railway does price to obtain as much profit as possible.

In his empirical work, Norrie looks at actual rates charged by varying degrees of disaggregation. He finds that the "general incidence of rates is low on goods exported from the Prairies" and that there "is no obvious bias in export rates on raw versus semi-processed or processed products, except in the case of rapeseed and feedgrains, and only here because of statutory rates that favour western farmers." Thus, the first complaint does not stand up to analysis. In addition, "charges on manufactured goods are higher on regional imports than on exports" so that the fourth and associated fifth complaints are also doubtful. He concludes that railway freight rates constitute a burden in the sense that manufactured goods cost more for western consumers as a result of railway pricing practices, but that they do not have the effect of favouring raw materials versus processing activities in the economy of the western provinces.

In his opening remarks, H.C. Eastmen, discussant for the above work, describes Norrie's research as "exceptionally clear and concise." The discussion of the paper that follows is filled with valuable points of clarification and the discussant finds no call for substantial criticism of Norrie's study, in part or in whole.

*   *   *   *   *

Professor Leslie's concern is whether the substance of public policy is affected by the kind of constitution we have. In principle, he says, constitutional change can have six kinds of influence, on respectively: the careers of politicians and bureaucrats, the costs of administering and developing government policies, the degree of sensitivity of government policies to regional needs, the distribution among regions of the costs and benefits of public policies, and the size and role of government as a whole. Leslie uses his taxonomy to distinguish six viewpoints about the importance of constitutional change, according to whether a person gives credence only to the first influence, to the first and the second but not the other four, and so on through to a belief in all six. He also notes, on page 7, which interests are affected by constitutional change in each case.

The Great Depression seemed to show at the time that the constitution was a serious barrier to implementing needed social

policies. However, after World War II a great deal was achieved
without in fact amending the constitution in major ways, though in
the process some resentment of federal powers was created in Quebec
and the west. Nevertheless, Leslie argues, the constitution does
affect policy in significant ways. It determines, for example,
which community has the main voting say in particular policy areas,
and a parallel is drawn here between the effects of constitutional
change and the effects of gerrymandering. A minority interest in a
large jurisdiction can be a majority interest in a smaller one.
Although that in itself suggests benefits from decentralization of
powers, good policy may sometimes require joint action by both
levels, more easily achieved without too much decentralization.

The question is then taken up of whether interests divide along
regional lines, because decentralization will only be an important
political issue if they do. Examples are studied: of transportation
and western interests, and of labour policy and Quebec interests.
Even if there are significant regional interests, it may nevertheless
pay the regions to agree on a central authority, since the periodic
gains from the exercise of this authority may more than offset the
periodic losses also caused by it. It is also noted that the forms
of the constitutional structure do have a certain importance, e.g.
how powerful the Senate is and what the precise role of the Supreme
Court is.

Leslie concludes that constitutional change has a real and
important effect on what governments do and do not do, and on which
interests get what they want and which do not, and closes with an
appeal for more empirical work on these matters.

Bernard Bonin directs his energy towards a re-emphasis of
several points raised within Leslie's paper concerning the possible
benefits to be derived from decentralized political decision making.
He asserts that centralized decision making and strong regional
interests cannot be easily reconciled.

*   *   *   *   *

The paper by Professor Irvine offers a new federal electoral
system designed to give provinces better representation in the caucuses
of the two major parties. Governments, he argues, need legitimacy,
which involves the four attributes of representativeness, sensitivity
to the popular will, ability to mobilize social forces, and capacity
to manage conflicts between different groups in society. They also
need responsiveness to make policy as demanded and to change it as
necessary and to provide redress for grievances such as the unfair

exercise of administrative discretion. A well designed electoral
system can improve both legitimacy and responsiveness and does this
through its effects on representativeness, party strength, policy-
making and the capacity for redress.

Four types of existing electoral system are described. The
plurality system is one, and Canada is an example of it. Another is
the single transferable vote system, as in Ireland, in which three
to five people are elected per constituency, with voters indicating
their relative preference among candidates, these preferences being
used in helping to determine who wins. A third is the list electoral
system, with the Netherlands an example. Here there are several
representatives per constituency, but each party must now offer a list
of candidates for each constituency equal to the number of representatives it will have. The assignment among parties of seats to each
constituency is such that: "without going into details, each party
can count on receiving a number of seats closely corresponding to
its proportion of the constituency vote and will fill those seats
starting with the top of its constituency list." (p.6). Finally,
there are compromises between the plurality and the list system, as
in the Federal Republic of Germany. In general, list systems lead
to representation of political parties roughly in proportion to the
votes cast for them, in contrast with the plurality, first-past-the-
post, system.

Irvine then provides details of his proposed new system. Its
general characteristic is that, while retaining the present "one man
represents a constituency" character of Canada, albeit with somewhat
larger constituencies, a number of additional members will be elected
to the house as party representatives of each province. Among these
members, who would represent just under half of the total, parties
would usually achieve representation within provinces fairly close
to their percentage of the provincial popular vote. The exceptions
might occur either with very small parties or with very small provinces.
Irvine "re-runs" the 1974 election with his system, showing that,
for example, Quebec elects a substantial minority of conservative
members, and Alberta of liberal members.

Since Irvine's proposal involves a new system that compromises
between the present plurality and a list variant that introduces
elements of proportional representation, he is concerned to meet the
common criticisms that proportional representation tends to weaken
governments and make them indecisive. He addresses these arguments
in general terms as well as in the Canadian context and finds them
unconvincing.

The system's main benefit would be in improving the representation within the party caucuses in a special kind of way. It would allow representation of the concerns of large blocs of voters whose views *qua* members of provincial communities, in contrast with their views *qua* members of the wider Canadian community, are not presently receiving adequate consideration within those caucuses. Once again, there are the examples of conservatives in Quebec and liberals in Alberta. One could say of the present system that it tends to make provinces look more unanimous than they really are, to sharpen regional cleavages, and thereby to exacerbate the problem of the Canadian community as a whole.

The criticisms of K.Z. Paltiel in his discussion of the Irvine paper are directed towards the lack of consideration given to technical problems which he feels would arise in any attempt to implement Irvine's proposed electoral system. He argues that adoption of such a system would only exacerbate the representational shortcomings of the existing Canadian electoral structure.

* * * * *

In their preface Professors Rabeau and Lacroix (R and L) emphasize the persistence of regional economic disparities as a prime factor in the doubts felt by the provinces, notably Quebec, regarding the distribution of power and jurisdictions within confederation. One key regional disparity is that unemployment is much more severe in some regions, including Quebec, than elsewhere. These same regions also bear a disproportionate share of the burden of extra unemployment during economic recessions and therefore have a strong interest in improving the effectiveness of stabilization policy, not only in general but also in such a way that the stimulating effect of that policy is especially enhanced in regions where cyclical unemployment tends to be high. R and L's paper seeks to find methods to improve stabilization policy along these lines, with particular stress on making it more effective in combatting regional unemployment disparities.

R and L begin by discussing stabilization "instruments." These are particular taxes or categories of government expenditure which can be changed in order to increase or decrease production and employment. They maintain that categories of expenditure are technically more efficient instruments than changes in income tax and corporation tax. Moreover, the types of expenditures most suitable for stabilization purposes are under provincial or municipal jurisdiction, not federal.

In section 2 a number of different issues are taken up. In
2.1, R and L estimate how much would have to be borrowed by a
government wishing to increase employment in Quebec by 1 per cent.
This borrowing is called the "net cost to the treasury," and Table
2.1 shows how it varies according to the level of government stabilization instrument used, an example being that annual borrowing
of $891 million would be needed if the Quebec government created
the jobs via increased spending on gross capital formation.

In parts 2.2 and 2.3, R and L discuss causes and remedies for
unemployment in Quebec. Of the 3 percentage point average discrepancy
between Quebec and Ontario, one-half of a point is seasonal, with
the rest attributable to labour immobility and institutionally caused
wage rigidity. Since downward wage flexibility is impractical for
political reasons, according to the authors, and a mobility solution
to unemployment "has always been, and will always remain, unacceptable
to the Quebec elite, and perhaps to the Quebec people as a whole,"
jobs must be created in place. This should be done by a combination
of long-term structural adjustments, short-term regional stabilization
measures and "concerted action (on wages) by the major social partners,"
with the last measure being needed because "these policies would not
have a truly lasting effect on employment through productivity unless
wages in the under-privileged regions continued to rise at a slower
rate in other regions, despite the fact that the unemployment rate
had abandoned past trends."

The final part of section 2 discusses whether the federal or
provincial governments should have the responsibility for stabilization.
Arguing in favour of federal responsibility, say R and L, is the need
from time to time to apply restrictive policy in some provinces
simultaneously with expansionary policy in others, and the need for
the stabilizing authority to carry a considerable budget deficit over
a long period of time. Arguing in favour of provincial responsibility
is the technical efficiency of provincial stabilization instruments.

Section 3 now proposes a new organization of stabilization
policy intended both to permit its regionalization and to resolve the
"Canadian dilemma" -- that the effective stabilization policies are
at the provincial government level while the effective financing and
co-ordinating power is at the federal level.

The authors begin by stressing that their

> ...proposal does not actually intend to increase
> transfers from one region to another, but rather
> to increase their economic effectiveness.

Under our proposal, transfer payments made for
purposes of stabilization would also be designed
to restructure the regional economies. Over the
medium term, these stabilization policies would
lead to a reduction or even a complete disappearance of some other transfers.

Only the broad outlines of the proposal can be described here. The
provinces would vary capital expenditures counter-cyclically, using
a federally financed fund. Access to the fund would be controlled
by a method related to economic indicators, coupled with a political
decision, through a federal-provincial committee, on the stabilization
and other objectives to be met by use of the fund. The latter is
intended to be quite large, for they foresee its existence and use
gradually leading to "an extensive reorganization of Ottawa's main
expenditure items," including the disappearance of certain federal
programs, such as the Department of Urban Affairs, Manpower Training,
and the Department of Regional Economic Expansion.

A key criticism raised by Pierre Fortin in his analysis of
the L and R paper is that insufficient discussion is afforded to the
question of what are or should be the goals of Canadian stabilization
policy. Though Fortin concurs with L and R on their grading of
previous Canadian stabilization performance, he finds "some overselling"
of the proposition that the federal budget is ill-suited for pursuing
effective stabilization measures. He argues that their proposals for
future stabilization measures rely too heavily on the capital expenditure device, the authors having too quickly dismissed the usefulness
of tax cut measures.

*   *   *   *   *

A controversial and interesting thesis is put forward by Professor Martin in collaboration with A. Moroz. It is that pure
decision making can be as potent a force in regional development as
expenditure policies like equalization payments and fiscal and monetary
stabilization.

Pure decisions include regulatory activities, international
trade agreements and tariffs, and the location of federal government
activities and purchases of goods and services. From 1867 to 1940,
the authors argue, pure decisions were the cornerstone of federal
intervention in the economy, the main ones being Prairie settlement,
the all-Canadian transportation system, and industrialization by
protected tariffs. Only in the more recent period have expenditure
policies come to the fore, beginning with general stabilization policy

and moving on to the addition of equalization payments and expenditures like those now coming under the Department of Regional Economic Expansion. Within Regional Economic Expansion, however, there is now a move to exploit once more the potential of pure decisions. Martin and Moroz (M and M) go farther that qualitative argument and try to demonstrate empirically just how pure decisions can influence the location of economic activity. They choose two examples, the Canada-United States Automotive Agreement and the impact on one small industry, flour and breakfast cereals, of the regulation of railway freight rates in Canada.

The authors begin by updating previous work on the national impact of the Automotive Agreement. To calculate this they need to specify what would have happened in the absence of the agreement, to rewrite Canadian economic history, as it were. What they specify is that fiscal and exchange rate policy would have been used instead of the Automotive Agreement to try to keep unemployment and other economic variables at values as close as possible to those actually obtained by use of the Agreement. In performing the necessary calculations underlying this exercise they made use of a great deal of work previously done by the Economic Council in explaining the general functioning of the Canadian economic system, work summarized in what is known as "the CANDIDE econometric model" of the Canadian economy. Using procedures that are standard with such models, they find that the Automotive Agreement generated improvements in employment, production, and other indicators of economic success that would have been difficult to achieve by use of more conventional expenditure-type policies. They conclude that this particular "pure decision" was a very potent one.

They then consider the effects of the Automotive Agreement on output in individual regions, in comparison with what would have happened under alternative policies. The key results are found in Table 2. The central panel of that table, labelled alternative strategy 6, is especially interesting because it comes closest, for Canada as a whole, to achieving the beneficial effects of the Automotive Agreement by other means. Even so, the table shows that Canada's gross domestic product was an average of $250 million a year higher as a result of the Agreement than it would have been with alternative strategy 6. In the last row of this central panel of Table 2 it is shown that the Canada wide gain involved a gain of about $500 million a year for Ontario, twice the national gain, and actual losses in all the other provinces, e.g. about $120 million a year loss in Quebec, about $45 million a year loss in British Columbia. It should be noted, however, that if one compares the Auto Agreement, not with the best alternative federal policy, but with a much worse alternative policy, the "passive" scenario, all provinces gain, though Ontario far more than the others. M and M's conclusion is that the Automotive Agreement was a very powerful "pure decision" and that it had strong effects on the regional distribution of Canadian economic activity.

In examining the effect of decisions concerned with railway freight rate setting, M and M's focus shifts to the west. They wish to distinguish between distance and discrimination as variables influencing industrialization and, like Norrie, they recognize no obligation on the federal government to use pure decisions to offset the economic effects of distance, but do recognize an obligation not to compound those effects by discrimination. Their approach to the problem is to make two different calculations of how much protection central Canadian producers receive on account of transport costs from actual or potential western competition. A measure of that protection, called an "effective protection rate," is first calculated using actual freight rates, and then using theoretical freight rates that approximate the full costs of moving the relevant merchandise. For flour and breakfast cereals,the actual effective protection for central Canadian producers turns out to be far higher than the theoretical full cost protection (22.5 per cent versus 4.8 per cent). M and M conclude that "the ability of the railways to set prices above their true full costs which in turn are determined by their accounting practices allowed by the government results in an incentive to locate the processing plants in Ontario." Unlike Norrie, they do not attempt to decide whether the railway's ability to set prices above costs is generally used in such a way as to inhibit industrialization in the west; their purpose is simply to show, via the flour and breakfast cereals example, the power of pure decisions to influence location, regardless of whether all the potential power has actually been made use of in one way or another.

Michael Walker, in his opening comments on the M and M paper, attempts to redefine the regional development problem from the standpoint of a classical economist, providing a valuable alternative insight. He goes on to criticize M and M for the distinction they draw between pure decisions and expenditure decisions, feeling their taxonomy distorts the essential issues of efficiency and equity which arise in the choice between these decisions. He expresses his skepticism over attempts to simulate the non-existence of the auto-pact.

*   *   *   *   *

In studying matters of pressing current urgency it is easy to forget that the problems may be more comprehensible in the perspective of history. Professor Durocher does not feel that the present crisis is unique but he does consider, as a historian, that it

> constitutes one of the most serious challenges
> that Canada has faced since 1867. The present
> crisis over federalism is all the more serious
> because it has been building up for a long
> time. This crisis is deeply rooted in the
> history of the country, which explains my
> interest in a study of the evolution of
> federalism since 1867.

Durocher's thesis may be interpreted as showing that the Canadian government system has oscillated since confederation between centralization and decentralization. In a historical perspective there is nothing sacred or unchangeable about the particular division of relative power between the federal and provincial governments which can be and has been modified according to the needs and pressures of each historical period. Confederation began in 1867 as a compromise between the French and the English who had different purposes--the French to survive and the English to secure control of the Canadian territory. The intent was to create a highly centralized federal system, but the centralizing dream of the Fathers of Confederation, says Durocher, received a rude awakening.

From 1873 to 1896 several factors modified the federation in the direction of more relative power to the provinces, with Ontario under Mowat playing a leading role. Thus, except during World War I, federalism after 1896 came to emphasize provincial sovereignty, with the federal government limited to powers enumerated in article 91 of the BNA Act. It was a system in which the two levels of government were co-equal, rather than one being subordinate to the other.

The problems of the 1930s revealed difficulties with this kind of federalism and paved the way for a return to centralization. World War II completed the rupture with the years since 1896. After the war's end the federal government had a quasi-monopoly of direct taxes. It planned to implement a vast social security program, either directly or via conditional grants; to Canadianize several institutions; to follow a dynamic cultural policy for Canada; and to make use of Keynesian economics to avoid problems of unemployment and depression. All these policies greatly increased the degree of centralization of the confederation.

Starting in the middle of the 1950s, however, several political and economic factors began restoring provincial autonomy, most notably in Quebec. These included the coming to power of the Liberals in that province, marking the beginning of the "quiet revolution" there, and massive use of the opting out provision. People began to speak of "co-operative federalism," but as time went by the system took on, Durocher argues, more of an appearance of "competitive federalism."

In 1965, Quebec and Ottawa positions had rigidified. Constitutional negotiations in 1968 and 1971 ended in failure. Since 1970 the other provinces have shown signs of discontent and of wanting more power to assure their own development. With regard to the provinces in 1976, Durocher concludes, that

> they have formed the beginnings of consensus
> on several points, and the new Quebec
> Government is now actively participating in
> the elaboration of what might become a new
> federalism.

In discussing this paper, Stanley Ryerson suggests that Canadian federalism has evolved from a basically equivocal premise. Canada's two founding peoples are ostensibly partners in Confederation, but underlying socio-economic inequalities, which are rooted in the country's past, have only led to increased ethnic cleavage. He feels that Durocher could have looked closer at the impact of property, private business and labour on this basic structure on inequality.

SOME OPENING REMARKS

by

Sylvia Ostry, Chairman

Economic Council of Canada, Ottawa

I am delighted to take part in this workshop, which is
jointly sponsored by the Economic Council and the Institute of Intergovernmental Relations at Queen's. I feel I should stress that the
papers presented by the Council within this Conference do not represent the views of the Economic Council; they represent the views of
the authors, whether they be staff members or academics who are hired
on contract by us. The views of the Economic Council are as diverse
on the issues examined here as those of any other group of Canadians;
indeed they are probably more so because there are a number of economists on the Economic Council now!

The papers presented here through the Queen's Institute
are part of a far larger project entitled "The Future of Canadian
Communities," which is being funded by the Donner Foundation.

I would like to open the Conference by providing some
kind of background for it, if you'll bear with me for a few minutes;
then, we will move on to the papers prepared for this morning's
session.

We have almost reached an anniversary at this Conference:
it has been about two years since the P.Q. government was elected in
Quebec. At that time, it appeared that a referendum might take place
at about now. It looked as though we would be facing, at this time,
the most momentous decision point in this country's history. Many
individuals and organizations felt an urgent need to communicate to
the Quebec public and to the Canadian public at large, and to say
what they thought it was important for people to know before
Quebecers voted one way or another. After a few months' lag, there
was a flurry of conferences; there was the setting up of a National
Unity Task Force; there was the setting up of a unit within the
Quebec government to analyse and produce studies on various forms of
sovereignty-association and their implications; and, within the
federal government, a "Co-ordination" group was formed in the Federal-
Provincial Relations Office to develop a federal position; the
C. D. Howe Institute set up an ambitious program of about a dozen
studies, many of which have been published; Canada West Foundation
initiated a work program, as did many other individuals and groups
around the country.

The members of the Economic Council discussed the matter at some length and felt that they, as a Council, wanted to contribute. It became obvious that the Council could not give a rounded view of the issues as a whole, since so many of the relevant questions in the national unity debate were outside the realm of economics; there were issues of language, of culture, of political structure, and there was philosophical cleavage on whether the ideal country must coincide with a nation, or whether more than one nation could co-exist within a country.

But the Council felt that it could contribute economic information or "intelligence," to put the economic aspect of the debate on as accurate a factual base as was possible in the circum- stances. The studies presented here are a result of that under- taking, which began early in 1977. I would like to give some per- spective on whether a good factual base is in fact possible, and on the relative importance of economic and non-economic factors.

An extremely important purpose of such economic intell- igence work is to inform voters in a Quebec referendum of rele- vant economic facts, as well as citizens in the rest of the country, to the extent that their readiness to accept changes in federalism might influence the relative attractiveness of the alternatives facing Quebec voters. The ideal technique is fairly clear. It would involve contrasting the expected performance of a fractured country, however each of these is defined. How do these alterna- tives look for Quebec? For the West? For other parts of the country? A second purpose, stressed by the Council, was to analyse possible changes in those aspects of the Canadian economic system whose alleged malfunctioning may have been influential in leading to the present crisis. Both sides in the debate could presumably subscribe to such an aim "without prejudice," as the lawyers say.

The first task -- that of providing information -- requires some attempt to define relevant alternatives or scenarios. Let me deal briefly with that before coming to my main theme. Two alternatives are federalism and separation. In the latter case, we did not consider it useful to give extensive consideration to sovereignty with association, since it rapidly became obvious that "Rump Canada," in Clarence Barber's superbly inelegant phrase, would have so little to gain from association over the long run that this alternative seemed very unlikely to happen. In addition, the concept of association is very difficult to define with any accuracy. Nevertheless, let me emphasize that it is quite easy to apply our analysis to the sovereignty-association alternative. We also considered that the possibility that our present "fédéral- isme" could be radically "renouvelé" was most unlikely. But that

does not mean that improvements are impossible in the economic
sphere -- far from it. Nor does the improbability of sovereignty-
association mean that no links whatsoever would exist.

     It was our view that contrasting various alternatives for
the system as a whole would be less useful than keeping in mind alternatives for control over each of four economic variables that largely
define how much economic "sovereignty" or "independence" a province
or a nation has. Moreover, sovereignty in the economic sphere is
not only multidimensional, it is also continuously variable, rather
than being there or not there, in the four economic dimensions.
These dimensions are the tax expenditure system, the external trade
system, the monetary system, and the conventions regarding factor
mobility.

     In the case of the tax expenditure system, the present
federal arrangement gives Quebec a partial say on taxes and expenditures in that province and a partial say on taxes and expenditures outside; independence, with or without association,
would give Quebec full say within its own borders and no say outside;
a Swiss-style confederation would fall in between.

     In the area of external trade, Quebecers at present share
power with others in Canada to decide upon a common external tariff
and commercial policy; with independence, Quebec might gain zero
extra sovereignty in this area (a Common Market agreement); some
extra sovereignty (a free trade area); or full extra sovereignty
(no trade association at all).

     As for the monetary system, the shared jurisdiction of
Quebecers with other Canadians might be left as it is, with no gain
in sovereignty (that is, a monetary union), or there could be a
partial increase in sovereignty, by means of a separate currency but
a fixed exchange rate, or a bigger increase, by means of a separate
and floating currency.

     In the area of factor mobility, the Quebec government
exercises no present control over movement of people and capital
into Quebec from Canada, while the Quebec people share control with
other Canadians over immigration from abroad. Independence could
go with varying degrees of sovereignty here, depending on whether
Quebec control on foreign immigration of people was supplemented by
control over migration from the rest of Canada or control over
capital movements, or both.

     Whenever we did research on a particular issue concern-
ing change in constitutional arrangements, we took into account only
those changes, in each of these four dimensions of economic sovereignty, that were relevant to the issue at hand. For example, in
studying the implications of changes in control over the tax-expendi-

ture system for taxes paid by Quebecers, it is not very important
what one assumes about monetary union. But for trade flows, a
wider spectrum of changes in the economic components defining independence needs to be examined. You will see, therefore, that we have
varying scenarios or alternatives according to the topic considered.

Let me now return to the main thrust of my argument. An
uneasiness that I, personally, have always felt about economic analysis of the issues at stake, by anyone --including the Economic
Council -- is that some of the relevant economic facts cannot be uncovered by the current tools of economic analysis, powerful though
they be. And if these particular facts were important, in that they
could seriously influence living standards and unemployment in Quebec
or elsewhere, they would dwarf into insignificance the conventional
facts that analysts like ours, C. D. Howe's, Mr. Bonin's, Mr. Tellier's,
are capable of uncovering.

What I mean by that is what Maynard Keynes called "the
animal spirits" of entrepreneurs, and the unpredictability of
human reactions in crises, which could play a key economic role in
the event of separation -- one that essentially cannot be analysed.
If businessmen withdrew capital from Quebec or, indeed, from Canada,
in large amounts, the impact on employment and income in Quebec --
and in the rest of Canada -- could be far more significant than any
other economic factor we analyse in these three days. Equally, if
independence liberated a spirit of dynamic co-operation within Quebec,
as some pēquistes have argued, that could also be of dominating importance. My point is that there are *dynamic factors whose impact
is both potentially large and in practice unknowable*. How do we
account for such dynamic uncertainties? I don't know, but I confess
to great uneasiness that we cannot do so and that we have not done
so in these papers. I would caution you, therefore, to take the
excellent economic analyses presented here as incomplete stories.
They could be less significant than these other, "undoable"
analyses.

As you know, the Council is sponsoring this workshop
jointly with the Institute of Intergovernmental Relations at
Queen's. I am grateful that we have the chance to work with the
Institute, because a myopic focus on the economics of the issues would
be more than just misleading; it would, in my view, be positively
distasteful. Misleading, because for many Canadians the really important issues in Confederation, as I said earlier, concern language,
culture, political structure, and philosophy about what a country
is, and, in particular, emotional commitment. Distasteful also, for
the question of whether it is worthwhile or not to preserve this
country we call Canada must surely transcend our pocketbooks.

As long as these reservations are kept very firmly in

mind, economists can contribute something to the debate. What they
can do is give perspective concerning the size of some of the economic problems associated with separation, if that should come, and
on some non-problems that people think are problems. They can also
give a limited number of ideas about what to do to improve the
system we have.

As you will note, the focus in today's sessions is mainly
on economic issues, whereas tomorrow it will be on political issues,
and Friday on history, politics, and economics.

Separation would alter trade and "aid" flows among
provinces. By "aid" flows, I mean flows of cash in the form of
equalization and other transfers. The first three papers today
tackle these questions. Dr. Hazledine's examines the economic costs
and benefits of the present system -- a customs union -- as measured
by what the system is worth in terms of real output available for use
by the citizens, relative to separation-type alternatives. He measures this value for each province taking into account both trade and
aid flows within Canada. His time horizon is the medium term,
defined as a period within which policy adjustments could occur in
the form of changes in the values of any new currencies associated
with separated provinces, and in the wage levels in those provinces,
in order to cope with employment and balance-of-payments problems
that might occur as a result of separation.

Dr. Auer's focus is narrower in scope but thereby richer
in detail. He looks at the short run, and only at trade flows in
the manufacturing sector. His basic concern is how big the short-
run manufacturing employment losses would be in each province, if
current tariff protection were modified by either going to free trade
or to tariffs between Quebec and the rest of the country, how big the
corresponding consumer gains would be, and how the gains and losses
would balance out in each province.

Mr. Glynn's focus is also narrower than Mr. Hazledine's,
but this time richer in detail on the "aid" flows -- equalization as
mentioned, the federally subsidized portion of transfers to persons,
such as old age security, unemployment benefits, and transfers to
business from DREE, IT & C and other departments. If any province
left the system, how much would the Finance Minister have to think
of changing taxes and spending on the morning after? And what
would be the implications for families at various income levels in
that province? Mr. Glynn's paper will be presented by Mr. Baxter
MacDonald. On the other economics paper today, Baxter will present
his own research, on a question often raised in the debate -- the
quantitative importance of scale economies associated with providing certain government services federally rather than in two or more
separate jurisdictions.

        The focus of the economics papers tomorrow and Friday is
rather different. Professor Norrie, tomorrow, will present his
views on economic grievances in the West. On Friday, the focus shifts
somewhat, away from emphasis on economic facts about our present
system as compared with separation-type alternatives, to an emphasis
on economic problems <u>within</u> the present system, a careful examination
of which could lead to possibilities for improvement. Professors
Rabeau and Lacroix deal with the problem of cyclical unemployment,
which impacts especially severely on Quebec, and develop the concept of a regionally targeted stabilization policy. Professor
Martin believes that regionally targeted policies should go beyond
conventional manipulations of taxes and expenditures, in that federal decisions in the economic sphere should be actively used to
equalize regional disparities.

THE ECONOMIC COSTS AND BENEFITS OF

THE CANADIAN FEDERAL CUSTOMS UNION

by

T. Hazledine*

Economic Council of Canada

*Frank Flatters, Harry Postner, Bob Thompson and, especially, Neil Swan have contributed very useful criticisms and suggestions.

I. INTRODUCTION

There are at least three features of the Canadian confederation which might not survive should one of the member provinces
leave.

First, Canada is a "customs union" -- that is, an arrangement
whereby the provinces agree to impose no tariffs on trade between
themselves and a common tariff on goods imported from foreign
countries.

Second, it is a monetary union, sharing a common currency.

Third, it contains a federal government, which taxes economic
activity in the provinces and then redistributes the revenues
amongst them; not, in general, in the proportions in which they
were received.

It is the implications of this system which I will attempt
to uncover and compare with the conceivable alternatives for each
of the five regions of Canada.[1] It turns out that a good deal
depends on two characteristics of each region's economy under
confederation: its total balance of trade (i.e., its trade
position vis-à-vis foreigners and other Canadian regions combined)
and its balance on just the regional component of the total. A
region is likely to gain from running a deficit on its total trade
account, since it is then consuming more than it produces, with
the difference made up by transfers from other regions. It may
lose, however, having a deficit on its regional trade account if
it is, therefore, buying more Canadian-produced goods from other
regions at tariff-protected prices than it is selling to them.

Of the five regions of Canada, two (Quebec and the Atlantic
provinces) run an all-trade deficit, and three (British Columbia,
the Prairie and Atlantic provinces) have a deficit on their
regional account. Thus, from this point of view, Quebec unambiguously should be a gainer from confederation, and British Columbia
and the Prairie region losers. For Ontario, we cannot, *a priori*,
know whether the opposing effects of running surpluses on both
total and regional trade net out to a gain or a loss; nor for the
Atlantic region, although the size of the latter's deficit on all
its trade makes it fairly safe to predict the net effect.

Nevertheless, these numbers cannot be taken very far as
indicators of the regional costs and benefits from confederation.
In particular, we should note that the transfers received by

---

1 The Prairie and Atlantic provinces are aggregated into two regions, in
   order to impose some sort of order-of-magnitude comparability of the
   economic size of the units being analysed.

Quebec and the Atlantic provinces are associated with lower, not higher, incomes -- there they come in the form of equalization and unemployment insurance payments reflecting the lower productivity and employment rates in Eastern Canada. Much of these regional disparities, no doubt, can be blamed on deep-seated structural imbalances, the resolution of which is beyond the medium-term horizon of the present work (though, probably crucial to the future of Canada).

However, we will be able to look at the sensitivity of regional output and employment to some important macroeconomic variables. Perhaps the Canadian tariff structure does not best meet the requirements of particular regions, nor, perhaps, does the Canadian currency -- might an independent Quebec, for example, be able to increase employment by devaluing its currency against the rest of Canada and the World?

These and related questions are the subject of the work reported in this paper. I do not expect that they are all-important to the future of confederation, but they are certainly of interest.

Two "scenarios," or alternatives to the status quo, are examined for each region. The first might be called "simple-minded separation." In it, each independent region retains the present Canadian tariff structure and imposes it on the other regions. While not in itself particularly likely, this scenario gives us a way of evaluating the consequences of the customs union as presently constituted.

The second scenario supposes unilateral free trade -- the abolition by Canada of all its tariffs on foreign imports. Which regions, if any, would gain, and which lose?

In addition, for Quebec, we will look at a third option, in which it retains tariffs on foreign imports which the rest of Canada abolishes, and in which free trade between the regions continues.

For the separation scenario we first compute the initial impact, then allow for compensatory adjustments in regional currencies and wage rates.

To quantify all this, I needed a mathematical "model" of the regional economies. In section II, this model is first outlined, then in section III documented in detail. We may just note here that a crucial feature of the model, and one which sets it apart from other work in this area, is its explicit rejection, for manufacturing industries, of the "law of one price." The main consequence of doing this is to make the numbers smaller -- to reduce the quantitative impact on production and employment of changes in trading arrangements.

Section IV contains a brief description of the database built up for the study. Section V brings together model, database, and scenarios, to generate the actual results, and Section VI summarizes these and concludes the paper.

II.   THE MODEL: OUTLINE AND CAVEATS

Outline

Goods and services produced in a Canadian region can have any of three destinations: they can be consumed within the region, they can be shipped to other regions, or they can be shipped abroad. Consumption within the region is supplied from three sources: from intraregional production, from other regions, or from abroad. Thus, we have five categories of flows of goods and services which summarize the "real" economic activity (that is, not considering capital account flows) of the region.

It is the analysis of these flows which is the concern of this paper. In particular, by considering the three production flows we can analyse gross regional product and employment, and by netting out the four export and import flows, we measure a region's balance of payments on its current account.

Each regional economy is broken down into up to twenty-seven industries, in each of which we observe some or all of the five sorts of shipment flows. Changes in these flows are, in the first instance, prompted by changes in prices induced by changes in tariff rates levied on interregional or foreign shipments. The price paid in other regions for an industry's regional shipments goes up with the imposition of the tariff, but the price received by the industry falls (since the new tariff is paid to the governments of the importing regions). The size of these changes may depend on the extent to which the local industry was, before separation, taking advantage in its pricing of the protection afforded it by the Canadian tariff. As well, the price in the local market will go up with the application of a tariff to shipments from other regions.

The effects of these price changes are as follows: the lower price received by regional shippers will put some of the highest-cost producers out of business. The demand for the output of the surviving shippers will fall with the increase in price paid. The local demand for foreign imports and for locally produced output will increase somewhat, as consumers substitute away from the now higher-priced regional imports. The net effect on employment and the balance of payments within the region depends on the relative magnitude of the various flows. For example, a region which finances its imports relatively more by exporting to other regions than to the rest of the world will probably experience a deterioration in its balance of payments and a fall in employment if the absolute value of the fall in regional exports is larger than either the fall in regional imports or the increase in domestically produced consumption.

In reaction to the initial impact on the trade balance and employment, market forces and/or government policies may change the exchange rate and the distribution of income in the region. The model will give us estimates of the size of the adjustments needed on the part of these macroeconomic variables to compensate for the effects of dismantling the customs union.

Limitations

The model should be placed in the context of its limitations -- in order to make useful sense of the numbers that will be discussed in later sections, we must know what questions the model does not cover; what factors are held constant. The important ones are:

1. This is a model of flows of goods and services only. No attempt is made to predict changes in capital account flows that might follow separation or free trade.

2. The time horizon of the model is "medium term," by which is meant a period long enough for any adjustment lags in changes in prices and costs to work through, and for a firm that finds it unprofitable to operate under the new conditions to exit from its industry, but not so long that new capital can enter an industry (though we allow existing firms flexibility in changing their levels of output).

3. Changes in quantity variables in the model are induced solely by changes in price variables. One implication of this is that the input-output linkages between the quantity produced of a finished good in a region, and the demand for materials and semi-finished inputs, does not affect outputs of other industries within that region. In a model of a closed economy, this property would be very restrictive, but for the rather open regional economies here modeled it should not matter so much.

4. A second property of a price-motivated model is that no recognition is given to possible multiplier effects on output and employment consequent to price change-induced changes in incomes. Again, we must hope that the openness of the regional economies is such that "leakages" to other regions and abroad dissipate multiplier effects.[2]

---

2 Multipliers in Canadian macromodels are around 2. In regional models they would be still smaller.

5. It is assumed (a) that Canada is small relative to the
rest of the world, and (b) that each region is small relative to
the rest of Canada, so that (i) no Canadian region can influence
its terms of trade by altering its exchange rate, (ii) each region
is modeled independently; that is, we assume no reaction to its
actions by other regions. This rules out such events as competitive devaluations between two or more regions.

These qualifications to the generality of the model are not,
of course, desirable in themselves, but are forced by the limited
resources (approximately one man-year) available to this project.
It would be quite feasible, and possibly useful, to go on to
merge my model with a regionalized macroeconometric model including
Input-Output relationships.

III. THE WORKINGS OF THE MODEL

We need two things: one, a database of "base-period" foreign,
interregional, and intraregional flows of goods and services , and
two, a model of how these flows would change if the customs union
were broken up. The database is described in Section IV; the
model in this section. First, the price change process is outlined,
and second, the relationships between prices and shipments.

Price Changes

(a) Manufacturing industries

Previous work on the national or regional implications of
Canadian tariffs has *assumed* the validity of the "Law of One
Price,"[3] which states that there is a single world market price
for each commodity, so that the equilibrium domestic price in any
country is simply equal to the world price times the country's
exchange rate plus any tariff imposed on imports of the commodity,
since any price differences will be arbitraged away.

---

3 James R. Williams, *The Canadian-U.S. Tariff and Canadian Industry*, Toronto,
   1978; Vittorio Corbo and André Martens, "Le tarif extérieur canadien et la
   protection de l'activité manufacturière québecoise," *CRDE*, Montreal, 1978;
   Clarence Barber, "The Customs Union Issue," Conference on the Future of the
   Canadian Federation, Toronto, October, 1977; Ontario Treasury "Interprovincial
   Trade Flows, Employment, and the Tariff in Canada," Supplementary material
   to the 1977 Ontario Budget; R. J. Wonnacott, *Canada's Trade Options*, Economic
   Council of Canada, Ottawa, 1975; H. M. Pinchin, "The Regional Impact of the
   Canadian Tariff," Economic Council of Canada Background Paper, Ottawa, 1977;
   Roma Dauphin, *The Impact of Free Trade in Canada*, Economic Council of Canada,
   Ottawa, 1978; Federal-Provincial Relations Office, *Trade Realities in Canada
   and the Issue of "Sovereignty-Assocation,"* Ottawa, 1978, L. Auer, *Confederation
   and Some Regional Implications of the Tariffs on Manufactures* (this Workshop).
   It is perhaps only fair to warn the reader that, although the evidence seems to
   refute this assumption, not making it makes a difference to our results that in
   one particular case -- the free trade scenario -- seems to be especially marked
   (on the basis of preliminary evidence). The direction of the difference is that
   free trade is considerably less productive of employment loss in the short run
   when the "one price" assumption does not hold.

This is a very strong proposition[4] and direct analysis of changes in time-series of manufactured traded goods prices appears decisively to refute it.[5] Differences in common-currency prices of the "same" traded commodity from different countries appear typically to exist and persist, even when commodities are classified at the 7-digit level of disaggregation.

In a background study, I have tested the proposition that price differences are consistent with a world of generally heterogeneous goods, in which each seller has some market power (non-infinite price elasticities of demand). Using a cross-section of Canada/U.S. relative common-currency domestic prices of manufactured commodities from the study by Frank,[6] I found that more than 60 per cent of the variation in the price ratio could be statistically explained by differences in tariff protection, market concentration and relative costs.[7] Protection and concentration (measured by the Herfindahl index) appeared to act multiplicatively, such that only in a highly concentrated industry[8] would full advantage be taken of tariffs. In an industry with many small firms, high cross-elasticities of demand apparently prevent domestic sellers from taking any advantage at all of the tariff -- competition chisels away any prices that are sufficiently higher than costs to generate monopoly profits. This result implies that the common assumption (found in all studies which assume the "law of one price") that the protection afforded a domestic industry is equal to the tariff rate is not valid.

---

4   For example, the law of one price implies that, since all domestic prices are already equal to the world price plus the tariff, imposing this tariff on interregional shipments would have *no effect* on the market price (though it would lower the supply price -- the price received by domestic interregional shippers -- by the amount of the tariff).

5   For recent evidence cf. Irving B. Kravis and Robert E. Lipsey, "Price Behavior in the Light of Balance of Payments Theories"; and J. David Richardson, "Some Empirical Evidence on Commodity Arbitrage and the Law of One Price"; both in the *Journal of International Economics*, May 1978. Reviewing these findings, R. Dornbusch and D. Jaffee conclude that "the evidence presented leaves that hypothesis [the law of one price] rather in shambles" (*ibid*, p. 159).

6   James G. Frank, *Assessing Trends in Canada's Competitive Position*, The Conference Board in Canada, Ottawa, 1977.

7   Tim Hazledine, "Protection; and Prices, Profits and Productivity in Thirty-three Canadian Manufacturing Industries," Economic Council of Canada Discussion Paper No. 110, Ottawa, 1978. The results used in the present paper are slightly different, reflecting work done since the publication of the Discussion Paper.

8   A Herfindahl value of 0.25 is needed for full pricing-up-to-the-tariff. The mean value of the Herfindahl index is about 0.10. The Herfindahl index is defined as the sum of the squares of the market shares of all the firms in an industry.

Differences in the Canadian/U.S. ratio of the cost of
producing a unit of output also appeared systematically to affect
price differentials. About one half of any cost difference seems
to be reflected in prices. That is, a Canadian industry with unit
costs lower, say, than the average for the U.S. industry producing
the same commodity, passes on about half of these lower costs in
lower prices to Canadian buyers, and keeps the other half. An
industry with higher costs absorbs about half of these, and passes
the rest on to consumers. In so doing it presumably suffers some
loss in market share, but not an *infinite* loss, as is required in
the law of one-price models.[9]

These findings are the basis for the model of pricing needed,
in this study, to begin predicting the impact for each region of
its separation from the rest of Canada. First, I assume that the
market structure input to prices survives separation. That is,
the degree to which a Canadian industry can take advantage of
tariff protection from the rest of the world stays constant when
further tariff barriers are set up between the regions. At least
in the medium-term context of the model, in which there are no
separation-induced capital movements (apart from liquidations
when high-cost fringe firms exit from an industry), this assumption
is probably reasonable -- the same firms will be doing business in
a dismembered Canada as operate across the country at present.

Second, I suppose that the 50/50 partition of cost differences
applies to separation-induced changes in market conditions such as
the imposition of interregional tariffs, the de- or re-valuation of
a region's currency, and changes in interregional costs following
independent movements in regional wage rates.[10] That is, for
example, a region which imposes a 10 per cent tariff on shipments
from other regions will find itself paying a 5 per cent higher
price for these shipments. Half of a 10 per cent devaluation in
a region's currency will be passed through to consumers in other
regions -- the other 5 per cent will go to the region's producers.
Half of a wage change-induced cost differential will be passed on.

We have, thus, hypotheses to account for price changes in two
of the five sorts of shipments flows -- flows to other regions and
from them. For "domestic" shipments -- that is, the price of goods
that are produced and consumed within a region -- I assume that the
relationship found in the Background Study between domestic and
world prices still holds after separation. This means that prices
of domestic output are affected by changes in the price of imports
and in domestic costs.

---

9 We may note that a 50 per cent pass-through of cost changes would be predicted by a monopoly model with constant marginal costs and linear demand.

10 Persistent wage differentials *may* require some limitations on the mobility
    of labour between regions.

The landed or domestic market price of imports is taken to reflect in full changes in the exchange rate, in accordance with the "small country" assumption -- that is, that Canada can change the quantity it buys from abroad without affecting the foreign currency price.

Finally, fluctuations in the price of goods exported to markets in other countries are assumed to match one half of fluctuations in exchange rates and costs, just like goods shipped to other Canadian regions.

There is thus an asymmetry between the treatment of shipments to and from Canadian regions and the rest of the world. The asymmetry may well be too clear cut; its validity depends on a postulate that, in a generally demand-constrained world, Canadian importers tend to have more alternative sources of supply than Canadian exporters have alternative sources of demand.

(b)   Primary commodities

The prices of primary sector commodities -- grain, petroleum, potash, and so on -- are likely to be more closely identifiable than are manufactured goods prices with a set of world market prices, given the generally greater degree of homogeneity of primary goods. I assume that for primary industries the law of one price holds, so that the price of exports to the world equals a given world market price, and the prices of imports and of domestic and regional shipments are set at the world price converted to domestic currency and with any tariff added on.

(c)   Construction and Services

The remaining sectors of the economy are characterized by an output which is not much traded, so that it is reasonable to assume that they price according to some percentage mark-up on domestic costs. The size of this mark-up probably varies across industries according to differences in market concentration, ease of entry of small firms, and other market structure factors, but so long as each industry's mark-up stays the same over the medium-term period here considered, we just need to know changes in costs in order to calculate changes in price in each sector.

Shipment Changes

The price changes discussed above will work through both the supply and demand side of the market to induce changes in the flows of goods and services.

It is assumed that commodities in the same industries from different supply sources are substitutable, but not perfectly so. Thus, changes in the demand for foreign imports are calculated as a weighted sum of price changes of foreign imports, regional

imports, and domestic shipments, with the weights being the own-
and cross-price elasticities of demand. Precise formulae, and
a description of the derivation of cross-price elasticities from
market shares and own-price elasticities are given in an Appendix,
which is available on request.

Changes in the demand for regional imports are computed
similarly. For these two shipment flows I assume that each region
is small enough relative to the world and to the other regions
for actual shipments to be demand-determined.

For shipments originating within a region, however, we must
consider possible supply effects of changes in the prices received
by domestic producers. The imposition of a tariff on regional
exports, for example, lowers demand by increasing the market price,
but also may affect supply by lowering the price received by
producers by the amount that they absorb the new tariff. For
manufacturing, I have estimates of the distribution of unit costs
relative to price for the establishments in each industry, and
use these "capacity elasticities" to predict the proportion of
pre-separation industrial capacity that would become unprofitable
(costs greater than price) for a given fall in price received.
I assume that these highest-cost establishments would exit from
the industry, and that a proportion of their sales, according to
pre-separation market shares, would go to the surviving firms.
The latters' output would be further affected by the change in
the price paid in their market, according to the demand elasticity,
and assuming that output of surviving establishments can be
expanded or contracted over the medium term, at constant average
cost.[11]

In the primary sector, with elastic world supply and demand,
domestic output is supply determined. At the going price,
individual producers supply up to the point where it is no longer
profitable (that is, to where marginal cost equals price). If
the sum of these supplies is greater than the region's consumption
demand, it will export the surplus; if not, it will be an importer.

There is no trade between Canada and the rest of the world
in construction and service industries shown in the Statistics
Canada Trade data, and I did not have any information on interregional flows. I, therefore, assumed these to be not significant,
or, at least, not significantly affected by tariff and other
changes, and focused on intraregional (domestic) output, taking
this to be demand-determined.

---

11 Constant unit costs is, if anything, a conservative assumption. Most
    econometric models (such as CANDIDE 2.0) find that Okun's Law holds --
    that is, that productivity *increases* with output in the short run. There
    is certainly little evidence for the upward sloping marginal cost curves
    required by neoclassical models in which producers *choose* output such
    that marginal cost equals price.

Employment Changes

We have data on the distribution of employment by the cost/price ratios of establishments, from which an estimate can be made of the change in employment consequent to the closing down of some capacity in a manufacturing industry. For surviving establishments, employment is assumed to change in the same proportion as output, in keeping with the assumption of constant unit costs over the medium-term time horizon of the model.

This assumption is made, too, for the construction, service, and primary sectors, with the exception of agriculture. In this industry hired labour makes up only a small proportion of the total labour force, which is largely families operating their own farms, whom we assume to remain in the industry over the medium term, whatever the fluctuation in agricultural prices.

IV. DATABASE

The model uses 1974 as a base year. This year was chosen because it was the most recent for which Statistics Canada provided data on provincial economic accounts[12] and because it was the only recent year for which data were available on interregional shipments from manufacturing industries.[13] Each regional economy is disaggregated into up to twenty-seven industries or sectors -- five primary sectors, up to twenty manufacturing industries, construction, and other industries (mainly services). Except for Ontario and Quebec, the number of 2-digit manufacturing industries for which complete interregional trade data were available was less than the possible maximum of twenty. It was possible, though, to calculate flows for the sum of the missing industries as a residual. These flows were assigned to a "residual manufacturing" industry. The gaps in the interregional data lead to a certain amount of "guesstimating" to ensure that the sum of regional flows matched the total Canada data which were available for all industries.

Data on regional value added, wages and employment for manufacturing, for the primary industries, and for construction, were taken from the appropriate Statistics Canada industry reports for 1974. To ensure consistency with the provincial accounts, the remaining "other" industry was measured as a residual so that value added in all industries would sum to the figure for gross provincial domestic product at factor cost calculated for each region from the Provincial Accounts publication.

---

12 Statistics Canada, "Provincial Economic Accounts, 1961-1974," Experimental Data, Ottawa, 1977.

13 Statistics Canada, *Destination of Shipments of Manufacturers, 1974*, Cat. No. 31-522, Ottawa, 1978.

No regional shipments from primary industries are included at present in the database, but this is currently being worked on, as is the disaggregation of the agriculture sector into four sub-sectors.

Goods and services go either to final "consumption" (consumer expenditure, capital formation, public authority expenditure) or as intermediate inputs to the production of other goods and services. I have calculated intermediate requirements for the output of each industry in each region by applying the 1971 Canada Input-Output coefficients[14] to the region's particular industrial structure. Regional final consumption was inferred by dividing up the all-Canada figures (calculated from GDP and foreign trade data, and the I-O tables) according to the size of gross regional product.

The elasticity estimates needed to work the model (Table 6) are culled from a number of sources. The derivation of capacity and employment elasticities from analysis of establishments within each manufacturing industry was mentioned in Section III. For non-manufacturing industries, the "capacity" elasticity, which is actually the supply (marginal cost) elasticity for the primary industries, was taken, arbitrarily, to be 2/3, so that an x per cent change in price is assumed to have a 2/3x per cent effect on output. Employment elasticities for non-manufacturing are put at 1 (implying a constant employment/value added ratio) except for agriculture, for which it is assumed that, over the medium term, there is no employment response to a price change.

Estimation of price elasticities of demand were arrived at by combining econometric estimates from several sources.[15] The "net rate of protection" is tariff protection net of protection on inputs as a proportion of selling price, aggregated by shipment-shares, from the 3-digit figures given by Dauphin.[16]

All elasticity data sources gave information only at the all-Canada level; therefore, the same numbers are used for all regions.

---

14 Statistics Canada, *The Input-Output Structure of the Canadian Economy, 1961-71*, Cat. No. 15-506E, Ottawa, 1977.

15 Elasticities were calculated by combining estimates of Z. A. Hassan and S. R. Johnson ("Static and Dynamic Demand Functions," Economics Branch, Agriculture Canada, November, 1977) with unpublished estimates by T. Schweitzer and Bobbi Cain of the CANDIDE Modeling group. The two sources tended to agree.

16 Dauphin, *op. cit.*, Table 3-2, pp. 50-5.

V.   RESULTS

We wish to have the reply, promised by the title of this paper, to the question: "what are the costs, or benefits, to each region of its membership in the Canadian confederation?" Now this is a rather difficult question, not just to answer, but even to pose, since we must specify the alternative with which we are to compare the present system. One possible comparison is with the initial impact of separation when this involves adding some restrictions to interregional trade, as in the first option con- sidered here. However, it is reasonable to expect that, in a newly independent region, other important economic factors would change from their present Canadian levels. In particular, I have proposed in the preceding sections a model in which a region's balance of payments and the change in its total numbers employed are functions of exchange rate and wage rate changes as well as the tariff structure. A useful property of the model is that these two functions are linear, or nearly so, and can, therefore, be re-arranged to give two expressions for exchange rate and money wage rate, each a linear function of the balance of payments (BOP), the change in employment (ΔE), and tariffs. With post-separation tariffs held constant, we can then solve the equations to find out what exchange and wage rate adjustments would be required to achieve any given BOP and ΔE situation.

I leave unsettled the question of how such changes would be effected. It could only be direct government policy action (pegged exchange rates, incomes policies), or by market forces, or by a combination of these. So long as the adjustments implied by the BOP and ΔE targets are not unusually large by, say, the standards of past experience, it is probably reasonable to suppose that, by one means or other, they could be achieved.

These "target equations" give us tools we can use to put a figure on the net effect on a region's well-being of leaving confederation (or, if you like, of staying in). We will calculate whether a separated region is better or worse off than before after its level of money wages and the exchange rate of its new currency have adjusted so that (1) employment in the region remains at its pre-separation level, and (2) its balance of payments on current account is the same, as a proportion of gross regional product, as was the Canadian balance of payments before separation. The second of these conditions (suggested to me by Neil Swan) requires some explanation. Its point is to net out interregional transfers, leaving an equal regional apportionment of the current account surplus or deficit of Canada with the rest of the world, which, we assume, could be maintained by a Canada of independent regions. That is, it is proposed that, after separation, each region no longer contributes to, or benefits from, a system of redistributing spending power in Canada among the regions through such federal mechanisms as equalization payments and unemployment insurance.

As the measure of changes in economic well-being, we will use the total annual "absorption" of goods and services in the region -- total private and public consumption and capital formation -- measured in constant (1974) dollars.

None of this is immune from controversy. A region might wish to increase employment over its pre-separation level, and, indeed, may, at least in part, wish to separate in order to do this. Regions' current account BOPs may differ from the Canadian average due to differences in capital account flows reflecting interregional variation in rates of growth and in foreign investment. The use of aggregate absorption as the welfare index, though admirable in its simplicity, glosses over, in particular, the consequences of separation for the division of income between private and public sectors; consequences which are strikingly revealed in the paper by Tony Glynn.

A limitation to the generality of this approach to the costs and benefits question is that the exchange and wage rates are both "expenditure-switching" variables. That is, they work through changes in relative prices to divert expenditure from one industry or source of supply to another. This is acceptable in the case of a region which finds itself, after separation, with a BOP deficit which must be worked off with the cutting-off of the transfers from the other regions which previously had financed it. In this case, a currency devaluation coupled, perhaps, with a fall in the wage level will switch consumption from imports to domestic production, and encourage exports, thus increasing employment and improving the BOP, both desirable results.

In the case of a region with a post-separation BOP surplus, however, expenditure-switching policies may not be the most appropriate, since they will tend to reduce the surplus by reducing exports and increasing imports at the expense of domestic production and employment. If so, "expenditure-augmenting" policies, such as aggregate monetary and fiscal policies, which boost demand for both imports and domestic production, will be preferable. The present model does not, as noted in Section II, incorporate these macroeconomic relationships.[17]

We will consider, too, a second option, namely unilateral free trade, in which all tariffs on world imports are abolished (and the present interregional customs union retained). I expect

---

17 However, they could be allowed for in an *ad hoc* way simply by multiplying absorption, production and import values by proportions according (a) to the size of the fiscal or monetary stimulus assumed, and (b) the different impact (different multipliers) such stimuli have on different industries and sources of supply.

that this is more likely or, at least, of more interest, as an option for a united Canada than for separated regions, excepting, perhaps, the Prairies. In any case, I have not yet calculated regional target equations for option 2.

For one region (Quebec), I have worked through a third option, in which it preserves the present tariffs on world imports and free trade with the rest of Canada, but in which the latter declares unilateral free trade, thus lowering prices of goods competing with Quebec's exports to the other regions.

Keeping in mind all the qualifications and cautions noted above, we proceed to the actual results. These are given, region-by-region in Tables 1 through 5, beginning in the west of Canada.

British Columbia (B.C.) had a deficit on current account in 1974 (Table 1), but this is probably not typical. In other recent years, the Provincial Economic Accounts reveal a surplus more often than not. In any case, "simple separation" (column 2 of the table) has a small effect on the deficit and on employment. The decline in interregional trade in manufactures (the only sector affected by simple separation in the present model) improves the BOP, since the value of the fall in regional imports is greater than the fall in regional exports; the latter being just over one half of the value of the former in 1974. Domestic shipments increase, but not by enough to prevent a fall in employment.

The target equations suggested that a devaluation of 6.5 per cent and an increase in money wages of 1.7 per cent would get the B.C. economy to the required situation of a BOP surplus of about 1.0 per cent of GDP (the all-Canada BOP situation in 1974) and no change in employment. Probably due to inaccuracies caused by non-linearities, the targets are not exactly met, but the finding that real absorption would fall by around $700 million is probably robust.[18]

Unilateral free trade (UFT) increases the deficit by nearly $200 million, mostly due to increased imports of manufactures. However, employment does not fall much as the prices of domestic output falls in competition with import prices.

The *Prairies* begin with a large BOP surplus -- equal to 14 per cent of their GDP in 1974. Simple separation slightly increases this, as the region gains from lower supply prices for regional imports. A hefty revaluation of 20 per cent wipes out most of the surplus, but this is largely done by reducing output in the high-productivity primary and manufacturing sectors rather than by consuming the surplus through increased absorption.

---

18 Of course, had 1974 been one of B.C.'s BOP-surplus years, there might have been no fall in consumption needed.

Clearly, expenditure-switching policies are not very efficient for the Prairies. Coupling revaluation with an expansion in aggregate demand should enable this region to increase absorption by more than its $3.7 billion surplus (the excess coming from the improvement revaluation implied in the terms of trade). UFT induces a small fall in the surplus and increase in absorption. Gross product hardly changes. Again, aggregate demand-augmenting policies are appropriate.

Ontario had a surplus equal to about 8 per cent of its GDP in 1974. About $1.25 billion of this is attributable to its position as a net exporter of manufactured goods at tariff-free prices to the other regions and disappears after simple separation. The target equations were not very accurate in eliminating the remainder of the surplus, but, unlike the Prairies, revaluation is a feasible method for consuming the gains from separation -- Ontario's manufacturing sector is large enough to benefit from a switch in demand away from regional imports, although there is still a net fall in manufacturing employment and a shift into construction and services. Expansionary monetary and fiscal policies could help in lowering the BOP without "de-industrializing" the province.

UFT does reduce Ontario's surplus on total (regional + world) trade in manufactures, but by only about half as much as does simple separation.

Simple separation reduces the BOP of *Quebec* by more than $700 million. This change is about the same as a proportion of GDP (2 1/2 per cent) as it is for Ontario, but the latter province has a comfortable overall BOP surplus to chip away at, whereas Quebec begins with a deficit. Employment falls by about 21,500. Devaluation of 9.3 per cent, along with a very small fall in wage rates, is enough to get Quebec's trade balance near to the required surplus of 1 per cent of GDP. The cost of doing this is a $1.5 billion drop in real absorption. That is, due to the worsening of the terms of trade, it costs about $1.50 to improve the balance of payments by $1, or 5 per cent of Quebec's GDP.

The two other options considered are less damaging to Quebec's BOP than simple separation. Under UFT, the real value of exports to the rest of Canada actually *increases*, a result that may surprise some. This happens because the demand-boosting effect of the lower prices Quebec manufacturers must charge when tariffs are removed from foreign imports is greater than the capacity-reducing effect of lower prices on the fringe of high-cost producers, in enough industries for the net effect to be positive.

There is an increase in productivity following this shift from higher- to lower-cost manufacturers which I have not yet tried to isolate, but which I will investigate further, since it has obvious relevance to the debate on the desirability, for Canada as a whole as well as its regions, of trade liberalization.

The third option, in which Quebec retains tariffs on world imports while living with UFT in the other Canadian regions, results, as one would expect, in a smaller increase in the BOP deficit than does full unilateral free trade.

The *Atlantic* region begins with an enormous deficit of about 40 per cent of its 1974 GDP. Simple separation increases this by another $100 million or so.

According to the target equations, a 30 per cent currency devaluation would eliminate most of the deficit and also induce an increase in employment of more than 13 per cent. Despite this increase in employment and GDP, however, real absorption would have to fall by 20 per cent. These are big numbers.

VI.   SUMMARY AND CONCLUSIONS

This paper reports an attempt to calculate the economic effects on the regions of Canada of some conceivable alternatives to the present federal system. For each region, figures are given for changes in exports, imports, production and employment in each sector. These figures are aggregated to show the effect on total employment, on a region's balance of payments with the rest of Canada and the world, and on the absorption within regions of goods and services, which is taken as a measure of the cost or benefit of membership in the present system.

Two important features of this system are (1) tariff-free movement of goods between regions and (2) interregional transfers, through the federal government, of disposable income. It appears that, with the possible exception of Quebec, the second of these features is the most important. Thus, Ontario loses more from its transfers to other regions than it gains from tariff-free access to their markets. The Prairies lose on both counts. Quebec, which receives transfers and runs a surplus on its inter-regional trade, thereby gains from both. British Columbia appears to gain from confederation, according to the 1974 data used in this study, but might not do so had another year been chosen, so that the *average* effect of confederation on this province may not be substantial and could be of either sign.

The Atlantic region does not appear to be viable as an independent economy, at least within the time-horizon to which the study is restricted. This limited "medium-term" focus of the model is perhaps the most important of the many qualifications and *caveats* strewn through the paper, and to which the reader can no doubt add his or her own list. The time scale matters particularly to our interpretation of these interregional transfers on which so much in the model depends. Canadian regions which receive subsidies from other regions may not enjoy doing so. They may wish to have the sort of industrial structure that would enable them to pay their own way, and may even see the confederate system, as it is presently arranged, as an impediment to long-term changes in their own economies which might achieve this.

Table 1

British Columbia Results[1]

| | 1974 | Option 1 | | Option 2 |
		$\dot{r} = 0.00$ $\dot{w} = 0.00$	$\dot{r} = -0.065$ $\dot{w} = 0.017$	Unilateral Free Trade
Balance of Payments	-435,716	-418,884	182,102	-630,580
Employment	996,000	995,072	992,803	994,314
Absorption, separation prices	15,710,016	15,651,326	15,537,529	15,833,896
Absorption, 1974 prices	15,710,016	15,544,025	14,983,760	16,181,960
Wage Bill	9,534,000	9,521,208	9,686,175	9,516,863
Profits	5,740,300	5,711,234	6,033,457	5,686,453
Gross Domestic Product, separation prices	15,274,300	15,232,442	15,719,632	15,203,316
Gross Domestic Product, 1974 prices	15,274,300	15,251,275	15,337,063	15,238,127
Primary				
Balance of Payments	1,203,999	1,203,999	1,637,229	1,197,239
Employment	73,513	73,513	77,743	73,513
Domestic Shipments	1,848,677	1,848,677	1,820,120	1,843,509
World Exports	1,417,133	1,417,133	1,710,242	1,416,573
World Imports	217,095	217,095	176,151	223,336
Absorption	410,647	410,647	218,401	418,800
Manufacturing				
Balance of Payments	-1,639,715	-1,622,883	-1,455,127	-1,827,819
Employment	143,964	143,036	146,275	142,278
Domestic Shipments	3,662,112	3,740,774	3,717,792	3,604,028
World Exports	2,954,392	2,954,392	3,029,894	2,954,392
Regional Exports	1,398,480	1,259,932	1,371,923	1,381,091
World Imports	3,797,483	3,835,299	3,693,555	4,029,977
Regional Imports	2,482,938	2,368,971	2,371,800	2,442,576
Absorption	5,032,258	4,866,267	4,625,600	5,496,049
Construction, Services				
Employment	778,523	778,523	768,784	778,523
Domestic Shipments	11,229,681	11,229,681	11,098,135	11,229,681
Absorption	10,267,111	10,267,111	10,139,759	10,267,111
Total				
Domestic Shipments	16,740,470	16,819,132	16,636,046	16,677,219
World Exports	4,371,525	4,371,525	4,740,136	4,370,965
Regional Exports	1,398,480	1,259,932	1,371,923	1,381,091
World Imports	4,014,578	4,052,394	3,869,707	4,253,312
Regional Imports	2,482,938	2,368,921	2,371,800	2,442,576

1 Figures are in thousands of dollars except employment, which is in natural numbers. Balance-of-payments figures are in current dollars (separation prices); other sectoral data are in constant (1974) prices.

Table 2

Prairies Results[1]

		Option 1		Option 2
	1974	$\dot{r} = 0.00$ $\dot{w} = 0.00$	$\dot{r} = 0.20$ $\dot{w} = 0.00$	Unilateral Free Trade
Balance of Payments	3,678,303	3,749,632	768,432	3,609,476
Employment	1,497,590	1,497,456	1,480,761	1,495,586
Absorption, seperation prices	20,476,212	20,378,694	20,111,083	20,461,684
Absorption, 1974 prices	20,476,212	20,191,237	21,166,891	20,715,519
Wage Bill	11,152,178	11,151,022	10,981,280	11,134,379
Profits	13,002,337	12,977,303	9,898,235	12,936,781
Gross Domestic Product, seperation prices	24,154,515	24,128,325	20,879,515	24,071,160
Gross Domestic Product, 1974 prices	24,154,515	24,150,076	22,716,105	24,118,246
Primary				
Balance of Payments	7,813,484	7,813,484	4,879,005	7,800,692
Employment	230,250	230,250	225,737	230,246
Domestic Shipments	2,591,217	2,591,217	2,867,184	2,603,355
World Exports	7,899,664	7,899,664	6,224,913	7,887,447
World Imports	86,842	86,842	126,951	87,417
Absorption	1,210,586	1,210,586	1,722,104	1,223,965
Manufacturing				
Balance of Payments	- 4,135,182	- 4,063,853	- 4,110,573	- 4,191,216
Employment	135,643	135,509	123,328	133,643
Domestic Shipments	5,494,246	5,643,972	5,532,028	5,420,204
World Exports	716,624	716,624	650,859	716,624
Regional Exports	1,810,660	1,599,844	1,135,962	1,799,460
World Imports	2,199,996	2,251,791	2,421,983	2,318,738
Regional Imports	4,632,929	4,434,557	4,440,627	4,594,649
Absorption	7,002,111	6,717,135	7,181,270	7,228,038
Construction, Services				
Employment	1,131,697	1,131,697	1,131,697	1,131,697
Domestic Shipments	13,847,002	13,847,002	13,847,002	13,847,002
Absorption	12,263,516	12,263,516	12,263,516	12,263,516
Total				
Domestic Shipments	21,932,465	22,082,192	22,246,214	21,870,561
World Exports	8,616,288	8,616,288	6,875,772	8,604,071
Regional Exports	1,810,660	1,599,844	1,135,962	1,799,460
World Imports	2,286,838	2,338,633	2,548,934	2,406,154
Regional Imports	4,632,929	4,434,557	4,440,627	4,594,649

1 Figures are in thousands of dollars except employment, which is in
   natural numbers. Balance-of-payments figures are in current dollars
   (separation prices); other sectoral data are in constant (1974)
   prices.

Table 3

Ontario Results[1]

	1974	Option 1 $\dot{r} = 0.00$ $w = 0.00$	Option 1 $\dot{r} = 0.07$ $\dot{w} = -0.035$	Option 2 Unilateral Free Trade
Balance of Payments	4,104,118	2,831,226	1,298,457	3,469,647
Employment	3,519,000	3,496,194	3,534,348	3,509,920
Absorption, separation prices	47,696,383	48,349,375	48,068,298	47,840,927
Absorption, 1974 prices	47,696,383	47,927,853	50,056,363	48,992,334
Wage Bill	33,001,003	32,790,258	31,940,857	32,919,968
Profits	18,799,498	18,390,344	17,425,898	18,390,606
Gross Domestic Product, separation prices	51,800,501	51,180,601	49,366,755	51,310,574
Gross Domestic Product, 1974 prices	51,800,501	51,373,833	51,504,435	51,649,244
Primary				
Balance of Payments	-954,048	-954,048	-1,310,803	-985,214
Employment	170,441	170,441	168,448	170,432
Domestic Shipments	4,926,698	4,926,698	4,883,510	4,895,120
World Exports	501,073	501,073	321,397	499,910
World Imports	1,465,732	1,465,732	1,745,389	1,496,091
Absorption	4,167,054	4,167,054	4,487,013	4,192,893
Manufacturing				
Balance of Payments	5,058,166	3,785,275	2,609,260	4,454,861
Employment	883,730	860,924	837,654	874,658
Domestic Shipments	26,107,301	26,382,878	26,323,998	25,778,599
World Exports	11,297,741	11,297,741	11,019,251	11,297,741
Regional Exports	11,991,029	10,740,585	9,841,059	12,020,211
World Imports	14,445,118	14,554,390	15,075,458	15,078,058
Regional Imports	4,758,684	4,525,734	4,391,330	4,586,803
Absorption	14,862,342	15,093,811	16,172,499	16,132,454
Construction, Services				
Employment	2,464,829	2,464,829	2,528,247	2,464,829
Domestic Shipments	31,927,758	31,927,758	32,684,692	31,927,758
Absorption	28,666,987	28,666,987	29,396,850	28,666,987
Total				
Domestic Shipments	62,961,757	63,237,334	63,892,201	62,601,477
World Exports	11,798,814	11,798,814	11,340,648	11,797,651
Regional Exports	11,991,029	10,740,585	9,841,059	12,020,211
World Imports	15,910,849	16,020,121	16,820,847	16,574,149
Regional Imports	4,758,684	4,525,734	4,391,330	4,586,803

1 Figures are in thousands of dollars except employment, which is in natural numbers. Balance-of-payments figures are in current dollars (separation prices); other sectoral data are in constant (1974) prices.

Table 4

Quebec Results[1]

	1974	Option 1 $\dot{r} = 0.00$ $\dot{w} = 0.00$	Option 1 $\dot{r} = -0.093$ $\dot{w} = -0.006$	Option 2 Unilateral Free Trade	Option 3 $\dot{r} = 0.00$ $\dot{w} = 0.00$
Balance of Payments	-774,048	-1,496,009	229,743	-1,175,625	-943,569
Employment	2,427,000	2,405,435	2,440,280	2,422,342	2,425,985
Absorption, separation prices	30,876,345	31,141,152	30,516,578	31,034,684	30,451,224
Absorption, 1974 prices	30,876,345	30,777,667	29,379,648	31,556,668	30,351,067
Wage Bill	19,739,000	19,565,131	19,754,042	19,698,619	19,733,436
Profits	10,363,296	10,080,012	10,992,278	10,160,440	10,304,705
Gross Domestic Product, separation prices	30,102,296	29,645,142	30,746,320	29,859,059	30,038,140
Gross Domestic Product, 1974 prices	30,102,296	29,780,973	30,376,129	30,057,185	30,114,293
Primary					
Balance of Payments	-1,527,941	-1,527,941	-1,241,544	-1,548,768	-1,527,941
Employment	155,726	155,726	158,514	155,683	155,726
Domestic Shipments	2,848,852	2,848,852	3,030,387	2,832,234	2,848,852
World Exports	0	0	0	0	0
World Imports	1,544,337	1,544,337	1,149,023	1,565,235	1,544,337
Absorption	3,173,746	3,173,746	2,886,886	3,202,342	3,173,746
Manufacturing					
Balance of Payments	753,892	31,931	1,471,286	373,143	584,371
Employment	541,500	519,935	544,349	536,885	540,485
Domestic Shipments	13,637,545	13,920,467	13,748,176	13,567,949	13,637,545
World Exports	4,790,121	4,790,121	4,967,854	4,790,121	4,790,121
Regional Exports	6,946,280	5,950,285	6,865,430	6,953,069	6,953,069
World Imports	5,385,168	5,395,881	5,051,204	5,658,295	5,385,168
Regional Imports	5,961,956	5,679,768	5,478,743	6,019,144	5,961,956
Absorption	9,290,954	9,192,276	8,000,449	9,942,682	8,765,676
Construction, Services					
Employment	1,729,774	1,729,774	1,737,417	1,729,774	1,729,774
Domestic Shipments	20,298,699	20,298,699	20,382,251	20,298,699	20,298,699
Absorption	18,411,645	18,411,645	18,492,313	18,411,645	18,411,645
Total					
Domestic Shipments	36,785,096	37,068,018	37,160,814	36,698,882	36,785,096
World Exports	4,790,121	4,790,121	4,967,854	4,790,121	4,790,121
Regional Exports	6,946,280	5,950,285	6,865,430	6,953,069	6,953,069
World Imports	6,929,505	6,940,218	6,200,227	7,223,530	6,929,505
Regional Imports	5,961,956	5,679,768	5,478,743	6,019,144	5,961,956

1 Figures are in thousands of dollars except employment, which is in natural numbers. Balance-of-payments figures are in current dollars (separation prices); other sectoral data are in constant (1974) prices.

Table 5

Atlantic Provinces Results[1]

	1974	Option 1 $\dot{r} = 0.00$ $\dot{w} = 0.00$	Option 1 $\dot{r} = -0.30$ $\dot{w} = 0.00$	Option 2 Unilateral Free Trade
Balance of Payments	-3,173,550	-3,290,588	844,205	-3,421,981
Employment	692,000	688,975	785,624	690,257
Absorption, separation prices	10,829,750	10,873,532	9,284,647	11,025,767
Absorption, 1974 prices	10,829,750	10,763,001	8,257,420	11,415,484
Wage Bill	5,099,000	5,071,731	5,952,184	5,083,051
Profits	2,557,200	2,511,213	4,176,665	2,520,734
Gross Domestic Product, separation prices	7,656,200	7,582,944	10,128,850	7,603,786
Gross Domestic Product, 1974 prices	7,656,200	7,594,058	9,208,929	7,618,168
Primary				
Balance of Payments	-43,569	-43,569	3,459,821	-54,950
Employment	66,431	66,431	144,261	60,431
Domestic Shipments	593,351	593,351	619,876	589,903
World Exports	918,210	918,210	3,351,945	917,580
World Imports	977,267	977,267	701,529	987,931
Absorption	913,711	913,711	-555,600	938,141
Manufacturing				
Balance of Payments	-3,129,981	-3,247,018	-2,615,616	-3,367,030
Employment	83,489	80,464	99,283	81,746
Domestic Shipments	1,850,439	1,932,641	2,233,743	1,782,492
World Exports	2,032,344	1,868,792	2,337,160	2,032,344
Regional Exports	777,964	651,965	943,297	755,662
World Imports	3,918,017	3,988,572	3,379,848	4,235,288
Regional Imports	2,393,605	2,260,957	2,146,502	2,279,682
Absorption	4,697,775	4,631,025	3,594,756	5,259,079
Construction, Services				
Employment	542,080	542,080	542,080	542,080
Domestic Shipments	5,760,154	5,760,154	5,760,154	5,760,154
Absorption	5,218,264	5,218,264	5,218,264	5,218,264
Total				
Domestic Shipments	8,203,944	8,286,146	8,613,774	8,132,549
World Exports	2,950,555	2,787,003	5,689,105	2,949,924
Regional Exports	777,964	651,965	943,297	755,662
World Imports	4,895,284	4,965,840	4,081,377	5,223,220
Regional Imports	2,393,605	2,260,957	2,146,501	2,279,682

1 Figures are in thousands of dollars except employment, which is in natural numbers. Balance-of-payments figures are in current dollars (separation prices); other sectoral data are in constant (1974) prices.

Table 6

Canadian Industry Parameters

Industries	Capacity Elasticity[1]	Employment Elasticity[2]	Domestic Demand Price Elasticity[3]	Import Demand Price Elasticity[4]	Export Demand Price Elasticity[5]	Net Rate of Protection[6]	Domestic Markup on World Price[7]
Agriculture	0.667	0.0	-0.50	--	--	0.003	--
Forestry	0.667	1.000	-0.50	--	--	-0.003	--
Fishing	0.667	1.000	-0.75	--	--	-0.026	--
Petroleum and natural gas	0.667	1.000	-0.75	--	--	0.001	--
Other inedible crude materials	0.667	1.000	-0.50	--	--	-0.014	--
Food and beverage manufacturing	1.399	0.951	-0.50	-0.50	-1.00	0.055	1.041
Tobacco and products industries	1.454	1.419	-0.50	-0.50	-1.00	0.169	1.352
Rubber and plastic products	1.079	1.148	-0.75	-1.00	-1.00	0.059	1.054
Leather products	1.008	1.066	-0.75	-1.25	-1.00	0.158	1.073
Textiles	1.084	1.156	-0.75	-1.25	-1.00	0.105	1.078
Knitting mills	1.231	0.981	-0.75	-1.25	-1.00	0.152	1.007
Clothing	1.140	1.062	-0.75	-1.50	-1.00	0.121	1.084
Wood industries	0.624	0.969	-0.75	-1.25	-1.00	0.039	1.005
Furniture and fixtures	0.723	1.091	-1.00	-1.25	-1.00	0.101	1.051
Paper and allied	1.496	1.248	-0.75	-1.00	-0.75	0.045	1.124
Printing, publishing and allied	0.671	1.225	-1.00	-1.25	-1.00	0.052	1.045
Primary metals	1.524	0.688	-0.50	-0.50	-0.75	0.027	1.033
Metal fabricating	1.038	1.065	-0.75	-0.75	-1.00	0.077	1.113
Machinery	1.216	0.999	-1.00	-1.00	-0.75	0.020	1.063
Transportation equipment	1.712	1.066	-0.75	-0.75	-0.75	0.007	1.005
Electrical products	1.157	1.144	-0.75	-1.25	-1.00	0.078	1.077
Non-metallic mineral products	0.969	1.194	-0.75	-1.00	-0.75	0.050	1.067
Petroleum and coal products	1.946	1.033	-0.75	-0.50	-0.50	0.081	0.993
Chemicals and products	1.012	0.986	-0.75	-1.00	-0.75	0.048	1.082
Miscellaneous manufacturing	1.143	1.092	-0.75	-1.00	-1.00	0.074	1.066
Residual manufacturing industries	0.923	1.000	-0.75	-1.00	-1.00	0.000	1.038
Construction	--	1.000	-1.00	--	--	--	--
All other industries	--	1.000	-0.75	--	--	--	--

1 Percentage change in domestic capacity from a 1 per cent change in price.

2 Percentage change in employment from a 1 per cent change in shipments.

3 Percentage change in Canadian demand for domestic output from a 1 per cent change in domestic price.

4 Percentage change in Canadian demand for imports from a 1 per cent change in import price.

5 Percentage change in demand for Canadian exports from a 1 per cent change in Canadian export price.

6 Effective tariff protecting Canadian output as a proportion of price.

7 0.436 + 3.94 ∗ Herfindahl ∗ net rate of protection + 0.547 ∗ relative Canadian/world costs.

Comments by R. Boadway, Department of Economics,
Queen's University, Kingston

Tim Hazledine has set for himself an extremely ambitious
task, that of predicting changes in resource allocation that would
occur subsequent to a change in the trading arrangements among
Canadian regions. He has done a most creditable job given the
time available and, especially, given the poor quality of the data
on interregional trade flows. My comments will be directed toward
two things:

1. Those aspects of the results and analysis which
    may be sensitive to the manner in which the model
    was formulated;

2. Suggestions for improvements in the modelling of
    the problem.

Most of them will be directed towards the technical economic aspects
of the problem rather than at the broader political economy aspects.

The Law of One Price

The author suggests that the so-called law of one price has
been universally adopted in all work investigating the effects of
tariff changes. This is not so. Those papers which have used
general equilibrium computational techniques to simulate the effects
of tariff changes in open economies have all rejected the law of one
price (e.g. the work of John Whalley and the recent paper on
Canadian tariffs by Boadway and Treddenick in the Canadian Journal
of Economics). These models have typically assumed imports to be
imperfect substitutes for domestically-produced goods as in the
current paper.

The reason for mentioning this explicitly is that I think the
general equilibrium methodology has a great deal to teach us about
these sorts of problems. The technique does not always have to be
applied or restricted to the seemingly sterile, neo-classical,
perfectly competitive models. They can be viewed as a systematic
way for solving simultaneously several supply/demand market
equilibrium conditions of the sort which is implicitly behind this
paper.

The Pricing Model

The analysis proceeds sequentially. First, price changes are assumed on the basis of some shifting assumptions. Then, output, demand, and employment changes are obtained from that. In other words, price changes are imposed independently of the output changes that accompany them. It is very difficult to justify this on theoretical grounds. I am tied to the view that prices have at least some market-clearing function so that price changes cannot be determined independently of quantity changes. Much of microeconomics would fall apart otherwise.

One of the advantages of the general equilibrium computational approach would be to allow prices and outputs on markets to be determined simultaneously from any assumed demand and supply elasticities one cared to postulate. Furthermore, this would allow one to perform sensitivity analysis very easily, something which has not been done here. It would be nice to know how sensitive the results are to the pricing and elasticity assumptions. My own work on Canadian tariffs indicates that results are sensitive to world trade elasticities but not to domestic production elasticities.

There are some particular pricing assumptions which puzzle me somewhat. Imports from one region of Canada into another are assumed to be not fully priced up to the tariff (unlike imports from outside Canada). This implies that the exporter bears part of the tariff imposed by a region. The pricing assumptions used to justify the price changes for import substitutes come from the author's own empirical estimates. However, those estimates are not relevant for determining the pricing mechanism for imports and exports between regions. The other peculiarity is that exports to the rest of the world are not priced up to cost changes. This seems inconsistent with the small open-economy assumptions and is in no way implied by the dropping of the law of one price. It would be worthwhile to make demand and supply elasticities explicit here as well.

Intermediate Goods

Data problems obviously preclude a full treatment of the role of intermediate goods flows between regions, but I suspect this to be an important part of the problem. Intermediate goods price changes have an important impact on prices for all other goods, whether they be manufacturing, primary, or non-traded. The latter industries use traded intermediate inputs so their prices would be expected to change upon a change in tariffs. Unfortunately, this has had to be ignored. Intermediate flows are also an important source of demand. If manufacturing in region A is increased in output due to tariff protection, intermediate purchases from B will be reduced and this will influence output and employment in the latter.

Non-Traded Goods

Tariff changes are assumed not to influence the output of non-traded goods. This is unrealistic for two reasons. First, their prices will change when tariffs on their intermediate purchases are changed. Second, the demand for them will change when the price of other (e.g. manufacturing) goods changes. The work that has been done using the general equilibrium technique has generally found that tariff changes have a large impact upon the output of non-traded goods.

Shipment Changes

The main problem with the calculation of output and shipment changes has already been mentioned: price changes are assumed to be determined prior to and independent of shipment changes. In general, price and output changes are determined simultaneously on markets. In this model some shipment changes are demand-determined and others supply-determined. When investigating the effects of a change in the customs union on a particular region, the regional imports are said to be demand-determined since each region is small relative to the world and to other regions. This does not seem to be consistent with the fact that the imports from other regions are not priced up to tariff changes (i.e. the elasticity of their supply to the importing region is not infinite).

Supply considerations are, however, important in determining shipment changes originating within a region's own manufacturing sector. The mechanism leaves me a bit uneasy. Consider, for example, a reduction in tariffs on manufacturing. The induced price fall is assumed to force some high cost firms out of business. Any demand changes induced by the lower price for manufacturing goods is then assumed to be met by an expansion of the output of the remaining firms in the industry at constant cost. What I find puzzling is why the low cost firms, if they can expand at constant cost, do not force the high cost firms out of business even without any tariff change.

Results

The results are much as one would expect on the basis of an inspection of the data on manufacturing flows among regions. Presumably the results on Quebec separation are the most interesting. The finding is that if Quebec separated, adopted the present tariff structure of Canada, and allowed its exchange rate and wage rate to change to maintain its employment level and balance its current account to correspond to that of Canada's before separation, its real absorption would fall by $1.5 billion per year. This is obviously no paltry sum and may be an underestimate due to the fact that factor movements, especially capital flows, are assumed away. Presumably what is happening here is that Quebec is made worse off due to the fall in exports to other regions (e.g. textiles) when tariff protection of markets in the rest of Canada is lost.

I have only three comments about these results in addition to those I have already stated. First, it would be interesting to know the effect of Quebec's separation on the well-being of the rest of Canada as well as the effects on Quebec which are reported here. It is certainly not obvious *a priori* whether they would be better or worse off. Second, some sensitivity analysis would be helpful to test the robustness of these results. Finally, the assumption that both Canada and Quebec would adopt the pre-separation Canadian tariff structure is a strong one. Other tariff structures might be experimented with.

CONFEDERATION AND SOME REGIONAL IMPLICATIONS

OF THE TARIFFS ON MANUFACTURES

by

L. Auer
K. Mills

Economic Council of Canada

Objectives of Study

This paper attempts to show how Canadian manufactures tariffs affect producers and consumers in each province today, and how alternative tariffs under a different set of federal-provincial arrangements -- including Quebec separation -- might affect them tomorrow.

Four distinctly different tariff scenarios are considered. One relates to tariffs under confederation and the other three to tariffs arising from a Quebec separation. Within confederation today manufactures of all provinces are protected by a common tariff wall and, therefore, all provinces are insulated to the same degree against competition from foreign imports. By examining the potential impact of a "free-trade" policy, it can be shown how vulnerable Canadian manufacturing industries are to free trade today; to what extent the current tariffs protect manufacturing employment in plants, small and large; how many plants might have to close if tariff protection were removed; what cuts in salary employees might have to accept if they wanted to keep these plants open; which industries would be threatened most and which ones least; and how in all these aspects the impact might differ from one province to the next.

On the consumer side the study examines how today's tariffs raise prices of some of the basic necessities, how that affects the "average family" and how it affects those families and unattached individuals whose incomes are close to the "poverty line." Then we compare producer "benefits," in short run pre-servation of jobs, to consumer "costs," in higher prices, showing which provinces would gain most and least if tariffs were elimi-nated. This information is essential background for understanding the issues at stake in the present debate on confederation, es-pecially as regards the stance the rest of Canada might wish to take on the issue of sovereignty-association. The analysis done here is short run, but revealing nevertheless.

In a similar vein, some trade policies are examined that might be imposed if Quebec were to separate from the rest of Canada. Looking at separation of Quebec as a process of economic disintegration,[1] separation leads in the opposite direction to that of the "Common Market experience":[2] Trade links between Quebec and the rest of Canada will weaken, tariff walls will arise between the two, and the markets now open to both will shrink in size. Since it is impossible to predict precisely which tariff policy the former trading partners might pursue after separation, three

---

1   Deutsch, A. "Quebec Libre and the Economics of Disintegration," in the *Journal of Canadian Studies*, February 1968.

2   Krause, B. *The Meaning of European Economic Integration for the United States*, Brookings Institution, Economic Studies, February 1968.

different trade scenarios will be considered: one represents a very "hostile" trade scenario, the second describes a "mixed" scenario, and a third is what one might call a "tit-for-tat" scenario. Not all three are equally likely to occur but each will be described in detail later and in every case the impact on employment in the short run will be estimated for Quebec as well as the rest of Canada.

This analysis is very limited in scope. It deals only with economic questions and ignores all social, cultural, and political aspects; it covers only the manufacturing industries and ignores all other goods-producing and service industries;[3] it ignores longer-run adjustments, such as alterations in exchange rates, in monetary and fiscal policy, in industrial structure and technology, as well as potential changes in flows of foreign investment that might accompany an event as traumatic as separation. No attempts are made to specify what action ought to be taken to overcome the potential adjustment problems. The analysis should provide, however, a fair indication of the size of the adjustment problem that awaits the manufacturing industries, should tariffs be removed today or should Quebec separate from the rest of Canada tomorrow.

The order of presentation is as follows: Canada's national tariff policy is described first, some regional aspects of tariff protection are presented next, then the provincial benefits and costs of the present Canadian tariffs are examined and, finally, it is shown what the initial losses or gains might be if Quebec were to separate.

Canadian Tariff Protection

In the past, Canadian governments have employed tariffs with the objective of stimulating the growth of the manufacturing industries of the eastern provinces, and of accelerating population growth and development of the resource industries of the western provinces.

During the early decades of this century, U.S. policy afforded U.S. producers a higher degree of protection than Canadian producers. Towards the end of the Great Depression of the 1930s, however, a reciprocal trade agreement was reached with the United States aimed at reducing tariffs. As well, attempts were made to lessen the role of bilateral agreements with the United Kingdom in favour of freer trade. Following the Second World War, even stronger support emerged for lowering the barriers of trade when all the major trading nations endorsed a "General Agreement on Tariffs and Trade." As one of its initiators, Canada accepted the underlying principle of the (GATT) agreement that national commercial policy measures should not primarily serve to achieve high levels of employment in protected industries at the expense of other trading partners, but should be used to promote growth of world trade, international specialization, and efficiency of national production. Canada participated in several rounds of tariff

---

3 Cf. the paper by T. Hazledine, also being delivered at the Workshop, which covers all sectors, not just manufacturing, and in which some possible effects of changes in the value of the currency and monetary and fiscal policy are considered as well.

negotiations under GATT and, along with other countries, reduced its tariff barriers substantially.

Table 1

Industrial Tariff Rates on Total and Dutiable Imports, by Commodity Group, Canada and Major Trading Partners, 1973

	Trading Nations			
	CANADA	USA	ECC	JAPAN
Total Import Average				
Raw materials	0.3	2.7	0.5	5.9
Semi-finished manufactures	8.4	7.6	8.1	8.6
Finished manufactures	10.2	7.9	9.3	11.2
All industrial products	7.7	6.7	7.2	9.4
Dutiable Import Average				
Raw materials	7.2	6.1	3.4	9.3
Semi-finished manufactures	12.7	9.0	9.6	9.9
Finished manufactures	14.7	8.3	9.6	11.5
All industrial products	13.7	8.1	9.1	10.7

Source   *Looking Outward: A New Trade Strategy for Canada*, Economic Council of Canada, Information Canada, Ottawa, 1975, p. 11. These tariff rates vary somewhat with estimation procedures but the variations do not alter the basic conclusion that some of the Canadian manufacturing industries are very highly protected -- much more so than in other countries -- while others are comparatively little protected.

Today, Canadian tariff rates, in comparison to those of other industrialized countries, fall in the medium to upper range. They rank high if averaged over finished manufacturing products, and higher yet if averaged only over those commodities that are dutiable. That is so because typically the primary Canadian industries, e.g., agriculture, forestry and mining, as well as some of the resource-based secondary manufacturing industries, have little or no tariff protection while others are very highly protected. As shown in Table 1, Canadian tariff rates range from a low of 0.3 per cent for the import average of raw materials to a high of 14.7 per cent for dutiable imports of highly finished manufacturing products.

Similarly, a wide range of tariff rates applies to the manufacturing industries. Judging by the effective rates, generous protection -- at a rate of over 20 per cent -- is granted to knitting mills, the textile and clothing industries, and the leather-products industry, and very limited protection -- at a rate of 5 per cent or less -- is given to about half of the remaining industries (Table 2). A very low rate of tariff is also listed for the transportation-equipment industry, but in this case subsidies to the shipbuilding and motor vehicle industries provide some additional shelter. This does not change the ranking significantly, however, because quotas, subsidies and tax concessions generally reinforce the protection afforded by tariffs, even to those industries that are already highly protected by tariffs.[4]

A ranking of manufacturing industries according to tariff rates does not necessarily correspond to their importance in the economy. Industries with high rates of tariff protection may account for very little of total output while others with low tariff rates may account for a large part of it. To assess the potential impact of tariff changes on domestic production and import flows, it is necessary, therefore, to take the size of the different industries into account. Weighting the tariff rates by value of manufacturing[5] ranks the food and beverage industries with 20 per cent of the total, first; the leather, textile, knitting and clothing industries with 19 per cent, second; and the paper and allied industries with 16 per cent, third. Together these three industry groups account for over half of the tariff protection and, if combined with the metal fabricating and electrical equipment industries, for three-quarters of the tariff protection of all manufacturing industries. Because of their larger weight in tariff protection, some of these industry groups will be examined more closely.

Historically, tariffs have been granted to industry for a variety of reasons. They have been granted to enable industries to compete with cheap foreign labour, to retaliate against restrictive tariffs imposed by other countries, to equalize the cost of production at home and abroad, to shelter an industry at the "peril point" from extinction, to improve the country's terms of trade, to help reduce high unemployment, to shift from a specialized to a more diversified economy, and to help promising infant industries

---

4 See, for example, B. W. Wilkinson and K. Norrie, *Effective Protection and the Return to Capital,* Economic Council of Canada, Information Canada, 1975, Table 3-4, pp. 42, 43.

5 Following traditional methods of estimation the degree of tariff protection is measured here by weighting of the individual commodity tariffs, at a more refined level of disaggregation, by the relative amount of value added. It implies that manufacturers price right up to the tariff barrier. In this general area see, for example, J. Melvin, "A Weighting Problem in the Calculation of Effective Tariff Protection: A Comment," in the *Economic Record* (June 1972).

Table 2

Tariff Rates and Tariff Protection
Afforded to Canadian Manufacturers, Canada, 1974

	Effective Tariff Rate	Percentage Distribution of Effective Protection
Food and Beverages	16	20
Tobacco Products	-1	0
Rubber Products	18	5
Leather Products	27	2)
Textiles	21	)
Knitting Mills	32	7) 19
		2)
Clothing Industries	29	8)
Wood Industries	5	2
Furniture and Fixtures	20	4
Paper and Allied Products	15	16
Printing and Publishing	2	1
Primary Metals	4	3
Metal Fabricating	14	12
Machinery	1	1
Transport Equipment	-2	-2
Electrical Equipment	15	9
Nonmetallic Minerals	4	1
Petroleum and Coal Products	5	1
Chemicals and Chemical Products	5	4
Miscellaneous	13	4
All Manufacturing	10	100

Source   The effective rates were based on the 1974 nominal tariff
         rates and the 1970 Input-Output Table of Statistics Canada;
         all estimates were derived from more disaggregated data.

acquire competitive strength. Most of these reasons for tariff
protection can be rejected as false, as a textbook on first
principles of economics will readily show.[6] A notable exception
among them, however, is the infant-industry argument whose advocates would favour a temporary protective tariff for those industries which have a strong potential for future growth once the
critical points of learning experience and scale of production
have been reached.

Although the objectives of Canadian tariff policy of earlier
years have never been clearly defined, statistical analysis suggests
that the existing Canadian tariffs are not designed for temporary
protection of promising infant industries but favour old-established
manufacturing sectors which rely heavily on low-priced labour.
As shown in Table 3, Canadian tariff rates are higher for labour-
intensive manufacturing industries which require more labour per
unit of output, employ labour of less skill with lower ratings in
education and work experience, produce in smaller plants, and lag
behind in productivity growth. During the past decade, for example,
manufacturing industries whose labour productivity was 10 per cent
below the national average received 4 per cent higher tariff protection. If, in addition, their growth rate was 10 per cent below
the national average, they received another 3 per cent protection.[7]
The inverse applied to the more efficient industries. The higher
the level of labour productivity and the greater the rate of growth,
the lower was the rate of tariff protection.

The explanation for this seemingly perverse incentive system
is quite simple. Low-productivity and slow-growth manufacturing
industries often have difficulty in attracting more capital investment, are unable to modernize their plants, and can not afford to
pay higher wage rates even at the best of times. Although often
they employ less-skilled and lower-paid labour, they are not able
to compete against cheaper imports. Tariff protection of such
industries is not likely to solve their long-run problems and may
only prolong the agony of adjustment. In the short run, however,
tariff protection of such industries will raise the returns to
capital, save jobs, keep people from being unemployed, and perhaps
enable families to maintain their incomes above poverty levels.

Regional Aspects of Tariff Protection

Within the context of federal-provincial arrangements or
re-arrangements, questions of tariff policy would hardly matter if
the size of the manufacturing sector and the industry mix were
the same in all provinces. But about one half of Canada's manufacturing output is produced in Ontario, not quite one-third in

---

6 See, for example, P. A. Samuelson, *Economics, An Introductory Analysis*,
   McGraw-Hill Book Company, Inc., Toronto, Ninth Edition, 1973, Chapter 35.

7 Estimates are based on regression results given in Appendix Table 1.

Table 3

Relationship between Tariff Rates and Selected Industry
Characteristics, Manufacturing, Canada, 1974

Rank of Industry's Tariff Rate[1]	Average Tariff Rate[2]	Labour Inten- sity[3]	Labour Product- ivity[4]	Labour Quality[5]	Plant Size[6]	Productivity Growth[7]
	(Per cent)					
High	280	166	60	85	112	94
Medium	153	94	106	102	152	98
Low	66	93	107	107	234	102

1   Among 19 (2-Digit SIC) manufacturing industries the six
    protected by the highest (nominal) tariff rates are ranked high,
    the next seven medium, and the remaining six low. The tobacco
    industry was excluded because its nominal and effective tariff
    rates differ widely.

2   All estimates are expressed in percentages of the (weighted)
    average of all manufacturing industries. The average tariff
    rate of 280 per cent of the high-ranking group, for example,
    implies that the nominal tariff rate of this group was 2.8
    times as high as that of all manufacturing in 1974.

3   Estimates of labour intensity are based on the ratio of workers
    (employees plus working owners) per unit of value added. A
    labour intensity of 166 per cent of the high-ranking group, for
    example, implies that it takes 1.66 times as many workers to
    produce a million dollars' worth of (value-added) output in this
    group as it takes on average in all manufacturing.

4   Labour productivity estimates are defined as the ratio of value
    added per worker, and are the inverse of labour-intensity estimates.

5   Labour-quality estimates are based on criteria of age, educa-
    tion and sex of manufacturing employment of the year 1970.
    Estimation technique and additional statistics are given in
    L. Auer, *Regional Disparities of Productivity and Growth in
    Canada*, Economic Council of Canada (forthcoming).

6   Plant size refers to the number of workers per establishment,
    averaged over the period 1970-73.

7   Estimates of 1961-74 end-point growth rates of value added per
    worker, in current dollars.

Quebec and the remaining fifth in the eight other provinces.
Since Canada's manufacturing industries are mostly located in
Ontario and Quebec, it would be a fair guess to say that these
two provinces rely more on tariff protection than other provinces
and, *vice versa*, if tariffs on manufactures were removed they would
be affected more than other provinces. To extrapolate this line of
reasoning, however, and to say that the provincial reliance upon
tariff protection is simply proportionate to the provincial shares
of manufacturing output, is to overstate the case. There are a
number of reasons why this is not so.

As shown in Table 4, the levels of tariff protection vary
greatly among provinces. The highest levels of protection are
afforded to manufacturers in Quebec and Manitoba. Compared to
Ontario, for example, Quebec's level of protection is one quarter
higher.[8] At the same time, Quebec and Manitoba are the only
provinces where all four characteristics of industry performance,
i.e., the level of labour productivity, the quality of the work
force, the size of plants, and the rate of productivity growth,
fall below the national average. Perhaps this does not come as
a surprise since it was shown earlier that Canadian tariffs rates
are highest for the labour-intensive manufacturing industries
which require more labour per unit of output, employ labour of
lower quality ratings, produce in smaller plants, and lag behind
in productivity growth. A tariff policy of this kind will, of
course, favour manufacturers of those provinces that rank lowest
in these performance characteristics.

While the provinces with the highest levels of tariff protection rank below average in all four measures of industry performance,
the opposite does not hold true. The provinces with the lowest
levels of tariff protection, i.e., Newfoundland, Alberta, and Ontario,
do not rank above average in all measures of performance. It is
clear from this that there are considerable variations in tariff
protection and industry performance and that it could be misleading
to estimate how a province might be affected by tariff changes by
considering only the provincial level of tariff protection or the
size of the provincial manufacturing sector.

The pattern of foreign and domestic trade also has a bearing
on the potential impact of tariff changes. The more efficient an
industry, the more likely it is that it can compete in world markets,
and, *vice versa*, the less efficient it is, the more likely that it
must depend on its tariff protected home markets. In 1974, Canadian
manufacturers shipped one fifth of their output to foreign markets,
a quarter to other provinces, and the remainder, about one half,
to their home province. British Columbia and three of the four
Atlantic provinces exceeded the national proportion of exports

---

8 This conclusion is based on the relative tariff rates of 118 and
   93, for Quebec and Ontario respectively (Table 4, col. 1).

Table 4

ariff Rates and Selected Industry Characteristics,
Manufacturing, Canada (=100) and Provinces, 1974[1]

Province	Nominal Tariff Rate	Labour Productivity	Labour Quality	Plant Size	Productivity Growth
	(Per cent)				
Newfoundland	76	93	100	98	106
Prince Edward Island	103	70	93	32	109
Nova Scotia	99	81	100	82	110
New Brunswick	104	98	98	92	113
Quebec	118	88	96	97	97
Ontario	93	106	102	123	99
Manitoba	107	84	98	71	96
Saskatchewan	86	103	101	41	96
Alberta	91	106	104	56	96
British Columbia	96	112	106	77	106
Canada[2]	100	100	100	100	100

1 The estimates of industry characteristics correspond to the
   national estimates described earlier in Table 3. Estimates
   in columns 1 and 2 relate to the year 1974, in column 3 to
   1970, in column 4 to 1974 and in column 5 to 1963-74.

2 Excludes Yukon and North West Territories.

to foreign markets, Ontario was right on average, and the other
five provinces -- including again Manitoba and Quebec -- fell
well below the national average. All provinces shipped their
manufactured goods to other provinces but only three provinces --
Newfoundland, British Columbia and Ontario -- shipped less than
half as much as they shipped to their home market to other
provinces. All other provinces in the Atlantic region, the
Prairie provinces and Quebec were relatively more dependent on
interprovincial trade. As will be shown later, it is partly this
dependence on interprovincial trade that makes the latter provinces,
including Quebec, more vulnerable to lower tariffs.

Table 5

Destination of Shipments of Goods of Own Manufacture
by Province of Origin, Canada, 1974

	Exports[1] (Per cent)	Shipments to Other Provinces (Per cent)	Shipments to Same Province (Per cent)	Total of All Shipments	
				(Per cent)	($ Millions)
Newfoundland	62	13	25	100	712
Prince Edward Island	8	44	48	100	94
Nova Scotia	25	37	37	100	1,696
New Brunswick	33	35	32	100	1,586
Quebec	14	30	57	100	22,397
Ontario	20	23	57	100	41,404
Manitoba	9	34	57	100	2,280
Saskatchewan	11	33	56	100	1,045
Alberta	7	32	61	100	3,821
British Columbia	38	14	49	100	7,411
Canadian Average[2]	20	25	55	100	82,446

1   Exports are based on province of lading.

2   Excludes Yukon and North West Territories.

To estimate what part of the provincial manufacturing would be affected by changes in tariffs, that is to say, what part of the industry would be "tariff-vulnerable," the industry characteristics and the patterns of trade need to be taken into account. Towards this end, we examine how many plants in each industry would have to close down and by how much the surviving plants would have to cut their output. At the same time, information on wage rates, price of material inputs, labour productivity, foreign and provincial trade, is brought to bear on these questions.

Analysis of the twenty major manufacturing industries shows that over the years 1963 to 1974 a change in the industry price often affects the smaller plants more seriously than the larger plants, that accommodating adjustments in wage rates could moderate this impact, and that concurrent changes in material prices could modify the impact on the whole industry. It is estimated, for example, that a 10 per cent cut in prices, brought about by an industry-wide cut in tariffs, would threaten the survival of plants in some industries much more than in others. Among the industries related to clothing, the leather-goods-producing plants would be hardest hit, with a 15 per cent reduction in the number of plants irrespective of plant size (Table 6). The textile plants would be a close second with anywhere from 8 to 15 per cent reduction in plant numbers, with small plants closing at nearly twice the rate of large plants. Among the furniture and fixture plants, the survival of small plants would also be threatened more than that of large plants. Indeed, the same holds true for most other industries. A striking exception, however, is the petroleum and coal products industry where an industry-wide cut in prices would not only affect a large part of the plants but would threaten the survival of large plants even more than that of smaller plants. Some other notable exceptions are the pulp and paper industry, the publishing industry and the primary metal industry where adjustments to price changes are not at all size-specific.[9]

The very unfavourable impact of tariff-induced price reductions on plant survival could be moderated substantially if labour was prepared to reduce its wage rates accordingly. Indeed, the estimates suggest that no plants, small or large, would need to close if labour reduced its wage rates at the same rate as tariff reduction reduced prices. If, for example, tariff removal would lower prices of shipments by, say, 10 per cent, no plants would need to close if labour reduced its wage rate by 10 per cent too. Or, if labour was not willing to lower wages by quite as much but by some intermediate amount, say by half the percentage cut in prices, e.g., 5 per cent, a little over half of the "endangered" plants would survive.

Over the past ten to fifteen years, wage rates and prices of material inputs have risen along with prices of shipments. Although the recent rise in energy prices may have given the impression that prices of material inputs have risen much faster than wage rates, analysis of the years 1963-74 shows that this is not so. Relative to the price of manufacturing output, annual wage rates have risen 82 per cent, while prices of material inputs have risen only 6 per cent.[10] At the same time, labour has obtained an increasingly larger share of the returns in manufacturing. This happened during a period of rapid economic growth. Should tariffs be removed and prices of manufacturing output fall, it is *not* likely that drastic downward adjustments in wage rates would accommodate this fall. To wit: the textile industry has recently encountered serious problems of meeting international competition, yet minimum wage rates have been raised at the same time, an action that might render the industry even less competitive.

In all further analysis of tariff changes, therefore, it is assumed that labour does not agree to lower (nominal) wage

---

9 Perhaps this is related to the fact that in these industries some large firms operate or control plants of varying sizes and, therefore, can withstand the competition of the market place better than others. This hypothesis, however, was not tested.

10 For details, see Appendix Table 2.

Table 6

Percentage Reduction in Numbers of Plants Resulting from a
10 Per Cent Reduction in the Price of Shipments,
by Plant Size[1]

Industry	Plant Size[2]								
	1-4	5-9	10-19	20-49	50-99	100-199	200-499	500-999	1000+
Food and Beverage	9	5	2						
Tobacco Products	1								
Rubber and Plastic Products	21								
Leather	15	15	15	15	15	15	15	15	15
Textile	15	14	13	12	11	11	10	9	8
Knitting Mills	4								
Clothing	9	7	6	4	2	1			
Wood	2								
Furniture and Fixture	12	10	10	9	8	7	7	6	5
Paper and Allied									
Printing, Publishing and Allied									
Primary Metal	1								
Metal Fabricating	1								
Machinery	3								
Transportation Equipment	6								
Electrical Products	17	7							
Nonmetallic Mineral Products	10	3							
Petroleum and Coal Products	20	23	24	26	29	30	32	33	36
Chemical and Chemical Products	3								
Miscellaneous Manufacturing	6	4	2						
Total Manufacturing	19	13	8						

1   Table based on regressions equations listed in Appendix Table 3.

2   Plant size groups are defined in terms of numbers of workers
    (employees plus working owners) per plant.

rates, even if the survival of some of the plants in the industry were at stake.[11]

Elimination of the less efficient and less competitive plants, however, would not accommodate the full impact of tariff removal. In all size groups average shipments per plant can be expected to fall off. For most industries a 10 per cent reduction in the price of shipments would mean a real output reduction of less than 10 per cent. It appears to be critical, however, whether or not the prices of material inputs are reduced at the same time. If they were reduced by the same proportion, i.e., 10 per cent, as shipment prices, they would have no additional effect. If, however, they were reduced by only five per cent or not at all, the impact could be very serious. Hardest hit, by far, would be the textile, food and beverage industries, but also the knitting, the primary metal, and metal fabricating industries would be threatened (Table 7).

Compared to the Canadian average, more plants in Ontario fall into the larger size groups than in any other province. According to one measure, for example, Ontario's plants exceed the size of the average Canadian plant in three out of four manufacturing industries. Quebec exceeds it in half of them, and all the other provinces exceed it by only one out of four or less. Since tariff and price reductions can be expected to hit small plants harder than large plants, the plant size distribution will favour Ontario and Quebec over the others.

As well, there are substantial provincial variations in labour productivity. Part of these come from provincial variations in industrial structure and part come from lower output per worker in each industry. After adjusting for industrial structure, manufacturing output per worker in Ontario, Saskatchewan, Alberta and British Columbia is greater than in Quebec, Manitoba and the Atlantic provinces. Output per worker in Quebec and Manitoba is 10 to 20 per cent, and in the Atlantic Provinces as much as 40 per cent, below that of the high-productivity provinces.[12] Since lower output per worker implies that more people are required to produce the same output, it also implies that more people will be laid off if production is cut. Should tariff-induced price changes lead to

---

11 It is interesting to note that improvements in production technology and labour productivity, leading to lower unit labour costs, might be more effective in helping plants survive than the lowering of wage rates. The efficacy of such measures, however, would depend on the long-run prospects of these industries. It is unlikely that adoption of new technology could save all industries, let alone all plants.

12 *Living Together: A Study of Regional Disparities*, Economic Council of Canada, 1977, pp. 66, 67.

Table 7

Percentage Reduction in Shipments per Plant
Resulting from a 10 per cent Reduction in Price,
under Various Assumptions of Material Costs[1]

| | Percentage Reductions of Shipments | | |
Industry	Price of Material Reduced by 10 per cent	Price of Material Reduced by 5 per cent	Price of Material Unchanged
Food and Beverage	16	50	71
Tobacco Products	6	11	15
Rubber and Plastics Products	10	19	28
Leather	7	9	11
Textile	7	66	88
Knitting Mills	3	31	52
Clothing	7	16	25
Wood	6	6	6
Furniture and Fixture	5	21	35
Paper and Allied	4	14	24
Printing, Publishing and Allied	11	16	20
Primary Metal	12	32	49
Metal Fabricating	10	32	50
Machinery	6	6	7
Transportation Equipment	15	15	15
Electrical Products	7	13	20
Nonmetallic Mineral Products	12	18	24
Petroleum and Coal Products	6	11	16
Chemical and Chemical Products	2	2	2
Miscellaneous Manufacturing	5	27	45
Total Manufacturing	13	26	42

1 Table based on regression coefficients listed in Appendix Table 4. The percentage estimates suggest by how much shipments per plant would be reduced if prices of material inputs were to fall at various rates relative to the price reduction in shipments.

production cuts, the low-productivity regions in Canada, including Quebec, will be hit harder by employment cuts than the high-productivity regions.[13]

Provincial "Benefits" and "Costs" of Canadian Tariffs Today

To assess how Canadian tariffs affect producers and consumers in each province today, industry-specific tariff rates, the size of the industry, the size of plants, plant survival, prices of material inputs, output per worker, industry structure, and the provincial pattern of domestic and foreign trade are brought together in a consistent framework. That makes it possible to estimate by how much manufacturing revenue would be reduced in each province and how many workers would lose their jobs, in the short term at least, if all tariffs were removed overnight. As shown in Table 8, gross revenue would drop by 23 billion dollars and nearly 275 thousand workers would be laid off. That is roughly equivalent to 15 per cent of all manufacturing employment and represents about 8.6 per cent of the employment in the goods-producing industries, and 3.2 per cent of the Canadian labour force. Ontario and Quebec would account for 83 per cent of all the employment losses, and the rest of Canada for the other 17 per cent. Although manufacturers' shipments of Quebec are only about half as large as those of Ontario, the employment losses of Quebec would come to within 10 per cent of those of Ontario. Indeed, Quebec would lose nearly 20 per cent of its manufacturing employment, one of the highest percentage losses among the ten provinces (Table 8).

A substantial part of the provincial variations in potential employment losses can be traced to industry-specific tariff rates and provincial industry structure. As mentioned earlier, tariffs granted to the food and clothing industries are much higher than those of most other industries. Since Quebec has a larger share of its manufacturing employment in these highly protected industries, its potential loss from tariff removal is correspondingly larger. With 14.5 per cent they account for nearly twice the percentage loss of manufacturing employment of 7.7 per cent in Ontario (Table 9). Thus, tariff protection of the food and clothing industries makes for different levels of protection of the individual provinces.

The benefits of tariff protection to producers, in terms of short-run preservation of jobs, can be compared to the costs to consumers, in terms of more expensive goods. Estimates along this line are based on the assumption that tariff-induced price increases on the industry side are passed on to consumers and increase consumer expenditures accordingly. Without the tariffs granted to Canadian producers, consumer expenditures would be substantially lower. The price of food, for example, would be nearly 10 per cent lower

---

13   This conclusion is based on the earlier assumption that workers will not opt for reduction in their nominal wage rates even if it would save the jobs of their fellow workers in the less efficient manufacturing plants.

Table 8

Estimated Revenue and Employment Losses in the Short Run
from Complete Tariff Removal, Canada and Provinces[1]

(Based on 1974 data)

	Gross Revenue Loss	Employment Loss		
			Percentage of:	
		Numbers	Manufacturing	Goods-Producing Industries
	(Million)	(Thousands)		
Newfoundland	62	1.5	9.6	2.3
Prince Edward Island	43	.6	22.5	3.6
Nova Scotia	318	5.2	13.9	6.0
New Brunswick	376	4.2	12.5	5.1
Quebec	7,942	108.9	19.5	12.7
Ontario	10,653	118.8	14.0	9.7
Manitoba	850	9.8	17.4	7.1
Saskatchewan	306	2.8	14.4	1.9
Alberta	1,135	9.2	15.1	3.6
British Columbia	1,435	13.0	8.4	4.0
Canada	23,120	274.0	15.3	8.6

1   Estimation procedures are described briefly in the Appendix
of this paper.

Source   Based on data of Statistics Canada.

Table 9

Estimated Employment Losses in the Short Run from Complete
Tariff Removal, Food and Clothing Industries, Canada and Provinces

(Based on 1974 data)

| | Employment Losses[1] | | | As per cent of Total Manufacturing Employment |
	Food	Clothing[2]	Food and clothing	
	(Thousands)			
Newfoundland	1.4	–	1.4	8.8
Prince Edward Island	.6	–	.6	22.6
Nova Scotia	2.9	1.3	4.2	11.2
New Brunswick	3.2	.1	3.3	9.9
Quebec	20.4	61.0	81.4	14.5
Ontario	28.5	36.7	65.2	7.7
Manitoba	4.3	2.9	7.2	12.9
Saskatchewan	2.0	.3	2.3	12.0
Alberta	5.3	.7	6.0	9.8
British Columbia	5.8	1.7	7.5	4.9
Canada	74.4	104.9	179.2	10.1

1 Estimates of employment losses have been derived as described
in footnotes 1 and 2 of Table 10.

2 Clothing industries comprise the leather, textile, knitting
and clothing manufacturers.

Source Based on data of Statistics Canada.

and that of clothing over 20 per cent lower.[14]   This reduction
could have saved the average urban family of four over 500 dollars
per year in 1974.   Since food and clothing are essential expenditure items, it is very difficult for low-income families to cut
down on these expenditures.   Savings on food and clothing, therefore, would have been of particular benefit to the low-income
families.   In 1974, for example, the savings could have lowered
the incidence of poverty in Canada by an estimated 25 per cent,
from roughly 1.4 million people living below the poverty line
before removal of tariffs to 1.0 million people thereafter.

     Consumer costs of tariffs, computed in this manner, can be
compared to the extra returns of producers and the government.
On the consumer side the annual costs are simply the extra expenditures on higher-priced tariff-protected manufactures and imports;
on the producer side the benefits are the extra wages and salaries
paid to labour as well as the extra returns to capital; and on the
government side they are the extra tax revenue from duties collected
on imports.   Some of these costs and benefits are listed side by
side in Table 10.   It shows that tariffs imposed on food and
clothing alone add over 2 billion dollars to consumer expenditures
annually and raise the level of poverty in Canada by over 350
thousand persons.[15]   The principal benefit of the same tariffs is
a saving of about 180 thousand jobs in the food and clothing industries.[16]   This does not yield a favourable cost-benefit ratio:
after allowance is made for 453 million dollars of customs duties
collected by the federal government, it costs $1.93 billion to save
these 180 thousand jobs, enough to pay every worker who would have
lost his job in these industries over 10,000 dollars annually.

     Provincially the costs and benefits of tariffs vary with popu-
lation size, income, manufacturing activities and productivity
performance.   Because the two central provinces account for over
half of Canada's population, one would expect that they account
also for over half of the costs and benefits of tariffs.   This is
confirmed in the case of food and clothing, for example, where
over two thirds of all consumer costs and benefits accrue to these
two provinces.   Although Quebec's population is only three quarters
the size and its manufacturing output is only about half
the size of Ontario's, Quebec's employment benefits, derived from

---

14   Assuming that removal of tariff protection would lead to corresponding
     price reductions at the retail level, the prices of food and clothing
     would have been reduced by an estimated 9.6 and 23.1 per cent, respectively,
     in 1974.   These price reductions would only hold if the "surviving" plants
     could produce food and clothing at world competitive prices, a necessary
     assumption which will be reconsidered at the end of this paper.

15   The corresponding estimates in Table 10 are the totals of 2,383 million
     dollars and of 357 thousand persons, and 179 thousand jobs lost.

16   The food and clothing industries include the food and beverage processors
     and the leather, textile, knitting and clothing manufacturers.

Table 10

Consumer Costs and Employment Benefits in the Short Run
of Selected Manufactures Tariffs, Canada and Provinces

(Based on 1974 data)

	Consumer Costs[1]		Employment Benefits[2]	
	Extra Expense on Food and Clothing	Increase in Poverty	Food and Clothing Manufacturers	All Manufacturers
	(Millions of dollars)	(Thousands)	(Thousands)	
Newfoundland	32	9	1	2
Prince Edward Island	5	1	1	1
Nova Scotia	49	9	4	5
New Brunswick	43	7	3	4
Quebec	699	148	81	109
Ontario	942	111	66	118
Manitoba	95	11	7	10
Saskatchewan	71	10	2	3
Alberta	170	24	6	9
British Columbia	265	27	8	13
Canada	2,383	357	179	274

1 Consumer costs are measured in terms of extra dollars spent on food and clothing because of tariff protection. The degree of poverty is estimated on the basis of consumer expenditure functions of the form $ln\ X_i = a + b\ ln\ Y + c(ln\ Y)^2 + d\ ln\ S$ where X_i is expenditure on item i (food, clothing, housing), Y is family income, and S is family size. The functions were converted to Engel's curve ratios X_i/Y, related to income distributions and poverty lines at which (urban) families spent an estimated 70 per cent or more on food, shelter and clothing. The authors are indebted to Ms. K. McMullen who estimated these consumer costs.

2 The employment benefits were estimated on the basis of plant-number and shipment-response functions (Appendix Tables 3 and 4) and translated into numbers of jobs saved, taking into account the provincial variations in plant-size distributions and labour-productivity performance. Estimation procedures are described in the Appendix.

Source Based on data of Statistics Canada.

tariffs on manufacturers are nearly as large as Ontario's. In
food and clothing, Quebec's producer benefits (measured by the
number of jobs saved) are even larger than Ontario's, but, at the
same time, the extra cost of tariffs puts a heavy burden on the
lower-income families in Quebec. For the 81 thousand jobs
protected in Quebec, the number of low-income people falling
below the poverty line increases, initially at least,[17] by an
estimated 148 thousand (Table 10).

In these comparisons of consumer costs and producer benefits,
the cost-benefit ratios vary greatly among provinces and are in
some cases much less favourable than Quebec's. In food and clothing,
for example, they are very unfavourable to Newfoundland, Saskatchewan,
Alberta and British Columbia. In these provinces, the number of
low-income people put below the poverty line by tariffs on food
and clothing outweighs the number of jobs saved by a far greater
margin than in Quebec. That is so because these provinces incur
the extra consumer costs without benefiting from the same job
savings in their manufacturing industries as Ontario and Quebec.

From the preceding analysis it is evident that tariffs protect
employment in manufacturing but that, at the same time, they impose
a burden on consumers, particularly on the low-income earners.

Quebec Separation

So far only the tariff protection has been described as it
exists under confederation today. The analysis can be readily
extended to the potential impact of separation of Quebec under
various trade scenarios.

If the Canadian confederation of provinces were ever to break
apart, far more manufacturing jobs could be lost if the former
"common-market partners" would adopt a very hostile attitude towards
each other than if they would find a more rational approach to
settle their differences. A "hostile trade scenario" would prevail,
for example, if Quebec and the rest of Canada boycotted each
other's trade. This could be a very discriminatory policy and
could have the same effect as if Quebec were to put a trade embargo
on all imports from the rest of Canada and the rest of Canada were to
put a trade embargo on all imports from Quebec. It could result
in a total job loss of close to 260 thousand workers. Nearly
60 per cent of that loss would occur in Quebec and a little over
40 per cent in the rest of Canada. Since Quebec's manufacturing
sector is less than half the size of that of the rest of Canada,
the burden of adjustment -- measured in terms of the proportion of
manufacturing employment lost -- would be at least three times as
heavy for Quebec as it would be for the rest of Canada (Table 11).

17 Subsequently, government welfare payments may ease the lot of some of the
    people.

Table 11

Potential Short-Run Employment Losses in Manufacturing
from a Separation of Quebec

(Based on 1974 data)

	Trade Scenarios[1]		
	Hostile Trade Boycott	"Mixed" Policy	"Tit-for-Tat" Policy
Employment loss in thousands of workers			
Quebec	152	41	41
Rest of Canada	107	165	23
Total Loss	259	206	64
Employment percentage of manufacturing employment			
Quebec	28.0	7.5	7.5
Rest of Canada	8.6	13.3	1.8
Total Loss	14.5	11.5	3.6

1 Under a hostile trade scenario Quebec is assumed to boycott all trade with the rest of Canada, while the rest of Canada boycotts all trade with Quebec. Under a mixed policy scenario Quebec would impose tariffs on the rest of Canada, while the rest of Canada would pursue a policy of free trade. Under a "tit-for-tat" scenario the former "common market" trading partners would impose the same tariffs upon each other's trade as Canada imposes today on imports from the rest of the world.

Source Based on data of Statistics Canada.

More likely, perhaps, than a trade embargo would be a scenario of a mixed commercial policy: tariff protection for Quebec industries and free trade for the rest of Canada. Assuming Quebec would continue the tariff protection which it has under confederation today, while the rest of Canada -- perhaps because of pressures from the western provinces -- shifted over to a policy of free trade, Quebec would encounter an employment loss of 41 thousand, while the rest of Canada would have to adjust to a loss of 165 thousand jobs. It would also mean that the consumers in the rest of Canada would have the benefit of tariff reduction, while consumers in Quebec would continue to carry the cost of tariff protection.

Different from these two policy extremes would be a "tit-for-tat" policy where, after separation, Quebec would impose tariffs on imports from the rest of Canada and the rest of Canada would impose tariffs on imports from Quebec. Under this arrangement both would treat each other like foreign countries. This would reduce the total adjustment problem of manufacturing employment to a low of 64 thousand workers. Quebec and the rest of Canada would continue with the same levels of tariff protection as before, but the burden of adjustment (measured by the proportionate employment loss in manufacturing) would be at least four times as heavy for Quebec as it would be for the rest of Canada because Quebec's manufacturing sector would lose 7.5 per cent of its employment, while the rest of Canada would lose 1.8 per cent (Table 11).

According to this analysis the potential short-run employment losses would be highest if Quebec and the rest of Canada imposed a trade embargo on each other, and they would be lowest if both implemented a "tit-for-tat" policy against each other. It could be simplistic to assume, however, that a commercial policy aimed at minimizing employment losses would be the only rational policy, and that any other, resulting in higher employment losses for one or both trading partners, would be irrational and nothing but "economic terrorism."

To be only concerned with employment losses and not with the impact of commercial policy on consumer expenditures and on the incidence of poverty, is to ignore half the economic issue. It was shown earlier that the costs of food and clothing have a significant impact on consumer welfare. It was also shown that the cost-benefit ratios of protective tariffs vary greatly among the provinces, with Newfoundland, Saskatchewan, Alberta and British Columbia being at a distinct disadvantage. Because of these regional variations the "mixed policy" scenario, with triple the employment loss of the "tit-for-tat" policy, could be far more attractive to the West and Newfoundland than either of the other two. Under this free-trade policy scenario, Ontario would face sizeable employment losses. In view of these losses, Ontario might have to opt for an industrial policy that encourages its more dynamic industries at the expense of the more traditional ones. To facilitate the adjustment problem of the latter, Ontario might have little choice but to impose tariffs or restrictive quotas against imports of the food and clothing industries of Quebec.

Appendix

Estimation Procedure

In estimating economic losses from tariff-induced price reductions, two aspects are taken into account: plant closings and output reductions of the surviving plants. Given the regression estimates for both (Appendix Tables 3 and 4), the revenue loss of each of 20 manufacturing industries and each of 9 plant size groups is estimated according to

$$\sum_s \Delta VS_s = \sum_s \{N_s(1 - (1-\tau)^{\alpha_s}\}(\frac{VS}{N})_s + \sum_s (\frac{VS}{N})_s(1 - (1-\tau)^{\beta}\{\frac{1-\tau}{1-\sigma}\}^{\gamma})N_s(1-\frac{\Delta N_s}{N_s})$$

where s denotes plant size group, ΔVS is the change in value of shipments, τ is the nominal tariff rate on industry output, σ is the tariff rate on material inputs, α is the elasticity of the ratio of output price to wage rate, β is the price elasticity of output, γ is the elasticity of the price ratio of industry output to material inputs, and $\Delta N/N$ is the change in plant numbers estimated by the first part of the summation.

Employment losses are estimated for each plant size, each industry, and each province by dividing ΔVS by the appropriate output-per-worker ratios.

Appendix Table 1

Relationship between Tariff Rates and Performance
of 43 Manufacturing Industries, Canada, 1970

| | Regression Coefficients | | $\bar{R}^2$ |
	Value added per worker	Growth Rate 1961-70	(df. = 40)
Nominal Tariff Rate	-.35*	-.00	.23
Effective Tariff Rate	-.40*	-.25*	.26

*Tested statistically significant at the 5 per cent level.

Note   This regression analysis was based on cross-sectional data of 43 manufacturing industries selected from B. W. Wilkinson and K. Norrie, Effective Protection and the Return to Capital, Economic Council of Canada, Information Canada, Ottawa, 1975, Appendix Table A-1, pp. 75-80.

Appendix Table 2

Regression Estimates[1] of Average Annual Changes in Wage Rates
and Prices of Material Inputs Relative to a 1 Per Cent Change in
Price of Shipments, Manufacturing, 1963-74

	Wage Rates		Price of Material Inputs	
	α	r^2	β	r^2
Food and Beverage	1.39**	.40	1.09**	.99
Tobacco Products	2.67**	.88	.85**	.93
Rubber and Plastics Products	2.14**	.76	.59**	.44
Leather	1.64**	.87	1.02**	.97
Textile	3.72[2]	--	1.07**	.96
Knitting Mills	6.54[2]	--	1.25**	.77
Clothing	1.95**	.86	.83**	.95
Wood Products	1.25**	.60	1.01**	.99
Furniture and Fixture	1.65**	.83	.93**	.98
Paper and Allied	1.38**	.36	.93**	.95
Printing, Publishing and Allied	1.64**	.89	1.02**	.99
Primary Metal	1.65**	.63	1.07**	.99
Metal Fabricating	1.83**	.84	1.01**	.99
Machinery	1.99**	.85	1.06**	.99
Transportation Equipment	2.12**	.65	1.13**	.98
Electrical Products	2.37**	.71	.93**	.97
Non-Metallic Mineral Products	2.08**	.97	1.04**	.99
Petroleum and Coal Products	.79	.04	1.04**	.99
Chemical and Chemical Prods.	1.08	.28	1.09**	.96
Miscellaneous Manufacturing	1.56*	.03	.93**	.91
Total Manufacturing	1.82**	.54	1.06**	.99

**, * indicates statistical significance at the 1 and 5 per cent
   levels (11 degrees of freedom), respectively.

1 The estimated regression equations were specified as in:

   lnPL = αlnPS; and lnPM = βlnPS

   where ln denotes natural logarithms, and PS, PL and PM are
   indexes of shipment prices, wage rates and material prices
   as defined in the preceding Appendix Tables.

2 Estimates based on 1963-74 end-points.

Source Based on data of Statistics Canada.

Appendix Table 3

Regression Estimates of Plant Number Response
to Changes in Prices of Shipments and in Wage Rates of Labour,
Twenty (2-Digit-SIC) Manufacturing Industries, Canada, 1963-74

Industry	Constant C	Ratio of Price Shipments to Wage Rates Interaction with Plant Size			Plant Size		Time Trend	Correlation Coefficients	
		$ln(PS/PL)$	$ln(PS/PL)lnS$	$ln(PS/PL)(lnS)$	lnS	(lnS)	t	$\bar{R}^2$	df
Food and Beverage	6.40**	1.25**	-.40*		-.43**	-.18**		.96	90
Tobacco Products	2.29**	.19	-.11		-.15	-.13**		.42	38
Rubber and Plastics Products	3.88**	.80	.87**		-.38**	-.02	2.33**	.75	78
Leather	4.44**	1.52*			-.43**	-.18**		.53	59
Textile	4.52**	1.59*	-.11		-.42**	-.13**	7.63+	.93	92
Knitting Mills	4.12**	.12	-.38**		-.41**	-.22**		.80	74
Clothing	6.17**	1.03**	-.18		-.54**	-.21**		.86	56
Wood	6.27**	.52	-.49+		-.52**	-.18**		.93	69
Furniture and Fixture	5.77**	1.23*	-.10		-.60**	-.16**		.93	74
Paper and Allied	4.77**				-.59	-.21**		.77	76
Printing, Publishing and Allied	6.15**				-.69	-.07**		.96	82
Primary Metal	3.68**	.55	-.81**	-.21**	-.24**	-.04+		.65	75
Metal Fabricating	6.59**	.02	-.02		-.60**	-.19**		.97	83
Machinery	5.00**	.59	-.16	-.17	-.47**	-.13**	2.50	.90	70
Transportation Equipment	4.14**	1.24	-.74**	-.24**	-.29*		3.28	.79	72
Electrical Products	4.47**	2.18	-.47*	-.18+	-.38**	-.14**	8.67	.84	65
Nonmetallic Minerals	4.74**	2.18	-.47**	-.18+	-.38**	-.14**	8.67	.84	65
Petroleum and Coal	2.96**	1.86**	.31+	-.51*	-.11**			.68	61
Chemical & Chem. Prods.	5.06**	.66	-.35**	-.21**	-.54**	-.10**	7.56+	.92	63
Miscellaneous Mfg.	6.14	.50			-.70**	-.11**		.96	72
Total Manufacturing	7.77**	2.26**	-.29**	-.11**	-.47**	-.10**	6.57*	.97	101

**, *, †, denotes statiscally significant t-tests at the 1, 5, or 10 per cent levels respectively.

Appendix Table 4

Regression Estimates[1] of the Response in Shipments per Plant to Changes in the Prices of Shipments and Materials Inputs, Twenty (2-Digit-SIC) Manufacturing Industries, Canada, 1964-74

Industry	Constant c	Price of Shipments ln PS	Price Ratio of Shipments to Materials ln PS/PM	Plant Size S	Ratio of Shipments to Value Added VS/VA	Time Trend t	Correlation Coefficients $\bar{R}^2$	df
Food and Beverage	3.44**	2.64**	10.16**	1.05**			.99	91
Tobacoo	1.28**	1.60**	.96	1.31**	.97**		.98	,38
Rubber	3.04**	2.02**	2.04**	1.06**			.99	59
Leather	2.61**	1.68**	.45	1.01**			.99	94
Textile	2.65**	1.66**	19.64**	1.09**			.99	94
Knitting	3.57**	1.29**	6.68**	.84**			.99	75
Clothing	3.42**	1.65**	2.12*	.84**			.99	57
Wood	2.57**	.56**	.03	1.14**		.05**	.99	69
Furniture	2.64**	1.48**	3.63**	1.05**			.99	75
Paper	3.10**	.36	2.23 †	1.08**		.05**	.99	74
Printing and Publishing	2.30**	1.10**	1.07	1.08**	.69**	.02**	.99	79
Primary Metal	1.70**	2.17**	5.18**	1.11**	1.37**		.99	76
Metal Fabricating	2.05**	1.96**	5.54**	1.07*	1.29**		.99	83
Machinery	2.89**	1.56**	.08	1.0**	.45**		.99	72
Transport Equipt.	2.37**	1.49**		1.14**		.06**[2]	.99	74
Electrical Prods.	2.72**	.69**	1.38**	1.02**	.59**	.04**	.99	66
Nonmetaliic Mineral Prods.	2.74**	2.2**	1.38	1.06**	.67†		.99	71
Pet. & Coal Prods.	2.51**	1.56**		1.09**	1.34**		.99	62
Chem.&Chem. Prods.	-2.35**	1.23**		.96**	.66**[3]		.99	66
Miscellaneous Manufacturing	2.61**	1.48**	5.23**	1.07**			.99	72
Total Manufacturing	2.98**	1.28**	3.82*	1.09**		.04**	.99	103

**,*,†, denotes statistically significant t-tests at the 1, 5, or 10 per cent levels respectively.

1. The regression estimates were specified as in

$$ln\frac{VS}{N} s,t = c + \alpha ln \text{ PS} + \beta ln \text{ PS/PM} + \gamma \; ln \text{ S} + \delta \; ln \text{(VS/VA)} + \varepsilon t + u$$

where ln denotes natural logarithms, S is plant size, t is time trend (t = ... -1, 0, + 1, ... for the years ... 1970, 1971, 1972 ... respectively), PS is the price of shipments (1971 = 100), PM is the price of material inputs, VS is the (nominal) value of shipments, VA is the (nominal) value added, and u is the residual error term.

2. In case of the transport equipment industry, the time trend variable is replaced by WAFT6 of the CANDIDE 2.0 data bank (it equals 0 for 1963 and 1964; 1, 2, 3, 4, 5 for the years 1965-69 and 6 thereafter), a variable designed to capture some of the impact of the Canada-U.S. auto agreement.

3. In this case the rates of shipments to value added VS/VA was replaced by 1963-74 manufacturing exports of the CANDIDE 2.0 data bank.

Source Based on data from Statistics Canada.

Comments by V. Corbo, Director, Institute of Applied Economic Research, Concordia University, Montreal [1]

The two objectives of Dr. Auer and Miss Mills' (A and M's) paper are, first, to quantify how present tariffs on Canadian manufactures affect producers and consumers in each province and, second, to simulate the effects of alternative tariff schemes on both.

A and M begin by measuring the protection afforded by manufacturing tariffs at the aggregate Canadian level and then examine some of the regional variations in the degree of protection. In their regional computations, the nominal tariff rates are weighted by the production of each of the provinces. With nominal tariffs as measures of protection, Quebec's manufacturing ranks as one of the most highly protected in the country. My own studies of Quebec's industry have shown this not to be true. They indicate that the Canadian tariff affords less protection to the manufacturing industry in Quebec than it affords to the rest of Canada.

A and M go on to examine the consequences for employment and manufacturing shipments when there are changes in the tariffs. They perform a regression analysis with a double-log function in which the number of plants is regressed against the price of shipments relative to the price of labour, and where the size of the plant is measured by employment. This double logarithmic function also allows for interaction terms and a time trend. Finally, it is fitted to Canadian data at the two-digit level of the Standard Industrial Classification. The difficulty with this type of analysis is that most of the conclusions derived from it are based on the specification of the function. In my opinion, the number of plants affected by a tariff change should not depend solely on the relative price of shipments to the price of labour, when there are other important variables such as the price of capital services and the price of raw materials. A and M conclude that a 10 per cent cut in tariffs, for example, would not affect the survival of plants as long as labour was willing to take a comparable cut in wages. If the wage rate moved in conjunction with the tariff, there could be no great change. Surely this is because of the way the equation is fitted and because of the fact that it is homogeneous at zero for the price and wage rate. It seems to me that this equation for predicting the number of plants affected by tariff changes does require further theoretical justification than provided by the authors.

The same can be said for the equation predicting changes in shipments of different industries. In this double-log equation, the dependent variable is shipments per plant and the explanatory variable is the price of shipments. A certain non-homogeneity is introduced into this price because it enters both by itself and as a ratio to the price of raw materials. In this specification labour plays no role and production is no longer homogeneous of degree zero. As a result, there is no need for a one-to-one correspondence between changes in price of shipments and price of materials to maintain output after a tariff-induced price reduction. Again, I would suggest that capital be included as a variable even though I am aware that there are limitations to capital input data. Aside from a separate role for capital, I would like to see more theoretical underpinning of this specification. My main point is simply the wisdom of drawing strong conclusions on the basis of parameters obtained from this type of function. With so much derived from it, this equation can not afford to be theoretically weak. Clearly, it should include capital, and *a priori* I would probably choose a function that would be homogeneous with respect to price. One could then test for non-homogeneity.

I have no real quarrel with A and M's methodology once they begin to look at the consequences of various degrees of trade suspension between Quebec and the rest of Canada. It is important to remember that this study is geared to the short-term and unencumbered by any hypothetical indirect effects. Unfortunately, we have not yet devised a well-developed, multi-regional, input-output model capable of taking such indirect effects into account.

THE NET PROVINCIAL EXPENDITURES

ASSOCIATED WITH FEDERAL GOVERNMENT EXPENDITURES,

AND FISCAL AUTONOMY

by

A. Glynn

Economic Council of Canada

In this study, we investigate for each province the likely short-term changes in both the level and distribution of taxes on families in the province, assuming fiscal autonomy.
Becoming fiscally autonomous means that the provincial government gains full control over all federal tax sources (personal income taxes, corporate income taxes, customs duties and sales taxes, etc.) but at the same time loses access to federal intergovernmental transfers (equalization payments, for example) and becomes responsible for continuing or eliminating all expenditures that are presently wholly or partially financed by the federal government. Such expenditures include federal transfer payments made directly to persons in the province (Old Age Security, for example); public services from which provincial residents may be presumed to benefit, whether or not the expenditures happen to be made in the province itself, such as national defence; and federal transfers currently being made to businesses in the province, such as those funded by the Department of Regional Economic Expansion.

We thus compare a hypothetical future situation under which each provincial government would be totally fiscally autonomous, with the current situation where each provincial government has a degree of fiscal autonomy but, at the same time, is fiscally tied to the federal government.

Of necessity our analysis relies on current data, which depend on the present set of fiscal arrangements, in drawing implications for a future which might be founded on a different set of arrangements. In addition, the analysis ignores the possibility of future structural changes and their influence on future tax revenues, for example. By thus concentrating on the short term, we ignore the possible influence of such factors or changes in the trend level of the unemployment rate and changes in the industrial structure which a province might experience in the future under fiscal autonomy. In essence we compare what is presently the case with what would be the case if nothing else changed other than the set of underlying fiscal arrangements. It seems fairly reasonable to assume that not much would change in the short term under fiscal autonomy and that the *ceteris paribus* assumption underlying our results is defensible.

This does not, of course, deny that such structural changes might occur and might alter drastically the tax revenues available to a fiscally autonomous province, and hence the conclusions drawn from the present analysis. Suffice it to say that the results presented here are based on a reasonable assumption as to the situation facing a fiscally autonomous province in the short term.

In allocating federal expenditures to the provinces, or rather to provincial residents, two basic approaches have been used--the benefits or consumption approach and the cash-flow or production approach. The benefits approach treats the federal government as a supplier of goods and services and attempts to measure the value of these goods and services consumed by the residents of each province. The cash-flow approach treats the federal government as a purchaser of factors of production from the provinces and measures its resulting impact. Transfer payments are treated similarly under both approaches since the beneficiaries, be they provincial governments or residents directly, are clearly identified.

In this exercise, we adopted the benefits or consumption approach in allocating the non-transfer items of federal expenditures. In using this approach, we employed the "costs incurred on behalf of principle" common to this type of exercise and equated the benefits and the costs incurred (the actual expenditures). We thus assumed that a dollar spent on health care provides a dollar's worth of benefits to those who receive the benefits.

The use of the benefits approach allows us to calculate the total benefits derived by the residents of each province from federal government activity. Having this total, we can compare it with the total each province would receive based on its share of total tax contributions to calculate a net expenditure total for each province. Since the provincial allocations of federal expenditures and taxes differ, some provinces receive a share of benefits (expenditures) that is larger than their share of federal taxes and hence run a net expenditure surplus with the federal government. Some provinces, on the other hand, receive a share of expenditures which is smaller than their share of taxes and hence run a net expenditure deficit with the federal government. To investigate the situation facing a province in the short term on assuming fiscal autonomy, it is necessary to calculate these current net expenditure totals for each province. All calculations refer to fiscal year 1974-75 and the expenditure and tax totals were taken from the Statistics Canada Financial Management Series publication, *Federal Government Finance*, Cat. no. 68-211.

We first allocated total federal taxes to the provinces using two basic tax-shifting assumptions. Under Experiment A we assumed that 50 per cent of the corporate income tax is shifted backwards to shareholders. In addition, we assumed that all indirect taxes (general sales, alcohol, tobacco and other commodities) and customs duties were borne by the consumers of the taxed products. All other taxes were assumed to be borne by those upon whom they are levied, that is no shifting is assumed to occur.

Given the uncertainty as to the portion of the corporate income tax that is shifted to consumers and hence that share borne by shareholders, we have used some alternative tax-shifting assumptions in Experiement B. Here, we assumed that

only 25 per cent of the corporate income tax is shifted to
consumers while the remaining 75 per cent is borne by shareholders. These shares have been used in the literature quite
frequently, although this is an area where the number of estimates is as great as the number of studies themselves. In
addition, we assumed that 50 per cent of the indirect taxes
were borne by consumers and 50 per cent by factor incomes, as
opposed to 100 per cent being borne by consumers which we used
in Experiment A. The details of these tax-shifting assumptions
along with the series used to allocate the national totals to
the provinces are shown in Table 1. We see under Experiment A,
for example, that the share of corporate income tax borne by
consumers has been allocated by province according to the
provincial distribution of total retail sales. The share borne
by shareholders has been allocated according to the provincial
distribution of dividends received, having first eliminated
those dividends accruing to non-resident shareholders. We
assumed that none of the tax passed on to consumers in the form
of higher prices is exported but is borne in full by Canadian
consumers.

The Canadian oil export tax as well as the hidden tax on
Canadian oil producers (who have to sell oil on Canadian markets
below world prices) receive controversial treatment in the
scenarios presented in the text of this paper. We did not
include either tax in the calculation of total federal tax
contributions which we allocated among the provinces.

Both taxes exist only so long as the price of oil in Canada
lies below world oil prices. Federal-provincial agreements,
committed to eliminating this price differential, have the effect
of relegating these taxes to the position of purely short-term
transitory phenomena.

Provincial allocations of total federal taxes paid which
include the export and hidden oil tax would be representative
only of that period that began with the world oil embargo of
1974 and will end when Canadian oil prices rise to world levels.
However, because such calculations would provide the most
accurate description of the current situation, they have been
performed and are available on request.[1]

Suffice it to say here that inclusion of these two taxes
in the federal tax total, and the provincial allocation of tax
contributions that results, differ significantly from the
results presented in the text only with respect to Alberta and
Saskatchewan. In the former estimates, Alberta appears in an
overwhelmingly deficit position (receiving far less in federal

---

1 Available from the Economic Council of Canada.

benefits than would be expected, based upon its federal tax contributions). Saskatchewan appears in the same estimates in a
marginally deficit position, while in the latter set of estimates
it attains a significantly surplus position (receiving more in
federal benefits than would be expected, based upon its federal
tax contributions). The net positions of the remaining provinces
are similar in both estimates.

The results of our experiments appear in summary form as
part of Table 2. This table contains the total federal taxes
borne by the residents of each province as estimated. Using these
totals we derive a percentage distribution which we will use to
calculate the net expenditure totals.

The provincial allocation of federal expenditures on goods
and services required many decisions as to the location of the
beneficiaries of these expenditures. We employed two basic
experiments in allocating these totals. Under experiment (i)
those expenditure items whose benefits could be said to accrue
to all, or rather to no one group or province in particular, were
allocated according to the provincial distribution of family units.
These included expenditures on general government, national
defence, courts, correctional services, other protection, health,
environment, recreation and culture, foreign affairs and research
establishments. Expenditures on transportation, communications
and the post office were assumed to benefit the users of these
facilities, while expenditures incurred in administering social
welfare programs were assumed to benefit the recipients of these
program payments. Expenditures on education were assumed to
benefit the students receiving instruction; expenditures on
natural resources, agriculture, trade and industry, labour and
employment were assumed to benefit those employed in these
industries. Expenditures on housing were assumed to benefit
those homeowners who received assistance; expenditures on
immigration, those provinces where the immigrants settle; and
expenditures on the supervision and development of regions, the
recipient provinces. Having thus identified the recipient groups,
the provincial allocations were derived by using appropriate distributive series, the details of which are contained in Table 3.

We altered some of the underlying assumptions as to the
recipients of federal expenditures on certain goods and services
in experiment (ii). Rather than assuming that the benefits
derived from general government, national defence, courts,
correctional services and other protection accrue to all families
equally, we assumed that the more income a family possesses the
larger the benefits it derives from these expenditures. We then
allocated these expenditure totals according to the provincial
distribution of personal income. We thus assumed that peace and
order and good government largely benefit those with higher
incomes mainly because they have more to lose in times of war
or strife or social unrest. We further assumed that farmers

benefit from agricultural expenditures in proportion to their income, that expenditures on research establishments mainly benefit those employed in this activity rather than all families, and that expenditures on labour and employment benefit employees in proportion to their earnings. Again these alternative assumptions and the distributive series used to allocate them by province are shown in Table 3.

The allocation of transfer payments to persons by province presents fewer difficulties if only because the recipients are more easily identified and the task is to find appropriate series with which to allocate the totals among the provinces. Some of the expenditure items cover categories already included under goods and services expenditures and similar distributive series have been employed, while other items are unique to this classification and their distributive series are explained in Table 4.

Under the expenditure item "Interest," we find those interest payments made by the federal government to holders of the public debt. We assumed that the real beneficiaries of this item are the holders of the debt itself. We thus allocated it according to the provincial distribution of federal debt outstanding.[2]

The total federal transfers to business have been allocated by province following the procedures outlined in Table 5. Expenditures on rail transportation have been assumed to benefit the users of these facilities rather than the recipient businesses and were allocated according to the provincial use of these facilities. Expenditures on agriculture have been assumed to accrue entirely to the producers of the assisted products. Given the size of the dairy subsidies, we divided total agricultural expenditures into a dairy component and a non-dairy component. The share of the total going to the dairy industry was then allocated by province according to data from Agriculture Canada, while the non-dairy portion was allocated according to the provincial distribution of all other agriculture expenditures.

Federal transfers to the provinces present no problems since the benefiting provinces and municipalities are by definition identified. This is sufficient information for our purposes. We do make the assumption that the benefits flowing from these

---

2 Based upon the regional distribution of federal debt as given by Jon Cockerline in "A Balance-Sheet to Federal-Provincial Integration and Implications for Divestment", Table 21, mimeo., Economic Council of Canada.

federal transfers accrue only to the residents of the province
in question. Thus, for example, we ignore the possible benefits
derived by non-resident motorists from federally supported
provincial highway maintenance expenditures. It is unclear how
restrictive this assumption is, but because of data limitations
it is one which we are forced to live with.

The results of all our calculations on the provincial distribution of federal expenditures are presented in summary form
in Table 2, with separate rows for expenditures on goods and
services, transfers to persons, transfers to businesses and transfers to local and provincial governments, respectively. We have
covered 98.5 per cent of total expenditures; hence, the results
can be said to be representative of the current situation.

Given these estimates of federal expenditures, hence benefits
received by the residents of each province, we can then determine
what these expenditures would have been had each province received
a share of expenditures equal to its share of total federal taxes.
Applying, in turn, the provincial distribution of total federal
taxes from Experiment A and B (in Table 2) to the national totals
(again in Table 2), we obtain four sets of estimates (Experiment
A(i), B(i), A(ii) and B(ii) of the "expected" expenditures.

Subtracting these expected expenditures from the provincial
distributions of actual expenditures, we obtain the current net
expenditure totals. These net expenditure totals are shown in the
first four rows of Table 6.

We see that these range from $2.2 billion in Quebec to
-$3.0 billion in Ontario. All of the Atlantic provinces, Quebec,
Manitoba and Saskatchewan appear with net expenditure surpluses,
while Ontario, Alberta and British Columbia appear with net
expenditure deficits. Thus, for example, Quebec is currently
(1974-75) receiving $1.9-$2.2. billion more than it would if it
was receiving expenditures equal to its share of taxes. Ontario,
on the other hand, is receiving approximately $3.0 billion less
than its share of taxes might entitle it to. These net expenditures are obviously based on a technique which is a zero sum game
in that the gains and the losses cancel each other. In examining
the net surpluses and deficits, we speak of entitlements to
benefits based on tax contributions only to illustrate the size
and sign of tax changes and/or expenditure cuts each province
would face under fiscal autonomy. We do not mean to imply that
the current political system is reducible to such an exercise,
with the gains and the losses offsetting, if only because of the
limited information obtainable from this type of investigation.
What the totals do tell us is that those provinces currently
experiencing net expenditure surpluses would be faced with similar
sized deficits under fiscal autonomy in the short term. Conversely,
those provinces currently experiencing net expenditure deficits
would be faced with similar sized surpluses under fiscal autonomy.

The magnitude of these future deficits and surpluses can be better appreciated if we look at the current net expenditures on a per capita basis, also shown in Table 6. We see that currently each person in Newfoundland is receiving close to $900.00; each person in Quebec is receiving close to $350.00; and each person in Ontario is contributing approximately $350.00. In this form, we see that the size of the required adjustments is likely to be greatest in Newfoundland and Prince Edward Island and smallest in Manitoba and Saskatchewan. The same story is evident when we look at the net expenditures per family unit. Here each family in Alberta is contributing approximately $600.00 while each family in New Brunswick is receiving about $1,800.00.

Now that we have some feel for the size of the current net expenditures and the corresponding net deficits and surpluses under fiscal autonomy, we consider possible ways by which these fiscally autonomous provinces might finance or disburse these net deficits or surpluses.

In Table 7 we present four possible scenarios by which the provinces might finance (disburse) their net deficits (surpluses) under fiscal autonomy. These results refer to the net expenditures as estimated in Table 6, Experiment A(i).[3] These net expenditures are related to present federal and provincial tax totals to yield the percentage tax changes shown in Table 7.

Under Scenario (i) we assume all of the net deficits are financed through increases in the personal income tax and all of the net surpluses are disbursed through personal income tax reductions. The table shows the size of the resulting tax increases which are all very large, ranging from 15.7 per cent to 342.0 per cent. The tax reductions range from 38.0 per cent in Ontario to 25 per cent in Alberta. The very magnitude of the resulting tax increases in the Atlantic provinces and Quebec makes it extremely unlikely that such a scenario would be used.

Scenario (ii) postulates splitting the net deficits (surpluses) equally between the personal income tax and the general sales taxes. The results indicate that while the resulting personal income tax increases are halved, the general sales tax increases are unrealistically large.

Scenario (iii) postulates splitting the net deficits (surpluses) equally between the personal income tax, the corporate income tax and the general sales tax. Under this scenario

---

[3] Similar results for Exercises A(ii), B(i) and B(ii) are available upon request from the Economic Council of Canada. Results do not differ greatly.

all of the Atlantic provinces, Quebec and Saskatchewan would be faced with personal income tax increases in excess of 12 per cent, corporate income tax increases in excess of 57 per cent and general sales tax increases in excess of 23 per cent. As before, the reductions in taxes in Alberta, Ontario and British Columbia remain substantial by conventional standards.

In Scenario (iv) we have not specified the manner in which the tax increases (decreases) would occur but, rather, included it to indicate the size of the resulting tax changes compared to the total taxes available to the province under fiscal autonomy. Here we see that financing the net deficit in the Atlantic provinces by way of tax increases would everywhere lead to an increase of at least 33 per cent in total taxes. The increase in Quebec would be of the order of 20 per cent. The size of the tax decreases range from 16 per cent in Ontario to 6 per cent in Alberta. Clearly, then, the Atlantic provinces, Quebec and, to a lesser extent, Manitoba and Saskatchewan would be facing high tax increases upon assuming fiscal autonomy, if that was the route chosen to finance their net deficits.

In view of the great size of many of the tax increases shown in Table 7, it is instructive to look at their effects on the distribution of income. The changes in taxes per family unit associated with scenarios (i), (ii), (iii) from Table 7 are shown in Table 8 for seven income classes.[4] We have not included Scenario (iv) because data limitations did not allow us to fully specify the effects of changes in all tax revenue sources.

We have had recourse to Survey of Consumer Finance data for 1975 in preparing the income distribution results presented in Table 8. These data contain information on the sources of income and total taxes paid by economic families cross-classified by total income. Thus we were able to obtain frequency distributions with which to allocate a given change in personal income taxes and dividends across income classes. The data refer to calender year 1975 but have been applied to our 1974 totals to yield the results shown.

In addition, we needed information on the pattern of consumption expenditures by income classes to allocate that share of the corporate income tax change and the general sales tax change assumed to be borne by consumers. Lacking current data we have made adjustments to some 1969 consumption series derived by Maslove,[5] adjustments which make allowance for the effects of increases in personal

---

4 The corresponding results for Experiments A(ii), B(i) and B(ii), are available upon request from the Economic Council of Canada.

5 Allan M. Maslove, *The Pattern of Taxation in Canada*, Economic Council of Canada, December 1972.

income per family between 1969 and 1974. This procedure assumes
that all families experienced the same increase in income, that
is, that the effects of inflation were distributionally neutral.

With a series on personal income taxes, dividends and consumption, we were able to translate the tax changes resulting from
each of the three scenarios in Table 7 into tax changes per family
in each income class. In Table 8 we see that for Newfoundland,
Scenario (i) implies a tax increase of $10. per family for each
family whose total income is less than $3,000 and over $11,000 per
family for families whose total income is $20,000 and over. Under
Scenario (ii), where both the personal income tax and the general
sales tax are increased, we find that families in the five lowest
income classes pay more than was the case under Scenario (i), while
those in the top two income brackets pay less. The inclusion of
the general sales tax, which under Experiment A(i) is assumed to
be borne in full by consumers, makes this scenario more regressive
than Scenario (i) where the progressive nature of the personal
income tax itself is evident. It appears as if the inclusion of
the corporate income tax, half of which is borne by consumers,
makes Scenario (iii) the most regressive of the three scenarios
presented in Table 8. This should not obscure the fact that
higher income classes do bear more of the tax increases so that
within each scenario there is a large degree of progressivity; it
is this degree of progressivity which changes as we move from
Scenario (i) to Scenario (ii). Much the same pattern is evident
for the other provinces as well, although for Ontario, Alberta
and British Columbia we are dealing with tax reductions so that
the terms progressive and regressive need to be interpreted with
care. For example, for Ontario Scenario (i) is technically the
most progressive in that the higher income classes experience the
largest changes in taxes. Since these changes are negative, however, the lower income classes obtain little benefit; thus, from an
equity point of view, Scenario (i) is hardly progressive. We will
limit our comments to those cases where tax increases are in prospect rather than discussing those provinces facing tax reductions.

Along with the changes in taxes per family, Table 8 also shows
the current situation facing families in each province. In Newfoundland, where we found that Scenario (i) would imply a tax
increase of $11,291 for families with total incomes of $20,000
or more, we find that presently they are paying only $5,218 in
personal income taxes. Thus, Scenario (i) implies a tax increase
of 216.4 per cent as seen in Table 7. While families in each
income bracket face similar percentage tax increases,[6] the absolute
size varies. The inclusion of data on current tax payments helps
to put the likely tax changes resulting from fiscal autonomy into
perspective. It is more instructive to know that each family in

---

6 This is due to the use of the same distributive series to estimate the tax
   increases and the current taxes paid by families in each income class.

the $12,000 to $14,999 bracket in Quebec would be faced with an added $869.1 on top of their existing tax obligations of $3,463, should a fiscally autonomous Quebec decide to finance its net deficit through equal absolute increase in personal income taxes, corporate income taxes and general sales taxes, than to know the percentage change in each tax revenue source implied by such a scenario.

Since the resulting tax increases everywhere appear very large, it seems reasonable to explore alternative ways in which these net deficits might be financed. One such alternative (Scenario (iv)) is presented for the Atlantic provinces, Manitoba, and Saskatchewan for Experiment A(i) in Table 9.[7]

In each instance we postulate a cut in expenditures and a change in taxes as a means of financing the net deficit facing each of these provinces. The nature of the expenditure cuts, their size relative to existing expenditures and the distributive series employed are shown in Table 10. In Newfoundland, for example, we postulate a cut in expenditures of $250 million comprised of cuts of $50 million in Unemployment Insurance benefits, Family and Youth Allowances, Primary and Secondary Education, Health and Transportation expenditures. The remaining net deficit is then financed by means of equal absolute increases in personal and corporate income taxes and the general sales tax.

We derived distributive series from the 1975 Survey of Consumer Finances to allocate the losses arising from the expenditure cuts. Data on recipients of Unemployment Insurance benefits and Family and Youth Allowances by income class were available directly. We used the distribution of the number of children of appropriate age to allocate the losses associated with the education expenditure cut, while the distribution of families across income classes was used to allocate the losses arising from both the health and transportation expenditure cuts.

The losses per family arising from these expenditure cuts appear to be more evenly spread across income classes than was the case for any of the tax scenarios considered to date. This is not unexpected given that the expenditure items which have been reduced benefit the lower income classes to a larger degree. In addition, we have allocated both health and transportation according to the distribution of families which tends to make the expenditure cuts regressive in nature.

The increase in taxes was then allocated in a fashion similar to that of Table 8, Scenario (iii), to yield the results as shown. Here we find a more marked degree of progressivity

7   The corresponding exercises for Experiments A(ii), B(i) and B(ii) were conducted and are available upon request from the Economic Council of Canada.

compared with the losses associated with the expenditure cuts.
The total loss per family is , then, the sum of the losses due to
the expenditure cuts and the tax increases. We see that families
with incomes less than $3,000 would lose $1,401 which compares
with a loss (tax increase) of $1,078.5 under Scenario (iii) in
Table 8, $1,202.0 under Scenario (ii) and $10.1 under Scenario (i).
Families in the highest income bracket, on the other hand, face a
loss of $6,660.9 compared with a minimum of $7,716 in Table 8. In
fact , the bottom four income classes appear to lose more under
Scenario (iv) than is the case under either of the three tax
scenarios of Table 8, while the reverse is true for the top three
classes. This same pattern holds for the other provinces except
Manitoba where only the top two income classes appear to lose less
under Scenario (iv) than under Scenarios (i), (ii) or (iii).

While it is still the case that families with higher incomes
lose more than families with lower incomes, the method chosen to
finance the net deficit does appear to have distributional implications which appear to be of some significance.

Given the attention paid to Quebec , we present in Table 11
two alternative scenarios by which a fiscally autonomous Quebec
might finance its net deficit. Under Scenario (iv), Experiment A(i),
we postulate expenditure cuts of $1,500 million and tax increases
totalling $595.8 million. The expenditure cuts consisted of $200
million in Unemployment Insurance benefits, Transportation expenditures and other welfare payments, $400 million in Primary and
Secondary Education and Health, and $100 million in Family and
Youth Allowances. We derived similar distributive series as
those employed for Newfoundland in Table 9 to allocate these
expenditure cuts to families in each income class , and the resulting
total losses per family are displayed in the first row of Table 11.
As was the case with Table 9, we note that the incidence of these
expenditure cuts is more regressive than that of the losses
resulting from the tax increases described in Table 8. For example,
families with incomes less than $3,000 lose $523 due to the cutback
in these expenditure items whereas they, at worse, lose $187.0 due
to the tax increases postulated under Scenario (iii) in Table 8.

The losses due to the increase in taxes (Table 11) display
the more normal degree of progressivity, and the total losses
under this scenario, while progressive overall, are more regressive
for the bottom five income classes than those found in Table 8.
Again , the top two income classes appear to lose less under
Scenario (iv) than under any of the three scenarios previously
considered. Thus , the distributional impacts vary according to
the method of financing chosen by the province under fiscal
autonomy. The desire to avoid large tax increases appears to
shift more of the burden to the lower income classes while still
retaining a basic degree of progressivity.

A second alternative to the three tax scenarios of Table 8
is also presented in Table 11. Here we limit the tax increases

to 5 per cent of the personal and corporate income taxes and to 25 per cent of the general sales tax. As previously noted, the tax increases facing these fiscally autonomous provinces far exceed what has normally been the practice of Ministers of Finance to adopt on their budgets. Scenario (v) attempts to limit the resulting tax increases to the range normally adopted while placing most of the onus for financing the net deficit on expenditure cuts. Given our experience with Table 9 and Scenario (iv) of this Table we then expect this scenario to be the most regressive of the five thus considered for a fiscally autonomous Quebec. This is in fact the case , with families in the bottom five income classes facing larger losses under this scenario than under any of the previous four scenarios. For example, families with incomes less than $3,000 face losing $536 compared with $572 under Scenario (iv). At the same time, families with incomes of $20,000 or more would lose $2,232 as opposed to $1,935 under Scenario (iv) and $4,340 under Scenario (i). Again , the method of financing displays a distributional component which is of importance in any evaluation of alternative strategies for financing the resulting net deficit.[8]

In summary, we can say that under fiscal autonomy the four Atlantic provinces would fare very badly, facing large tax increases and/or expenditure cuts. Although the four scenarios postulated in the text are by no means exhaustive, they do indicate the real difficulty each of these provinces would face under fiscal autonomy. In addition, the method by which the resulting net deficits are financed appears to have significant distributional effects, shifting the burden among income classes.

A fiscally autonomous Quebec would face tax increases and/or expenditure cuts substantially smaller than those facing the Atlantic provinces but still very large by conventional standards. As before, the distributional effects seem to be sensitive to the way in which the net deficit is financed.

The situation facing a fiscally autonomous Manitoba and Saskatchewan, while far better than that in the Atlantic provinces or Quebec, would still necessitate large tax changes.

Of the three provinces which presently experience net expenditure deficits and which consequently might be facing tax reductions (or expenditure increases) under fiscal autonomy, Ontario seems to be in the most enviable position. The province would be in a position to reduce all its present taxes by 16 per cent. British Columbia would be in a position to cut its total tax collections by 12.2 per cent and Alberta by only 6.3 per cent.

---

8 The corresponding exercises for Experiments A(ii), B(i) and B(ii) were conducted and are available upon request from the Economic Council of Canada.

Table 1

The Provincial Allocation of Federal Taxes -- Methodology

Tax	Shifting Assumption	Distributive Series Used
Experiment A		
Personal Income	No shifting	Total taxes payable -- Dept. of National Revenue, Taxation Statistics
Corporate Income	50 per cent borne by consumers	Total retail sales -- Retail Trade, Statistics Canada #63-005
	50 per cent borne by shareholders*	Dividends received -- Taxation Statistics
General Sales	Borne by consumers	Retail sales subject to the tax -- Retail Commodity Survey, Statistics Canada #63-526
Alcohol	Borne by consumers of alcoholic beverages	Sales of alcoholic beverages -- The Control and Sale of Alcoholic Beverages in Canada, Statistics Canada #63-202
Tobacco	Borne by consumers of tobacco products	Retail sales of tobacco -- Retail Commodity Survey, Statistics Canada #63-526
Other Commodities	Borne by consumers	Total retail sales -- Retail Trade, Statistics Canada #63-005
Customs Duties	Borne by consumers	"
Estate Income	Recipients of estate income	Estate Income -- Taxation Statistics
Unemployment Insurance Contributions	--	U.I. contributors -- Provincial Economic Accounts, Supplementary Tables
Universal Pension Plan Levies	--	Canada Pension Plan Contributors, 1974

---

* The allocation of those taxes borne by shareholders excludes that portion borne by foreign shareholders. The foreign portion was assumed to be equal to the share of foreign ownership of capital employed in the corresponding industry, as obtained from Statistics Canada Daily, August 27, 1976.

Table 1 (cont'd)

Tax	Shifting Assumption	Distributive Series Used

Experiment B -- The following tax allocations were altered as specified, the allocation of the remaining taxes was as specified in Experiment A.

Tax	Shifting Assumption	Distributive Series Used
Corporate Income	25 per cent borne by consumers	Total retail sales
	75 per cent borne by shareholders	Dividends received
General Sales	50 per cent borne by consumers	Retail sales subject to the tax
	50 per cent borne by factor incomes	Factor incomes -- National Income and Expenditure Accounts Statistics Canada #13-201
Alcohol	50 per cent borne by consumers of alcoholic beverages	Retail sales of alcoholic beverages
	50 per cent borne by factor incomes	Factor incomes
Tobacco	50 per cent borne by consumers of tobacco products	Retail sales of tobacco products
	50 per cent borne by factor incomes	Factor incomes
Other Commodities	50 per cent borne by consumers	Total retail sales
	50 per cent borne by factor incomes	Factor incomes

Table 2

Federal Government Expenditure on Goods and Services, Transfers to Persons, Transfers to Businesses,
Transfers to Local and Provincial Governments and Federal Taxes, by Province, 1974-75*

(Millions of dollars)

	New-foundland	Prince Edward Island	Nova Scotia	New Brunswick	Quebec	Ontario	Manitoba	Saskatchewan	Alberta	British Columbia	Ten-Province Total
Total Federal Taxes by Province											
Experiment A	380.5	87.4	751.6	557.4	5,218.2	10,773.0	1,085.4	948.2	2,143.4	3,365.7	25,310.8
%	1.5	.34	2.96	2.21	20.61	42.56	4.28	3.74	8.46	13.29	100.0
Experiment B	352.2	79.8	721.0	526.0	5,051.9	10,835.7	1,053.1	901.0	2,072.1	3,305.8	24,899.6
%	1.41	.32	2.89	2.11	20.28	43.51	4.22	3.61	8.32	13.28	100.0
Federal Gov't Expenditure on											
Goods and Services² Ex(i)	231.2	53.6	334.5	245.7	2,048.7	3,175.7	424.8	435.9	740.2	1,199.9	8,890.0
Transfers to Persons³ Ex(i)	607.9	72.8	448.8	377.2	2,908.4	4,051.5	492.6	453.8	741.3	1,375.5	11,229.8
Transfers to Business³ Ex(i)	6.4	7.3	37.3	17.6	331.0	408.0	52.4	68.9	99.2	98.5	1,146.6
Transfers to Local and Provincial Gov'ts³ Ex(i)	351.3	84.7	406.1	362.3	2,786.7	1,963.2	378.8	313.6	536.3	560.5	7,743.5
Total	896.8	218.4	1,226.7	1,002.8	8,074.8	9,598.4	1,348.6	1,292.2	2,117.0	3,234.4	29,009.9
Federal Gov't Expenditure on:											
Goods and Services Ex(ii)	220.3	46.3	312.2	221.0	1,916.2	3,376.9	407.3	467.0	719.1	1,180.3	8,865.6
Transfers to Persons Ex(ii)	306.9	72.5	447.3	375.2	2,891.9	4,086.5	490.3	450.7	735.8	1,366.3	11,225.7
Transfers to Business Ex(ii)	6.4	7.3	37.3	17.6	331.0	408.0	52.4	85.9	99.2	98.5	1,146.6
Transfers to Local and Provincial Gov'ts Ex(ii)	351.3	84.7	406.1	362.3	2,786.7	1,963.2	378.8	313.6	536.3	560.5	7,743.5
Total	884.9	210.8	1,202.9	976.1	7,925.8	9,834.6	1,328.8	1,320.2	2,090.4	3,208.1	28,982.4

*A further breakdown for taxation & expenditures figures into component parts is available upon request.

Sources   1   Federal Government Finance, Statistics Canada, Cat. No. 68-24,) Further Economic Council of Canada
2   Federal Government Finance, Statistics Canada, Cat. No. 68-211,) data available on request.
3   Federal Government Finance, Statistics Canada, Cat. No. 68-211, and Department of Finance Worksheets.

Table 3

The Provincial Allocation of Federal Expenditures on Goods and
Services -- Methodology

Item	Beneficiaries	Distributive Series Used
Experiment (i)		
General Government	All families	No. of families -- Income Distributions by Size in Canada, Statistics Canada #13-207*
National Defence	All families	No. of families
Courts and Correctional Services	All families	No. of families
Police	Residents of location of police personnel	RCMP wages and salaries
Other Protection	All families	No. of families
Air Transportation	Users of facilities	Consumer expenditures on air travel -- Urban Family Expenditure, Statistics Canada #62-544**
Water Transportation	Users of facilities	Consumer expenditures on boats, steamships and ferries
Telecommunications	Users of the services	Consumer expenditures on telecommunications
Post Office	Users of the services	Consumer expenditures on postage
Health	All Families	No. of families
Veterans' Benefits	Recipients of benefits	Veterans' benefits -- Provincial Economic Accounts, Supplementary Tables
Unemployment Insurance Benefits	Recipients of benefits	U.I. payments -- Public Accounts
Other Welfare Benefits	Recipients of benefits	Other welfare payments -- Provincial Economic Accounts, Supplementary Tables
Primary and Secondary Education	Primary and secondary students	No. of students -- Elementary and Secondary School Enrolment Statistics Canada #81-210 Vocational and Technical Training Statistics Canada #81-209

* The number of family units in each of the Atlantic provinces and in each of the
  Prairie provinces were not available for 1974. Applying the 1975 percentage
  distributions to the 1974 regional totals we estimated the missing provincial
  totals. The 1975 totals were taken from Statistics Canada #13-207.

** We assumed that the average consumption expenditure per family unit in each
   urban centre on the item in question was representative of all families in
   that province. In those instances where more than one urban centre was surveyed
   in any one province we calculated a weighted average expenditure per family,
   using the weighted number of families in each centre as the weights. With these
   provincial average expenditures per family and the number of families in each
   province we could calculate provincial total expenditures and from these obtain
   a provincial distribution to apply to the corresponding national total which we
   wish to allocate provincially.

Table 3 (cont'd)

Item	Beneficiaries	Distributive Series Used
Post Secondary Education	Post secondary students	No. of students -- Fall Enrolment in Universities, Statistics Canada #81-204
Special Retraining Services	Trainees	No. of Canada Manpower trainees -- Vocational and Technical Training, Statistics Canada #81-209
Fish and Game	Employees	Employment in fishing -- Regional Databank
Mining	Employees	Employment in mining -- Regional Databank
Other Natural Resources	Employees	Employment in primary industries -- Regional Databank
Agriculture	Employees	Employment in agriculture -- Regional Databank
Trade and Industry	Employees	Employment in manufacturing and trade -- Regional Databank
Environment	All families	No. of families
Recreation and Culture	All families	No. of families
Labour and Employment	Employees	Total employment -- Historical Labour Force Statistics, Statistics Canada #71-201
Immigration	Province of intended destination	Province of intended destination -- Canada Year Book
Housing	Homeowners	CMHC loans -- Canadian Housing Statistics
Foreign Affairs	All families	No. of families
Supervision and Development of Regions	Recipient provinces	Transfers to provincial and local governments -- Department of Finance
Research Establishments	All families	No. of families

Experiment (ii)   The following allocations were altered as specified while the remaining expenditure items were allocated as specified in Experiment (i)

General Government	Persons in proportion to their income	Personal income -- National Income and Expenditure Accounts, Statistics Canada #13-201
National Defence	Persons in proportion to their income	Personal income
Courts and Correctional Services	Persons in proportion to their income	Personal income
Other Protection	Persons in proportion to their income	Personal income
Agriculture	Farmers in proportion to their farm income	Farm income -- National Income and Expenditure Accounts, Statistics Canada #13-201

Table 3 (cont'd)

Item	Beneficiaries	Distributive Series Used
Labour and Employment	Employees in proportion to their earnings	Wages and salaries -- <u>National Income and Expenditure Accounts</u>, Statistics Canada #13-201
Research Establishments	Employees in these establishments	Expenditures on research -- <u>Federal Government Activities in the Human Sciences</u>, Statistics Canada #13-205

Table 3 (cont'd)

Table 4

The Provincial Allocation of Federal Transfers to Persons -- Methodology

Item	Distributive Series Used
Public Service Pensions	Public Service Pension payments -- Provincial Economic Accounts, Supplementary Tables
Old Age Security	Old Age Security payments -- Public Accounts
Veterans' Benefits	Veterans' Benefits -- Provincial Economic Accounts, Supplementary Tables
Unemployment Insurance	U.I. payments -- Public Accounts
Family and Youth Allowances	Family and Youth Allowances -- Public Accounts
Assistance to Disabled etc., plus Other Welfare	Other welfare payments -- Provincial Economic Accounts, Supplementary Tables
Health	No. of families -- Statistics Canada #13-207
Post Secondary Education	No. of students -- Statistics Canada #81-204
Agriculture	Farm income -- Statistics Canada #13-201
Recreation and Culture	No. of families -- Statistics Canada #13-207
Labour and Employment	Total employment -- Statistics Canada #71-201*
Foreign Affairs	No. of families -- Statistics Canada #13-207
Research Establishments	No. of families -- Statistics Canada #13-207**
Interest	No. of families -- Statistics Canada #13-207***

---

*As an alternative we used the provincial distribution of wages and salaries (Statistics Canada #13-201) to allocate this item.

**As an alternative we used the provincial distribution of federal expenditures on the human sciences (Statistics Canada #13-205) to allocate this item.

***Here we assumed that the true beneficiaries of this item are those for whom the borrowing was incurred on behalf of and who benefited from the subsequent expenditures, rather than those recipients of interest payments themselves.

Table 5

The Provincial Allocation of Transfers to Business -- Methodology

Item	Beneficiaries	Distributive Series Used
Rail Transportation	Benefits passed on to users of the facilities	Consumer expenditures on rail travel -- Statistics Canada #62-544
Agriculture	Producers of agricultural products	Provincial share of total agricultural subsidies going to dairy and all other products -- Agriculture Canada
Trade and Industry	Employees in subsidized industries	Employment in manufacturing and trade -- Regional Databank
Labour and Employment	Employees in subsidized industries	Total employment -- Statistics Canada #71-201*
Housing	Recipients of housing assistance	CMHC loans -- Canadian Housing Statistics

*As an alternative we used the provincial distribution of wages and salaries (Statistics Canada Cat. No. 13-201) to allocate this expenditure item.

Table 5

The Net Expenditures, Per Capita, Per Family Unit, Associated with
Federal Government Expenditures, By Province, 1974-75

	Newfoundland	Prince Edward Island	Nova Scotia	New Brunswick	Quebec	Ontario	Manitoba	Saskatchewan	Alberta	British Columbia
Net Expenditures					(Millions of dollars)					
Experiment A										
(i)	461.6	139.2	368.0	361.7	2,095.8	-2,748.2	107.0	207.2	-337.0	-621.0
(ii)	434.7	112.2	345.0	335.6	1,952.5	-2,500.3	88.3	236.2	-361.5	-643.6
Experiment B										
(i)	487.8	125.6	388.3	390.7	2,191.6	-3,023.8	124.4	244.9	-296.6	-618.1
(ii)	476.2	118.0	365.3	364.6	2,048.2	-2,775.6	105.7	273.9	-320.9	-640.8
Net Expenditures Per Capita					(Dollars)					
Experiment A										
(i)	851.5	1,169.6	452.6	546.3	341.6	-339.4	105.8	228.4	-196.6	-259.2
(ii)	802.0	958.9	424.3	506.8	318.3	-308.8	87.3	260.4	-210.9	-268.6
Experiment B										
(i)	899.9	1,073.4	477.5	590.1	357.2	-373.5	123.0	270.0	-173.1	-258.0
(ii)	876.5	1,008.5	449.3	550.7	333.9	-342.8	104.5	301.9	-187.3	-267.5
Net Expenditures Per Family Unit					(Dollars)					
Experiment A										
(i)	3,369.3	4,350.1	1,502.6	1,836.0	2,060.2	-969.4	309.2	690.0	-569.3	-713.1
(ii)	3,172.9	3,506.3	1,406.7	1,703.5	907.7	-861.9	-255.1	766.5	-609.6	-739.0
Experiment B										
(i)	3,560.5	3,925.1	1,585.5	1,983.2	1,108.7	-1,529.7	-359.5	815.5	-500.1	-706.7
(ii)	3,475.9	3,687.6	1,634.6	1,850.7	1,036.1	-979.0	-205.4	912.1	-541.2	-735.8

Source Further Economic Council of Canada data available on request.

Table 7

Possible Scenarios by which Fiscally Autonomous Provinces Might
Finance (Disburse) their Net Deficits (Surpluses) Associated
with Federal Government Expenditures, Experiment A(i), by Province, 1975-75

	Newfoundland	Prince Edward Island	Nova Scotia	New Brunswick	Quebec	Ontario	Manitoba	Saskatchewan	Alberta	British Columbia
					(Millions of dollars)					
Scenario (i)										
Personal income tax change	461.6	139.2	368.0	361.7	2,095.8	-2,748.2	107.0	207.2	-337.0	-621.0
Percentage tax change	216.4	342.8	87.3	117.1	46.5	-38.9	15.7	36.0	-25.2	-29.7
Scenario (ii)										
Personal income tax change	230.8	69.6	184	180.5	1,047.9	-1,374.1	53.5	103.6	-168.5	-310.5
Percentage tax change	108.2	171.4	43.6	58.5	23.2	-19.4	7.8	18.0	-12.6	-14.9
General sales tax change	230.8	69.6	184	180.5	1,047.9	-1,374.1	53.5	103.6	-168.5	-310.5
Percentage tax change	145.3	202.3	79.1	94.0	52.9	-46.4	16.7	34.4	-47.5	-33.5
Scenario (iii)										
Personal income tax change	153.9	46.4	122.7	120.6	698.6	-916.1	35.7	69.1	-112.3	-207.0
Percentage tax change	72.1	114.2	29.1	39.0	15.5	-12.9	5.2	12.0	-8.4	-9.9
Corporate tax change	153.9	46.4	122.7	120.6	698.6	-916.1	35.7	69.1	-112.3	-207.0
Percentage tax change	206.0	246.8	75.6	104.8	52.1	-36.2	14.7	37.6	-19.2	-26.7
General sales tax change	153.9	46.4	122.7	120.6	698.6	-916.1	35.7	69.1	-112.3	-207.0
Percentage tax change	96.8	134.8	52.7	62.7	35.2	-30.9	11.1	23.0	-31.7	-22.3
Scenario (iv)										
Total tax change	461.6	139.2	368.0	361.7	2,095.8	-2,748.2	107.0	207.2	-337.0	-621.0
Percentage tax change	74.7	102.1	33.5	40.8	19.8	-16.4	64.2	12.2	-6.3	-12.2

Source Table 1. Further Economic Council of Canada data available on request.

Table 8

The Changes in Taxes Per Family Unit Associated with Possible Scenarios by which Fiscally Autonomous Provinces Might Finance (Disburse) their Net Deficits (Surpluses), by Family Income Classes, Experiment A(i)

	Less than $3,000	$3,000 - 5,999	$6,000 - 8,999	$9,000 - 11,999	$12,000 - 14,999	$15,000 - 19,999	$20,000 and over	Total
Newfoundland								
Fiscal Autonomy Financed by:								
Change in Taxes Per Family Unit								
(i) Increase in personal income taxes	10.1	176.6	808.8	2,282.5	3,694.6	5,629.0	11,291.1	3,369.3
(ii) Increases in personal income and general sales taxes	1,202.0	1,136.4	1,982.3	2,744.9	4,287.1	4,712.5	7,716.0	3,369.3
(iii) Increases in personal income, corporate income and general sales taxes	1,078.5	1,371.9	1,644.9	2,164.9	3,264.0	4,296.0	10,068.0	3,369.3
Current Situation								
Taxes Per Family Unit								
(i) Personal income taxes	5	82	374	1,055	1,707	2,601	5,218	1,547
(ii) Personal income and general sales taxes	828	803	1,460	2,158	3,585	3,907	6,643	2,698
(iii) Personal income, corporate income and general sales taxes	1,089	1,121	1,794	2,499	3,878	4,494	8,172	3,240
Prince Edward Island								
Fiscal Autonomy Financed by:								
Change in Taxes Per Family Unit								
(i) Increase in personal income taxes	10.2	348.6	1,394.4	3,063.1	5,170.8	8,515.6	17,289.2	4,350.1
(ii) Increases in personal income and general sales taxes	1,220.9	1,281.8	2,661.7	3,766.8	2,760.8	7,064.2	12,067.0	4,350.1
(iii) Increases in personal income, corporate income and general sales taxes	1,361.2	1,817.8	3,155.2	3,939.5	4,940.8	7,029.4	10,736.0	4,350.1
Current Situation								
Taxes Per Family Unit								
(i) Personal income taxes	3	102	407	899	1,509	2,486	5,046	1,253
(ii) Personal income and general sales taxes	603	649	1,377	1,999	3,080	3,874	6,748	2,314
(iii) Personal income, corporate income and general sales taxes	878	994	1,922	2,589	3,732	4,724	7,756	2,894

Table 8 (cont'd)

	Less than $3,000	$3,000 - 5,999	$6,000 - 8,999	$9,000 - 11,999	$12,000 - 14,999	$15,000 - 19,999	$20,000 and over	Total
Nova Scotia								
Fiscal Autonomy Financed by:								
Change in Taxes Per Family Unit								
(i) Increase in personal income taxes	3.5	88.5	481.8	1,083.9	1,731.8	2,606.3	4,947.3	1,502.6
(ii) Increases in personal income and general sales taxes	427.4	484.7	985.6	1,424.7	1,828.9	2,245.5	3,386.7	1,502.6
(iii) Increases in personal income, corporate income and general sales taxes	386.2	576.2	1,051.1	1,357.1	1,672.3	2,051.6	3,705.9	1,502.6
Current Situation								
Taxes Per Family Unit								
(i) Personal income taxes	11	101	551	1,241	1,982	2,983	5,663	1,720
(ii) Personal income and general sales taxes	549	658	1,493	2,356	3,198	4,174	6,816	2,669
(iii) Personal income, corporate income and general sales taxes	803	1,019	2,030	3,013	3,921	4,955	8,174	3,330
New Brunswick								
Fiscal Autonomy Financed by:								
Change in Taxes Per Family Unit								
(i) Increase in personal income taxes	15.7	123.1	555.7	1,215.2	1,926.3	2,892.4	6,204.3	1,836.0
(ii) Increases in personal income and general sales taxes	516.7	699.8	1,359.4	1,542.4	2,006.0	2,504.7	4,237.3	1,836.0
(iii) Increases in personal income, corporate income and general sales taxes	407.9	894.2	1,268.7	1,532.3	1,984.1	2,224.6	4,584.2	1,836.0
Current Situation								
Taxes Per Family Unit								
(i) Personal income taxes	13	105	474	1,037	1,644	2,469	5,297	1,570
(ii) Personal income and general sales taxes	554	784	1,624	2,031	2,753	3,595	6,504	2,547
(iii) Personal income, corporate income and general sales taxes	746	1,191	2,141	2,569	3,393	4,196	7,704	3,132

Table 8 (cont'd)

	Less than $3,000	$3,000 - 5,999	$6,000 - 8,999	$9,000 - 11,999	$12,000 - 14,000	$15,000 - 19,000	$20,000 and over	Total
Quebec								
Fiscal Autonomy Financed by:			Change in Taxes Per Family Unit					
(i) Increase in personal income taxes	6.1	54.5	263.1	565.8	870.3	1,653.9	4,340.4	1,060.2
(ii) Increases in personal income and general sales taxes	187.0	310.7	568.6	878.0	982.6	1,483.5	3,218.5	1,060.2
(iii) Increases in personal income, corporate income and general sales taxes	175.8	438.2	613.8	866.1	869.1	1,422.9	3,249.1	1,060.2
Current Situation			Taxes Per Family Unit					
(i) Personal income taxes	13	117	566	1,218	1,873	3,560	9,343	2,264
(ii) Personal income and general sales taxes	361	653	1,392	2,342	2,907	4,800	11,323	3,286
(iii) Personal income, corporate income and general sales taxes	528	1,056	1,897	2,992	3,463	5,637	13,053	3,965
Ontario								
Fiscally Autonomous Disbursements			Change in Taxes Per Family Unit					
(i) Reduction in personal income taxes	7.8	45.3	202.0	361.9	660.7	1,056.7	3,236.7	969.4
(ii) Reductions in personal income and general sales taxes	174.5	285.7	418.7	659.4	856.8	1,076.5	2,446.8	969.4
(iii) Reductions in personal income, corporate income and general sales taxes	163.2	433.7	538.9	735.8	800.5	974.7	2,373.2	969.4
Current Situation			Taxes Per Family Unit					
(i) Personal income taxes	20	116	519	929	1,697	2,714	8,312	2,488
(ii) Personal income and general sales taxes	387	682	1,202	1,959	2,834	3,894	10,095	3,530
(iii) Personal income, corporate income and general sales taxes	597	1,230	1,819	2,763	3,593	4,708	11,788	4,375

Table 8 (cont'd)

	Less than $3,000	$3,000 - 5,999	$6,000 - 8,999	$9,000 - 11,999	$12,000 - 14,000	$15,000 - 19,000	$20,000 and over	Total
Manitoba								
Fiscally Autonomous Disbursements								
Change in Taxes Per Family Unit								
(i) Reduction in personal income taxes	1.4	23.0	89.8	184.8	308.8	446.9	971.7	309.2
(ii) Reductions in personal income and general sales taxes	86.8	104.4	184.7	243.2	302.0	428.5	724.8	309.2
(iii) Reductions in personal income, corporate income and general sales taxes	79.4	148.8	217.1	242.3	310.5	399.2	685.1	309.2
Current Situation								
Taxes Per Family Unit								
(i) Personal income taxes	9	146	570	1,171	1,952	2,833	6,159	1,961
(ii) Personal income and general sales taxes	523	701	1,404	2,073	2,836	4,059	7,587	2,885
(iii) Personal income, corporate income and general sales taxes	790	1,178	2,036	2,662	3,539	4,903	8,808	3,581
Saskatchewan								
Fiscally Autonomous Disbursements								
Change in Taxes Per Family Unit								
(i) Reduction in personal income taxes	5.6	30.4	166.2	402.9	578.0	867.5	2,225.6	690.0
(ii) Reductions in personal income and general sales taxes	174.3	198.3	407.3	565.6	699.9	957.3	1,557.8	690.0
(iii) Reductions in personal income, corporate income and general sales taxes	144.6	270.1	432.7	552.4	654.6	794.5	1,650.5	690.0
Current Situation								
Taxes Per Family Unit								
(i) Personal income taxes	16	84	461	1,117	1,602	2,405	6,171	1,906
(ii) Personal income and general sales taxes	515	615	1,401	2,174	2,794	3,924	7,462	2,903
(iii) Personal income, corporate income and general sales taxes	704	961	1,904	2,729	3,408	4,595	8,669	3,512

Table 8 (cont'd)

	Less than $3,000	$3,000 - 5,999	$6,000 - 8,999	$9,000 - 11,999	$12,000 - 14,999	$15,000 - 19,999	$20,000 and over	Total
Alberta								
Fiscally Autonomous Disbursements			Change in Taxes Per Family Unit					
(i) Reduction in personal income taxes	11.4	30.9	142.0	290.4	467.4	684.9	1,493.7	568.3
(ii) Reduction in personal income and general sales taxes	152.7	159.2	267.7	437.6	586.3	700.5	1,138.8	568.3
(iii) Reduction in personal income, corporate income and general sales taxes	132.2	212.0	295.5	443.9	547.9	613.5	1,179.5	568.3
Current Situation			Taxes Per Family Unit					
(i) Personal income taxes	45	123	563	1,150	1,851	2,712	5,915	2,250
(ii) Personal income and general sales taxes	354	425	976	1,765	2,592	3,465	6,739	2,847
(iii) Personal income, corporate income and general sales taxes	683	950	1,623	2,668	3,613	4,468	8,514	3,833
British Columbia								
Fiscally Autonomous Disbursements			Change in Taxes Per Family Unit					
(i) Reduction in personal income taxes	4.3	26.7	162.3	284.9	515.5	911.9	2,525.4	713.1
(ii) Reductions in personal income and general sales taxes	140.8	155.3	302.4	439.5	668.3	982.7	1,893.7	713.1
(iii) Reductions in personal income, corporate income and general sales taxes	121.8	224.2	377.8	463.9	589.3	868.0	2,000.5	713.1
Current Situation			Taxes Per Family Unit					
(i) Personal income taxes	15	90	546	958	1,734	3,067	8,492	2,395
(ii) Personal income and general sales taxes	429	514	1,206	1,845	2,959	4,639	10,376	3,458
(iii) Personal income, corporate income and general sales taxes	554	916	1,812	2,535	3,740	5,582	12,544	4,346

Source Table 1. Further Economic Council of Canada data available on request.

Table 9

The Losses Per Family Unit of an Alternative Scenario by which Fiscally Autonomous Provinces Might Finance
Their Net Deficits Associated with Federal Government Expenditures, by Family Income Classes, Experiment A(i)

	Less than $3,000	$3,000 - 5,999	$5,000 - 8,999	$9,000 - 11,999	$12,000 - 14,999	$15,000 - 19,999	$20,000 and over	Total
Newfoundland								
Scenario (iv)								
Deficit financed by:								
-- expenditure cuts of $250 million	907	1,465	2,100	2,065	1,998	1,813	2,049	1,813
-- the remaining $211.6 million equally by increases in personal income, corporate income and general sales taxes	494.4	628.9	754.0	992.4	1,496.2	1,969.5	4,611.9	1,534.2
Total loss per family unit	1,401.4	2,093.9	2,854	3,057.4	3,494.2	3,782.5	6,660.9	3,347.2
Prince Edward Island								
Scenario (iv)								
Deficit financed by:								
-- expenditure cuts of $50 million	804	1,082	1,594	1,904	1,890	1,961	1,739	1,543
-- the remaining $89.2 million equally by increases in personal income, corporate income and general sales taxes	872.3	1,164.8	2,021.9	2,524.4	3,160.1	4,504.5	6,879.7	2,752
Total loss per family unit	1,676.3	2,246.8	3,615.9	4,426.4	5,050.1	6,465.5	8,618.7	4,295
Nova Scotia								
Scenario (iv)								
Deficit financed by:								
-- expenditure cuts of $250 million	527	951	1,061	1,160	1,025	1,164	1,036	1,021
-- the remaining $118.0 million equally by increases in personal income, corporate income and general sales taxes	123.8	184.7	322.3	435.1	536.3	657.8	1,188.3	481.7
Total loss per family unit	650.8	1,135.7	1,383.3	1,595.1	1,561.3	1,821.8	2,224.3	1,502.7

Table 9 (cont'd)

	Less than $3,000	$3,000 - 5,999	$6,000 - 8,999	$9,000 - 11,999	$12,000 - 14,999	$15,000 - 19,999	$20,000 - and over	Total
New Brunswick								
Scenario (iv)								
Deficit financed by:								
-- expenditure cuts of $250 million	854	1,178	1,350	1,349	1,371	1,371	1,373	1,271
-- the remaining $111.7 million equally by increases in personal income, corporate income and general sales taxes	125.9	276.1	391.8	473.2	612.7	687.0	1,415.7	567.8
Total loss per family unit	979.9	1,454.1	1,741.8	1,822.2	1,983.7	2,058	2,788.7	1,838.8
Manitoba								
Scenario (iv)								
Deficit financed by:								
-- expenditure cuts of $50 million	77	112	132	157	155	173	185	144
-- the remaining $57.6 million equally by increases in personal income, corporate income and general sales taxes	42.3	79.2	115.6	129.1	165.3	212.7	364.9	164.8
Total loss per family unit	119.3	191.2	247.6	286.1	320.3	385.7	549.9	308.9
Saskatchewan								
Scenario (iv)								
Deficit financed by:								
-- expenditure cuts of $100 million	174	192	32	39	41	49	38	332
-- the remaining $107.2 million equally by increases in personal income, corporate income and general sales taxes	74.8	139.7	223.9	285.8	338.6	411.0	853.6	355.6
Total loss per family unit	248.8	331.7	255.9	324.8	379.6	459.0	891.6	687.6

Source   Table 1.   Further Economic Council of Canada data available on request.

Table 10

Postulated Expenditure Reductions and the Series Employed
to Allocate the Losses by Income Class

	Expenditure Item	Reduction	Reduction as a per cent of total Expenditures on Item	Distributive Series Used
Newfoundland		($ Millions)	(Per cent)	
	Health	50	30.6	No. of families
	Primary and Secondary Education	50	35.6	Children 0-17
	Transportation	50	47.3	No. of families
	Unemployment Insurance	50	39.9	UI recipients
	Family & Youth Allowances	50	89.3	F&YA recipients
Prince Edward Island				
	Health	10	34.5	No. of'families
	Primary and Secondary Education	10	31.3	Children 0-17
	Transportation	10	46.1	No. of families
	Unemployment Insurance	10	50.3	UI recipients
	Family & Youth Allowances	10	98.0	F&YA recipients
Nova Scotia				
	Health	100	42.7	No. of families
	Primary and Secondary Education	60	46.5	Children 0-17
	Transportation	25	17.5	No. of families
	Unemployment Insurance	20	20.0	UI recipients
	Family & Youth Allowances	20	29.3	F&YA recipients
	Other Welfare	25	27.3	Provincial social assistance recipients
New Brunswick				
	Health	70	40.2	No. of families
	Primary and Secondary Education	70	41.4	Children 0-17
	Transportation	50	38.4	No. of families
	Unemployment Insurance	20	17.3	UI recipients
	Family & Youth Allowances	20	34.1	F&YA recipients
	Other Welfare	20	20.0	Provincial social assistance recipients

Table 10 (cont'd)

	Expenditure Item	Reduction	Reduction as a per cent of total Expenditures on Item	Distributive Series Used
		($ Millions)	(Per cent)	
Manitoba				
	Health	10	3.2	No. of families
	Primary and Secondary Education	10	6.1	Children 0-17
	Transportation	10	7.7	No. of families
	Unemployment Insurance	10	42.3	UI recipients
	Family & Youth Allowances	10	12.3	F&YA recipients
Saskatchewan				
	Health	25	10.6	No. of families
	Primary and Secondary Education	25	18.5	Children 0-17
	Transportation	10	5.8	No. of families
	Unemployment Insurance	20	44.7	UI recipients
	Family & Youth Allowances	20	26.2	F&YA recipients

Note   The distributive series employed were obtained from the 1975 Survey of Consumer Finances public release tape.

Source   Appendix Tables 7,8,9,10 and 13 and Provincial Government Finance, Statistics Canada Cat. No. 68-207, 1974.

Table 11

The Losses Per Family Unit of Alternative Scenarios by which a Fiscally Autonomous Quebec Might Finance its Net Deficit Associated with Federal Government Expenditures, by Family Income Classes, Experiment A(i)

	Less than $3,000	$3,000 - 5,999	$5,000 - 8,999	$9,000 - 11,999	$12,000 - 14,000	$15,000 - 19,000	$20,000 and over	Total
Scenario (iv)								
Deficit financed by:								
- Expenditure cuts of $1,500 million	523	772	709	733	721	865	1,012	759
- The remaining $595.8 million equally by increases in Personal Income, Corporate Income and General Sales Taxes	49.9	124.5	174.4	246.2	247.1	404.5	923.7	301.4
Total loss per family unit	572.9	896.5	883.4	979.2	968.1	1,269.5	1,935.7	1,060.4
Scenario (v)								
Deficit financed by:								
- Expenditure cuts of $1,366.0 million	440	700.0	653.6	648.4	617.4	799.2	1,193.6	701
- 5 per cent increases in Personal Income and Corporate Income Taxes and a 25 per cent increase in General Sales Taxes	96	160	260	374	380	530	1,049	399
Total loss per family unit	536	860	913.6	1,022.4	997.4	1,329.2	2,242.6	1,100

Source: Table 1 and Appendix Tables 24.

Table 12

The Expenditure Reductions Postulated for Quebec under Scenarios (iv) and (v), the Associated Tax Changes and the Distributive Series Employed

Expenditure Item	Reduction ($ Millions)	Reduction as a per cent of total Expenditure on Item (Per cent)	Distributive Series Used
Scenario (iv)			
Health	400	20.0	No. of families
Primary and Secondary Education	400	29.8	Children 0-17
Transportation	200	22.5	No. of families
Unemployment Insurance	200	24.9	UI recipients
Family & Youth Allowances	100	20.1	F&YA recipients
Other Welfare	200	21.1	Provincial social assistance recipients
Scenario (v)			
Experiment A(i)			
Health	150	7.5	No. of families
Primary and Secondary Education	150	11.2	Children 0-17
Postsecondary Education	102.9	17.2	Children 17+ in school
Transportation	283	31.8	No. of families
Unemployment Insurance	300	37.4	UI recipients
Family & Youth Allowances	200	40.3	F&YA recipients
Other Welfare	200	21.1	Provincial social assistance recipients
Experiment A(ii)			
As A(i) except Postsecondary Education	108.9	18.2	Children 17+ in school
Experiment B(i)			
As A(i) except Postsecondary Education	331.1	55.5	Children 17+ in school
Experiment B(ii)			
As A(i) except Postsecondary Education	215.0	36.0	Children 17+ in school

	Tax Changes		
	5 % Personal Income Tax	5 % Corporate Income Tax	25 % General Sales Tax
Experiment A	225.6	67.1	494.8
Experiment B	225.6	59.7	496.7

Source   Appendix Tables 7, 8, 9, 10, 13, and Provincial Government Finance, Statistics Canada Cat. No. 68-207, 1974.

96

Comments by D.B. Perry, Research Associate,
Canadian Tax Foundation, Toronto

It is now evident that decentralization in both taxing and
spending powers has changed from the possible to the probable.
Decisions about the new division of powers must be placed in a
financial perspective, as they have been in the preceeding paper.
In this context, I am reminded of the amalgamation studies done
at the local government level to show how some local property tax
rates would rise and others would drop. They serve to indicate
areas where a change in status would create severe hardships and
areas that could easily afford the change. Nice, precise studies
are produced to show how union would equalize the burdens, but
unfortunately none of the predictions come true; the shifts in
policy in the level, quantity and quality of government are more
significant in determining the fiscal outcome than the reorganization
of existing government.

The tips of two icebergs are evident in the development and
conclusions of Mr. Glynn's paper. The first and most visible is,
of course, the problem of distributing federal revenues and
expenditures by province. There are alternative approaches, as
noted by Glynn and Gerard Belanger of the C.D. Howe Institute; this
approach, using Statistics Canada Financial Management Series data,
is the appropriate one. However, I would suggest that the analysis
has been carried out at too high a level of aggregation. Specific
examples, where a finer breakdown of revenue items would have
yielded better results, include the distribution of customs duties,
taxes on other commodities (mainly on "luxury" items), the tax on
building materials used in residential construction, and non-tax
revenue.

Certain expenditure categories could have been broken down
further with recourse to the Public Accounts. The Interest item is
partly gross in the FMA; interest earned on lending to Crown
corporations, fishermen, small business, municipalities, and a
multitude of borrowers shows up on the revenue side in the FMS but
not here. Also excluded from this analysis is the book transfer
of interest to the public service pension plans. Given the
assumptions of the paper, this item represents an obligation to be
assumed by the provinces. The study does not examine the effect on
federal Crown Corporations of this hypothetical shift of responsibilities, although many of them concentrate their activities in

particular areas of the country, using federal funds to underwrite losses.

The author does not discuss the problem of choosing a year for the exercise. The year chosen was influenced by the oil export tax and import compensation, a program designed to be transitional in nature. The author can be excused for ignoring them. Had he studied a year or a decade earlier, the Ottawa Valley line policy would have been seen to give some benefit to the Western oil producer apparently at the expense of Ontario. The two-price wheat program was not in effect that year. The following year, $189 million was provided to subsidize a low domestic wheat price, a clear advantage to bread eaters as opposed to wheat growers. Should the world price fall below $3.25 per bushel, the benefit would go to the farmer.

The FMS federal figures for 1974-75 showed a surplus, offset to some extent in this study by the concentration on tax revenue. The surplus or deficit is nevertheless something that should be tackled in a study such as this. In one sense, the difference between expenditure by province distributed on the basis of revenue and expenditure by province distributed on the basis of benefit (expenditure) automatically distributes the surplus or deficit between the provinces, yielding a nationally balanced figure. Two drawbacks are apparent, first that the surplus or deficit as included above distorts the results; there should be an attempt to distribute the surplus or deficit itself. Secondly, as shown in the Council publication "Living Together," regionally differentiated fiscal policies, whether accidental or intentional, can have significant impacts on particular areas. These impacts should at least be touched on in an analysis such as this, with a reference to the options available for distributing the surplus or deficit.

The second iceberg, barely showing on the surface, but potentially much more dangerous in this study, is the distribution of federal tax revenue and expenditure by family income by province. Again, the literature is not extensive; many of the assumptions, not closely examined in the work, are open to debate. I must question one operation, where Maslove's figures for 1969 are escalated to 1974 assuming that inflation effects are distributed neutrally. In its 13th Annual Report, the Council presented quite a different picture. Tax incidence studies are very tricky, demanding full scale studies on their own. The patterns of income, consumption and provincial and local taxation change too much to assume constancy over periods of five years or more.

This brings me to a general comment on the conclusions and format of the study. The operations performed are technically complex in terms of public finance, and much of the work presupposes a familiarity with the general subject. In addition, as noted earlier, some of the assumptions are debatable. I question both the value and the wisdom of providing a summary by expressing the results in terms of gain or loss, increase or decrease, in tax or expenditure, in terms of dollars per family at each income level. How confident can we be about these dollar figures, given all that has gone before? How much are the income distribution final results influenced by the choice of certain income distributions used in the allocative process? The alternative scenarios help to illustrate the variety of results possible and the influence of various sets of assumptions. This form of condensation is unnecessary for the audience that the paper is intended for and can be dangerous when put into general circulation. To suggest 'per family' figures taken to the nearest whole dollar is deceptive when such figures can only be accurate to the nearest $25 to $50 per family, at best.

I would suggest that this study should not be interpreted as predicting fiscal outcomes because I feel that the *ceteris paribus* assumption is not realistic. If the underlying set of fiscal arrangements in Canada is changed, it is obvious that each province will immediately assess its own priorities. The minimum costs involved in maintaining what provincial residents regard as a "presence," nationally and internationally, will vary greatly and adjustments will be made. For example, the Economic Council may be disbanded, but the Ontario Economic Council may not necessarily be expanded in proportion, according to any of the measures shown here. The Atlantic Provinces Economic Council may be considered adequate in the new age. The investment committees of the Alberta and Saskatchewan Heritage Savings Trust Funds may become the dominant economic experts in British North America. The maritime provinces will put more emphasis on defending the two hundred mile limit than a continental power might. Further, no one seems to have claimed the Territories. Should Confederation break down after 112 years, I find it hard to imagine that the provinces will not move immediately to pick up the customs duties abandoned reluctantly in 1867 and to adapt them to their particular industrial strategies. The diversity that is now present within Confederation is a sufficient indication that quick and significant changes in the quantity and quality of government will follow immediately on "fiscal autonomy."

It is possible to suggest the direction of some changes. Welfare levels (including unemployment insurance) in each province will probably change to reflect the variation in per capita income.

Health and education will obviously have some elements that vary inversely because the importance of basic services may be relatively more important in lower income provinces. The export of trained workers and the import of expenses (such as students and the unemployed) will cause adjustments in other areas. The importance of telecommunications, air transportation and broadcasting may be more important in the vast expanses of the west and northern areas. Obviously, cultural influences will govern Quebec's actions under fiscal autonomy. Thus we might see the rise in importance of provincial air services and the expansion of the educational television authorities in some areas. The areas of speculation are many. The provision of financil details in the Glynn study would help to put such speculation into perspective.

To return to the amalgamation studies, there is a presupposition that there are differences in the level of service or the prospects for growth, and re-organization is seen as a policy tool to solve the problems. Similarly, the examination of Confederation and the decentralizing tendencies are policy tools that could be used to solve specific economic, social and cultural problems. In the municipal amalgamation studies, the problems are also spelled out and quantified. This type of study could do the same at the federal level.

THE NOVA SCOTIA ELITE AND

THE PROBLEMS OF CONFEDERATION

by

G. Rawlyk
Department of History

and

G. Perlin
Department of Political Studies

Queen's University*

*Assisted by Mary-Pat. MacKinnon

It is never easy to select a small influential elite group from amongst the perceived and often self-perceived leaders of any community. Nevertheless, despite the manifold problems involved, an attempt has been made, by using a variety of criteria, to choose such a group in each of the four Atlantic provinces. Politicians and civil servants, however, have not been included since their attitudes and opinions are examined in a separate chapter. Fifty-one Nova Scotian leaders were interviewed.[1] The occupational status of these respondents may be categorized in the following manner:

			Per cent
Business and economic	--	7	15.7
Education	--	11	21.6
Professional	--	16	31.4
Religious	--	4	7.8
Labour and others	--	13	23.5

Most of the fifty-one Nova Scotia leaders interviewed made it abundantly clear that they were not in any way reluctant Canadians. Almost 80 per cent of the respondents regarded themselves as Canadians first and Nova Scotians second. This does not mean, however, that their attachment to their native province was weak. The interaction of the two identities did not seem to cause conflict or dysfunction. The sentiment of one university administrator captured well the general consensus:

> I don't consider the two identities to be
> conflicting. I think that part of my continuing
> identity as a Nova Scotian involves my Canadian
> identity. I would have to say that I feel
> Canadian first but this is accompanied by a very
> strong provincial identity. (028)

A Roman Catholic leader insisted that Nova Scotians felt no estrangement from their nation but rather were staunch Canadians. "I think Maritimers have a greater sense of being Canadians than do other parts of Canada," (013) he asserted. Given that national attachment was so strong, it is important to consider the nature of that attachment and its possible relation to provincial commitments.

---

[1] In this study, specific individuals will not be mentioned. A large number of respondents asked that their name should not be associated with their answers to explicit questions. To meet this reasonable demand, each respondent has been given a three-digit code number, which has also been affixed to the questionnaires which are in the possession of the author's at Queen's University. This study was originally commissioned in 1978 by the Task Force on Canadian Unity. It is published with the permission of the Task Force which, of course, is not responsible either for its contents or its interpretations.

Most of the respondents defined Canadians and Canada in a positive manner, and only a handful either in negative terms or in both positive and negative terms. A few were not able to respond, either because they believed Canada lacked an identity or because they felt that the country's essence was not definable. As one professional engineer explained, "The country is so diverse that it can't be defined except perhaps to say that diversity defines Canada." (026) A view frequently expressed was that a mixture of British, American, and French culture, tradition and history had produced a unique and valuable entity called Canada. In the words of a religious leader, "We have the free and easy ways of the Americans and yet the staidness and tradition of the British." (013) Or as expressed by a leading academic lawyer,

> Basically we are a mid-Atlantic country that tries
> to bridge the gap between the old world and the new.
> We are a biracial and bicultural country and we've
> tried to combine features of both cultures and
> societies ... we have British common law and French
> civil law. We are also shaped by our North American
> environment. (042)

Others stressed the view of Canadians as generous and moral people whose social conscience had contributed to advanced social welfare schemes. "Canadians have a strong sense of the collective. We are a community oriented people." (025) Also emphasized was the physical environment and its impact in shaping and colouring Canadian realities. As a prominent Halifax businessman explained, "Our environment, sharing in the geography of Canada unites us. We all have an appreciation for the outdoors and a closeness to nature." (010) Respondents who had difficulty defining Canada's identity often turned to the international sphere in an attempt to find some answers. These individuals referred to Canada's middle power status, her peace-keeping role, and what was described as a respected international reputation. Some claimed to be most aware of a Canadian identity when abroad. According to a member of Nova Scotia's Bar Society Executive, "It's a very hard thing to express but I think there is a Canadian identity. When I'm abroad I feel it most particularly. We are recognized within international circles." (041)

Negative perceptions of Canada focused on the lack of drive, enthusiasm and ambition shown by its citizens and the failure of Canadians to take pride in their country's achievements and potential. One academic complained that Canadians were "over cautious, never take a risk and are not adventuresome." (022) A religious administrator was annoyed with the absence of patriotism in Canada. "We have a Canadian identity but we don't spend enough time thinking about it. We have been too humble and have lacked pride and assertiveness." (033)

Although they may have considered themselves to be Canadians first, most Nova Scotian leaders had little difficulty in articulating their provincial identification in positive terms. Positive

respondents emphasized historical factors, the geography of
the peninsula, and certain social and demographic characteristics.
The province's rich reservoir of history, its early achievement of
responsible government and its stable population whose roots reach
generations-deep into Nova Scotian soil were frequently mentioned.
The remarks of one physician were typical of many comments made:
"People here have a close association with the land, their roots
in the land are strong. This relationship also involves the
consciousness of how long their families have lived here." (009)
Comments about the North Atlantic and its impact upon the past,
present and future shaping of Nova Scotia and its residents were
often made. "The people here have a great interest in the sea both
in work areas and play areas." (027) Respondents perceived the
province as a place where the rural character was still strong,
and the pace of life slow enough to allow people to have time for
one another and for the communities in which they lived. "Our
distinctive values," it was asserted, "are our strong family roots,
our extended family idea and generally our deep community
ties." (033) The clear impression given was that there was a
certain simplicity of life-style in Nova Scotia; there was a lack
of tension generally -- a tension associated with big-city living.
An important member of the economic elite offered this observation:
"There is a difference in how we run our daily lives. I think that
we are commercialized to a lesser degree than other parts of
Canada." (010) The province's smallness in terms of land mass and
population was thought to contribute to neighbourliness and honesty.
The weight of history and tradition had created a people somewhat
conservative in nature and generally "not as aggressive or outgoing
as Upper Canadians." (011) Several respondents mentioned the
significance of Scottish settlement to the province's development.
A university president pointed out that "in Nova Scotia's history
there has been much Scottish predominance," (007) and a Roman
Catholic leader asserted that many Nova Scotians "are very much
influenced by their Highland Scot background." (013) A number
qualified their descriptions of Nova Scotians by remarking that
there also existed a variety of local identities. One lawyer
insisted, "I am not only a Nova Scotian. I am also a Haligonian and
proud of it." (041) A university teacher cautioned outsiders
against assuming that all provincial residents were alike.
"Another distinctive thing about Nova Scotians, they are Pictou-
nians, Cape Bretoners, people from the Valley, Southshore people
or whatever." (024) A Sydney union leader described his provincial
identity in Island terms alone: "On Cape Breton there has always
been a strong sense of brotherhood and co-operation among
residents." (001)

Negative aspects of Nova Scotia's identity were usually traced
to the province's economic vulnerability. Persistent economic
hardship and "have not" status were blamed for breeding an
inferiority complex, a dependency syndrome, slight paranoia and a
loss of confidence and initiative. A prominent Halifax lawyer
described Nova Scotian distinctiveness in the following manner:

> I think that the long history of economic disparity
> here has created a sense of inferiority among the
> people. There is a certain Maritime paranoia found
> here -- the fear that the province is being taken
> advantage of. Speaking of the legal profession,
> because it is the one that I am closest to, I would
> say that many lawyers here have the feeling that
> they could not compete or cope with lawyers in
> Ontario. They feel they can get along very well in
> Nova Scotia but would not be able to cut any ice in
> Ontario. (030)

A few people were critical of Nova Scotians' acceptance of what
was considered to be intolerable conditions. A leading Cape
Breton union spokesman complained that residents "tend to be placid
in their acceptance of things which normally cause people to be
upset." (004) On the other hand, a university administrator felt
that residents complained too often and emphasized their "have not"
status too much.

> Nova Scotians tend to emphasize the have-not idea and
> this is dangerous because it can be a self-fulfilling
> prophecy.... Nova Scotians have to get rid of a kind
> of mentality that blames others for their
> misfortunes. (022)

Another criticism was what one respondent referred to as the
province's "tunnel vision." (017) A Halifax union official
complained of the "clannish" nature of Nova Scotians and their
"inwardness." (029) And according to a key Roman Catholic leader,
"The negative side of our identity is our parochialism. We have
encouraged rather passé myths about this province and the vision
of Nova Scotians is not, as a rule, very broad." (033)

Attitudes towards Confederation and its significance for Nova
Scotia shed more light on the relationship of some of its leaders
with their country and their province. Of the fifty-one
respondents, thirty-five (68.6 per cent) judged Confederation to
be a good thing for the province, eight (15.7 per cent) thought
it had a detrimental effect, and eight (15.7 per cent) did not or
could not make any overall assessment. Many of the affirmative
respondents referred to the benefits derived from being part of a
country as large, powerful, and wealthy as Canada. They asserted
that partnership with Canada had allowed Nova Scotia more latitude
for growth and broadening than would have been otherwise possible.

> Nova Scotia could not have developed as it did
> without being part of a larger unit. (037) At
> the time of Confederation Nova Scotia had
> reached a peak; it was ripe for some kind of
> change. In order to grow further it had to
> join something bigger. (034)

> In being part of Canada's development, we took part
> in something valuable -- more valuable than if we
> had been alone. (029)

> Confederation helped us because it gave us a
> larger identity, the opportunity of belonging to
> a great country. We couldn't have had that kind
> of identity if we had not joined Confederation. (028)

Belief in Confederation did not prevent Nova Scotians from
criticizing national economic policies developed and fostered by
Ottawa and Central Canadians, many of which policies were
considered inappropriate for the Atlantic region. The majority
did not blame Confederation, *per se*, for the economic decline
of their province, but did stress that centralist economic
policies had retarded provincial economic development. One
university president observed:

> I can't honestly say that I blame the province's
> economic decline after Confederation solely on
> the fact of Confederation. We would have
> encountered economic troubles with or without
> Confederation. However, there is no doubt that
> the national tariff structure was set up to help
> Ontario and that it hurts us. I also blame the
> federal government for not doing enough to give
> Nova Scotians the choice and opportunity of
> staying within their own province. (028)

A minority of respondents, however, took a more extreme view. A
past President of the Association of Professional Engineers of
Nova Scotia was far more outspoken and harsh in his criticism.
Confederation, he asserted,

> has hurt us severely in the economic field. We
> have not been able to develop our initiatives, our
> own resources, and manufacturing potential
> because we have been smothered by the more
> powerful central Canadian bloc. This discrim-
> ination is and was a very deliberate policy of
> the financial and political authorities. (023)

But a university president arrived at a very different conclusion.
He was unwilling to accept that Confederation had anything to do
with Nova Scotia's economic problems:

> I do not think we can blame the economic woes of
> Nova Scotia on Confederation. Confederation
> merely coincided with a bad time of development.
> Using this Confederation argument is a rational-
> ization for our own failure. We have ourselves
> to blame for much of what happened. (007)

Many leaders considered equalization grants and the standardization of social security programs as great advantages derived
from being part of Canada. Frequent mention was made of the
federal government's commitment to lessen regional disparity. An
executive of the Nova Scotia Teachers Union felt certain of the
country's "commitment to fight disparity. Equalization payments
and shared cost arrangements have helped.... The federal
government is putting more money into Nova Scotia than it is
taking out." (020) Others, although accepting the positive
aspects of the equalization process, warned that such assistance
was not without its negative effects. The remarks of one
businessman concerning the ramifications of continued subsidization,
although too strong to be representative, did indicate why some were
alarmed. "Because the federal level controls so much of Nova
Scotia," he maintained, "we have been sapped of our autonomy, lost
our self-respect, our creativity, our motivation and initiative. We
are no longer in control." (010)

A grievance more commonly expressed was that Ottawa had
not been energetic enough in fighting regional disparity, and that
federal economic policy continued to discriminate against the
region. According to one leading Halifax lawyer, "There has to be
more give and take in Canada, more recognition of the need to have
equal opportunity for all regions." (037) He was supported by
another legal authority who pointed out that "What the federal
government does in Nova Scotia is really patchwork; it is not
changing our situation." (041) Numerous complaints against
discriminatory economic policy, however, did not change the fact
that a majority of leaders seem convinced that Nova Scotia's gains
from Confederation had been far greater than its losses.

Questions dealing with national goals received rather pragmatic, non-philosophic answers from the sample. Less than a quarter
of the fifty-one respondents gave first priority to the necessity
of promoting and ensuring national unity. Almost half focused
attention on goals of an economic nature and insisted that the
current economic crisis required immediate remedial action,

> Economics has to take priority over all other
> concerns. We must get our economy back into shape
> and our business flourishing. This will resolve
> so many present concerns being expressed ... if
> people are making money and sharing in the joys of
> life all else will fall into place. (019)

Others, equally preoccupied with practical matters, accentuated the need for appropriate regional development policies
that would allow the "have not" regions to become full partners
in Confederation. According to one advocate of "regional
technologies," "we must ... provide the technological infrastructure and research to allow each region to develop the
appropriate technology for itself.... We must change the
assumption that every thing has to be in Ontario." (027)

Reinforcing this opinion were the words of a Halifax businessman, "Our first goal should be to work out national and regional economies that provide a standard of living and a way of life that we should have in Canada." (010)

Those who stressed the importance of national unity argued that it was urgently necessary to come to grips with the disharmony arising between the two founding races. The comments of a union official accurately reflected the sentiments of this group.

> Obviously Canadians must try to obtain unity of
> purpose. We will go nowhere if we continue our
> constant fighting between the founding races.
> If this fighting continues, it will tear the
> country apart and that is nothing we can afford
> to let happen....   The attempt to mend the
> split in Canada must take priority. (029)

An influential engineer, in voicing concern over federal-provincial differences, provided a variation on the unity theme,

> The survival of the country must be our primary
> goal. We must allow regional identities to
> exist but we must also search for a common
> Canadian identity....   I am worried about the
> destruction of the cohesive forces of this
> country. We are too concerned with the parts
> and not enough with the whole. (026)

Very few of those interviewed elaborated upon the virtues and advantages of national unity. Most seemed to take the country's continued existence very much for granted. Those that did comment stressed that the alternatives to federal union were not promising:

> As for why to remain united, I don't see any
> more attractive alternatives to Canada....   It
> is nice to be part of a bigger thing and being
> so does not detract from the region. (027)

> ... As for why we should preserve the country,
> well as Nova Scotians alone I don't think we
> cut a very wide swath in the world. As
> Canadians we are respected and have a useful
> role to play in world politics. (007)

When dealing with Quebec and the possibility of separation, the Nova Scotia leaders revealed a strong desire to avoid the partition of Canada. Of the fifty-one respondents, forty-five (88.2 per cent) feared that Quebec's separation would have a somewhat or very harmful effect on Nova Scotia. When asked to state what course of action they preferred to take should Quebec decide to become independent, almost the same number expressed the desire to remain in Canada. This group reasoned that "Nova Scotia could not exist on its own, it is too small and not a viable entity" (037) and also that "many people here feel a definite allegiance to Canada." (035) Most respondents observed that "Nova Scotia would be better off economically within Confederation" (007) and were therefore hopeful of the province's ability "to get a better deal in a new federation. I think the rest of Canada will want to keep us." (023) The prospect of an independent Nova Scotia or an independent Atlantica was scoffed at by a majority of the leaders. It was argued that Nova Scotia lacked the resources, funds, infrastructure and power to go it alone. This contention was accompanied by a tendency to rely on Canada as a source of security.

> There would be extreme difficulties associated with independence. We would be just too vulnerable.... Nova Scotians feel an allegiance to Canada and would be too frightened at the prospects of independence to go it alone. (019)

The reluctance to consider independence seriously was also evident in their second preference. Only ten opted for joining the United States and twelve for Atlantic union; four individuals favoured an independent Nova Scotia.

There were a variety of responses to Nova Scotia's future economic prospects. Many of these revealed hostility towards large-scale industrialization unrelated to the provincial resource base. The industrial experiments of the 1960s and 1970s, the efforts of DREE, IEL, and a number of other public agencies to entice industry to Nova Scotia appear to have produced an elite cautious in its hopes for a revitalized province. Most of those interviewed seemed to envisage a future where the province's natural resources would be used to their fullest extent, combining new sophisticated technology with expert marketing techniques and skills. The opinion of one engineer captured this sentiment.

> I have been a close observer of IEL and I have to conclude that our industrial strategy has not worked and not because of lack of talent and effort. We have to go back to a reliance on our natural resources, on fishing, lumbering, mining, agriculture and on tourism. (026)

Cautious as respondents were about the economic future, quite a number indulged in a bit of excitement and speculation when discussing the potential of the fisheries and the gains to be made from the extension of the 200-mile limit:

> The 200-mile limit provides vast economic potential. We could develop a huge fishing fleet complete with factory ships, small craft and all the infrastructure that goes with it. We could get into the manufacture

of fishing gear, into the refrigeration process and
general processing. By improving marketing techniques
we could be selling to an international market. (023)

It is interesting that in their discussion of planning for the
province's future, few leaders turned to industrial Ontario or
booming Alberta as development models. Scandinavian countries
were thought to be far more appropriate models for a province
like Nova Scotia. Nor, warned a number of respondents, was the
standard of living of the wealthier provinces necessarily to be
envied or emulated. One academic protested that "we must realize
that we don't need the same standard of living as Ontario," (027)
while another commented that "our unemployment levels will go
down although we will never enjoy the prosperity that Ontario,
British Columbia and Alberta do." (038)

Increasing dependence on government equalization and transfer
payments had to stop, many argued. It was felt that the
provincial economy was far too concentrated in the service sector
and far too dependent on government money and not sufficiently
productive. "We have to accept the fact that we have to work hard
and increase our productivity" it was explained. "In other words,
get the work ethic back and convince ourselves that we can do it
and it will pay off." (035) Another concern expressed related to
the need for more entrepreneurial leadership and business expertise.
It was pointed out that the potential for development existed but
what was lacking was qualified and adventuresome entrepreneurs to
accept the challenge.

The most fundamental thing needed to get the economy
going is leadership. In the past we have not had
effective leadership and we have lost year after
year potential entrepreneurs. This is what is
needed yet. (036)

It was also stressed that more sensitive national policies in
transportation, taxation, tariff rates and marketing were needed
as a precondition of economic recovery. With appropriate policies
in place, the region would have less need for transfer payments.
"We must change many of our national policies," it was asserted,
"so that they reflect regional needs." (041)

The provincial identity of those interviewed reflected a
healthy regionalism founded upon a positive attachment to Nova
Scotia and the Atlantic region. For the most part, individuals
believed that their province provided special psychological, social
and physical advantages but within a Canadian context. An awareness of the very serious problems confronting the province was also
an important aspect of their "Nova Scotianess." Their attachment to
the nation was correspondingly strong. Collectively, the Nova
Scotia leaders gave the impression that Canada provided a larger
stage upon which they could actualize their greater ambitions and
full potential. Most stressed that creating an independent

province was neither possible nor desirable. It was also clear
that the nationalism expressed was not without its critical edge.
All those interviewed expressed some frustration with federal
policies. It was contended that Ottawa was callously indifferent
to the Atlantic region, and it was bitterly resented that Nova
Scotia in particular was often overlooked in the corridors of
power. As one Maritime historian has quite succinctly expressed
it, "Maritime eschatology ... has not been predicated upon the
destruction of the national policy but upon its fulfilment."[2]
Respondents obviously intended to remain Canadians, but Nova
Scotian Canadians, living in a respected and viable and productive
corner of Canada.

Respondents' perceptions of the federal and provincial
governments were quite varied. When asked about contacts with the
federal government, twenty-six of the fifty-one replied that they
did have such contacts, fourteen said that they did not, and
eleven did not respond. Provincial contacts, as might be expected,
were more frequent. Thirty-seven respondents had dealings with the
provincial government and only four had no contacts. In the
federal sphere, twelve had dealings with public servants, one
individual dealt strictly with politicians and twelve with both
politicians and bureaucrats. The remaining twenty-eight did not
respond. At the provincial level, two dealt exclusively with
politicians, six with public servants, twenty-seven with both
groups and sixteen did not answer. Twelve claimed to have been
negatively affected by federal government policy, six felt that
they had suffered no ill-effects and thirty-three did not respond.
Provincial government actions were not considered as being
especially harmful. Of the thirty-two individuals responding,
twelve felt they had experienced negative effects from provincial
government policy while twenty regarded such actions as relatively
harmless. When asked to decide which level of government was
easier to deal with, a majority chose the provincial government.
Of the twenty-one people answering this question, seventeen
preferred to deal at the provincial level, two favoured the
federal government and two saw no difference in dealings with the
two governments. A question about the impact of jurisdictional
conflict produced twenty-five answers. Of these, fifteen said
that they had been affected by jurisdictional conflict, and ten
suggested that they had felt no such thing.

Opinions concerning the extent of Ottawa's understanding of
Nova Scotia's problems were evenly divided. Twenty-eight
respondents believed that the federal government understood Nova
Scotia's problems, while twenty-one disagreed with that conclusion.
Two did not find an answer. When asked about the provincial
government's ability to communicate problems to Ottawa, thirty-six
(70.6 per cent) replied that Halifax was doing a good or adequate
job with only eight (15.7 per cent) ranking provincial efforts as

2   T. W. Acheson, "The Maritimes and 'Empire Canada'" in Bercuson, *Canada and
the Burden of Unity*, p. 109.

poor. The remaining seven did not respond, claiming they did not
know enough to answer intelligently. When asked to decide whether
federal-provincial conflicts were mainly the result of different
policy orientations or of a power struggle, respondents gave a
variety of answers. Of the forty-six individuals responding,
twenty-nine suggested the conflict involved a power struggle,
eleven saw issue differences to be more crucial, and six felt
conflict involved both issues and power.

It is necessary, it seems clear, to elaborate somewhat on
the above findings. From an examination of answers, it is evident
that the leaders were more likely to have contacts with the
provincial government than with the federal government. It is
notable that only one individual preferred dealing with the
federal government. Accompanying remarks suggested that
respondents perceived the federal government as a huge, very
complicated and quite inaccessible machine. The provincial
government, on the other hand, was considered more accessible,
much less complex and more humane. The comments of one Halifax
lawyer captured well the general view. "Naturally, I find the
provincial government much easier to deal with ... it is so close
and it is smaller." (030) The existence of personal contacts
within the provincial government was a factor frequently referred
to. The following remarks indicate something of the extent to
which that personal element was considered important.

> I have a good rapport with the government both
> because of the size of it and because of the
> fact that I know them personally. This
> personal element makes a fantastic differ-
> ence. (019)

> Well, it is easier for me because I have
> personal contacts with a number of politicians
> and bureaucrats. I play tennis with Gerry
> Regan. I must say that I am well-received and
> have continuous contact both at a professional
> level and a social level. (012)

In discussing the most effective way to handle obstacles or
difficulties with the provincial government, this personal
element was frequently mentioned. Although respondents advocated
following conventional grievance channels when dealing with
problems associated with the federal government, they emphasized
a different method with respect to the provincial government. In
the latter case, individuals remarked that it was best to take the
matter to a minister, some influential person in the government
or perhaps to the Premier himself. In the words of one business
leader, "Well, in Nova Scotia, I would be more inclined to go to
the politicians than I would at the federal level.... I have no
hesitation in going to the Premier if need be." (010) According
to a leading lawyer, "If I have serious difficulties I have no
hesitation about going to the Minister or the Premier. This is
the most effective route to go." (018)

This preference for dealing with provincial officials did not necessarily mean that the federal government was perceived totally in negative terms. That twenty-eight individuals, 54.9 per cent of the total sample, thought Ottawa understood Nova Scotia's problems is both noteworthy and significant. Scrutiny of accompanying comments, however, revealed that although a majority felt Ottawa to possess adequate understanding, many also felt that it lacked the will to deal effectively with provincial problems. As one engineer put it, "I think they perceive the scope and nature of the problems but that does not mean they act on that knowledge." (026) Others qualified their affirmative responses by adding that if Ottawa understood Nova Scotian problems, it understood even better the political realities of Canada, and that was that the province carried little real political weight. In the blunt words of one union leader, "They are quite aware but they won't do anything because they are too concerned with the interests of Ontario and the West." (001) Still others suggested that problems arose not from Ottawa's lack of awareness, but rather because it applied inappropriate solutions. As one academic explained:

> Ottawa does try to understand the problems here.
> Their error is in thinking that they alone have
> the solutions. There is an arrogant attitude in
> the federal public service that seems to say
> that they know better what has to be done than
> people here. (025)

A number of respondents, in discussing Ottawa, clearly differentiated between political Ottawa and bureaucratic Ottawa. Most perceived the bureaucracy to be rather unsympathetic and hard to reach. It was observed that the Ottawa mandarins had lost "contact with reality" (034) and were far too removed from the situation in Nova Scotia to understand it. A doctor, formerly an Ontario resident, argued that few officials in Ottawa had any comprehension of what the province was all about. "I myself did not understand until I moved here." (024) Others based their arguments on an assessment of federal government actions in the province. According to a university president, "It's difficult to generalize ... about all the people in Ottawa but the results and actions witnessed don't lead one to believe that Ottawa does understand." (028).

Most respondents considered the provincial government's attempts to communicate with Ottawa to be good or at least adequate. This did not mean, however, that they believed Halifax's pleas were always given a fair hearing or were acted upon. They did believe, however, that Halifax was persistent and very vocal in demanding recognition of the province's particular problems. As one hospital administrator put it, "the provincial governments have been vocal and active. They do a good job of taking their prayers to Ottawa." (011) A lawyer reiterated this opinion, adding a frequently-mentioned complaint. "Our people here make lots of noise. They try to get through to Ottawa. There is a problem at the other end -- those receiving the information leave something to be desired." (018)

The majority of respondents had no difficulty in delineating areas of conflict between the federal and provincial governments. As might be expected, most conflicts were thought to arise because of economic difficulties. Aside from a few individuals who mentioned Constitutional reform as a contentious issue, most emphasized funding arrangements, natural resource utilization and control, transportation policy, tariff and trade arrangements, energy, regional development, and unemployment rates. Tension in these areas, it was argued, was triggered by the power struggles between politicians and bureaucrats. It was "Basically ... a power struggle between the two levels of governments to see who can get the most credit, who can get the votes." (007) Also stressed was a government desire to accumulate and solidify power. "Neither side wants to give up any of their power," (029) it was observed. Individuals believing that different policy orientations were at the root of the tension explained that "it is a case of Ottawa trying to keep the national interest in mind while the province is trying to push its provincial interests. It is quite natural." (030)

Taken as a group, the leaders appeared to feel more comfortable and relaxed in their dealings with the provincial government. This ease resulted from the proximity and accessibility of that government. The federal government, although certainly not condemned, was criticized for its insensitivity to regional needs. Nonetheless, comments concerning Ottawa were usually reasonable in tone and lacked bitter invective.

The general reaction to Quebec and the possibility of separation revealed tolerant and compromising viewpoints. Forty-nine (96.1 per cent) respondents considered the French language and culture to be valuable contributions to Canadian culture. Special constitutional status for Quebec was accepted by twenty-eight (54.9 per cent) and rejected by twenty-one (42.9 per cent). Reaction to the proposal outlining economic union (sovereignty-association) was not so positive. Twenty-one (41.2 per cent) accepted the proposal, while twenty-three (45.1 per cent) rejected it and seven were uncertain. Forty-one (80.9 per cent) believed that a third option was possible. Guaranteeing the right of French-speaking Nova Scotians to be educated in their own language and to have trials conducted in their mother tongue posed no problem for the majority of respondents. Thirty-eight (74.5 per cent) agreed with educational and legal rights while nine (17.6 per cent) disagreed with the education guarantee and ten (19.6 per cent) rejected the legal guarantee. Although disapproval of the federal government's implementation of bilingualism in the public service was widespread, respondents looked favourably on the principle of bilingualism. The actual implementation of bilingualism was criticized by thirty-one (60.8 per cent), approved by thirteen (25.5 per cent) and seven

(13.7 per cent) were unable to answer. The principle itself received acceptance from thirty-eight (74.5 per cent) and was rejected by twelve (21.5 per cent). The generally conciliatory attitude of respondents is better understood when one realizes that forty-five (88.2 per cent) feared that Quebec's separation would have a somewhat or very harmful impact upon Nova Scotia.

It was felt that the linguistic factor was not a major cause of Quebec's unrest. Forty-five (88.2 per cent) stated that "something else" lay at the root of the Quebec problem. A majority perceived the struggle in Quebec as a struggle of the people striving to achieve "equality." A few individuals referred to Quebecers as "white niggers," while others described them as "second-class citizens." Most expressed sympathy for Quebec's demands, and tried to understand their grievances in the context of historical and cultural factors unique to that province. The comments of an executive member of the Nova Scotia Registered Nurses Association were typical of many opinions expressed:

> Their discontent results from their historical
> difficulties. I have sympathy for Quebecers
> and do think they have been subjected to
> injustices by English Canadians. They have
> been frustrated in the past, and the Church
> worked to maintain their subjection. They
> want equality. (017)

A number of other Nova Scotians stressed the traditional economic inferiority of the French-Canadians and Quebec's current financial difficulties. According to a Teachers' Union Official:

> They [Quebecers] are frustrated because of
> their inability to progress in economic
> fields. They want to be able to run their
> own province and maintain their identity.
> The federal government responded wrongly
> to their needs by concentrating on
> language. (020)

Respondents rejected bilingualism in the public service, not because they opposed increased use of French in Canada, but because they considered the program to be grossly expensive and a total failure. Some protested that funds spent on the policy would have been better spent if channelled into the school system in the hope of making the next generation bilingual. "The money could have been spent in better ways such as beginning French at the grade Primary level." (034) Others accepted the goal of a bilingual public service but considered the methods employed by the government to achieve this goal to be "absurd, ineffective, a farce and absolutely stupid." Many complained that the wrong individuals were sent away for language training, that too many in bilingual positions never had reason to use French, and in general that the government was less than sincere in its efforts to promote French.

In summary, it seems obvious that most Nova Scotia leaders were willing to concede certain rights and special privileges, however undefined, to French Canadians. And most, moreover, expressed concern for Quebec's needs and seemed confident that compromise was indeed possible.

Reactions to possible reform proposals revealed interesting and varied opinions, many of them shedding light on the current provincial-federal debate. A proposal for administrative decentralization received favourable answers from twenty-six (51.0 per cent) individuals, negative replies from twelve (23.5 per cent); six (11.8 per cent) were ambivalent and seven did not respond. A proposal advocating jurisdictional decentralization provoked a different reaction. Thirty (58.8 per cent) disliked the proposal, twelve (23.5 per cent) favoured it, three were ambivalent and six did not answer. Many felt that administrative decentralization would bring the government closer to the people, improve decision-making and the administration of programs, and spread some of Ottawa's wealth around the country. According to a leading member of Halifax's financial elite, "government departments could be just as effective outside Ottawa as they are inside. If departments were spread out that way, it could mean a great deal to the area they were decentralized to." (008) Many also expressed concern that change should truly be change and not mere tokenism. As one union leader stated, "I agree with administrative decentral-ization as long as it is truly decentralization, that is when offices are moved, the power to make decisions goes with them. I don't want to see regional desks set up with no real power." (034) It was suggested that administrative reform would encourage people to identify more with the nation. "I favour administrative decentralization of government services. This will act to strengthen the regions and also to help them identify more with the whole of Canada. Canada will no longer be something up in Ottawa." (029) A main complaint of those opposing the reform proposal was that administrative decentralization was an imprac-tical, unworkable scheme which, if implemented, would remedy no existing problems. One engineer referred to the reform as "a political gimmick to get votes," (023) and a lawyer was concerned about a loss of efficiency. "I have grave doubts about its efficiency. I don't think it will work, it will lessen government efficiency." (018) Others stressed that the reform's effects would be largely irrelevant. "Administrative decentralization is not significant. The decisions would still be made in Ottawa anyway." (038)

Opponents of jurisdictional decentralization based their rejection on one or both of the following arguments. The first argument usually took the following form:

> I don't want to see a change in the power distribution between the provinces and Ottawa. We need a strong central government in order to keep this country together. (007)

I am a federalist and I believe that the survival of
the country depends upon a centralized government.
(012)

The second argument was more specific:

We would be financially hurt in the Atlantic region
if Ottawa was no longer in a position to grant
subsidies here. (037)

Weakening Ottawa might hurt us because certainly
Ontario would have little desire to develop our
economic potential. (035)

Most respondents were less concerned with balancing jurisdictional powers than they were with improving the consultation
process between the two levels of government and ensuring that
Nova Scotia's voice was heard and considered in a serious manner.
As one individual explained, "it would be better if we had a
strong Ottawa that gave more recognition to Nova Scotia." (023)
A chartered accountant pointed out that "the problem today is not
with jurisdictional balances but rather with the attitude of
Ottawa." (014)   The seriousness of the problems confronting the
provinces, argued many respondents, required a sharing of skills,
expertise and knowledge.   A generalized conclusion was that
"provincial interests can be better protected through a consultative, co-operative process." (024)   People were not particularly
responsive to questions dealing with specific delineations of
federal and provincial powers.   One union leader in answering the
above question curtly stated, "it's not where the power is that
counts but how it is administered." (001)   Many individual expressed
general satisfaction with the *status quo*, although they added that
they would not be necessarily opposed to change, provided it
occurred through a consultative process.   Seven respondents wanted
to have fisheries changed to a provincial jurisdiction, while
eleven felt that education should be turned over to the federal
sphere.   The latter group sought the change as a means of standard-
izing curriculum and avoiding glaring qualitative differences in
educational systems.   A few believed the province should have
control of all its natural resources, and some proposed that the
provinces "be allowed to decide where the money it receives should
be spent." (019)   Overall, one could certainly not claim that those
interviewed were strong advocates of provincial rights, or of a
radical alteration of the B.N.A. Act.   The general consensus seemed
to be captured in the following cogent statement:

It's not so much a matter of jurisdictions prevailing
as it is of more meaningful consultation between the
two levels; more provincial input.   We don't have to
have an across-the-board national policy; we need
policy with regional variations. (041)

Proposals suggesting that the Senate be reformed, to give it more power in federal-provincial matters and to have its members chosen from the provinces, drew mixed reactions. Nineteen (37.3 per cent) supported the suggestion, eleven (21.6 per cent) rejected it, eight (15.7 per cent) wanted the Senate abolished, and thirteen (25.5 per cent) did not respond. The prospect of an elected Senate drew nineteen (37.3 per cent) advocates, twenty-three (45.1 per cent) opponents, and nine (17.6 per cent) uncertain individuals. A proposal for an appointed Senate chosen by provincial governments received a response rather similar to the above reaction. Twenty-nine (51.9 per cent) opposed the reform, twelve (23.5 per cent) supported it, and ten (19.6 per cent) were unsure. A final option, having Senators appointed by all parties in the provincial legislatures, produced no more favourable a response. Only eight (15.7 per cent) desired the change, twenty-seven (52.9 per cent) rejected it, and sixteen (31.4 per cent) did not answer. Few leaders indicated any enthusiasm for Senate reform, many seemed somewhat bored and unconcerned with the topic. Others, desiring Senate reform, were unsure of how it should be achieved. As one union leader said "I have not thought out the particulars but I do think change is necessary." (029) A number of those who failed to respond to the reform options explained their hesitancy by saying that in their opinion the cart was being put before the horse. In the words of one lawyer:

> Before we can talk of giving it more power we have to define its role. That has not been done and is crucial to any discussion of the Senate. The selection system can be worked out after the role is determined. I can't answer these questions until that is done. It is obvious that something has to be done. (042)

Abolitionists called the Senate "an old man's club" (028) and complained that "Senators have outlived their usefulness. We don't need two governments up there playing games." (039)

Respondents were more favourably disposed to reform proposals that advocated increasing provincial influence in federal institutions and policies. A proposal suggesting that provincial governments have more influence in appointing Judges to the Supreme Court was accepted by twenty-six people (51.0 per cent), rejected by eighteen (35.3 per cent) and was not reacted to by seven (13.7 per cent). Supporters who elaborated upon their choices tended to stress that "regional representation is important" (037) and that the Court needed "a better balance" (021) than it currently had. Others admitted that allowing provincial appointments would not eliminate political favouritism, but insisted that nonetheless the reform would bring about a Court "better than what we have now." (041) A major complaint of reform opponents was that "the Supreme Court was not meant to represent provincial interests or regional interests." (018) In the opinion of this group, provincial input "would create a political body.

The Supreme Court should not be political." (030)   "Its function," it was contended, "was to represent the law." (007-8)   Those who failed to respond either said that they "did not know enough about" the issue or they pointed out that appointments would be political anyway so they did not care who made the selection. "I see them as purely political appointments so I don't care who is making them." (002)

A proposal to permit provincial governments a role in appointing individuals to federal regulatory agencies received affirmative answers from twenty-nine (56.9 per cent) individuals, negative responses from sixteen (31.4 per cent), and six declined to answer.   Advocates maintained that it was very important that federal agencies keep "in touch with provincial concerns" (022) because the impact of their actions was felt right across the country.   Provincial input on the various agencies was considered to be absolutely essential.   Reform opponents complained that involving provincial governments would accomplish very little and would do nothing to alter the fact that many appoints were based on considerations of political affiliation rather than merit.   As one university president argued, "although the immediate response is yes, on second consideration it is evident that this would accomplish little.   The province would be making political appointments just as the federal government." (036)

Supporters and critics of a proposal advocating greater involvement of provincial governments in the determination of monetary policies were very evenly balanced.   Twenty-five (49 per cent) desired an enhanced role for the provinces, twenty-two (43.1 per cent) did not, and four could not or did not respond. Supporters insisted that the different regions of Canada required special attention and policies, policies more likely to be developed if provincial input was increased.   "It would be desirable to have monetary policies that suit us rather than having to abide by national policies which are not applicable." (029)   Opponents warned that involving provincial governments would only create a "confusing" situation and that "the perils inherent in allowing the provinces in on this policy are greater than the advantages.   It would balkanize the country." (007) Another criticism voiced was that "provinces don't have the expertise to become involved" (011) in shaping national monetary policy.

More provincial involvement in federal fiscal policy, specifically in the determination of the federal budget, was sought by twenty-nine (56.9 per cent) and rejected by twenty (39.2 per cent).   Only two individuals did not respond to this reform proposal.   Although the majority supported the reform, many qualified their support by adding that final authority in policy determination should always be the federal government. "The provincial governments should be consultants in this matter and not full partners, that is, the federal government must have the final say." (026)   Reform opponents complained that monetary control had to be centralized. In their opinion, allowing the provinces a greater role would open up an enormous can of worms. As one academic put it:

> The idea is great but I think there would be great problems of implementation ... there is the danger of its becoming too political and of the national good being ignored because of bargaining between the two levels of government. (028)

From an examination of the response to the various reform proposals, it is clear that Nova Scotia leaders were not over-whelmingly in favour of provincial rights. A majority did support greater involvement of provincial governments in a variety of federal functions. The opposing minority was, however, significant in numbers and quite articulate. Comments suggested that what was desired was not a weakening of federal powers but rather a sensitive, aware Ottawa able to act on Nova Scotia's special needs. At no time did respondents give the impression that they sought the aggrandizement of provincial powers at the expense of the federal sphere.

Atlantic union received support from twenty-three (45.1 per cent). The remaining twenty-eight (54.9 per cent) were opposed. Twenty-two (43.1 per cent) supported Maritime Union, twenty-eight (54.9 per cent) rejected it, and one individual declined to answer. Although some did support both union proposals, most did not "think it ... likely to occur in the near future unless some traumatic change occurs in the region." (010) Many believed that if Quebec separated, the region would be practically forced into such a union. Even union opponents stated that in the event of Quebec independence they would support the joining together of the four Atlantic provinces. As one opponent remarked, "I don't think it [union] is likely to occur and I would not favour it unless some radical change happened such as Quebec's separation." (011) Political amalgamation was considered unlikely for two main reasons. One factor involved the provincial identity of Atlantic residents. "We are too traditionally bound by our provincial love affairs. We don't want to give up these identities." (008) As one academic put it, "the psychology of the people in the Maritimes prevents or inhibits any such union." (038) A second reason preventing union was thought to be the reluctance of political leaders to promote the idea in earnest. "We don't have the leadership to bring it about. They are too interested in their own empires." (010)

Respondents considered the following as advantages to be gained from Atlantic or Maritime union: "more political clout with Ottawa" (018), "standardization of services and savings in administrative costs" (038), enhanced ability to "devise a common strategy for development in economic, educational and social areas" (010), "avoid needless duplication" (012), "increase our bargaining power with companies" (027), and finally, "de-emphasize

petty politics and strengthen our government, improving the
quality and competence of those involved." (033) The following
were listed as disadvantages associated with union: "rather than
having less bureaucracy we might have more" (036); "government
would become too remote, we would lose the feeling that we are
able to influence people in government" (019); it would "water
down some of our political clout with Ottawa" (012); "politically
impossible to administer" (014); "Nova Scotia might lose a bit
since we would have to redistribute funds to the poorer
provinces" (009); and finally, "there would be a loss of identity
for people in the region and also a loss of pride in provincial
identities." (018)

Opponents of union proposals protested that co-operation
would be more difficult to achieve within a union. They
complained that political union was unnecessary and directly
opposed to the wishes of the people. "I believe we can achieve
better co-operation without a formal political union. No one
wants it anyway." (041)

Respondents' appraisal of existing co-operation among
governments in the region varied. A small group considered co-
operation to be poor. They complained that politicians were
unwilling to pursue objectives common to the whole region and
were too concerned with maintaining their own power. As one
religious leader bluntly stated, "the co-operation that exists is
just tokenism. All of the governments are primarily interested
in maintaining their power and protecting their bureaucracies."
(033) An economic leader predicted that co-operation would not
improve until "we improve our political leadership and political
life." (010) A second, more numerous group, although not
satisfied with the degree of co-operation, conceded that
provincial governments were at least making an attempt to
communicate and co-operate. This group accepted that some
competition would always exist because it was a part of the
political system, but hoped that it would lessen in the years
ahead. "Co-operation has been reasonably good in those areas in
which there are common interests. Disagreements arise because of
the political system we have to work with. Each politician must
be responsible to his own constituency." (038) Others worried
that recent economic setbacks would inhibit or retard improved
relations. "They are beginning to work together, but recently
I've detected a certain backing off, a reappraisal of co-operation.
I have a feeling that co-operation is beginning to decline." (029)
The smallest group, numerically speaking, was composed of
individuals generally satisfied with the extent of government co-
operation in the region.

Attention must be drawn to the fact that many in referring to
Atlantic co-operation really meant Maritime co-operation. Quite a
few respondents saw Newfoundland as a self-declared outsider,
unwilling or unable to share concerns with the other three Atlantic

provinces. As one union leader said, "Newfoundland does not get very involved with the other three provinces and is inclined to be aloof." (029)

When questioned about APEC, most respondents reacted by saying they thought it fulfilled a necessary role in Atlantic Canada. They also stressed that its publications provided relevant information. "APEC is good. It attempts to gather information on a regional basis. It allows us to compare things and to see where we are going." (027) The single most common complaint against the institution by both admirers and critics was that it lacked power and consequently was less effective than it could be. "APEC is a good idea but it doesn't have much power and thus can't accomplish a great deal. It has to receive more recognition from the government." (024)

The Council of Maritime Premiers (CMP) evoked fewer detailed responses from the sample than did APEC. While most individuals were more positive than negative about CMP, many were rather vague about the Council's specific achievements. Comments like "the CMP have done a number of useful things" (032) were common. Others did not differentiate between the CMP and APEC, making statements like this one, "Both APEC and CMP are very relevant and needed. They do a good job in certain areas of co-operation." (022) Criticism of the Council paralleled that of APEC, that is, some respondents questioned CMP's effectiveness given its lack of power. "As far as CMP is concerned, it seems that the three Premiers have backed down on co-operation. In the end it is a political matter. None of the provinces will give up anything." (018) Others worried that the original intentions of the Council were being neglected or misdirected. "The CMP was a good first step but lately they have been regressing. The Premiers are more concerned with politics." (010) Those who were completely unimpressed with the Council referred to it as "an entertainment society" (041) which had a "big bash three times a year." (034)

Nova Scotian leaders seemed united in their conviction that meaningful co-operation and sensitive consultation provided the answers not only for the region's problems but also for those facing the Canadian nation. Despite a strong attachment to the constitutional *status quo*, there was some willingness expressed to accept some changes, provided that these did not undermine a strong federal presence in Ottawa.

Comments by Peter E. Gunther, Task Force on Canadian Unity,
Ottawa

It is impossible to do justice to this year's efforts by
Professors Perlin and Rawlyk in a paper such as we have just heard.
It is but a single cell in a much more encompassing opus which
includes the historical themes of Confederation, the interpretations
of the press for the last decade, a mass survey and an elite one.
Although these preliminary Nova Scotia results still await more
sophisticated statistical treatment, they contain the heart of what
I might dub the Canadian irony; national allegiance midst provincial
preference.

The resilience of Nova Scotian national allegiance is quite
remarkable. The paper correctly recognizes the necessity at
Confederation, midst the decline of wood and sail, new world wide
competition for the British Empire and the cancellation of reciprocity,
for Nova Scotia to enter a larger trading entity but it could also
harken back to the options of Maritime union, union with the United
States and a British Empire parliament of which Joseph Howe was the
main exponent. The new allegiance to a parliament dominated by land
lubbers intent upon a national, not international policy, meant that
the dead hand[1] of national policy would be upon the Atlantic region
for at least 100 years. Next year, do not ask the ghosts who remain
to celebrate its centennial.

As recently as 1961-1971, it contributed to a net emigration
of 129,000 people from the Atlantic region. The scars of this
emigration will remain with us for two generations through a depleted
tax base, low demand for housing and the transfer of income of those
migrants to established central Canadian land owners in the form of
increased land prices elsewhere in the country. Although these cuts
have been sutured by net immigration of 30,000 from 1971-1976, many
economists and politicians alike are poised to rip open the stitches
with little understanding of regional or provincial preferences.

Perhaps Ottawa bureaucrats who protest about their guilded
cages being moved as far away as Hull should recognize that others
feel strongly about their domestic nests. By their own protestations
it is certainly clear that the bureaucrats prefer the Versailles of
Ottawa to life amongst those whose interests they purport to serve.
Yet Nova Scotians maintain allegiance.

---

1 Harold Innis, *Complementary Report Nova Scotian Commission*,
  Provincial Economic Inquiry, King's Printer, Halifax 1934, p. 133.

Although I live in Halifax, there is no one else listed on this programme as residing east of Montreal. Yet, omitted from the discussion table, Nova Scotians remain loyal.

This unconscious omission has been historically typical of Dominion attitudes. In his review of the "Literary Standing of the Dominion" in 1877, the leading critic of his time, Jean Talon Lesperance, admitted "I am not sufficiently acquainted with the literary movement in the Maritime Provinces to enter into an account of it, but I know...the names of." A century later Central Canadian attitudes have not changed. Witness *Quill and Quire*, from its advertising, the obvious darling of the Canadian publishing industry,

> "...Atlantic provinces could become a solid
> front against what Karl Webb, Nova Scotia's
> youth director refers to as 'The Central
> Canada Syndrome'. 'Writers are writing books
> as if Canada stopped short at the Quebec border.'
> Insularity, it should be said, is not confined
> to the Maritimes.[3]

Note that according to *Quill and Quire* it is Maritimers who are insular not Central Canadians who simply ignore part of the country's heritage when writing texts. Yet allegiance more than lingers among the elite.

Perlin and Rawlyk assure us of that. Almost 80% of the respondents were Canadians first and Nova Scotians second. I am not sure that 80% is a large number. I suspect it would be higher in Ontario. More important, is Nova Scotian allegiance based upon positive factors? The basic thrust of the paper suggests to me that it is not. There is the inferiority complex made deeper by the maintenance transfers which are the major means for distributing benefits of the economic union. Development policies are preferred. Only 68.6% see Confederation as being a good thing, so it is not surprising that less than a quarter give national unity as their priority objective, although most recognize a net gain stemming from Confederation despite Ottawa's perceived callousness. The Honourable Eugene Whalen's recent comment that Nova Scotia's election was no more important than a municipal one will do nothing to improve Ottawa's image in a province that, should it join the United States, would be the 41st in population size. The response to Ottawa's

---

2 Jean Talon Lesperance, "The Literary Standing of the Dominion," *Canadian Illustrated News*, 1877.

3 Loren Lind, "Geography lessons in text adoptions," *Quill and Quire*.

policies is singularly unenthusiastic, 12 injured and 6 not injured, no one helped and 33 not responding. Suggestions for reform ought not to fall on deaf ears.

Most (17 of 21) preferred to deal with the province; in the language of Scott and Breton, signalling costs to provinces were clearly less than to Ottawa. For example, even an application of their principles of total costs would have dictated that the Atlantic Restoration Center remain in Moncton in order to avoid serious costs and risks in transporting Acadian and Atlantic artifacts and resultant destruction of our heritage. But that is of little concern to Ottawa.

My purpose here is not to summarize or to add colourful particulars; it is to highlight the Canadian irony and suggest to economists that the analytical framework based upon neo-classical economics is wholly inadequate to deal with the issues at hand. Economics has little to say of allegiance and regional social preferences. The propositions of neo-classical economics require mobility of labour and capital as well as complementary tax structures as outlined by Johnson.[4] Perlin's and Rawlyk's findings, sustained discrepancies in income and linguistic barriers, suggest that these assumptions are not met. Indeed, until we social scientists come fully to grips with much broader but equally specific models, we shall continue to recommend policies which politicians and poets alike will rightly regard as being non-optimal. When neo-classists speak of "non economic costs," there is an admission of inadequacy. At the micro foundation level, Lancaster[5] and Becker[6] have begun to form a broader, more detailed theoretical base, but their work needs to be expanded to include a perceptual function between activities and utility. We need to make models compatible with those of perceptual psychologists if we are to have anything to say about vesting education and communications. Only in such models can all the avenues for development become clear; only then can the constraints imposed by government and the division of power be examined completely. Only then can we clearly delineate the social costs and see how they are borne by government and individuals. Economists will then be able to discuss the tax structure as a vehicle for transferring social cost back to those creating the costs and, within that framework, the allocation of power which is what is at stake in federal-provincial conflict.

These are the best of times; they are the worst of times; it is an age of foolishness; it is an epoch of belief; it is the season of

4 This theory is developed by Harry G. Johnson, "The Implications of Freer Trade for the Harmonization of other Policies" in *Aspects of the Theory of Tariffs* (London: Allan and Unwin, 1971).

5 Kevin J. Lancaster, "A New Approach to Consumer Theory," Journal of Political Economy, Vol. LXXIV, 1966, pp. 133-157.

Light; it is the season of Darkness. Income per capita is higher
than it has ever been; soaring unemployment leads to unrest. Glass
palaces tower over dinosaurs in Calgary and cover the old guilded
cage of the Bank of Canada in Ottawa. Mirror windows reflect cold
steel and the art of technocrats. In Montreal, buildings stand
naked and gutted; Expo is gone, and the big O is all that remains
of the Olympic rings. The Prime Minister's pretty lady is splashed
all over films, and people know that pretty is not beauty. Some
rip off the UIC, and others lose self-respect.

Economic models that worked by sleight of hand do not work
in more sophisticated times. The depression gave us Keynes and
economic management for a quarter of a century.

If we are **lucky**, the crisis in federation will give us a
viable theory of federalism and particularly of Canadian federalism.
It has taken us a century to travel from Joe Howe to Joe Who. We
do not have another century to find Joe Why. The two Georges do us
a service in tackling this problem, but I wonder what the results of
a survey in the France of 1773 would have revealed?

****

This comment is that of the author alone. It in no way
reflects the opinion of any of his employers or the direction of
their research.

---

6 Gary S. Becker, "A Theory of Social Interactions," Journal of
  Political Economy, Vol. LXXXII, 1974, pp. 1063-1093.

DECENTRALIZATION AND PROVINCIAL REPLICATION

OF THE CANADIAN FEDERAL PUBLIC SERVICES

by

B. MacDonald

Economic Council of Canada

PART I

INTRODUCTION

Either significantly increased decentralization of federal powers or separation of Quebec would mean that some presently federal public services would be provided by two or more jurisdictions. Some argue that such a change would, on balance, be beneficial, while others argue that it would be harmful to the general interest of Canadians. Four sets of arguments have commonly been advanced in this connection, which are presented and summarized below.

1 Varying Tastes

Decentralization of public services from the federal to the provincial level would mean that each of these smaller political jurisdictions could put forth a personally designed package of services to reflect the peculiar preferences of each constituency. Given perfect interprovincial mobility, individuals could relocate on the basis of their preferences for various provincial programs, and the general level of satisfaction derived from the services offered within a province and the nation as a whole would rise. Some argue that many would benefit from such an arrangement, while none would be made worse off.

2 Allowing for Spillovers

Decentralization or greater provincial autonomy over public services would erode the ability of the federal government to correct for the existence of externalities arising as interjurisdictional spillovers.

Production externalities may arise, for example, when Ontario produces pulp and paper, and pollutants are emitted as a by-product. Suppose these pollutants are passed into waterways shared with the province of Quebec. It is unlikely that Ontario would, of its own accord, compensate those consumers of the waterway whose utility has been affected by the pollution and who do not reside in Ontario.

If, however, some central authority exists, such as the federal government with its control over reallocative tools like taxation and subsidy, then these externalities may be accounted for. The federal government could place a tax on the sale of pulp and paper products so that the price of this product would reflect all costs, including that for polluting the riverway. It could then, if desired, compensate directly those affected most by the pollution.

The development and enforcement of such solutions by individual persons and provinces could be prohibitively expensive, and similar spillovers and associated allocative inefficiencies would go on uncorrected.

---

1 G. Tullock, "Federalism: Problems of Scale," *Public Choice*, Spring 1969, pp. 19-29.

3   Presence of Scale Economies

Decentralization may mean the loss of certain cost advantages which accrue from the centralized production of goods and services because of positive scale economies in the production process. Of course, where negative scale economies dominate the provision of a public service, exactly the opposite will hold true, and lower average unit and total cost will be attained by dispersing the production facilities among the provinces.

4   Possibilities of Duplication

Within the federal-provincial political framework it might well be possible that competition or lack of consultation between the federal and provincial levels of government could result in certain public service operations being performed more than once, implying wasteful duplication.

These four arguments have received considerable analytical attention. Two or more of them have often been considered within the context of a trade-off situation where, for example, the potentially positive gains from decentralization associated with argument 1 are weighed against the potentially harmful effects of decentralization associated with argument 2.

We shall be devoting most of our attention to argument 3 which concerns economies of scale, and argument 4, involving the possibilities of duplication, is briefly examined.

Our study is different from previous works on the subject of decentralization because of its empirical approach to the analysis of decentralization. We adapt our analysis to a novel Canadian institutional framework with quite revealing results.

In Part II, entitled "An Industry Synopsis," we examine the nature of the production processes underlying the provision of those public services in Canada which are now provided by the federal government. In Part III, "The Regionalized Services," we consider alternative scenarios under which decentralization might occur. These scenarios are not individually exhaustive, but we hope that, together, they may capture the range of possible costs associated with decentralization. In Part IV, "Economies of Scale in the Regionalized Services," we discuss our empirical estimation procedures, as well as results generated concerning economies of scale in the provision of the regionalized public services. In Part V, "Decentralization of the Regionalized Federal Public Services," we combine our estimates of economies of scale from Part IV with out scenarios of decentralization outlined in Part III and arrive at some estimates for the cost of decentralizing the federal, regionalized public services in the province of Quebec. In Part VI, "The Unregionalized Federal Services," we discuss the decentralization of the unregionalized federal public services, and in Part VII we provide a summary of our results and some conclusions.

PART II

AN INDUSTRY SYNOPSIS

Roughly $47 billion will pass through the hands of the federal government in 1978. Much of this money is simply transfers, so that, of the $47 billion, approximately $17 billion constitutes the real operating costs of the federal government which is here viewed in a role analogous to that of a private sector industry, supplying goods and services. These costs include such things as supplies, salaries, buildings and equipment, etc.

Provincial government expenditures on goods and services, which surpassed similar expenditures by the federal government in 1971[1], are relevant to this study as well. The degree of similarity between Federal and Provincial programs suggests that infrastructure and expertise existing at the provincial level may well be capable of absorbing federal responsibilities.

In Canada the majority of public services result from the combined effort of head office and field operations. The head office activity may usually be separated from the field operations, both in terms of descriptive function and in expenditures.

In Table 2-1 we outline the production process which characterizes the majority of federal services. We have divided this overall production process into six distinct stages which we then attempted to align with their counterparts in private industry.

While we expect to find Stages 1 through 6 occurring to some degree at both head office and field levels, we expect activities within Stages 1, 2, 3 and 6 to be more predominant at the head office level. Policy directives, research and development, interprovincial co-ordination, etc., all occur within these stages of production. Stages 4 and 5 are predominantly field operations.

We analysed the actual field-head office allocation of occupational groups in an attempt to affirm our expectations of such a division. The occupational category we expect to be most prevalent in Stages 1, 2, 3 and 6 would be the scientific-professional group which, as expected, is distributed more heavily to the head office level. We would, in turn, expect operations under Stages 4 and 5 to involve the technical and operational categories of employees. We find a preponderance of these occupational groups at the field level, which again supports our proposed division of operations between the two levels.

---

1   Statistics Canada, *Canadian Statistical Review*, Pub. No. 11-003E, vol. 53, no. 7, July 1978.

Table 2-1

Production Stages of a Public Service

Stage 1	Stage 2	Stage 3	Stage 4	Stage 5	Stage 6
		(Public sector)			
Analysis of electoral support research and development (Exec, Sci-Pro*)	Analysis of production, distribution and administrative costs (Sci-Pro,Tech, Af, Afs)	Delegation and co-ordination of senior administrative and executive responsibility and actions (Exec, Af)	Physical production and servicing (Tech, Sci-Pro,Oper,Af, Afs)	Distribution and administration (Oper, Tech, Af,Afs)	Program effectiveness analysis (Sci-Pro, Af, Exec)
		(Private market counterpart)			
Analysis of market demand research and development	Analysis of production, distribution and marketing costs	Delegation and co-ordination of senior administrative and executive responsibility and actions	Physical production and servicing	Marketing and distribution	Profit analysis

*Occupational group most prevalent in above stage.

The executive component, as expected, is almost exclusively located at the head office level (our units of measurement were not fine enough to capture the occurrence of small numbers of this category at the field level).

Significant numbers of administrative and administrative support categories are employed in Stages 3 and 5 and are associated with both head office and field output.

When we analysed the distribution of occupational groups disaggregated to the level of the individual program, we found distribution of occupational groups among the provinces to be virtually identical. This suggests that there is little variation amongst the provinces in the field operations they use for any particular program.

An examination of the regionalized component of numerous federal departments revealed, as well, that the field operations between any two provinces were largely independent of one another. For example, the field operations of the federal department of agriculture in Saskatchewan serve largely, if not exclusively, the residents of that province.

The separability of head office and field operations, along with the independence of field operations among the provinces for operations of the same federal program, carries implications for the direction of our research.

First of all, we shall be advancing in Part III a scenario of decentralization in which Quebec takes responsibility for all ongoing federal field services within that province, and maintains these programs in their existing form. Essentially, we are proposing that field operations are already decentralized, and the division established between these and head office operations allows us to focus our attention exclusively upon the cost implications of further decentralization of this head office component.

Secondly, as the federal field services in any two provinces are independent of one another, we can safely assume (in the case of an autonomous Quebec, for example) that the post-decentralization level of field services would be the same as the original level of field services, everything else being equal.

The functional division between head office services and work performed in the field may be extended to the level of provincial services as well. The "general administrative" operations of most provincial programs perform a function highly similar in many respects to that of the head office at the federal level. Though both federal and provincial head office components fulfil a general steering function, federal head office operations expend considerably greater resources on R & D and policy development.

We divide federal programs into two categories. The first category involves programs in which the head office operation is largely concerned with steering and co-ordinating field operations, with the bulk of head office output arriving in the form of policy directives, financial management, research and development information and program co-ordination. These services flow directly to the field offices. The field operations are then responsible for manufacturing the final goods and services and delivering them to the public. Where the head office fulfils such a function, we expect its expenditure to be dwarfed by the expenditure of the field components. We label this group the "Regionalized Programs." Examples of regionalized programs are Agriculture, Transport, and Health and Welfare.

The second group of programs are composed largely of the head office operations themselves. These head office operations are not occupied to any great extent with the administration of their field operations; indeed field operations for these programs are a relatively minor component of the total service, if they exist at all. Such programs as Treasury Board, Energy Mines and Resources, and Urban Affairs fall into this category.

The head office for such programs would be primarily concerned with the production of goods and services which do not lend themselves to a regional implementation. These goods and services may be quite indivisible on a provincial basis, as would be the promotion of a national policy on energy conservation. They may be oriented mostly towards Research and Development with either a theoretical or a practical bias, or they may be constituted in such a way as to be best disseminated and administered by a single central authority. An example would be Canadian foreign relations.

A large number of smaller commissions and agencies whose fully centralized activities are directed to serving other agencies and departments fall into this category. Such agencies or commissions tend not to deal with any large cross-section of the Canadian public, but rather deal with specific industries, interest groups, or directly with other institutions.

Both regionalized and unregionalized federal programs are listed in Table 2-2 under Canadian Federal Program. In the same table, under Quebec Provincial Program, we have alligned with the federal institution a program at the Quebec provincial level which performs a similar operation.

The pairing of federal and provincial programs presented in Table 2-2 suggests that the regionalized vs. unregionalized division of federal programs may be extended to the level of provincial programs as well. In fact, this disaggregation can be as effectively applied to provincial as it can to federal programs. The Quebec department of the treasury, like its federal counterpart, is largely a head office operation, while the Quebec department of agriculture, like its federal counterpart, is largely field-oriented or regionalized (within the province).

We will first examine in detail those programs which are regionalized in nature.

Table 2-2

Canadian Federal Programs (Regionalized)
and Most Similar Quebec Provincial Counterparts

Canadian Federal Program	Quebec Provincial Program
A - Regionalized Programs	
National Defence	
Public Works	Public Works
RCMP	Justice I[1]
Transport	Transport
Indian and Northern Development	Tourism, Fish and Game
Health and Welfare	Social Affairs
Agriculture	Agriculture
Environment	Environmental Protection
Employment and Immigration	Manpower and Employment
Post Office	
Taxation	Revenue
Customs and Excise	
Regional Economic Expansion	
Correctional Services	Justice II[2]
Veterans Affairs	
B - Unregionalized Programs	
Secretary of State	Cultural Affairs
External Affairs	Intergovernmental Affairs
Urban Affairs	Municipal Affairs
Parliament	National Assembly
Communications	Communications
Privy Council	Executive Council
Treasury Board	Treasury Board
Consumer and Corporate Affairs	Consumers, Co-operatives and Financial Institutions
	Education
Finance	Finance
Civil Service Commission	Civil Service
Industry, Trade and Commerce	Industry and Commerce
Energy, Mines and Resources	Natural Resources
	Lands and Forests
Labour	Labour and Manpower

1 Justice I includes certain programs within the Quebec Department of Justice, with appropriate pro-rated share of internal management and support. These programs include (a) Securité du Quebec, and (b) Inquiries into Scientific and Specialist fields in assistance of judicial performance, and (c) appropriate share of management and support.

2 Justice II includes (a) custody of prisoners and detained persons, and (b) the appropriate share of management and support.

PART III

THE REGIONALIZED SERVICES

In this part we discuss the decentralization of the regionalized services. We attempt to formulate a framework within which we can estimate the costs of decentralizing these programs.

Similarity between ongoing federal and provincial services, and the existing capacity of the provinces to assume responsibility for federal programs, along with the nature of scale economies in the production of these services, will determine jointly the costs of decentralization.

With the exception of defence services the larger provinces maintain numerous programs which cope with problems similar to those dealt with by federal institutions.

In order to determine with any degree of accuracy the significance of existing capacity at the provincial level we would have to compare all federal and provincial programs, their roles, objectives, organizational framework, etc., as they were stated and as they appear to be. This approach is outside the scope of this paper.

However, we can assume various degrees of existing capacity and test for the significance of these assumptions on the impact of the size of cost associated with decentralization.

An upper cost boundary will be generated by Assumption 1 -- that no provincial capacity exists in Quebec due to the lack of similarity between federal and provincial programs.

A lower cost boundary will emerge from our second assumption, that the Quebec and federal departments paired in Table 2-2 are perfect substitutes for one another, so that production and responsibility for a particular federal program (for which a substitute exists) can be transferred to the provincial program.

In order to clarify the implications for decentralization costs of scale effects and existing provincial capacity, we shall provide a hypothetical exercise.

Assume the nature of scale economies in program X to be determined; we depict the cost output relationship characterizing field and head office operations in Figure 3-1, (a), (b) and (c). (Note that the scale economies governing head office operations, Figure 3-1(a), are not the same as those describing field operations in Figure 3-1 (c).)

Though in practice long-run average cost curves may slope upwards or downwards or lie horizontal, the long-run average cost curves in our hypothetical example, given in 3-1(a) and 3-1(c), fall to the right, as positive scale economies are assumed to characterize both field and head office production.

Figure 3-1(b) repeats the story told by 3-1(a) in terms of total costs.

In the world "before" decentralization, the federal government and provincial government are both in the business of providing public service X. At the level of field operations, both the Quebec and Canadian governments serve a Quebec population of 600, each spending $100 in the province, so that both governments produce at M along $LRAC_F$ in Figure 3-1(c). The federal government maintains an expenditure of $100 in all ten provinces, so that total federal field expenditure equals $1,000, as indicated in Figure 3-1(a) by point F_1.

To administer these operations, the federal and provincial governments, respectively, spend $500 and $110 on head office operations, as shown in Figure 3-1(a) and 3-1(b). F_1 represents the initial federal position, P_1 the initial Quebec operation, in both figures.

These "before" expenditure values, as well as total federal and provincial expenditures obtained by addition, are provided in Table 3-1.

Upon decentralization Quebec combines federal and provincial field operations into a single field unit, serving the total combined population (600 + 600 = 1,200, as indicated by point N in Figure 3-1(c)). Quebec, however, does not double its field expenditures to $180. Because of economies of scale in field services it is able to serve a population of 1,200 for $180 (1,200 x 15) at the original level of services -- see Figure 3-1(c). Along the "after" row of Table 3-1, 180 is entered in column 6 and a zero is entered for federal field expenditure in Quebec in Column 3. Total federal field expenditure falls to 900 in column 2.

The decline of the federal field expenditure allows the federal government to reduce its head office expenditure, while Quebec must enlarge its own head office facilities. Though the absolute change in the level of federal field services (-) and provincial field services (+) is equivalent, the absolute and proportionate increase in size of the Quebec head office that follows is substantially greater than the associated decrease in the size of federal head office operations. Federal head office expenditure falls to 486 (column 4), adjusting to a new field expenditure of 900. Quebec head office expenditure rises to 160 for a field expenditure of 200. The new points of federal and provincial head office production, F_2 and P_2 respectively, are indicated in Figure 3-1(a) and 3-1(b).

140   MacDonald

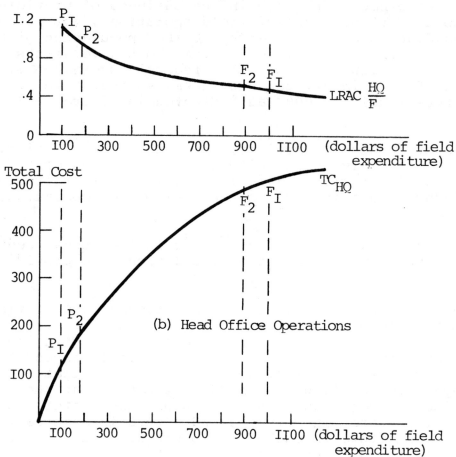

$Head Office expenditure
$Field expenditure

Figure 3-I

Head Office Operations   (a)

(b) Head Office Operations

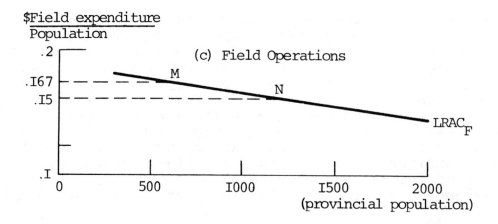

$Field expenditure
Population

(c) Field Operations

All remaining spaces in Table 3-1 may be ascertained through simple addition or multiplication.

The change in total cost for providing the same level of services is shown in column 12. In this case, the change is positive.

Decentralization will imply higher costs for head office administration (given: $HQ_{j,f} > HQ_{j,0}$) and economies of scale at the field level will exert a negative influence on the change in total cost. The larger the initial fraction of head office to total operating costs, the more likely is the head office effect to outweigh the field effect, and vice versa.

This exercise, then, is typical of the other exercises we will carry out under alternative assumptions.

We must now estimate the slope and nature of the long-run average cost curves at the level of head office and field operations. This will be done in Part IV within the context of the regionalized public services.

Table 3-1

Numerical Exercise
(Dollars)

Program Federal Provincial			Federal				Provincial (Quebec)				
			$C_{J,F}$ Total Operating Expenditure	$F_{J,C}$ Field Operating Expenditure (All Canada)	$F_{J,Q}$ Field Operating Expenditure (Quebec only)	$HO_{J,F}$ Head Office Operating Expenditure	$HO_{J,Q}$ Head Office Operating Expenditure	$P_{J,Q}$ Field Operating Expenditure	$C_{J,Q}$ Total Operating Expenditure	Combined Federal and Provincial Operating Expenditure	Change in Combined Federal and Provincial Operating Expenditure
			(1)	(2)	(3)	(4)	(5)	(6)	(7)	(8)	(9)
x	x	Before	1,500	1,000	100	500	110	100	210	1,710	
x	x	After	1,386	900	0	486	160	180	340	1,726	+ 26

PART IV

ECONOMIES OF SCALE IN THE REGIONALIZED SERVICE

We are interested in determining whether a systematic relationship exists between cost and output in the regionalized public services. We use cost-function estimation to examine the cost-output relationship in terms of the output of both head office and field operations.

Cost Functions

Introduction

We made use of several alternative cost functions in our analysis at both head office and field operations levels, meeting with varying degrees of success. We began by estimating the most general textbook equation:

$$TC = A_0 + A_1 x + A_2 x^2 \qquad (1)$$

where TC was made equal to either head office or field costs, and x made equal to either field expenditure or population (as proxy for market size).

This equation format allows for the presence of internal economies and diseconomies of scale arguments. Positive scale effects are generally suspected to arise, at least in the initial stages of increased production, from the division and specialization of labour, combined with the more efficient use of indivisible capital inputs with these labour resources. Negative scale economies may be expected to arise at some point due to labour management or other organizational problems which may bottleneck specific areas of the production process. As long as the positive scale effects dominate, average costs fall over the long run. If, however, negative scale economies surface more as production increases, then the average costs will first level out and then perhaps begin to rise.

From the total cost equation we may derive the average cost equation by dividing both sides of (1) by output x:

$$AC = \frac{A_0}{x} + A_1 + A_2 x_1 \qquad (2)$$

Whether average costs generated over various levels of output will take on the image of a U-shaped average cost curve, or that of either a constantly increasing or declining average cost curve, depends upon the sign and size of the right-hand terms in equation (2). The typical U-shaped curve will surface from the presence of positive first and third terms. Constantly falling average costs would result from a positive first term and a negative second term. On the other hand, constant average costs would appear if the first and third terms were either small and/or insignificant.

We also estimate a linear form of cost-output relationship, as given below, in total and average cost terms:

$$TC = A_0 + A_1 x_0 \tag{3}$$

$$AC = \frac{A_0}{x} + A_1 \tag{4}$$

The straight-line average cost curve generated will fall if the first term is positive, rise if the first term is negative, and be horizontal if this term is small or insignificant.

The second type of general relationship we estimate is in Log format, so that scale elasticities are generated. For example, testing the following equation:

$$\text{Log } TC = A_0 + A_1 \text{ Log } x \tag{5}$$

the value arrived at for A_1 is the elasticity coefficient relating the percentage change in output to the percentage change in costs that result.

Head Office Cost Functions

We had no explicit measurement for head office output and therefore employed a proxy for this variable -- the size of field expenditure administered by head office. Equation (1) thus becomes:

$$HQ_F = A_0 + A_1 F_F + A_2 F_F^2 \tag{6}$$

HQ = expenditure at the head office level and F = field operating expenditures (subscripts F and 2 denote federal and provincial institutions, respectively).

We tested equation (6) for a cross-section of all federal programs with field size >0 and then tested it separately for those programs which constitute the regionalized services. The results are presented in Table 4-1, lines 1 and 2.

We also tested equation (6) using provincial data, the costs of the general administrative component for provincial programs serving as our estimation of head office costs. The sample of provincial programs used to test equation (6) was limited to those programs which coincided with the regionalized federal programs. The results are in line 3 of Table 4-1. We then attempted to test (6) for regionalized federal and provincial programs.

Once A_0, A_1 and A_2 were estimated for the various populations tested, they were placed in our average cost curve equation

$$AC = \frac{A_0}{x} + A_1 + A_2 x.$$

Table 4-1

Empirical Results -- Economies of Scale
at Head Office

	A_0	t	A_1	t	A_2	t	R^2, $\bar{R}^2$
$HQ = A_0 + A_1F + A_2F^2$							
1.1 All federal programs F>0	39,233	(3.8)***	.17	(3.5)***	.1(-07)	(.64)	.76, .75
1.2 Regionalized federal programs	85,672	(1.7)**	.06	.53	.3(-07)	(1.0)	.77, .73
1.3 Regionalized provincial programs	1,736	(1.3)*	.03	(1.7)*	.1(-07)	(.47)	.37, .32
$HQ = A_0 + A_1F$							
1.4 Regionalized federal programs	45,715	(1.4)*	.19	(6.0)***			.76, .75
1.5 Regionalized provincial programs	2,006	(1.9)***	.02	(4.2)**			.37, .35
$Log\ HQ = A_0 + A_1\ Log\ F$							
1.6 Regionalized federal programs	2.4	(.94)	.71	(3.5)***			.51, .47
1.7 Regionalized provincial programs	2.2	(1.8)	.51	(4.4)**			.40, .8
$Log\ HQ = A_1\ Log\ F$ + Dummies							
1.8 Regionalized provincial-departmental dummies	(All dummies)***		.60	(3.8)***			.46, .33
1.9 Regionalized provincial-provincial dummies	(All dummies)***		.53	(5.8)***			.78, .68
$Log\ (O.C.) = A_0 + A_1\ Log\ F$							
2.0 Exec.	-8.8	1.26	(2.6)**				.35, .30
2.1 Sci. Pro	-1.9	.85	(2.03)**				.25, .19
2.2 Af.	1.3	.66	(4.1)***				.58, .55
2.3 Tech.	-2.9	.86	(1.65)*				.19, .12
2.4 Afs.	3.3	.47	(2.4)***				.32, .36
2.5 Oper.	-.69	1.14	(1.5)*				.15, .08

*Significant at a 90 per cent level of probability.

**Significant at a 97 per cent level of probability.

***Significant at a 99 per cent level of probability.

The results for equations tested showed the presence of large, significant first terms for 1.1 and 1.2 (Table 4-1), and small and insignificant third terms for the same equations. This suggested definite scale economies for both samples of federal and provincial head office operations.

Because the third term in all equations proved insignificant, it appeared that a linear specification may have been more appropriate to capture the cost-output relationship. We tested equation (7):

$$HQ = A_0 + A_1 F \tag{7}$$

for regionalized federal and provincial programs.

As shown in Table 4-1, lines 1.4 and 1.5, the R^2 was unaffected by the change to linear format, and the levels of statistical significance for the coefficients in each equation improved.

The results of these equations are graphically illustrated in Figures 4-1 and 4-2. The relative sensitivity of average costs to changes in the level of output is quite similar for federal and provincial samples. We would expect, therefore, our Log equations to yield similar coefficients for provincial and federal programs. However, the absolute size of the provincial head office operations at any one level of field output is close to one-tenth that of its federal head office counterpart. This reflects facts pointed out in our earlier discussion, relating to the relatively higher federal head office expenditures on R & D, interprovincial co-ordination, policy development, etc.

Testing our Log specification of the cost-output relationship given below

$$Log\ HQ = A_0 + A_1\ Log\ F \tag{8}$$

we found highly significant cost-output elasticity coefficients for provincial programs (.51) and federal programs (.71). Both elasticity coefficients indicate a high degree of scale economy in head office operations. The federal coefficient suggests that a 1 per cent change in field operations results in a .71 per cent change in head office expenditure, while the reaction of provincial head offices is only a .51 per cent change in expenditure for the same 1 per cent change in the level of field operations.

As indicated by both $LRAC\frac{HQ_F}{f}$ and $LRAC\frac{HQ_P}{f}$ in Figures 4-1 and 4-2, average costs first decline rapidly and then gradually decrease to become almost constant after field size surpasses $300 million expenditure. Provincial field or head office operations are on average less than one-tenth of the size of the average of our sample of federal head office or field operations with almost all

Figure 4-I

Economies of Scale at
Head Office Level
(Federal)

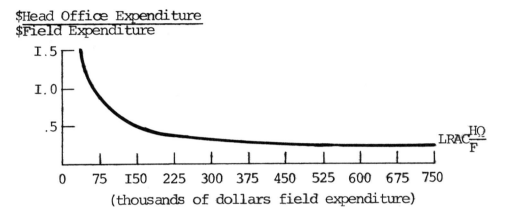

Figure 4-2

Economies of scale at
Head Office Level
(provincial)

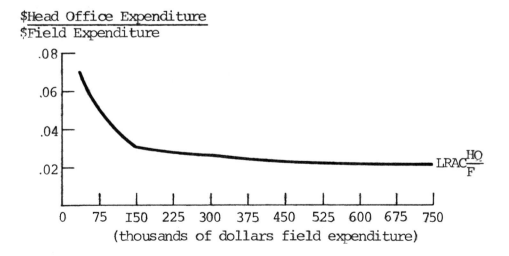

observations on field size falling below the expenditure level of $300 million. This explains the higher degree of scale economies generated from the provincial sample. This is the range of field-size with which scale effects appear to be most significant.

We introduced two sets of dummy variables into equation (8) for the provincial sample. The first set of dummy variables represented the province of the program. The second set of variables represented the type of program.

While the introduction of the first set of variables had little effect upon the explanatory power of the equation, the elasticity coefficient went from .51 to .60. The introduction of the second set of dummies markedly raised the overall explanatory power of the equation, leaving the elasticity coefficient about the same, .53 (vs. .51). These results are outlined in Table 4-1, lines 1.8 and 1.9. All dummy variables were significant.

Finally, we had to know whether a particular component of head office employees might be more or less responsible for the head office economies of scale. Thus, we tested

$$\text{Log O.C.} = A_0 + A_1 \text{ Log F} \qquad\qquad (9)$$

for all six occupational categories, where O.C. equals expenditure upon any one of six individual occupational groups.

As might be expected, the scientific-professional category of labour reflected a significant scale response to field size, suggesting that a 1 per cent increase in the level of field activity resulted in only a .85 per cent increase in the requirement for scientific and professional employees. The strongest scale effects, however, were exhibited by the administrative and administrative support category, while the executive and operational categories exhibited a negative scale response. The results for all occupational groups are given in Table 4-1.

Economies of Scale at the Level of Field Operations

The form of equation we employed at the field operations level was essentially the same as the one we had used to test for economies of scale at the head office level.

We tested the following equation in Log format:

$$\text{Log F} = A_0 + A_1 \text{ Log M} \qquad\qquad (10)$$

where F = field expenditure within a particular province, and
      M = the market size served within a particular province.

We first tested this equation cross-sectionally across all provinces for all federal programs with operations in each province. The number of observations was 210. We included in our equation dummy variables for the program type. The results generated are in line 1 of Table 4-2. As can be seen, all results were highly significant for all coefficients and the overall explanatory value of the equation was very good. The coefficient of .85 attached to the second term (POP) suggests that a 1 per cent increase in the population served results in a .85 per cent increase in expenditure.

Equation (9) was then tested cross-sectionally over 10 provinces for 21 individual federal programs, all of which had operations in all provinces. Despite the limitations of sample size, the results from these estimations are often significant and revealing. All results are presented in lines 2 to 29 of Table 4-2. Where possible we retested this equation for the individual programs, substituting alternative proxies for market-size served, as indicated in Table 4-2.

Taking only those results which were most successful in terms of the overall explanatory value of the equation, we found 13 out of 21 programs showed elasticity coefficients of less than I (positive economies of scale), while 6 showed coefficients greater than one. Two programs showed coefficients equal to I, suggesting no scale effects.

Seven of the 13 coefficients that were less than one proved to be *significantly* less than 1, while 3 of the elasticity coefficients that were greater than 1 proved to be *significantly* greater than 1.

From these results we conclude that economies of scale do exist in field operations, but are not consistently exhibited within all programs. Some programs operate under negative scale effects.

No correlation between a particular occupational category and the existence of scale effects in a particular service could be found.

Summary

Given our empirical results pertaining to economies of scale both at the level of head office and field operation, the possibility of positive scale economies at both these levels cannot be rejected; in fact, there is considerable evidence that significant scale economies characterize the cost-output structure of the provision of federal and provincial services.

Table 4-2

Economies of Scale in Field Services

All Departments

	A_0	t	A_1	t	R^2, $\bar{R}^2$
1. Log F = A_0 + A_1 Log POP + (A_2 ... A_{11}) departmental dummies	.93	(2.5)***	.85	(3.75)***	.88, .85
			(all dummy coefficients)		

	Log F = A_0 + A_1 Log POP	A_0	A_1	R^2, $\bar{R}^2$	Proxy	Significantly different from 1
2.	Defence	4.2 (2.22)*	.79 (2.97)**	.56, .49	POP	No
3.	Post Office	2.7(12.25)***	1.09(35.4)***	.99, .99	POP	Yes
4.	" "	- .48(-1.73)***	1.01(25.8)***	.99, .98	Postal Receipts	
5.	Transport	5.3 (4.43)***	.61 (3.67)***	.65, .61	POP	Yes
6.	Public Works	4.1 (4.02)***	.64 (4.5)***	.74, .70	POP	Yes
7.	Public Service Commission	-4.1(-1.41)*	1.42 (3.46)**	.63, .57	POP	No
8.	RCMP	3.8 (3.17)**	.47 (2.78)**	.52, .45	POP	Yes
9.	Manpower and Immigration	2.87(5.4)***	.88(11.9)***	.95, .94	POP	Yes
10.	" " "	9.0 (2.9)**	.83 (1.53)*	.25, .14	Clients	
11.	Unemployment Insurance Commission	1.93(2.06)*	.95 (7.6)***	.88, .87	POP	
12.	" " "	1.84(2.5)**	.89(10.74)***	.94, .93	Claims	No
13.	Indian and Northern Affairs	4.4 (3.4)***	.68 (3.8)***	.67, .62	POP	Yes
14.	Taxation	1.49(2.4)**	1.06(12.2)***	.95, .95	POP	
15.	"	-4.3(-5.5)***	1.00(16.9)***	.97, .97	T4's	
16.	Customs and Excise	- .48(-.54)	1.25(10.3)**	.93, .92	POP	Yes
17.	" " "	3.9 (1.1)	.87 (2.5)**	.46, .39	Revenues	
18.	Environment	4.98(3.3)***	.59 (2.8)**	.53, .46	POP	Yes
19.	Agriculture	4.8 (4.0)***	.59 (3.5)***	.63, .53	POP	Yes
20.	Health and Welfare	1.4 (1.29)	.97 (6.2)***	.84, .83	POP	No
21.	Industry, Trade and Commerce	-1.97(-1.79)*	1.01 (6.58)***	.86, .84	POP	No
22.	Veterans Land Act	- .69(-.04)	1.16 (5.15)***	.79, .76	POP	No
23.	" " "	7.5 (3.9)***	.88 (2.9)**	.68, .60	Claims	
24.	Canadian Pensions Commission	1.73(2.5)**	.47 (4.9)***	.77, .74	POP	
25.	Labour	1.15 (.38)	.72 (1.8)*	.31, .21	POP	No
26	Supply and Services	.60 (.49)	.99 (5.8)***	.83, .80	POP	No
27.	" " "	4.5 (4.0)***	.75 (5.2)***	.79, .77	Civil Servants	
28.	Communications	.84 (.78)	.81 (5.3)***	.80, .77	POP	No
29.	Consumer and Corporate Affairs	- .12 (.18)	1.00(10.8)***	.94, .94	POP	

*Significant at a 90 per cent level of probability.

**Significant at a 97 per cent level of probability.

***Significant at a 99 per cent level of probability.

PART V

DECENTRALIZATION OF THE REGIONALIZED
FEDERAL PUBLIC SERVICES

It is now our objective to integrate our evidence of positive
economies of scale with two alternative scenarios of decentralization
to the province of Quebec. These scenarios reflect different
assumptions as to the existence of scale effects in head office
and field operations and the degree to which Quebec possesses the
capacity to absorb ongoing federal programs. They are the following:

Scenario I

In Scenario I we postulate that Quebec provincial and federal
public services are distinct from one another, both in terms of
their product and methods of provision and administration. Quebec,
therefore, has no existing capacity with which to absorb ongoing
federal programs.

Scenario II

Scenario II develops from our pairing of federal and provincial
institutions in Table 2-5. Where a suitable Quebec counterpart for
a particular federal program is given, we assume that production for
that particular service may be simply transferred from the federal
to the provincial program. Where no substitute at the provincial
level is indicated, as is true with respect to Defence, the Post
Office, Customs and Excise, etc., no existing capacity is assumed
to exist, and treatment identical to that received in Scenario I is
received by these programs.

Scenario II is further divided into parts (a) and (b). Under
part (a) we assume that Quebec maintains the existing federal field
services in the original form so that no scale effects at the field
level are considered through the merging of federal and provincial
field operations.

In part (b) we assume that federal and provincial field
operations are indeed merged into one single operation; hence we
allow for economies of scale effects from both the head office and
field levels.

We have chosen to reflect our assumptions regarding the degree
of scale economies present at head office and field operations level
in terms of an elasticity coefficient, α. *Alpha* is the percentage
change in head office expenditure associated with a given percentage
change in field operations, or the percentage change in field
expenditure associated with a given percentage change in the size of
population served.

Though we conducted our exercises using several alternative values for α, we present here results for exercises conducted with α = .7 only. An α value of .7 provides a liberal estimate of existing scale economies. The results, in terms of changes in program expenditure under Scenarios I and II for α of .7, are provided in Table 5-1 in summary form.

The values for "Total Change in Expenditures" range from a positive $447.0 million in Scenario I to a negative $179.0 million in Scenario II(b).

It should be pointed out that positive scale effects at the level of field operations will result in a reduction in the average cost of providing ongoing Quebec services when federal and provincial field services are combined. There is no inversely related increase in average cost of remaining federal field services, however, as federal field services in Quebec are in no way operationally connected to federal field services in the other provinces.

Because field services as a proportion of total program expenditure far outweigh head office expenditure, the supposition of equivalent scale effects at both levels necessarily leads to a net reduction in total costs, with the negative field effect.

Our estimates for total expenditure change were sensitive to the value of α. Using α = .8, values for total expenditure change ranged from positive $280.00 million to negative $143.00 million. Using α = .9, these respective values were positive $134.00 million and negative $80.00 million.

These total expenditure increases or decreases, financed across all Canadian households, would entail, for α = .7, an increased burden of $59.00 per household under Scenario I, $36.00 per household under Scenario II(a), and a reduction in the burden per household of $24.00 in Scenario II(b).

Besides values for total change in Canada, we calculated net costs in Quebec attributable to decentralization *per se*. Total expenditures by the federal government on regionalized services for Quebec can be estimated as $2,545 million (field expenditures plus an appropriate share of head office spending). After separation, using Scenario I as an example, provision of the same services would cost $2,851 million. The difference of $306 million is, then, the cost of decentralization in Quebec. Table 5-2 shows the net costs calculated similarly for all scenarios, in total and on a 'per family' basis.

The total net costs of decentralization for the Province of Quebec range from $306 million to -$320 million for Scenarios I and II(b) respectively. Expressed in terms of dollars per family unit, this range is $155 to -$162 between Scenarios I and II(b).

Table 5-1

Change in Expenditures Associated with
the Decentralization of the Regionalized Services in Quebec,
The Rest of Canada and Canada Including Quebec

	Change in Expenditure in Quebec	Change in Expenditure in Rest of Canada	Total Change in Expenditure Canada Including Quebec
	(Millions of dollars)		
Scenario I	2,851	-2,404	+447
Scenario II(a)	2,676	-2,404	+272
Scenario II(b)	2,225	-2,404	-179

Table 5-2

Net Costs of Decentralization of the
Regionalized Services in
the Province of Quebec

	(Million dollars)	(Dollars)
Scenario I		
Total Cost	2,851	
Net Cost	306	
Net cost per family unit		155
Scenario II(a)		
Total Cost	2,676	
Net Cost	131	
Net Cost per family unit		66
Scenario II(b)		
Total Cost	2,225	
Net Cost	-320	
Net Cost per family unit		-162

When these net costs to Quebec are viewed in terms of dollar change per family unit, both absolutely and relative to current federal expenditures on regionalized services in Quebec of about $1,300 per family unit, they are seen to be quite small.

As well, Scenarios I and II are both extreme in that Scenario I assumes no existing provincial capacity and Scenario II assumes perfect substitutability between most federal and provincial programs. Clearly, neither of these scenarios adequately reflects reality, and the results obtained under them can only establish a set of possible boundaries between which the true costs can be expected to lie.

Outright Duplication

Apart from scale economies, it is important to consider, even if briefly, the possibility of outright duplication between federal and provincial programs. Duplication can result when both the federal and provincial governments participate in programs which fall within an area of dimly sketched jurisdiction. With each government ignoring the other's activities, certain functions may be performed twice. Duplication may also arise when two levels of government compete for the dominant position within a given sphere of influence.

Though the degree of, or possible degrees of, provincial-federal overlap in Canadian services has never been adequately researched, the "Report of the Western Premiers' Task Force on Constitutional Trends"[1] provides a detailed delineation of the arenas of federal-provincial conflict among the federal services. Areas of conflict ranging from agricultural and transportation programs to Consumer and Corporate Affairs activity have been identified.

Because the activities of the larger provincial governments are similar in both scale and development, the trends attested to at the Western Premiers' Conference can probably be extended to the public service operations of the Province of Quebec.

Within Scenario II Quebec spends approximately $1,658 million on services within its boundaries.

Ignoring scale effects associated with any overall federal reduction in Quebec service expenditure upon the average cost of such services at the field and head office level, since we have shown that they are relatively small anyway, let us consider the possible consequences of an existing federal-provincial duplication in Quebec upon the estimate of decentralization costs.

A degree of overlap as small as 8 per cent would be sufficient to turn the expected total increase in cost estimated in Scenario II(a) for Quebec to a zero figure.

---

1 Report of the Western Premiers' Task Force on Constitutional Trends, May 1977.

Alternatively, if we assume a 20 per cent degree of existing federal-provincial overlap in Quebec, Quebec could save $330 million by curtailing operations in areas of overlap. The total cost change to Quebecers, originally given as an increase of $306 million under Scenario I, would now involve a small decrease.

PART VI

THE UNREGIONALIZED FEDERAL SERVICES

In the unregionalized services the head office component is itself the final producer and distributor of goods and services. Either these goods and services do not lend themselves to regional implementation, or the cost-saving of centralized provision outweighs the advantages of regionalization. This would be the case for research programs such as Science and Technology or the National Research Council, for central government steering bodies such as Treasury Board, or the Department of Finance, and for other intergovernmental bodies. Total expenditure on such programs is approximately 2.5 billion dollars, compared to 13.6 billion dollars for the regionalized services.

We do not attempt any rigorous empirical estimation of head office decentralization costs in the following analysis, but rather set out to establish a more general framework of analysis, more for the purpose of laying the groundwork for discussion than for arriving at any one figure

The unregionalized programs may be categorized on the basis of the general duties they perform. Occasionally, one program may qualify for two different categories. Table 6-1 specifies six categories of "Duty" and lists the appropriate federal institutions under each category.

Expenditures within Categories I, II and VI account for the largest portion of the non-regionalized expenditure bill -- approximately 1.3 billion dollars (double counting corrected for) -- while expenditures related to Regulatory, Funding and Representative bodies are very small by comparison.

In column 2 of Table 6-1 we indicate whether or not there is evidence of similar operations performed at the Quebec provincial level. Outside the "Research-Related" category Quebec does indeed have many similar programs. The actual Quebec counterpart is not given as this would often require the lengthy description of an individual provincial program within a given department.[1]

Quebec does not have any existing capacity outside of Category V in either the science fields or international relations, but it does have considerable capacity within the category "Intergovernmental Support Bodies." This is not surprising given the similarity between the scope and organization of federal and Quebec provincial programs. The sum of expenditures associated with Research-Related Bodies and all other programs for which little indication of existing capacity

---

1 The list of actual Quebec counterparts is available upon request.

Table 6-1

Breakdown of Federal Unregionalized Programs by
Broad Classification of Duty

		Head Office Operating Expenditure	Possibility of existing capacity in Quebec
		($ thousands)	
I	**Intergovernmental Support Bodies**		
	Finance	27,865	Yes
	Auditor General	18,850	Yes
	Statistics Canada	126,107	
	Supply and Services	120,510	Yes
	Treasury Board	33,844	Yes
	Library of Parliament	5,302	Yes
	Public Archives	17,006	Yes
	Canadian Intergovernmental Secretary	1,127	Yes
	Justice	54,025	Yes
		404,636	
II	**Research-Related Bodies**		
	National Research Council	178,036	
	Atomic Energy Control Board	14,303	
	Atomic Energy of Canada	120,215	
	Statistics Canada	126,107	
	Medical Research Council	1,373	
	Status of Women	1,153	
	Economic Council of Canada	5,398	
	Science and Technology	6,128	
	Anti-Inflation Board	22,746	
		475,459	
III	**Regulatory**		
	Communications	55,912	Yes
	Canadian Radio-Television Commission	15,188	Yes
	Consumer and Corporate Affairs	35,631	Yes
	National Energy Board	10,970	Yes
	Tariff Board	1,436	
	Foreign Investment Review Agency	3,793	
	Canadian Labour Relations Board	2,265	Yes
	Canadian Transport Commission	22,065	Yes
	Canadian Dairy Commission	2,952	Yes
		150,212	
IV	**Central Funding Bodies**		
	Canadian International Development Agency	28,500	
	Federal Development Bank	9,036	Yes
	Medical Research Council	1,373	
	Canadian Film Development Corporation	3,562	Yes
	National Film Board	46,727	Yes
		89,198	
V	**Representative Bodies**		
	Senate	12,729	Yes
	House of Commons	78,225	Yes
	Privy Council	24,725	Yes
	International Joint Commission	1,260	
		116,939	
VI	**Policy Development and Implementation**		
	Secretary of State	64,974	Yes
	Science Council of Canada	2,468	
	External Affairs	108,277	
	Justice	54,025	Yes
	Labour	26,258	Yes
	National Energy Board	10,970	Yes
	Industry, Trade and Commerce	100,693	Yes
	Energy, Mines and Resources	139,966	Yes
	Consumer and Corporate Affairs	35,631	Yes
	Urban Affairs	14,144	Yes
		557,406	

Table 6-2

Net Costs Associated with Decentralization
of the Federal Regionalized Services,
and Replication of Certain
Unregionalized Services; Quebec

Regionalized Services		
Scenario I	306	155
Scenario II(a)	131	66
Scenario II(b)	-320	-162
Replication of Unregionalized Services Research		
Scenario I	238	120
Scenario II	158	80
Foreign Affairs	70	35
Total Combined Costs		
Scenario I	614	311
Scenario II(a)	359	182
Scenario II(b)	- 92	- 46

in Quebec appears is approximately $600 million, and research
service expenditure alone accounts for roughly 80 per cent of this
amount. We discuss the decentralization of these services separately
as the peculiar nature of their product merits a separate analysis.

Due to certain technical aspects of these services analysis
of their decentralization *per se* can only be performed at a very
general level.

The technical aspects we refer to are those which characterize
and qualify these services as public goods. Two such characteristics
are first, the non-rival nature of consumption of these services and,
secondly, the high cost or inefficiency of applying the "exclusion
principle"[2] to these services.

We say the consumption of these services is non-rival because,
for example, the consumption or utilization by Province A of research
reports from the National Research Council of Canada does not reduce
the benefits which may be derived by other provinces from the same
information.

If Quebec were to become autonomous, the expenditure necessary
to maintain these existing benefits to a Canada without Quebec would
be equivalent to the expenditure currently being made. We would
expect no reduction in the public service operating expenditures of
the federal government were Quebec to become autonomous with respect
to the provision of the services.

The second characteristic of these programs is the high cost
of exclusivity associated with the consumption of their services.
How might the federal government prevent a Quebec which has achieved
formal autonomy from utilizing the services of Statistics Canada
which produces freely available information? The price of excluding
an autonomous Quebec from the consumption of these services would be
prohibitively high. It is quite possible that Quebec could "free-
ride" on these formerly federal services at no additional cost.

Were Quebec to decide for non-economic reasons, however, that
it should provide these essential research-associated services with
no reliance on spillovers from the rest of Canada, the level of
services equivalent to that received by Quebec before autonomy
could only be generated by expenditures in that province equivalent
to the existing levels of expenditures for the whole of Canada
(475 million dollars). This follows from the first characteristic
of public goods discussed, the non-rival nature of the consumption
of these goods. This characteristic implies that Quebec is currently
free to consume without limit the benefits of these services.

---

2 R.A. Musgrave and P.B. Musgrave, *Public Finance in Theory and Practice*,
  McGraw-Hill, 1973, Chapter 3.

Neither zero nor one hundred per cent free riding seems plausible. Subsequently, we have adopted a compromise situation. For the calculations underlying Table 6-2 we assumed in Scenario I that 50 per cent of the value of present federal research services would be replicated, and 33 1/3 per cent in Scenario II. The implied additional Quebec research costs are $238 million and $158 million, respectively.

The remaining federal expenditures, attributable to services for which no capacity exists in Quebec, are accounted for by services of an international nature, the most significant of which is External Affairs itself.

There is certainly some element of the public good in these international service programs, but they are not characterized by either non-exclusivity or non-rivalry in consumption. For example, an autonomous Quebec government could be, with little cost, excluded from the use of Canadian diplomatic channels in foreign countries. It is equally likely that the Canadian Tariff Board would make greater efforts to import exemptions for goods produced and exported from the rest of Canada.

We make the somewhat arbitrary assumption that expenditure to replicate these foreign-service-related programs in an autonomous Quebec would amount to half that of current federal spending, ($139 million). The major part of this expenditure would contribute to the maintenance of Quebec diplomatic relations abroad under their own external affairs department. Expenditures within the federal department of External Affairs currently constitute well over two-thirds of the $139 million figure just cited.

In Table 6-2 we combine the costs of decentralization and replication, which together range from $614 million to -$92 million, or $311 to -$46 million on a 'per family' basis.

Although these combined costs relative to the costs of decentralization of the regional services alone are significantly larger, the absolute magnitude is still small, even under the extreme assumptions that Quebec has no existing capacity to absorb regionalized federal programs and that Quebec would have to replicate 50 per cent of federal expenditure on research programs.

There does not appear to be a sufficient basis on which to speculate as to the decentralization costs of the balance of the unregionalized services, presently accounting for some $1 billion of federal spending. Given that capacity exists in many provincial programs to absorb these unregionalized, federal head office operations, one may wonder whether similar scale effects observed among the

regionalized programs might entail definite cost increases to
Quebecers, should they have to assume responsibility for these
activities. On the other hand, a great deal of duplication within
these federal and provincial programs might set up a situation,
as we saw in Part V, in which decentralization could involve merely
marginal, if not negative, cost increases. Questions involving the
scale economy and the amount of existing duplication will require
considerable attention in any further study.

PART VII

SUMMARY

In our empirical estimation of the cost-output structure of Canadian public services we found significant evidence that positive scale economies are at work in this industry.

The existence of positive scale economies in the provision of public goods would lead one to conclude that centralized provision of these services, at least from a purely efficiency standpoint, would be desirable.

However, within the context of the existing Canadian institutional and political framework of public service production, where similar services are already being supplied at the provincial and federal level, we conclude that further decentralization of the majority of services (regionalized services) would involve relatively minor additional costs. Using middle-of-the-road assumptions, the additional cost burden on Quebec families would be very modest, in the order of $182 per family per year. Under more extreme assumptions in one direction, this cost increase climbs to a still relatively small $311 per family. Under extreme assumptions in the other direction, there is even the possibility of a small saving of $46 per family.

Economic arguments for or against decentralization which are based on economies of scale are insignificant. This should heighten one's concern over the possible economic consequences of decentralization that might arise from consideration of spillover effects, or taste patterns, discussed in Part I. It may be that only economic considerations of this nature can swing the balance one way or the other in favour of decentralized vs. centralized provision of public services.

The provision of certain federal services for which Quebec possesses little or no existing capacity could entail significant additional costs for Quebec. However, this conclusion is sensitive to speculation on how an autonomous Quebec might fill the gap in research-oriented services. We stated that Quebec might decide to free-ride on public goods produced in Canada. In this case there would be no additional costs to Quebec.

Comments by D. Usher, Department of Economics,
Queen's University, Kingston

    Much of the research into the economics of confederation has
to do with deciding what are the big numbers and what are the small
numbers. If one leaves aside the dynamic factors Sylvia Ostry
referred to this morning, there seem to be four numbers under
discussion at this conference, each representing an important aspect
of the gains or losses to the different regions from the existence
of an economic union. The first is the effect of the tariff; the
second is the effect of nontariff barriers to trade plus industrial
and consumer subsidies like that on oil; the third is direct transfers;
and the fourth is scale and overheads in the provision of public
services. The first three numbers have been discussed in other papers,
and if their results hold up to critical analysis, we can say i) that
the tariff is small; ii) that the effect of nontariff barriers is as
yet uncertain, and iii) that straightforward transfers are very
large. Now we have the fourth number, duplication of government
services, overheads, etc. The main result of this paper is to show
that, by comparison with the rest, this number is small. This is
quite an important result, because it means that one argument can be
virtually eliminated from the debate.

    There is, however, a major technical problem with MacDonald's
paper, a problem which is fundamentally insurmountable in any attempt
to develop numbers on this issue. The essence of the problem is that
we have no measure of output in government services. Economies to
scale are defined as the increase (or decrease, as the case may be)
of output per unit of input as output itself increases; we say there
are economies to scale if 10 men can produce 20 units of output but
15 men can produce, not 30, but 35. We can estimate cost functions
for automobiles, for instance, because we know the total cost of
production of automobiles and the number of automobiles produced each
year. We cannot do so for government services because we know only
what was spent by government and we do not know, except in a few
isolated cases, what is bought with the expenditure. Thus, to talk
about scale in the public services, you must make some assumption
about the relationship between what is spent and what you get for
what you spend. Mr. MacDonald has had to make three very strong
assumptions.

    First, for a large portion of government expenditure, Mr.
MacDonald assumed that a clear distinction could be made between head
office expenditure, which is independent of the amount of service

supplied, and field expenditure, which is directly related to the amount of service supplied. This assumption may or may not be valid, e.g. expenditures in Ottawa may provide direct services to people elsewhere, and some overhead expenditure may take place away from Ottawa.

The other two assumptions are even more questionable. They are that services per head are the same everywhere and that any observed difference in cost per head is attributable to economies of scale rather than to characteristics of the regions in which the costs are observed. On these assumptions and in the absence of economies of scale, expenditure in province A would have to be twice expenditure in province B, if the population of province A were twice that of province B. If less than twice the expenditure occurred, MacDonald would take it as evidence that scale economies existed. This rules out the possibilities that less real service is being provided per person served (e.g. fewer letters delivered per head by the Post Office) or that cost differs for reasons other than scale (e.g. low population density, as in the Yukon, which could raise costs per unit of service provided, regardless of whether the Post Office is organized in each village or in the Territory as a whole). It is hard to see how Mr. MacDonald could have avoided these assumptions in the absence of an independent measure of the output of government services, but the fact remains that these assumptions are dubious and that the validity of the results is correspondingly impared.

Finally, I would like to add to the discussion a fifth number, which is more difficult to estimate but could be larger than any of the other four. It is the value to Canadians of living in a country so situated that we spend virtually nothing on national defence. Canada spends 1.9% of its gross national product on national defence. The United States spends 6.0%, Egypt spends 37%, Chile and Argentina with a mountain range between them and only a ridiculous little island to quarrel about spend 6.6% and 2.8%. Canada has been so peaceful for so long that we have come to take our good fortune for granted and to imagine our peacefulness to be the consequence of a special virtue that we possess and others do not share. A radical change in our circumstances could well prove to use that this is not so. Increasing defence expenditure to the average in other countries would impose a cost to Canada or its successor countries far in excess of any of the costs we have so far considered. The cost would be greater still if the expenditure proved necessary.

THE ROOTS OF DISCONTENT

by

Jeff Evenson and Richard Simeon

Institute of Intergovernmental Relations

Queen's University

The "crisis" of Canadian federalism is said to threaten the future of the country. Significant changes in the constitutional/ institutional arrangements of the state apparatus have been proposed in an attempt to deal with the threat. And yet, even as it dominates the news media and political thinking of the country, its sources and nature remain unclear. This is in part due to the many problems that currently face Canadian economic and political life; relations between the two founding language and cultural groups, as well as the conflicts between national and regional development goals and priorities and those between the governments that promote them, define the crisis of federalism itself. The crisis in turn interacts in complex and little-known ways with the faltering economy, inflation, the value of the dollar, and the intolerable number of unemployed people. This paper does not attempt to explain every dimension of the crisis. It is about that part which, while perhaps not as important in day-to-day life as inflation, unemployment, or French-English relations, nevertheless lies at the root of the current discontent so many government people and academics feel with the federal system of government in Canada

We need to be clear about what the crisis is *not*. Most important it is *not* a crisis of the fundamental social and economic order of Canadian society. It is a political crisis -- a crisis of governmental institutions. At the root of discontent lies the problem of the relation of governments to one another in the federal system. It is about functions that governments are going to perform and the tools with which to perform them, about the sharing of authority and the making of decisions. It embodies a competition concerning where and how interests are to be represented and how accommodations are to be worked out.

Responsibility for most policy areas is currently shared by both levels of government. The political interests of the provincial governments demand that they share in the decision-making process and policy development of the central government and that they assert greater control of social and economic development within their own jurisdiction. The political interests of the central government similarly lead it to assert the importance of national leadership. Yet no formal -- constitutionally defined -- linkage exists for the sharing of responsibility in the federal system. This is why we have demands for constitutional change and why it is impossible to divorce changes in central institutions from the crucial question of the division of powers. Thus, the question of institutional failure must be dealt with before any attempt can be made by the federal and provincial governments to deal with the more fundamental problems of cultural and linguistic harmony and economic recovery. Substantial erosion in the support for the current system of government is due to the fact that governments cannot seem to agree to do anything. Business interests call for certain measures and grow impatient as the federal and provincial governments bicker between themselves about

who should do what. According to working people, government acts
in pretty much the same way as it always has, yet unemployment
continues, inflation rises and taxes get higher all the time.

     Commonly, there are held to be two central elements in insti-
tutional failure. The first is the failure of the institutions
of central government to represent and develop effective policy
to meet regional aspirations -- a failure of Parliament, the
cabinet, the bureaucracy, and political parties to act as an
arena for representation and accommodation of diverse regional
interests. This perspective defines one set of prescriptions for
change: to develop ways to improve this representative and
integrative capacity of central institutions. Such changes appear
to be a necessary prerequisite for continued or enhanced federal
leadership in many policy fields. What is often neglected is the
fact that the institutions of the central government as constitutionally defined in the British North America Act were not designed
to operate in the reality of twentieth century Canadian economic
and social conditions. Substantial modification in the role of
our particular set of institutions has occurred both through
judicial decisions and through an evolution of accepted practices,
but the basic institutions themselves in their current form remain
inadequate. This is nowhere more apparent than in the lack of
formal, workable mechanisms for intergovernmental co-operation,
joint representation, and collective decision-making.

     The second element of institutional failure is related to
the first, and is expressed in the failure of the mechanisms of
federal-provincial relations to develop means of reconciling
regional and national aspirations and federal and provincial
interests in the making of collective policy. These mechanisms,
described in the literature on Canadian federalism as "co-
operative federalism" and subsequently as "executive federalism"
and culminating in a highly developed federal-provincial
conference, refer to the accepted practices mentioned above.
They are attempts to mold the policy-making and decision-making
process to the realities of the twentieth century Canadian life
without fundamentally altering the constitution.

     The two elements of institutional failure are essentially
two sides of the same coin. Our analysis leads us to frame the
nature of the crisis in institutional terms and to propose
institutional solutions. Currently, this historically indelible
problem has been complicated by the election of the Party
Québécois in November 1976 and by the severe economic problems
of inflation and unemployment. It remains to be seen whether
government can solve these economic problems, which are not
restricted to Canada alone, and the cultural problems, which are
presented by the bi-national character of the Canadian polity.
Very few will submit that one level of government can do it
alone. This is why we have centred our analysis in the institutional character of government.

There are three major approaches to the problem of analysing conflict in the federal system. Those who follow the sociological/ cultural model of W.S. Livingston[1] see diversity as largely territorially based. Differences in language, ethnicity, religion and/ or historical experience distinguish one community from another within the federation. Federal institutions are rooted in federal societies; the dynamic force in shifts between federal and provincial governments lies primarily in changes at the level of cultures and attitudes.

Such analyses typically suggest that just as the sources of conflict lie in clashing values and loyalties, so their solution lies in changing or reconciling them. This leads to proposals in the short run for more "understanding" and, in the longer run, for changes in the educational system and mass media in order to seek accommodation through attitudinal change. The most fundamental question for those who take the cultural approach revolves around the sense of community and identity that exists in each part of Canada. When a Canadian says "us," who does he mean?

The second approach sees the strain in the federal system as a result of the interaction between the various government structures and institutions and the political and bureaucratic leaders who run them. The major source of strain in this view lies in the inter-bureaucratic competition for support, prestige, and territory. The changing nature of demands and substantive conflict are seen to reflect the emergence of new elites or new priorities and interests. Government and those who run it, and their interests, shape society, rather than *vice versa*.

This approach is perhaps the dominant one in political scientists' analysis of Canadian federalism, as reflected in the work of D. V. Smiley, who writes of "executive federalism," Richard Simeon in *Federal-Provincial Diplomacy* , and E. R. Black. It leads to suggestions for change in the constitutional and institutional structures of the federal system. By changing the framework within which political competition takes place, it is hoped, the demands of governments can be more adequately accommodated and conflicts made more constructive.

Another approach is that of political economy. It goes beyond simple recognition of a regionally diversified economy to relate the uneven and sectoral development of the Canadian economy to the needs and interests of specific economic groups among the Canadian and American bourgeoisie. A continental division of labour among these groups is seen to result in the use

---

1 W. S. Livingston, "A Note on the Nature of Federalism," *Political Science Quarterly,* vol. 62, no. 1, March 1952; and *Federalism and Constitutional Change* (Oxford: Clarendon Press, 1956).

of American capital to finance exploration and extraction of
Canadian natural resources. Canadian capital, it is felt, is
interested only in facilitating the transfer of these resources
to foreign markets where they are processed and returned to Canada
as finished goods. Regional development goals that run counter
to the continental system of production seem to be systematically
frustrated by market conditions and the activities of the central
government and financial institutions. Regional disparities are
thought to be created and maintained by economic and political
conditions that benefit the dominant economic groups in Canada.
The historical dynamic of Canadian federalism is thus seen to lie
in the particualar development of Canadian capitalism and its
relation to the international economic environment.

By focusing on institutional failure, we do not deny the
relevance of these other factors. The underlying conditions of
regional and cultural conflict are to be found in the historical
development of the cultural and economic factors of the societies
that make up Canada. These factors are defined culturally and
territorially and the pervasiveness of regionalism and linguistic
conflict is a well-known fact of Canadian political life. Political institutions to a great extent reflect these conditions.
They are not neutral; the way they are structured benefits some
more than others and denotes a particular image of the country --
an image that is not now shared by provincial governments and
many citizens for a variety of well-known reasons.

That institutional rearrangement has been the focus in many
of the proposals for change put forth since 1976, and indeed long
before that, gives us an indication of the political character of
the conflict. We cannot ignore linguistic duality and regional
diversity; indeed, these are the central social forces at work in
Canada. They are reflected in competing attitudes, values, and
identities on the one hand and in important economic differences
and inequalities on the other. But the political debate in
Canada centres on institutions and the underlying forces are given
expression through governments. Thus the language question
focuses on whether linguistic duality will be reflected in national institutions and through a pan-Canadian bilingualism or in a
unilingual and perhaps fiscally and culturally separate Quebec.
Similarly, the debate about regionalism turns on the question of
whether it will be expressed and accommodated *within* the institutions of the central government or in relations *between* governments.

How have conditions changed in the last hundred years, and
why is the current system of government institutions felt to be
inadequate for solving the concrete problems that face Canada
today?

One way to explore these questions is to see Canadian history
and current problems as lying in the interplay of three distinct
political drives or dynamics, an understanding of which explains
and summarizes the many dimensions of strain and conflict within

Confederation and which incorporates the salient features of each
of three modes of analysis outlined above. These are what we can
call country-building, province-building, and Quebec nation-
building. The history of Canada has been shaped by the interplay
and tension between these three dynamics and the images of culture,
society, and economy they entail.

Each of these drives has a strong institutional base in the
country -- in Ottawa, in the provinces, especially in the West,
and in Quebec city. Each implies a different sense of community,
of collectivity across which benefits are to maximized and to
which primary loyalty or identity will be given. Each, moreover,
implies a different direction for reform in the federal system
and a different perspective on the nature of institutional failure
in Canada. The federal government and each of the provincial
governments can be seen to represent and in many cases articulate
these drives through their policies, priorities, and solutions to
problems. Thus, these drives include a strong normative element.

Country-Building

Country-building activities have taken different forms over
the past hundred years. In the initial or Confederation stage,
country-builders sought to weld together the various colonies in
British North America under a centralized institutional structure
and through certain integrative economic provisions. The British
North America Act reflects the country-centred view in the creation of a single Parliament "charged with matters of common
interest to the whole country" and in those provisions that made
it quite clear that Canada was to have a strong central government. The general power to make laws for the Peace, Order and
Good Government of Canada, the regulation of interprovincial
trade, the unilateral right to reserve or disallow provincial
legislation, the declaratory power and the right to appoint judges
and senators, are all examples of this intention. The provisions of the Act that removed tariff barriers between the various
units underlie the country-building drive in the economic sphere.
Western land settlement plans, a transcontinental railway scheme,
and a system of protective tariffs were further country-building
initiatives of the federal government in the first stage.

The second country-building stage picked up where the
MacDonald-Laurier National Policy left off and was implemented
under the guidance of Keynesian economic theory. Stretching from
the end of the Second World War to the mid-1960s, this era was
the heyday of federal dominance. Under the principle that firm
central control of the fiscal system was absolutely essential to
the maintenance of economic stability and growth, the federal

government, through its comprehensive reconstruction proposals,[2] sought to institute a broadscale vision for social and cultural development in the post-war era. The role of a strong and effective central government was "to ensure appropriate levels of aggregate demand through generalized fiscal and monetary policies and through lowering barriers to international trade and investment."[3] It was apparent that the federal government sought, in this stage, to substantially reduce the degree of direct state intervention in the economic development and instead to maintain its legitimacy through policies designed to maintain a good "climate" for private enterprise.

Today, country-building activities have shifted from financing the development of the welfare state towards a much greater concern with direct economic regulation. In addition, country-builders residing largely in the federal government and its agencies have become increasingly concerned with altering federal institutions so that they might better serve the national and provincial interests from the centre. Indeed, since 1968, it appears that this task has been the principal country-building activity.

In each of these stages, federal policies have entailed a specific image of a pan-Canadian community, a definite idea of the role the central government should play in the life of the nation, and specific blueprints for national economic, social, and cultural developments. In addition, certain characteristics define the nature of the country-building impulse. The federal government and national institutions are seen to be the chief instruments of national development. Problems are defined nationally and solutions are given in national terms. The need to establish and maintain a Canadian common market is stressed throughout, as is the need for a national standard level of public services and national leadership in the development and implementation of social policies. The federal government is seen as the primary vehicle through which to maximize overall economic growth, to create and promote the development of complementary regional economies and to distribute political costs and benefits in a nationally advantageous manner.

Yet, in each of these specific areas, national institutions, the economy and the development of social and cultural policy, the federal government has met with regional resistance and

2 *Proposals of the Government of Canada to the Dominion-Provincial Conference on Reconstruction* (Green Book), (Ottawa: August, 1945).

3 Donald Smiley, "Canada and the Quest for a National Policy," *Canadian Journal of Political Science,* vol. 3, no. 1, p. 47 (March, 1975).

discontent. The roots of this discontent lie in no single policy but in the content -- that is, the net effects of country-building activities as a whole.

Whatever else the national policy of MacDonald and Laurier accomplished, its net effect in Canada was to create a regionally structured economy based upon mercantilist relations between central Canada and the western and eastern regions.[4] The use of *generalized* fiscal and monetary policy in the reconstruction era could only serve to heighten the regional bias in the Canadian community. Lowering the barriers to international imports and actively seeking foreign, largely American, investment in resource extraction and sales further accentuated the regional character of the economy, and contributed to the growth of regional and provincial power in Canada and therefore directly to the current crisis in the federal system. By defining problems nationally and seeking to implement national solutions, the federal government has ignored the fact that economic problems in Canada vary from region to region just as their causes do and as their solutions must.[5]

This weakness of the federal government and its activities cannot be attributed solely to the mistakes of one government or to the deficiencies of particular policies. It must be seen as due in part to the failure of federal *institutions* to adequately represent the particular needs and interests of the various provinces and regions of the Canadian community. The result has been the weakening of the country-building drive on one hand and the strengthening of the province-building and Quebec nation-building drives on the other. The representative failure of the federal system is a powerful element in the rhetoric of many western spokesmen. This is, in part, due to the steady decline from 23 per cent in 1931 to 16 per cent at present in the Prairie provinces' share of the national population.

This lack of political representation is, however, more than just a problem of population. It is also a product of broader institutional failure of the federal government to effectively develop support across all regions, to reflect within itself Canada's regional diversity, and to serve as an arena for the accomodation of regional interests. The classic model of "brokerage politics" in Canada suggested that the critical integrative institutions were to be political parties, winning support

---

4   *Ibid.*, pp. 43-44.

5   Maurice Lamontagne advanced just this argument in his speech to the conference on national priorities convened by the federal Liberal Party at Queen's University in 1960, noted in Smiley "Quest for a National Policy," p. 49, footnote 41.

across the country. As coalitions of regional interests, the
parties would need to formulate policies with broad national
appeal. Their caucuses -- and the cabinet of the party in power --
would be arenas in which regional (and other) compromises would
be hammered out. This model no longer corresponds to reality.

Regional interests today seek their expression less through
federal parties -- or even through third parties -- and more
through provincial governments; the federal-provincial conference
has replaced caucus and cabinet as the primary bargaining arena.

Party failure is accentuated by the Canadian electoral system,
which greatly exaggerates the regional imbalance in party support.
As Table 1 shows, the discrepancies in national party support
across the country are much more dramatic at the level of seats
than in votes. The electoral system greatly exaggerates regionalism in an already regionalized society by denying to certain
regions representation in the governing party and caucus. Given
that so much power is concentrated in the cabinet, the lack of an
effective voice here is likely to render policy-making less
sensitive to regions that are under-represented. Tables 2 and 3
underline the dimensions of this problem. This failure of the
party and electoral system, especially when it leads to long-term
exclusion of regions or provinces from power in Ottawa, profoundly
weakens the integrative and nation-building impulse and has
contributed to the character of Canadian politics whereby relations take place between strong governments rather than within
central institutions.

Nor does the cabinet, bound by the norms of solidarity and
unity, allow ministers to act as effective regional spokesmen. To
the extent that ministers operate in a federal government, their
priorities and perceptions are gradually shaped to a national
perspective. The complexity of policy forces ministers to play
the role of policy manager to the detriment of that of regional
spokesman.

Parliament fails to provide an effective arena of adjustment
between national and provincial interests. David Bercuson has
noted that "since the House of Commons is elected on the basis of
population only it will reflect the interests of the most populous
part of the country."[6]

Party discipline, too, prevents regional caucuses of MP's
from crossing party lines in order to form new ones. In the
Canadian situation, the Senate has little policy-making significance and even less of a function in the relations between federal

---

6   David J. Bercuson, "Elected Senate," Brief to the Task Force on National
    Unity, Calgary (November 17, 1977).

and provincial governments. Accommodation in Canada has come to take place not within governments but between governments and this has important consequences for the extent to which federal institutions can be said to act as arenas for the adjustment of regional interests.

In Canada today, the form of the federal system precludes effective provincial voice in determining the structure and function of national political institutions. In turn, the way these institutions operate denies the provincial governments and interests sufficient influence in setting national priorities. In this context, it becomes clear why a growing sense of remoteness and alienation from the central government runs through much of what has been said at the task force hearings and various symposia that have been held in the last two years.

This analysis suggests that any country-building strategy for overcoming the threat to the current federal system must focus heavily on restoring Ottawa's ability to represent and reconcile within itself Canada's regional diversity. Restoration of its representative ability is a prerequisite for policy leadership. Several proposals along these lines have been suggested. They include changing the electoral system to create a more proportional system, restructuring the civil service on regional and ethnic lines, strengthening the regional role of the Senate, and reforming the House of Commons in the direction of the American congressional system, which gives members greater latitude to pursue local interests.

But it is unlikely that provincial governments will soon give up the role they have acquired, however representative Ottawa becomes. Quebec nation-builders would find nothing to please them in such a revamped federalism; indeed, the independentist movement has grown dramatically at the same time as Ottawa's sensitivity to Quebec's interests in both policy and representation terms has grown.

In Canada, we are past the stage when one level of government can seek to unilaterally develop policies for renewing the federal system. The breakdown of intergovernmental bargaining mechanisms, under the weight of shared responsibility, political interest, and major economic, social, and cultural problems, has put a strain on the constitutional arrangements of Confederation and made all the more pressing a concentrated effort at "renewal." Given the many linguistic, cultural, religious, geographic, and economic cleavages in Canada, the country-building interests must seek to reconcile these through joint effort with the forces that give political expression to this diversity.

Province-Building

The province-building drive is fuelled by grievances and frustration at unfair federal policies and unrepresentative national institutions, but it is much more than this. It is based on a strong sense of regional community and identity backed by the wealth of provincially owned resources and driven by the desire of provincial societies to develop unhindered according to their own needs and priorities.

Provincial governments provide a strong institutional expression to this impulse. Most important new activities of government have developed in the area of provincial jurisdiction. With the progressive decentralizing of taxing powers and the wealth of natural resources, the provinces have developed a significant fiscal clout and have become larger, more aggressive, and effective. The strength of the province-building drive is a reality of the Canadian political scene. It has arisen over the years in response to specific economic, governmental/ institutional, and cultural conditions. The current crisis in Canada, and a great many of the problems of governing the country, stem from the inability of the current federal system to accommodate this reality.

The province-building drive was not always strong. Writing in 1940, Alexander Brady argued that "the socio-economic forces of modern industrialism tend to quicken the pace from federation to legislative union." [7] Professor J. A. Corry felt that an interdependent economy with nationally oriented big business, big labour, and other national associations would inexorably drive Canadian federalism in a centralist direction. [8] Economic realities in an age of nascent monopoly capitalism, it was argued, would lead to integration at the level of politics, economics, and culture. Certainly this has been the case in the United States and Germany. It has been less evident in Australia. The explanation of the rise of provincial strength is to be found in the particular pattern of industrialization fostered by the federal government's reconstruction policies -- that is, in the institutional provisions of the Canadian federal system and in the inability of federal fiscal and monetary policies to sustain full employment beyond 1957 through the maintenance of appropriate levels of aggregate demand.

---

7 E. R. Black and Allan Cairns, cited in "A Different Perspective on Canadian Federalism," in *Canadian Public Administration*, vol. 9, no. 1, p. 38 (March, 1966).

8 *Ibid.*, p. 38.

Table 1

Ratio of Percentage of Seats
to Percentage of Votes, Canada, 1974

	LIBERAL	PC	NDP	OTHER
	Political Party			
Canada	1.24	1.02	0.39	0.76
Newfoundland	1.22	0.98	0/9.5**	0/02
Nova Scotia	0.45	1.53	0.81	0/0.5
Prince Edward Island	0.54	1.52	0/4.6	0/0.1
New Brunswick	1.27	0.91	0/8.7	1.23
Quebec	1.50	0.19	0/6.6	0.82
Ontario	1.39	0.81	0.48	0/0.7
Manitoba	0.56	1.45	0.65	0/15
Saskatchewan	0.75	1.09	0.49	0/1.3
Alberta	0/24.8	1.63	0/9.3	0/4.9
British Columbia	1.04	1.35	0.38	0/1.7

SOURCE   W. P. Irvine, "Does Canada Need a New Electoral
System?", Unpublished Mss., 1978, p. 7. Entries
of the form O/x.y indicate no seats. The x.y
indicates per cent of the vote in that province
received by the party.

Table 2

Proportion of Seats Held by Each Province in Governing Party, 1957-74

	Proportion of Seats in Parliament	1957 PC Minority	1958 PC Majority	1962 PC Minority	1963 Lib. Minority	1965 Lib. Minority	1968 Lib. Majority	1972 Lib. Minority	1974 Lib. Majority
Newfoundland	2.6	1.8	0.9	0.9	5.4	5.3	0.6	2.8	2.8
Nova Scotia	4.5	8.9	5.8	7.8	3.9	1.5	0.6	0.9	1.4
Prince Edward Island	1.5	3.6	1.9	3.4	1.6	0	0	0.9	0.7
New Brunswick	3.8	4.4	3.4	3.4	4.7	4.6	3.2	4.6	4.3
Quebec	28.3	8.0	24.0	12.1	36.4	43.0	36.0	51.3	42.6
Ontario	32.0	54.5	32.2	30.2	40.3	39.0	41.0	33.0	39.0
Manitoba	5.3	7.1	6.7	9.5	1.6	0.8	3.2	1.8	1.4
Saskatchewan	6.4	2.7	7.7	13.8	0	0	1.3	0.9	2.1
Alberta	6.4	2.7	8.2	12.9	0.8	0	2.6	0	0
British Columbia	8.3	6.3	8.7	5.2	5.4	5.3	10.3	3.7	5.7
Total Number of Seats		112	208	116	129	131	155	109	141
Total Number of Seats in House of Commons		265	265	265	265	265	264	264	264

SOURCE   Calculated from election results, various sources.

Table 3

Proportion of Seats Held by Each Province in
Caucus of Official Opposition, 1957-74

	Proportion of Total							
	1957 Lib.	1958 Lib.	1962 Lib.	1963 PC.	1965 PC.	1968 PC.	1972 PC.	1974 PC.
Newfoundland	4.8	10.2	6.0	0	0	8.3	3.7	3.2
Nova Scotia	1.9	0	2.0	7.4	10.3	13.9	9.3	8.4
Prince Edward Island	0	0	0	2.1	4.1	5.6	2.8	3.2
New Brunswick	4.8	6.1	6.0	4.2	4.1	6.9	4.7	3.2
Quebec	59.0	51.0	35.0	8.4	8.2	5.6	1.9	3.2
Ontario	20.0	30.6	44.0	28.4	25.8	23.6	37.4	26.3
Manitoba	1.0	0	1.0	10.5	10.3	6.9	7.5	9.5
Saskatchewan	3.8	0	1.0	17.9	17.5	6.9	6.5	8.4
Alberta	0.9	0	0	14.7	15.5	20.8	17.8	20.0
British Columbia	1.9	0	4.0	4.2	3.1	0	7.5	13.7
Total Number of Seats	105	49	100	95	97	72	107	95

SOURCE Election results, various sources.

Writing in 1966, Black and Cairns attributed "the continuing power and influence of the provincial governments in Canadian federalism to the importance of their considerable economic functions."[9] That certain tasks, unimportant when placed under provincial jurisdiction in the BNA Act in 1867, had become, by the mid-20th century, considerable is largely due to the changes that had occurred in the process of industrialization.

American investment [10] in the resource industry prompted provincially based growth and was the prime mover in the considerable expansion of the economic functions of the provincial governments. The need to provide infrastructural necessities for rapid development prompted government participation in public utilities, railways, highways, and in research and technological development, complementary to that imported from the United States. This resulted in a shift in the weight of technical competence, assertiveness, and activism as the provincial governments came to deal more and more with situations and activities specific to their provinces alone, as with natural gas and oil in Alberta, potash in Saskatchewan, and lumbering and timber in British Columbia.

The United States ownership of Canadian industry sets up particular trading linkages between the United States and Canadian economies and results in the north-south integration of provincial economies to U.S. markets. The weakening of the ties between the provinces and Ottawa and obversely the strengthening of the provinces, is in part a function of the fragmentation of the Canadian economy and a reason for the persistence of regionalism in Canada. In addition, the most rapid expansion of government activities in the post-war period took place in areas where the provinces had primary constitutional responsibility -- health-care, education, and public welfare. While Ottawa became heavily involved in all areas, through hospital insurance, medicare, grants for vocational and post-secondary education, and sharing of the welfare burden, it was the provinces that directly provided the services and obtained the political credit.

Industrial developments in turn affected the institutional character of provincial government. In the pursuit of specific development plans unrelated to the national interest and not

9 *Ibid.*, p. 38.

10 Two books by H. G. J. Aitken *The American Economic Impact Upon Canada* and *American Capital and Canadian Resources* provide much valuable data on the form of the American presence in Canada. See also, Wallace Clement *Continental Corporate Power: Economic Linkages between Canada and the United States* (Toronto: McClelland & Stewart, 1977), pp. 80-85.

integrated with other provinces, the institutions and structures of the provincial governments grew substantially in the post-war period. The number of employees in provincial employment increased 81 per cent between 1959 and 1971. If local government growth is included, the figure reaches 104.2 per cent.[11]

The growth of provincial governments is further reflected in the substantial shifts in the fiscal balance between the provinces and Ottawa, which began immediately following the Second World War and have continued to the present. Provincial expenditures on goods and services rose to 8.1 per cent of the GNP from 5.8 per cent in the 1955-65 decade and to 12.4 per cent in 1976. Correspondingly, federal expenditures in the same area fell from 9.3 per cent in 1946, to 8.3 in 1955, to 5.1 in 1966, and have stayed roughly the same in the last decade.[12] Federal taxes declined as a percentage of the total collected from 77 per cent in 1946 to 71 per cent in 1955, to 58 per cent and 53 per cent respectively, in 1965 and 1976. Provincial taxes, on the other hand, have climbed from a post-war low of 13 per cent of total taxes collected in 1946, to 15 per cent in 1955, to 27 per cent in 1965, and to 31 per cent in 1976.[13] Conditional and unconditional transfer payments to governments, which E. R. Black suggests have been the most realistic indication of the political strength of the provinces within the federation[14] increased from $465 million in 1955, to $1,379 million in 1955, and to $8,342 million in 1976.[15] Moreover, in recent years, the proportion of this aid in unconditional payments has grown rapidly relative to the proportion in the form of conditional grants, further weakening central control over provincial priorities.

While these general factors give some indication of the changes involved in the growing province-building drive, the specific elements of the impulse varied substantially across Canada. Substantial inflows of foreign investment to the resource sectors

---

11 D. Cameron, in J. P. Meekison, ed., *Canadian Federalism* (3rd. ed.) (Agincourt, Ontario: Methuen, 1977), p. 314.

12 *The National Finances* 1977-78 (Toronto: The Canadian Tax Foundation, 1978), Table 2-10, p. 22.

13 *Ibid.,* Table 2-5, p. 17 (our calculations).

14 E. R. Black, *Divided Loyalties* (Montreal: McGill-Queen's University Press, 1975), p. 87.

15 *The National Finances*, 1977-78, Canadian Tax Foundation, Table 2-7, p. 19.

of the western provinces provided the original impetus for the
expanding economic functions of the provincial governments. In
the Atlantic provinces, that impetus came from the federal government and transfer payments in the form of unemployment insurance,
children's allowances, and old age pensions, augmented by federal
cost-sharing agreements in the 1950s and, after 1957, by equalization payments and DREE grants, which alleviated the worst
poverty in the Atlantic region and which strengthened social
institutions. However, T. W. Acheson argues, "In the course of
achieving these gains, the Maritime provinces were transformed into
client states of the federal government."[16] If the West's
aspirations were based on the confidence engendered by new wealth,
the Atlantic provinces demonstrate the frustrations of dependency.

Furthermore, the difficulties surrounding any attempt to amend
the constitution and the particular way in which the constitution
has been interpreted by the JCPC greatly eroded the centralist
bias of the BNA Act. The proportionate strength of the central
Canadian provinces gave to Ontario and Quebec the necessary lever-
age to resist any attempt by the federal government to legitimize
and consolidate in law certain centralizing measures, even when
there existed major public support for them.

Thirdly, the growth of provincial governments and the matura-
tion of provincial societies is related to the attenuation of
federal dominance and the loss of legitimacy that the federal
government suffered as a result of the inability of its institutions
and policies to provide appropriate levels of aggregate demand and
thus ensure full employment, growth, and the alleviation of
regional disparities. Rather than argue, as Paul Phillips does,
"that the Canadian government has lost the policy tools to attack
the problem of regional disparity,"[17] one could seriously doubt
that it ever had them. Under the Keynesian policies of the
Reconstruction Proposals, the major tools of the federal government
were the generalized use of fiscal and monetary policy. It is
doubtful that generalized fiscal and monetary policies can be
useful when applied to an already regionally specialized economy
but, when the economy is largely foreign-controlled and dependent
on foreign markets, fiscal and monetary tools are even less
effective.

The centralist argument of Phillips states that "without the
active participation of the federal government the hinterland
regions are unable to combat the economic forces that produce and

16 T. W. Acheson, "The Maritimes and Empire Canada," in D. J. Bercuson, ed.,
    Canada and the Burden of Unity (Toronto: Macmillan, 1977), p. 105.

17 Paul Phillips, "National Policy, Continental Economics, and National
    Disintegration," in Bercuson, *Canada and the Burden of Unity* (Toronto:
    Macmillan, 1977), p. 20.

reinforce these disparities." [18]   However, it must be recognized before anything else, that it is precisely because the federal policies have been unable to combat the economic forces that produce and reinforce disparities that provincial governments have had to take independent action to protect what they believe to be their legitimate interests.

The growth of provincial priorities and strength has led to increasing conflict with the country-building character of federal government activities. The inability or perceived unwillingness of the federal government to develop national policies that appear to benefit the western and Atlantic regions is a fundamental source of grievance in the provinces. National transportation policies, federal resource policies as they affect Alberta oil, Saskatchewan potash and uranium, and Labrador hydroelectric power, agricultural, and fisheries policy all promote criticism from the various provincial governments. Yet a listing of regional grievances -- and there are many -- almost suggests that no one benefits from Confederation. In fact, it is extraordinarily difficult to measure with any precision how the benefits and costs are distributed; the debate surrounding Quebec's presentation of its "economic accounts" illustrates the problem. Politically, it is the *perceptions* that are most important in the immediate case.

Perceptions of grievances enunciated by provincial governments fall into three interrelated categories. Economic grievances revolve around general federal policies and attitudes that appear "by the very nature of Confederation to be directed in a central Canadian way." In Alberta's view, the classic case is Petrosar. No distinction, however, seems to be made between the vagaries of the market economy and the policies of the federal government. [19] Economic grievances help to shape political attitudes and therefore are important, but often they are not based on an objective analysis of the facts.

The second category is policy grievances that refer to policies of the federal government that are seen to be unfair. Generally, these result from Ottawa's pursuit of a unilaterally defined national interest and in places from its intrusion into areas of provincial jurisdiction. The deductibility of resource royalties

18 *Ibid.*, p. 20.

19 For an illuminating if somewhat classical, discussion of western economic grievances see, Kenneth Norrie, "Some Comments on Prairie Economic Alienation," in Meekison, *Canadian Federalism*, 3rd. ed., p. 325.

from federal corporate income tax, various two-price systems, and transportation policies that discriminate against certain modes of transport come under this heading.

The third category relates to structural problems of the Canadian federal system. Under-representation in national political institutions, inadequate representation and input into federal regulatory boards, inadequate consultative mechanisms, problems relating to appointments to the Supreme Court, and problems of the constitution all reflect the confused political situation. The suffocation and frustration that Alberta, Quebec, and the other provinces feel in attaining full partnership in Confederation stems largely from the inability of the federal system to accommodate an effective provincial role in the decision-making process.

Province-building has not generated such clear-cut programs for change as has the Quebec nation-building drive. This is partly because the provinces themselves are so much more diverse in their needs and interests and partly because provincial identities and grievances, though strengthening, are weaker than those in Quebec.

Yet the province-building impulse does imply some major changes. Some of these have already been occurring in the growth of provincial fiscal power, and in the dramatic move away from shared-cost programs as seen in the abandoning of the shared-cost device in hospital and medical care, aid to post-secondary education, and more recently, social services. All are being replaced by tax transfers and unrestricted cash transfers.

Province-builders seek several other things. First is greater autonomy and fiscal resources in a variety of areas. The clash is sharpest in the area of economic development and regulation in which, as they seek to promote their own development, provincial policies come up against federal policies and against the jurisdiction of the federal government over interprovincial trade and other matters. Second, province-builders seek to limit Ottawa's ability to "intrude" on their interests through use of its constitutional power to spend, or under the "Peace, Order and Good Government" clause. Such powers, they argue, should be either abolished or subjected to clear-cut provincial veto.

Finally, the provinces demand a much greater say in the exercise of federal powers that have major impact on them -- for example, in transportation, foreign trade policy, the activities of federal regulatory agencies, and the like. Such policies, it is argued, should be made jointly by the federal and provincial governments acting together rather than by Ottawa alone. Indeed, given the current distribution of constitutional and fiscal powers, it may be argued that broad policies can *only* be made jointly, since no single government possesses full authority.

More broadly, the province-building drive implies that, to the extent there *is* a national interest, it is the sum or resultant of a group of provincial interests. Moreover, it assumes that these provincial interests cannot be fully understood or promoted by Ottawa or by federal parties. The provinces are the legitimate spokesmen. Pushed to its extreme, this suggests a movement towards a confederal pattern of decision-making in which the federal government has only limited authority on its own.

Quebec Nation-Building

Quebec is the central focus of the contemporary political crisis in Canada. Important as they are, neither the other regional grievances nor the general administrative problems of the federal system actually call into question the basic political arrangements of Canadian federalism. "Solutions" that fail to address the related questions of the relations between French and English speakers and between Quebec and the other governments are irrelevant. It was the election in 1976 of the Parti Québécois, which was committed to establishing political sovereignty in Quebec, that precipitated the present constitutional crisis. Whatever the precise reasons for this victory -- and they are many -- the presence of an independentist government in Quebec radically transformed the debate.[20]

But the crisis did not begin with this election; nor would it end with a PQ defeat. Ethnic tensions have been a central preoccupation of Canadian politics. More recently, every Quebec government since 1960 has pressed for more or less fundamental changes in the operation of the federal system. It was this pressure from Quebec that triggered the extensive constitutional review between 1968 and 1971; similarly, it was the inability or unwillingness of other governments to meet these goals that led to failure. During the same period, there were two types of federal response.[21] On one hand, increased equalization and tax-sharing strengthened all provinces as measures such as the "opting out" legislation of 1964 and the establishment of a separate

---

20 This section owes much to the analyses presented in Richard Simeon, ed., *Must Canada Fail?* (Montreal: McGill-Queen's University Press, 1977) esp. James de Wilde, "The Parti Québécois in Power." A convenient summary of recent developments in Quebec is found in André Bernard, *What Does Quebec Want?* (Toronto: James Lorimer and Co., 1978).

21 For a brief account of these negotiations, see Richard Simeon, *Federal-Provincial Diplomacy* (Toronto: University of Toronto Press, 1972), Ch. 5. For a more detailed account, see Secretariat of the Constitutional Conference, *The Constitutional Review* (Ottawa, 1974).

Quebec pension plan were moving towards a *de facto* -- if not
constitutional -- special status for Quebec. On the other hand --
and increasingly after 1968 -- Ottawa sought to better represent
French-Canadians at the centre through a variety of policies, such
as the Official Languages Act. The differences between the two
strategies reflect a number of competing perspectives that have
not yet been resolved. Is the conflict between French-speaking
Canadians and English-speaking Canadians, or between Quebec and
Ottawa and the other provincial governments? Is the redress of
grievances to take place primarily at the level of language policy
and, if so, is it to follow the principle of national bilingualism,
or of territorial unilingualism? Is the stress on individual or
on collective solutions?

There are many ways to look at the relations between French-
and English-Canadians; and the choice of analysis and even
terminology (Quebec-Canada or Francophone-anglophone) is intimately
related to the solutions proposed.

One might begin by locating the conflict within the simple
difference between two languages and cultures by arguing that the
fact of linguistic and cultural difference in itself can generate
conflict. Alleged cultural differences between French- and
English-Canadians have generated a large literature, yet they
remain elusive. In any case, their relevance to political conflict
is unclear at best. Indeed, it may well be argued that cultural
convergence, rather than difference, increases conflict. Thus,
the process of modernization and its accompanying ideological and
value changes in Quebec, it may be argued, represents a growing
similarity between French- and English-Canadians -- a similarity
that increases both contact and conflict because now both groups
are in competition for the same things, such as posts in the
corporate or bureacratic structure. So long as Quebec culture
was seen to be rural, anti-industrial, and anti-étatiste, little
contact was necessary. "Two solitudes," by definition, seldom
fight.

More important, linguistic and cultural differences become
politically relevant only when they are associated with clear
differences in other political-economic interests. Thus, we need
to examine the grievances or disadvantages faced by French-
Canadians in the Canadian system.

First are economic grievances.[22] Per capita income in Quebec
has historically lagged behind that in Ontario. Even within

---

22 For a summary of the findings of the Royal Commission on bilingualism on
    these points, see Hugh R. Innis, *Bilingualism and Biculturalism* (Toronto:
    McClelland and Stewart, 1973). See also Bernard, Ch. 2. A careful analysis
    of the economic data is also found in *Living Together: A Study of Regional
    Disparities* (Ottawa: Economic Council of Canada, 1977).

Quebec, the average income of French-speaking Canadians is below
that of virtually all other ethnic groups in the province.[23]
Unemployment rates are historically above the average. English-
speaking Quebecers are greatly over-represented in the upper-
income levels and under-represented at the bottom.

These gross differences are related to the structure of
ownership of Quebec industry. The most profitable and productive
sectors of Quebec industry are owned by foreign or Anglo-Canadian
interests. While "foreign ownership" is an important issue in
English-Canada, too, the linking of language with foreign ownership in Quebec gives the question much more edge. The ownership
structure is also related to the employment structure. English-
Canadians predominate in the upper management echelons; the
relatively few French-Canadians at these levels must often work
in English. More generally, within the Canadian system, French-
Canadians make up only a small proportion of the "economic elite,"
as studies by John Porter and Wallace Clement demonstrate.[24]

Increased education, together with recent political pressures
in Quebec, have eroded the differences somewhat. Nevertheless,
the visibility of the concentration of economic power in Quebec
in the hands of a minority ethnic group is a powerful stimulus to
nationalist feeling. It underlies the linguistic policies of
successive Quebec governments. It helps account for the recent
emphasis by Quebec governments on economic planning and state-
sponsored enterprise. And it contributes to the desire for more
political autonomy.

Within the national political system, French-Canadians have
also been disadvantaged.

First has been the denial of French-language education and
other government services in the other provinces. Anti-French
policies in Ontario, Manitoba, and other provinces at the turn
of the century[25] may be an important reason why French-Canadians
remained highly concentrated within Quebec and, to a lesser extent,
in bordering areas of Ontario and New Brunswick. More recently,
French-language rights have been significantly extended in New
Brunswick and, to a lesser extent, in Ontario. Recent federal
policies, including constitutional proposals in 1968 and 1978, have
tried to encourage provinces to extend French-language rights.[26]

23 Bernard, p. 59.

24 Wallace Clement, *The Canadian Corporate Elite* (Toronto: McClelland and
    Stewart, 1975), pp. 233-237.

25 For a list of such actions, see Bernard, p. 27.

26 For a full statement of current federal language policy, see *A National
    Understanding*. A statement of the Government of Canada on the official
    languages policy (Ottawa: 1977).

Their success has been limited. On the one hand, English-Canadians
have strongly resisted such developments. On the other hand, it
may be argued that even very clear government policies are
powerless in the face of the massive economic and cultural pressures leading to the assimilation of francophones outside Quebec.
The result is that the assimilation proceeds apace, lending
strength to the assertion that only in Quebec, where French-
Canadians constitute a critical mass, where they are fully supported by an elaborate network of public and private institutions,
and where they have the unqualified support of government, can
francophone culture be protected.[27]

Within the federal government, the picture is more complex.
In Parliament, French-Canadian representation has been proportionate to numbers. Indeed, the historic Liberal dominance has
meant that, in purely numerical terms, French-Canadians have been
over-represented in the government party. But many qualifications
must be added.

Given the current party system, this representation is
fragile; it is to a large extent dependent on continued Liberal
pre-eminence. Even if representation is proportionate, French-
Canadians necessarily remain a minority at the centre. So long
as the primary issues of political debate do not pit French-
against English-Canadians -- and, in most cases, they have not
done so -- this does not pose severe problems. However, Canadian
history does offer several examples, such as the Riel crisis, the
conscription crises of the First and Second World Wars, and, more
recently, the issue of bilingualism in air traffic control, where
issues directly paralleled linguistic lines. If most issues did
so, or were believed to do so, the survival of Confederation
would be highly problematic.

Proportionate representation in the House of Commons has not
prevented under-representation in other political institutions.
Historically, cabinet ministers from Quebec have tended to hold
posts of lesser importance: only very recently, for example, has
a French-Canadian been Minister of Finance. More important has

---

27 The best discussion of the situtation of French-speaking Canadians outside
Quebec remains Richard Joy, *Languages in Conflict,* Carleton Library ed.
(Toronto: McClelland and Stewart, 1972). For a persuasive argument that
these demographic facts render national bilingualism policies ineffective
and irrelevant to the central need to maintain French dominance in
Quebec, see Hubert Guindon, "The Modernization of Quebec and the Legitimacy
of the Canadian State," in Daniel Glenday *et al.,* ed.,*Modernization and
the Canadian State* (Toronto: Macmillan of Canada, 1978) pp. 212-246.

been under-representation within the bureaucracy,[28] a fact of increasing importance as the size and influence of the bureaucracy itself has grown. Thus, French-Canadians were under-represented within the civil service and armed forces and tended to be concentrated at the lower levels. Indeed, in the upper ranks of the civil service, and especially in the ministries that were the architects of the Keynesian welfare state, Canada has had an essentially anglophone civil service. Those few francophones with it usually had to work in English.[29] This had three kinds of effect; the direct effect of barring francophones from an increasingly important avenue of employment, and the indirect effects of limiting the bureaucracy's ability to serve French-speaking clients and of giving short shrift to francophone values in policy formation.

In recent years, under-representation in the cabinet and the civil service has been reversed. The Office of the Commissioner of Official Languages was created; minority language services were extended through bilingual districts; a massive language training program was aimed at increasing the bilingual capacities of both French and English speakers. Major efforts were made to increase the number of French-Canadians in the civil service and to enable them to work in their own language. Between 1967 and 1976, the proportion of French speakers in the federal bureaucracy rose from 12 to 26 per cent. Between 1966 and 1976, the proportion in the officer category doubled from 10 to 19 per cent.[30] Nevertheless, these programs have provoked tensions among anglophone civil servants. The effectiveness of the language training schemes has been questioned and, despite its more bilingual public face, most of the civil service remains English.

More important, it is argued that federal policy formation has failed Quebec and French-Canadians. Earlier studies, such as the Tremblay Report of 1960, criticized federal policy primarily on the grounds that it infringed Quebec autonomy and that it embodied values and aspirations at odds with traditional values in Quebec. The autonomy theme has, of course, remained but critiques of federal policies by the PQ and others have shifted. They form an important part of the Parti Québécois indictment of federalism and have been echoed by many other Quebec spokesmen.

---

28 See Richard Van Loon, "The Structure and Membership of the Canadian Cabinet." Report prepared for the Royal Commission on Bilingualism and Biculturalism, 1966, pp. 56-57.

29 None of the Deputy Ministers holding office in 1944-5 was a French-speaking Canadian. See R. V. Wilson and W. A. Mullins, "Representative Bureaucracy: Linguistic Ethnic Aspects in Canadian Public Policy." Paper presented at Conference on Political Change in Canada, Saskatoon.

30 Bernard, p. 64.

First, it is argued that the federal government drains
resources from Quebec by taking more out in taxes than it returns
in federal spending. The bases for such analyses remain highly
controversial, but most agree that, following a long period of
deficit, federal taxing and spending do redistribute some resources
to Quebec from other parts of the country. Quebec spokesmen argue,
however, that this surplus is accounted for mainly by income
maintenance programs that do little to promote economic development.
They also argue that federal development spending (DREE) has not
been oriented to their perception of Quebec's needs.

It is also felt that basic structural policies benefit Ontario
and hurt the weak areas of the economy. The St. Lawrence Seaway
diverted trade from Montreal to the Great Lakes. Agricultural,
transportation, and other policies are oriented more to Ontario
than to Quebec, and so on.

The Quebec nation-building impulse derives from other sources
as well. Redress of grievances and under-representation would not
eliminate the drive for autonomy and self-determination within the
province itself. To focus on grievances is to ignore that
autonomy may be sought for its own sake or that a highly self-
conscious people, united by a common language, a common historical
experience, an elaborate network of social institutions, and with
institutional resources provided by control over a provincial
government, might wish to achieve sovereignty and so become a
complete "nation-state."

Only recently has Quebec nationalism generated the demand for
independence and sovereignty. Duplessis and the Union Nationale
government resisted federal incursions in the social field and
jealously guarded the province's tax resources but were content
to leave economic power in federal hands. The government of Jean
Lesage focused on expanding provincial tax shares in responding
to federal intitiatives, such as the Canada Pension Plan, with its
own programs and in seeking freedom from federal controls through
cost-sharing programs. Under the slogan "egalité où indépendence,"
the 1965 Union Nationale government expanded the cultural and
foreign roles of the Quebec government and called for fundamental
constitutional revision that would recognize the existence in
Canada of two distinct nations. In the late 1960s, attention
shifted somewhat to language policies, motivated partly by the
sense of threat to francophone majority status in Montreal and
partly by the desire to attack more directly the barriers to
francophones in the private sector.[31]

---

31 Guindon, *op. cit.*

Under Robert Bourassa's Liberal government, the emphasis
shifted to a greater Quebec role in social policy and to the
demand for "cultural sovereignty." The trend since 1960 is clear.
Each government has sought major change in the federal system and
in each case this has *not* taken the form of a demand for increased
French language rights across the country or for more power for
French-Canadians in Ottawa. All have argued instead for greater
authority centred in the Quebec government, the principal political voice of and spokesmen for francophone interests.

The process of industrialization in Quebec throughout the
1950s brought to the fore of events an organized, militant, urban
working class and a new technologically based middle class.
"Nationalist developments," such as Hydro Quebec and other state-
run enterprises, are seen by analysts like Albert Breton to result
from the desire of the new middle class to create for itself
managerial, professional, and technical positions, which they
had been unable to attain in the anglophone milieu.[32] Thus, the
new middle class is seen both as the creature and creator of the
expansionist Quebec state.

As the state attempts to organize the interests of the new
middle class, it undergoes an expansion. In Quebec's case, much
of the public sector growth represented a "catching up" with other
jurisdictions. The expansion requires massive resources and,
more importantly, policy levers that Ottawa influences or controls.
Competition, then, develops between federal and provincial
governments for the allegiance and support of the general population -- each level feeling it can deliver what the population
wants.

As the one instrument that could be turned to this purpose,
the Quebec state apparatus has become a device for preserving
Quebec's cultural identity and for asserting control over its
own economic life. Federalism, it was asserted, placed far too
many constraints on Quebec's ability to reach these goals.

---

32 Albert Breton, "The Economics of Nationalism," *Journal of Political Economy*
    72 (1964), pp. 376-86. For related analysis, see Guindon, "Social Interest,
    Social Class and Quebec's Bureaucratic Revolution," *Queen's Quarterly* 71
    (1964), pp. 150-62;and Charles Taylor, "Nationalism and the Political
    Intelligentsia," *Queen's Quarterly* 72 (1965). Breton's argument has an
    important twist: the middle class expansionism works to the disadvantage
    of working class interests in Quebec, because it leads to inefficient
    allocation of resources. This assumes, of course, that the previous
    allocation was efficient. In any case, notes must be taken of the broad
    penetration of separatist ideas in all Quebec milieux, though it does
    remain strongest among the younger, more educated and more urban elements.

In the process of modernization, the cultural and economic spheres have become fused. Economic control is seen as necessary for cultural control. The demands of the Parti Québécois for sovereignty and autonomy are in line with the development of past demands and consistent with the integration of cultural, economic, and political forces in the modern state.

None of this should imply that the Quebec population is united behind the drive for independence. As the variability of the polls concerning support for independence shows, much of the population supports continued federation, and many other are undecided. The same remains true of important interest groups, most notably the labour movement. The internal political debate is intense; its outcome is uncertain.

Several contending groups have emerged. The committed federalists, among whom Prime Minister Trudeau remains the primary spokesman, have a fundamental distrust of ethnically based nationalism and instead place reliance in valuation of individual rights. For these reasons, Quebec separatism is seen as dangerous. Humanist values are far better preserved in a multilingual and multicultural state. French-Canadians must look beyond their province to play a role in the larger country. Accordingly, English-Canadians too must be more willing to accept the rights of French-Canadians to live with their own language throughout Canada. Moreover, there must be a fundamental distinction between linguistic group and provincial government. Reform implies the promotion of individual French-Canadian interests everywhere, not the strengthening of the government of Quebec. Indeed, the fundamental objection to any form of special status is that, in so weakening the links between Ottawa and Quebec citizens, it becomes a snowball whose only logical stopping place is complete independence. It is this viewpoint that separates the Trudeau federalists from most other Quebec federalist political spokesmen. While prepared to work towards a "renewed federalism," this group argues for strengthening of minority language rights and for ensuring full francophone participation in national institutions. This has been the direction of federal policy in recent years and it underlies the recent constitutional proposals of the federal government.

The third-option federalists, perhaps best represented today by Liberal leader Claude Ryan,[33] remain committed to a federal system, partly for the same principled reasons, such as commitment to a bilingual Canada, that animate the first group. They also tend to argue for federalism on the grounds of expediency -- best

---

33 For recent statements of Ryan's views, see Claude Ryan *Une Société Stable* (Montreal, Editions Héritage, 1978).

summarized in former Premier Robert Bourassa's phrase "profitable federalism." In this view, Quebec benefits from the larger Canadian market, from redistributive federal policies, and from the political strength of a larger unit. An independent Quebec might suffer economically and would, in any case, be at least as vulnerable as it is now to outside economic forces. This group tends to differ somewhat from the present language policy; while strongly supporting the need for the federal government to be fully bilingual, it tends to be more accepting of a territorial strategy elsewhere, in which the position of the French language is strengthened within Quebec. But, most fundamentally, the third-option federalists adopt a conception of Canada as a binational state, in which Quebec is and must be the primary political voice of Quebecers. Hence, it requires legislative and fiscal powers that are not required by the other provinces, which lack this national role. From this flow the general arguments for some form of special status.

The independentists include the PQ party, which takes the view that Canada is binational and that Quebec must have full sover- eignty. Federalism is rejected for several reasons. It is a mask for continued centralization. It treats Quebec as merely one among ten provinces. The unnatural joining of two nations within a single political system is responsible for continual conflict and bitterness, which frustrates both French and English Canadians. Far better, they argue, to cut the ties and allow each majority to act alone. Yet, continued interdependence is accepted, so that economic association is expected to follow.

All three positions offer a challenge to English-Canadians and to Canadian political institutions. The last two orientations may be called Quebec nation-building strategies. As with province- building elsewhere, they depend crucially not only on the territorial concentration of the linguistic group but also on the existence of the political institution of the provincial government, which has provided the resources for the growth of nation-building and the focus for loyalty and support. It is hard to conceive of successful modifications to the federal system that do not recognize and respond to the nation-building drive.

Conclusion

The political crisis of Canadian federalism thus comes down to a clash between rival governments, each tending to speak for one of the three drives we have surveyed: for national leader- ship, for greater provincial control, or for a special role for Quebec as the political expression of a distinct national community. Each of these drives leads governments to act in virtually all policy areas and to use aggressively the policy tools available to it. Each "intrudes" on the other. The drives also suggest that each government has quite distinct policy priorities, which are often, though not always, in conflict.

This rival community-building activity is one prime reason
for the increased overlapping of federal and provincial responsibilities. It is reinforced by the vagueness or obsolescence of
the powers set out in the British North America Act. These
categories neither reflect accurately the role of contemporary
government in Canada nor provide strict rules delimiting the
responsibilites at each level. Overlapping is also reinforced
by the character of modern policy itself, since all policy domains
are now so interconnected, and by the competition of all governments to respond to changing citizen demands.

The result of this interpenetration of federal and provincial
policies is a high degree of interdependence and much opportunity
for mutual frustration. Policy activities are so shared that
"national" policies in fields from economic policy to culture can
only result from the activities of both levels of government.
Paradoxically, however, this *policy* interpenetration is not
accompanied by *political* integration. That is, there are sharp
discontinuities between politics at the two levels: provincial
voting patterns differ from federal voting patterns; provincial
parties have few ideological or organizational links with federal
parties; and there is little movement of political leaders from
one level to another. All this helps to explain the continued
conflict and why intergovernmental relations are conducted largely
at the executive level, reminiscent, indeed, of *international*
relations.

Quite outside the constitution, a huge network of intergovernmental relationships and techniques have grown up in relation
to these realities. Shared-cost programs, administrative delegation, and five-year fiscal arrangements are some of the instruments
of joint activity. Hundreds of federal-provincial conferences are
held each year, ranging from the set-piece, increasingly televised
First Ministers Conferences to a myriad of ministerial meetings
and to both multilateral and bilateral officials' meetings. In
fields such as energy and education, Councils of Ministers have
been created with small secretariats. A joint body, the Canadian
Intergovernmental Conference Secretariat, has been created to
administer the many meetings. The federal and several provincial
governments have responded internally to the heightened priority
of intergovernmental affairs through the creation of cabinet
committees and new central-control agencies or ministries. As a
counterweight to federal-provincial meetings, there has been
a considerable growth of interprovincial meetings, with the
annual Premiers' Conference now being an important forum for the
elaboration of joint provincial positions. Regional groupings of
Premiers in the West and the Atlantic provinces have grown in
importance. On several issues, including the fiscal arrangements
in 1975-76 and the debate on patriation and amendment in 1975-76,

the provinces, acting together, generated common fronts. Increasingly, the processes tend to be politicized and to move intergovernmental relations to the summit of the political system, where political competition and conflicting general strategies become most evident.

Extensive as this process is, and successful as it has been in many fields, it suffers from severe weaknesses. It is largely secret. It is sporadic. It has few firm procedures or decision rules. It cannot guarantee co-operative action. The inadequacies of the machinery and the degree of interpenetration create three kinds of frustration: the federal government is frustrated in its attempts to plan overall national development and to operate the tools of Keynesian fiscal policy. Province-builders often feel frustrated in their own planning by the constraints imposed by the federal system. And citizens are often frustrated by the lack of accountability, delay, uncertainty, and inconsistency engendered by intergovernmental conflict. Business groups are often frustrated by provincial barriers to the Canadian common market, by conflicting norms on such matters as consumer protection, and the like. Labour, too, is frustrated by variations in labour policy and by the inability of Ottawa to engage in national planning.

All this suggests that the primary agenda for constitutional discussion should focus on the relationship between governments, and this leads to a focus on the division of powers and on the machinery of intergovernmental relations.

The first goal of a search for a new division of powers might be to reduce entanglement and the potential for mutual frustration by redefining governmental powers in such a way that each is responsible for a given list of functions that it can carry out without reference to other governments. This "watertight compartments" view, however, seems unrealistic. In no modern federal system does it obtain; everywhere the pattern is one of mutual interpenetration. The character of modern policy, the undifferentiated demands of citizens, and most important, the community-building aspirations of governments render this strategy impossible in Canada. Much disentanglement is, no doubt, possible, as the ending of several major shared-cost programs recently attests, but the prospects are limited. Many, if not most, of the fundamental activities of the modern world can only be carried out through a process of collaborative or joint decision-making. Existing mechanisms for such collaboration are far too underdeveloped and the search for institutional change must focus on improving it.

Nor is it possible through the division of powers to meet fully the goals of any one of the three drives. Massive decentralization, increased centralization, and special powers for Quebec all have strong supporters and strong opponents. Some flexibility is possible, but it seems more likely to come about through a greater range of concurrent activities, through provisions for delegation of power, and through various opting-out strategies than it does through a move back to watertight compartments.

Whether it is possible to design new machinery for intergovernmental relations, which would maximize the incentive for harmony and agreement and which would maximize the chances for public accountability, is unclear, but several means have been suggested recently.[34]

Thus, while underlying factors of ethnic, economic, cultural, and historical diversity are crucial for understanding the Canadian political crisis, they are all manifested through governments. Reform of the Canadian system, therefore, while no doubt helped by stress on common symbols, values, and the like must concentrate on governments and on their capacities to develop policies in which the dynamic balance between national and regional forces is able to evolve continually. This search must focus first on the representative and integrative capacity of the federal government itself; second, and more important, it must focus on the relationship between it and the provincial governments.

Population factors alone make it hard for Ottawa to be fully representative. Under a system of majority rule, inevitably, the numbers in central Canada can defeat the numbers on the periphery, and the numbers of English-Canadians can defeat the French-Canadians. So long as political cleavages in Canada tend to pit English against French, or centre versus periphery, that is a problem impossible to reconcile.

---

34 Among them are: *Towards a New Canada,* Report of the Committee on the Constitution, the Canadian Bar Association (The Canadian Bar Foundation, 1978); David Elton, F. C. Engelman, Peter McCormick, *Alternatives: Towards the Development of An Effective Federal System for Canada* (Calgary: Canada West Foundation 1978); Richard Simeon, *Statement to the Joint Committee of the Senate and House of Commons on the Constitution, 13 September 1978,* Ontario Advisory Committee on Confederation, First Report (Toronto, April 1978); and *What is British Columbia's Position on the Constitution of Canada* (Victoria, 1976).

Comments by S. Roberts, President, Canada-West
Foundation, Calgary

Evenson's and Simeon's paper on "The Roots of Discontent" is
analytically perceptive and an excellent general description of
the very real malaise currently affecting our nation. It is a great
shame that so many provincial premiers ignore the kind of information
that is available in a paper such as this. I hope my elaboration
of one or two points will stimulate further discussion.

First of all, our current crisis is most definitely one of
government institutions. We can discuss any number of economic problems but we cannot ignore the faults of the Canadian federal system.
Western discontent with this sytem is not limited to government
people and academics; it is also rife amongst the masses. Westerners feel that they are alienated, and it matters little whether their
feelings are based on fact or only on what they perceive to be fact.
If the discontent is there, it can only be harmful to the nation.
Evenson and Simeon concentrate on the Quebec - Canada crisis, but
discontent is just as great in Western Canada and in the Atlantic
Provinces, for that matter, as it is in Quebec. Accordingly, we would
appear to be in the midst of a Region - Canada crisis. Western Canadians have their own particular perspective on many of the issues
raised by our current national dilemma.

They are primarily concerned with more effective regional
representation in the central government. To this end, they are not
afraid to talk of a "new deal" or even of a new constitution that
would allow them greater political clout at the national level. As
Evenson and Simeon have noted, such cries for proportional representation become louder as polarization increases. They are now
particularly loud because it is clear that, if another Liberal government is elected, there will be virtually no Liberals in Western
Canada. Conversely, there will be very few Conservatives in Quebec.
Aside from increased representation in the House of Commons and in
a new, reformed Senate, it is also vitally important that Westerners
have greater representation on all relevant regulatory agencies.
These are of special significance to the people of Western Canada.

It is interesting to note that Western Canadians do not
want the provincial governments running Canada; they do not believe
in small - "c" Confederation. If you look at the provincial voting
patterns in British Columbia, for example, you will note that there
is a strong Social Credit - NDP polarization, while neither party
has a particularly strong representation in the federal House. Western

voters want to elect provincial governments to run the provinces and, independently of this, a federal government with a strong regional component to run the nation.

Evenson and Simeon speak of country-building, province-building and Quebec nation-building. They could, perhaps, have looked more closely at government-building because this has been a major preoccupation at both the federal and provincial levels for the past twenty years. By and large, Western Canadians are thoroughly annoyed with big government because it is so insensitive to peoples' needs. Integral weaknesses in government structure are only magnified by expansion.

There are many peculiar ironies in the western response to the issues of the day. Westerners are opposed to bilingualism, but they demand french language training for their children; they favour unity, but oppose the price-tag that might accompany it; they demand control over their own natural resources and the funds which accrue from them, yet participate willingly in equalization payments to other parts of the country; they consider the Supreme Court to be made up of fine, impartial judges who regularly rule improperly and irregularly on constitutional matters in favour of the central government; and, finally, they're incensed at their poor representation in Cabinet, and mad at Jack Horner for changing sides. These are the paradoxical statements that emerge from meetings of the Canada-West Foundation in every part of Western Canada.

Evenson and Simeon state: "it is impossible to divorce changes in central institutions from the crucial question of the division of powers." I must disagree and suggest that Ottawa can begin to eradicate the roots of discontent by putting its own house in order without provincial government approval. A reformed House of Commons could allow for more regional input and proportional representation as well. It is the emending formula which cannot be divorced from the division of powers, and the November "First Ministers' Conference" ground to a halt over this very issue.

As the party system is failing, the Senate watchdog impotent, and the nation increasingly difficult to govern, it is time for the Federal Government to move on to unilateral reform of the House of Commons. There must be some kind of accomodation that will give Westerners a greater say in the Parliament of Canada. I shall frame my conclusion in the form of a gentle warning. There is an ambivalent mood in the West today. While committed to the ideal of one Canada, Westerners are also taking a pragmatic and somewhat envious look at Quebec's success in obtaining the things she holds dear. Western Canadians too are taking a long, hard look at their future.

WESTERN ECONOMIC GRIEVANCES:

AN OVERVIEW WITH SPECIAL

REFERENCE TO FREIGHT RATES

by

Kenneth H. Norrie*

University of Alberta

* I gratefully acknowledge comments by Dave
  Gillen and the research assistance of
  Yolanda Van Wachem. The usual disclaimer
  applies.

INTRODUCTION

The current preoccupation with the economics of Confederation stems from the election of the Parti Québécois government, and the publicity surrounding its claim that that province is a net loser under the present fiscal arrangements. Regional economic grievances are not unique to Quebec of course, nor have they been restricted to the balance sheet of federal taxation revenue versus expenditure by geographical area. It seems to have taken the emergence of the Parti Québécois though to create a climate in which the entire economic and political basis of Confederation is open to discussion. Topics that were unthinkable a few years ago have become the stuff of current research and debate.[1]

The Prairie Provinces[2] have always contended that Confederation, the national policy and most of the subsequent economic policies were designed by and for central Canada. Decades-old grievances over tariffs and freight rates have been supplemented more recently by disputes over resource taxation and industrial development strategies. Their dissatisfactions have been repeatedly expressed through submissions to Royal Commissions, through the election of strong provincial governments and the rejection of government candidates in federal elections, via federal-provincial conferences more recently, and most notably during the special Western Economic Opportunities Conference in Calgary in July, 1973. Ironically enough however, it has taken the threat of secession by one of the provinces the West has long considered to be favoured economically by Confederation for these claims to be viewed seriously. The so-called western viewpoint now makes a regular appearance in discussions of national economic concerns.[3]

Western economic grievances[4] must be viewed in light of the two main goals of the region's political and economic leaders to be properly understood.[5] The first concern is with maximizing the level of real per capita income from the existing economic base of the region. In the context of federal-provincial relations this means western opposition to federal policies that are construed as restricting the generation of income from these sectors, or its retention regionally, and to those that increase the cost of goods and services to residents. The other goal is a desire for greater economic diversification, meaning essentially expanding the industrial base of the region. In this regard, there is a belief that federal economic strategies are, and always have been, deliberately designed to develop Ontario and Quebec based on the resources of the outlying regions. The presumption is that with more neutral federal economic policies the industrial, financial, and commercial activities of the country would be more widely diffused among the regions. Natural disadvantages in these respects are sometimes recognized, but the belief persists that the western provinces are more dependent upon raw material exports than they otherwise would be because of the century-old Canadian development strategy.[6]

Note: See footnotes on p. 222.

The present paper is an attempt to analyse these two general areas of concern.[7] It is useful to adopt a criterion employed in an earlier paper. The term regional economic discrimination is reserved for demonstrated economic losses emanating from distortions initiated or tolerated by the federal government. In other words, the actual allocation of resources given the particular policy in question must be shown to be inferior from a western standpoint to an hypothetical one predicted to result from a more neutral policy environment. This criterion is specifically intended to exclude allegations of economic discrimination that stem in fact from the inevitable position of a small, geographically remote natural resource based economy within a larger industrial North America.

The paper cited in the previous paragraph argued that many of the western economic grievances are precisely of this latter type. Examples given were the general lack of secondary industry in the region (as distinct from a few specific industries), the fact that transport charges on both exports and imports are borne locally (and would be even with a perfectly competitive transport system), the lending policies of commercial banks, and the regional impact of tight monetary policies. In each of these cases, the grievance is more properly directed at the inevitable operation of a market economy where geographical distances are great, and in which regions are vastly different in size and proximity to other industrial areas of the world.

The other type of western economic complaint distinguished was distortions in the economy, caused by the federal government or at least tolerated by it, which have possible regionally discriminatory effects. Instances such as these qualify as grievances because the source of the dispute lies with the federal government, and because recourse lies in lobbying to have the distortions removed. Examples of this sort are western grievances over tariffs, freight rates and federal taxation of natural resource rents. Before it can be concluded that the West can and should press for changes in these areas, however, two additional criteria need to be satisfied. It must be shown first of all that the assertions are valid, and that the alleged losses are significant ones. In addition, it should be clear that the changes proposed would unambiguously benefit the residents of the region. A slightly less restrictive version of this would be that any changes involving income redistributions within the region should be ones that can be condoned through the usual political process. The remainder of this paper discusses each of these areas in turn, with a special empirical effort being devoted to allegations concerning freight rates.

TARIFFS

Western complaints about tariffs stem from the recognition that they operate to redistribute income from the western provinces and the Maritimes to central Canada. All Canadians pay the costs of the tariffs in the form of higher prices on protected goods, but the benefits are distributed unequally due to the concentration of industry in Quebec and Ontario. The question though is whether or how this can be construed as a legitimate regional burden. The main impact of the tariff is to create a larger number of industrial jobs within Canada than would otherwise exist, with the bulk of these accruing to Ontario and Quebec. The regional impact of the tariff then is essentially that persons living outside the industrial heartland pay a share of this excess wage bill through higher prices but receive a disproportionately small percentage of the jobs.

The usual recourse to this is to argue that there are no formal barriers to labour mobility within the country, so there is nothing to prevent workers of all areas from migrating to the industrial centres to take these jobs.[8] But this assumption of costless adjustment of factors is not tenable. Land and natural resources are not mobile by definition, so owners of these factors will have their incomes reduced below those potentially available, as Mackintosh recognized long ago.[9] Recent work in the economics of migration or job search has highlighted the importance of adjustment costs. Unless a factor has some degree of market power, which is unusual, it bears the full brunt of these costs.

An analogy can be drawn to the literature dealing with the reallocation of income between capital and labour due to tariffs or minimum wage legislation, between black and white or male and female due to discriminatory hiring practices, among income classes due to publicly funded education and so forth. The presumption in these cases is that one is dealing with mutually exclusive groups and perfect immobility; the full burden must be borne because there is no way of avoiding it. But if this is generally accepted as the basis of an interesting economic problem, then so is any policy such as tariffs that demonstrably shifts the costs of adjustment to a specific, identifiable subset of the population. It thus seems worthwhile to attempt to specify and estimate the exact regional effects of the Canadian tariff, as has been done in some recent studies.[10] Space limitation preclude any additional estimates here.

A related concern is the belief that western-based resource industries face a negative effective rate of protection because there are duties on inputs but not outputs. This means that value added in these sectors is less than it would be under free trade, implying in turn lower payments to labour, to capital or to the owners of specialized resources. In each case the result is a reduction in the aggregate income generated from the existing economic base of the region. In practice, though, the effective rate of protection is rarely significantly negative[11], so it is unclear how significant a point this really is.

Yet another contention is that the existence of the tariffs adds to the transport costs paid by westerners. The Canadian tariff ensures that deliveries of many manufactured consumer goods are from Quebec and Ontario, with the significant distances and therefore transport costs added on. In the absence of these barriers, it is argued, the west could purchase these products from geographically more proximate areas of the U.S. or even from Japan and face a lower total freight bill. It should be noted that this argument is made independently of claims that actual freight rates are discriminatory; it is a point about distance alone. This point is almost certainly correct to some extent, although to measure the size of the loss would be a nearly impossible task.

A final specific claim with respect to Canadian commercial policy is that the federal government has been lax in attempting to negotiate reciprocal trade arrangements with the U.S. and other countries for products that would benefit the west primarily. The American tariffs on petrochemical products are one example of a perceived barrier to the expansion of petrochemical capacity in the West. American and Japanese duties on processed products of agriculture, forests and mines are other examples. The federal role in securing the Autopact or the Defence Sharing Agreement is usually mentioned by way of contrast. Western interest in this area is evidenced by the very active role they have taken in shaping Canada's position in recent GATT negotiations. It is important to realize, though, that the real targets in these cases are foreign tariff structures and all the interest groups behind them rather than the Canadian tariff structure *per se*.

FEDERAL TAXATION AND EXPENDITURES

The reference in this section is to the so-called "balance sheet" question, made current recently by the Quebec-Ottawa dispute. There has long been a presumption in the western provinces, particularly in Alberta and B.C. that they contribute significantly more in taxes to the federal government than they receive back as government services and income transfers. In fact, the second volume of the "Costs of Confederation to Alberta" studies attempted to measure the size of this income transference via the tax system, and found it to be significant.[12] It is also the issue that is emphasized by nearly all of the variety of western independence parties currently campaigning in the region.

On this question though, it is important to define clearly what is at issue. Some provinces obviously will pay more in federal taxes than they get back in the way of services, and others less, simply because of disparities in regional incomes, the progressive

nature of the personal income tax and the goal of uniformity of
government services across the country. Furthermore, if the idea
of progressivity in taxation is accepted, then this is in fact how
it should be. It is unclear what it means to say that Alberta or
B.C. bear a burden in this respect. To argue that each province
should be exactly in balance in this respect is to deny the principle of progressive taxation applied to Canadians as a whole.

This question is an interesting issue, though, for a provincial
or regional jurisdiction contemplating political independence.
For then there is a need to examine the tax base of the region under
a variety of assumptions about dynamic effects to see if it could
support an equivalent level of government services once independent.
It would be equally interesting if it were discovered that the
poorer regions of the country were the ones in a deficit position.
But merely to show that residents of B.C. or Alberta or Ontario are
in total taxed relatively more heavily really only amounts to con-
firming that there is in fact some progressivity in the Canadian
tax system.

The argument could be made, however, that the above arguments
are valid in the case of taxation of incomes that have accrued
to companies and individuals, but not to federal interception of
resource revenues that would otherwise have gone to provincial
governments in the first instance. The western position along
these lines has been stated rather succinctly by two leading political figures.[13] The BNA Act divides powers and responsibilities
into areas of exclusive federal concern, those solely in the
domain of the provinces, and those such as agriculture that are
shared between the two levels. Areas assigned to the provinces
are unassailable, except in cases of true emergency and then
only by act of Parliament. The authority given to the provinces
under the BNA Act to own and manage the development of land and
natural resources is one such example of an exclusive provincial
prerogative. Thus, in the absence of a clearly recognized national
emergency the federal government has no constitutional right to
implement any special kind of taxes or regulatory provisions for
these sectors.

These are the grounds on which the western premiers have
opposed the federal export tax on crude oil, the 1974 budget
decision to disallow royalty payments to provinces as a tax deduction for resource companies, and Ottawa's active intervention
against Saskatchewan in challenges to the province's oil and potash
policies. In each case, the actions are seen as unwarranted and
grossly discriminatory. They ask why there was no similar export
tax on hydroelectric power transmitted to the U.S. or on shipments
of timber, gold, or nickel. The fact that the energy royalties
have been designated to aid in the industrial diversification of
the province in the case of Alberta, or in the repatriation of
the potash industry in Saskatchewan, makes the federal actions
doubly onerous. Ottawa is not only seen as taking an unfair share

of provincial resource revenues, but also is seriously impeding what may well be the West's last chance at achieving the elusive economic diversification.

To assess these claims requires resolving which level of government has the right to control and regulate the natural resource industries and act as the initial collector of the resource rents, and how much if any of these rents should be redistributed to other jurisdictions within Canada. The hitherto most complete attempt to examine these issues is by Anthony Scott.[14] He first examines what he calls institutional criteria - constitutional law, the province as landlord, and the notion of an optimal size of income redistribution jurisdiction - and finds no clear criteria as to how the resource revenues should be allocated. A second criterion, dubbed allocational factors, does not yield any firmer conclusions. He concludes by suggesting a division of revenues according to the share of special services provided by the respective governments, with the federal government also collecting a share in preparation for the interprovincial population movements that will likely result from exhaustion. In a similar kind of review Helliwell concurs that "nothing is 'right' when it comes to political division of authority and revenues."[15]

Any estimate of the size of the burden borne by the western provinces with respect to resource taxation depends crucially on what is viewed as "proper" allocation of economic rent. If the producing provinces are assumed to have exclusive rights, then the simplest estimate of provincial government revenues foregone from oil and gas is equal to the current production rate times the difference between world and domestic prices times the relevant marginal royalty rate. The companies' share of foregone income (equal to one minus the royalty rate) can then be allocated among provinces according to the distribution of shares. A calculation of this sort shows that income foregone by the province itself or by its share-holding residents in 1974/75 was equal to $310 million in the case of Saskatchewan, and $2,309 million for Alberta.[16] If the benefit the provinces' residents derive as consumers of lower-priced fuels is taken into account these figures drop to $214 million and $2,129 million, respectively. The net figure for Manitoba is a gain of $63.6 million.

These calculations could be refined in several ways. A similar exercise for a later year would yield a smaller figure for instance, since domestic oil and gas prices have been gradually approaching world prices by federal-provincial agreement.[17] The implicit assumption of a perfectly inelastic demand curve for fuels is almost certainly unrealistic.[18] The view that at least some portion of the resource rents properly belong to the nation as a whole could be accommodated by reducing the figures by an appropriate amount.[19] The historic pattern of preferential tax treatment of the industry could be taken into account, since this certainly increased the amount the provinces collected in the form of exploration and development rights.

Finally, it might be argued that current royalty rates in the producing provinces are a direct consequence of early federal initiatives in the area and that, in the absence of this demonstration effect by Ottawa, Alberta and Saskatchewan would never have revamped their taxation efforts in the manner they did. All these adjustments would reduce the estimates of the interprovincial income transfers.

In total, though, the issue of resource taxation does seem to be a legitimate area for provincial concern. The federal government has clearly collected a significant amount of the economic rent from the oil and gas industry and redistributed it to residents of other provinces. While there may not be a clear constitutional prohibition against this, it certainly does contravene the understanding the provinces have of the position of natural resources in the BNA Act. Alberta and Saskatchewan are also entitled to ask, as they do, why just their resource industries have been singled out for this special treatment. The fact that the economic rents were obvious and large and administratively rather easy to tax may explain the phenomenon, but it does not justify it.

FREIGHT RATES

This is perhaps the longest-standing issue of western alienation, stretching back to pre-CPR days. In the early years, western concern was focused mainly on the level of rates on grain exports. But as the economies have matured and developed, the criticism has become more comprehensive and sophisticated. The target at present is the National Transportation Act of 1967, with its near exclusive reliance on competition to set rail freight rates. Aside from a minimum charge equal to average variable costs, a maximum one for captive shippers, and the retention of the statutory grain provisions, the market was to be relied upon as the best judge of what rail tariffs should be.

The West's position as regards the implications of this system can be summarized as follows. The widely recognized joint and common product nature of railway operations makes it difficult or impossible to identify costs uniquely with each of the services provided. This means that the companies price so as to maximize the profits of the operation as a whole, with individual commodities often moving at rates at or near average variable costs and others at well above average total costs. Given the high ratio of fixed to variable costs in railroads, the consequent variation in rates can be quite large.

A discriminating monopolist faced with this situation will maximize profits by charging what the market will bear or, in other words, according to the price elasticity of demand for transportation services. Goods with no alternatives to rail transport will pay rates substantially in excess of average total costs, making up for the portion of fixed costs lost on rate-sensitive traffic moving at less than total cost. The National Transportation Act, relying as it does on intermodal competition to set rates in all but a few instances, creates and sanctions such discriminatory pricing by the railroads.

The western provinces feel that they inevitably have relatively inelastic demands for transportation services because of the lack of competing water transport, the high-bulk, low-value nature of their exports and the long distances involved in the import and even intraregional movement of goods. These latter factors are thought to restrict the competitive ability of trucking. As a result the region views itself as bearing a disproportionate share of railway fixed costs at the expense of real incomes of the region's residents. In addition, this value of service pricing together with statutory rate limitations on some agricultural products results in a structure of rates over commodities that actively discourages further processing within the region.

The specific complaints are five in number. It is held first that rates on the export of raw materials are significantly lower than those for processed products, creating an incentive to export the former rather than the latter and thus destroying otherwise natural industries for the West. Examples most often cited are the rates on feed grains as opposed to livestock and meat products, and those on rapeseed versus rapeseed oil and meal products. A second charge is that the West does not receive the same kind of zone or blanket rates on incoming goods that the East does. Smaller centres pay additional rates to those charged to the main cities, thereby discouraging the decentralization of economic activity within each of the provinces that is a major goal of all prairie governments. Thirdly, the rates on goods shipped to the provinces are said to be higher than those for the same product shipped the greater geographical distance to Vancouver. This is the familiar long-short-haul discrimination, and results from the railways' need to compete with ocean delivered supplies from other countries to B.C. The most common examples here are steel and canned goods. The higher prices reduce real incomes in the West and also inhibit the establishment of western wholesaling and distribution centres on the prairies. The fourth allegation is that rates on westbound manufactured goods are lower than those on eastbound ones, compounding western difficulties in competing with eastern producers in both local and central Canadian markets. Finally, it is argued that the horizontal rate increases of recent years, whereby a constant percentage increase has been applied to all rates, has increased the absolute rate spread, and thus exacerbated the above problem.

The West has proposed to replace the present value of service scheme with one based as closely as possible on the actual

costs incurred in providing individual railway services. To this
end Alberta has designed and lobbied for the so-called Equitable
Pricing Policy,[20] while Manitoba has suggested an alternative
method dubbed the Destination Rate Level Technique.[21] There has
been an understandable unwillingness to see the Statutory Grain
rates be abolished, however, at least until an alternative form of
compensation can be agreed upon.

Western claims about the divergence between rates charged
and costs incurred by the railroads cannot be investigated directly,
due to the absence of any reliable cost data. One recourse is to
try and infer what the structure of rates would be under the
assumption that the companies practise discriminatory pricing
efficiently. These predictions can then be checked against actual
freight revenue data together with any information on variables
likely to reflect cost differences over commodity movements.
This procedure is less precise of course, but is about all that
can be done with present data availabilities.

SOME THEORETICAL CONSIDERATIONS

The sensitivity of any given commodity movement to the level
of railway freight rates depends on two separate factors. The
first, and the one stressed by western spokesmen, is the presence
of competing transport modes. Water transport can be an effective
competitor to rail for bulky, low-value products moving long
distances, at least in season and where speed is not essential.
For higher-value, lower-bulk items moving shorter distances,
trucking is a main competitor. In addition there is competition
from airlines, pipelines and the like for more specialized product
movements. But there is another important determinant of demand
elasticity that is often overlooked in western submissions. Un-
reasonably high freight rates on products with no alternative
mode available can force the industry out of business, with the
railroad losing the traffic entirely. If they have excess
capacity and the rate they can charge covers some of the fixed
costs, then it is obviously to their advantage to price appropriately to ensure the industry survives. Thus even where railroads
are the only feasible mode, this product competition as it is known
can bring about rates at or below actual total costs.

There are two factors that determine how much of a freight
rate any specific industry can absorb without forcing it to shut
down. The first is the price elasticity of demand for the product
itself. The more inelastic this is, the more the industry will be
able to shift forward any transport charge, and thus the less is the
effect on producer prices. Conversely, a highly elastic demand
curve means that the producer will bear the brunt of the transport
charges. For a producer or industry in this latter situation
the ability to bear a transport charge depends on the margin between
the given world price and the average production cost. Producers

with highly elastic supply curves with intercepts at or slightly
below the world price would not be able to bear very large transport costs, for example. On the other hand very profitable ones
would be able to absorb the freight charges, and industries with
relatively vertical supply curves would accept additional transport
charges without reducing output significantly.

It is clear that there is a general lack of intermodal competition in western Canada. One ocean port, isolated and icebound
for most of the year, provides no competition to the railways.
In addition, most of the products shipped out of the region are
low-value, high-bulk raw materials for which trucking costs would
be prohibitive. The higher-valued manufactured imports from eastern
Canada and abroad generally move at such great distances that
trucks again cannot compete, although their disadvantage is apparently becoming less significant over time. The only area where the
effects of intermodal competition should be discernable is in
intraregional commodity movements of high value goods, where the
shorter distances make trucks a viable competitor.

Product characteristics are relevant,though,in setting rates
on western products, and the pattern that one would predict on
these grounds is exactly opposite to what the West describes the
current one to be. One example is the contention that freight
rates on raw materials are generally lower than those on processed
goods. Both would move by rail if at all due to their bulk and
the distances involved. In addition, one can safely assume that
external demand for both categories was highly elastic, given
the small share Prairie producers have or would have in world
markets. Thus there is little or no opportunity to shift freight
charges forward in either case. Any exceptions to this would be
more likely in raw materials rather than processed products,
Saskatchewan potash being one example perhaps. Thus any difference
here would point to higher rates on raw materials.

The ability of producers to bear a price decrease is different,
though. Manufacturing and processing plants on the Prairies are
necessarily small, marginal concerns operating on the fringe of
the larger North American Industrial heartland The margin between
average costs and world prices is generally rather small. In
addition, they are typically price takers for capital and labour
and purchased inputs, given their relatively small size and the
geographical mobility of factors, so any move towards reducing output would have little or no impact on factor prices and thus unit
costs.

Natural resource industries,on the other hand,have a unique
and immobile factor of production in addition to capital and labour.
The return to the latter factors may be immutable in the face of
factor mobility, but that to land or to the resource site is not, so
long as any Ricardian rent is being earned. In other words,

the presence of specific factors of production gives the raw
materials industries a much more inelastic supply curve than the
processing industries. A lower price at the farm gate or mine
site is reflected backwards into a lower capitalized value for
land or for the exploration rights. Only units at the margin
will be squeezed out, leaving intramarginal ones still operating.
A discriminating monopolist will recognize this and will attempt
to extract some of this economic rent.

In the absence of any regulatory distortions,then, such as
statutory rates on export and feed grains, one would expect any
divergence between freight rates and costs to be greater for raw
materials than for processed products, rather than the reverse
as is alleged. This is the first case then where the theoretical
prediction is at variance with the western position.

The same basic point applies to the claim that manufactured
goods move more cheaply from east to west than vice versa.
The elasticity of demand for western manufactured products in
eastern and world markets is likely very high given the easy
availability of substitutes. In addition,the marginal nature of
most western manufacturing industries suggests there would be
little room to absorb transport charges at the producer's end.
Thus if the traffic is to move at all,the railways would have
to provide relatively lower rates, not higher ones,as is advocated.

Commodities shipped east to west would likely be put into two
separate categories by railways. Manufactured goods not produced
in the West would move at quite high rates, given the relatively
inelastic demand for them in the region due to the absence of
easily available substitutes. Thus western prices of these products
would be higher than under a cost of service freight rate system.
For commodities that are produced locally,the railway would have
to compare the relative competitiveness of eastern and western
firms. Goods where the East had an apparently strong competitive
advantage could move at relatively high rates and still compete
in the West with western products, while for the more footloose
type of products, the reverse is true. In general, though, one
would expect the average rate on manufactured products to be
higher from east to west, and not vice versa, as is argued.

The presence of long-, short-haul discrimination is,in fact,an
example of the application of the above principles by the railroads. Rates are higher to the Prairies than to B.C. for some
commodities because of the absence in the former region of competing suppliers able to produce these products within the region
or land them there cheaply by competing modes. The alternative to
high-priced Ontario steel in B.C. is Japanese products landed by sea.
In the Prairies the local producers cannot offer the quantities
and varieties necessary, so it must be shipped in by rail regardless. The same is true for canned goods, with the B.C. alternatives
being ocean shipments of Australian and California products.

A COMPARISON OF FREIGHT RATES BY REGION

The actual pattern of freight charges can be seen by examining the Waybill publications published by the Canadian Transport Commission (CTC).[22]   Table 1 gives a matrix of revenue per ton-mile earned by the railroads for each of the five rate classes by region. The first category, class rates, is an effective ceiling rate for any good moving anywhere in Canada. In 1976 only 0.46 per cent of the total ton-miles moved came under this rate. Commodity non-competitive rates, or normal rates as the railways prefer to call them, cover cases where the railroad is the only feasible shipper but where the rate must be set so as to allow the commodity to compete in Canadian and world markets. Commodity competing rates are ones set in competition with other potential carriers. Agreed charges are an explicit contractual arrangement between the carriers and the shippers whereby a fixed rate is given in exchange for a specified volume of traffic moved during the contract period. Statutory grain rates are the ones from the 1925 agreement covering maximum rates on export grains.

Even at this very broad level of aggregation there are several interesting observations to be made. In the first place, the over-all incidence of freight rates on the western economies is apparently relatively low. In 1976, some 36.75 per cent of originating traffic from the West was statutory grain (Table 2) which moved at the very low rate of 0.50 cents per ton-mile. Another 33.34 per cent moved in the commodity non-competing class, at rates which are among the lowest of the entire table. Thus about 70 per cent of all traffic shipped from the western region is moved at the lowest rate categories. Assuming as is likely that the transport costs are borne by the producers in these cases, this seems to indicate that there is no large burden on these incomes.

It must be stressed, though, that this does not demonstrate that there is no discriminatory pricing being practiced on these com-modities. The rate on statutory grains is well below even average variable costs, as the Snavely Commission has recently shown.[23] But in the commodity non-competing class it could be that unit costs are unusually low and that even the low rates per ton-mile shown are in excess of what a true cost of service rate would be. Given that this category involves such things as unit coal trains, and that the average distances travelled by western products are greater, it is quite possible that costs are in fact lower. What Table 1 does indicate then is how much lower these costs would have to be for the thesis to be correct. It also demonstrates that for the bulk of the commodities moving out of the Prairies the average freight rate for non-competing commodities is well below that charged on the movement of all other commodities in Canada.

A second feature is that the rates on western products shipped under the commodity non-competing category are the lowest of all the groupings for each of the three destinations, excluding statu-

tory grains as a special case. This is the case in spite of the
fact that the average distance travelled is less in two of the
routes and only slightly higher for internal movements. This
illustrates the danger of regarding these as non-competitive and
of suggesting that the lack of a competing mode of traffic
necessarily implies excessive charges by the railroads. Carriers
have apparently responded to the competition faced by these
products in external markets by providing rates that are low in
comparison with traffic moving under supposedly more competitive
categories. Again, though, the point has to be stressed that in the
absence of good cost information, it cannot be concluded that
these rates are not in excess of total costs incurred in moving
the products. The data only illustrate that the magnitude of the
cost differential between products moving under this classification
and those under other ones would have to be substantial for this
to be true.[24]

Some further interesting patterns emerge from a look at specific geographical pairings. The commodity competing group[25]
includes most of the manufactured products shipped by rail.
Within this category eastern internal shipments move at cheaper
rates than western ones in spite of shorter average hauls, which
is consistent with the relative lack of intermodal competition in
the latter region. But when the east-to-west rates are compared with
the west to east ones the pattern is reversed. Western producers
of products shipped under this classification apparently have
access to eastern markets at rates lower than their eastern counterparts do to markets in the West. This is consistent with the theoretical analysis above, but runs exactly counter to the stated
Prairie position. The assertion is strengthened by the fact that
the east-to-west rate is higher than the west-to-east one in all
four categories reported, with the average hauls about equal in
all cases. The comparative figures for agreed charges are especially interesting since it is often argued that the much larger
size and influence of eastern industries allows them to negotiate
better rates with the carriers. In this respect too, it is interesting to note that the average revenue per ton-mile from agreed
charges within regions is lowest in the West, although the much
longer average length of haul probably accounts for this.

The conclusions to this point though are subject to qualifica-
tion as noted, because of the very high level of aggregation and the
absence of any specific reference to costs. It is possible to
circumvent the former problem somewhat by looking at a second set
of commodity flow data published by the CTC.[26] Data for province-
by-province flows for seven basic commodity groups are summarized
in Tables 3 through 7. The commodity group of most interest in
light of western concerns is manufacturing and miscellaneous. The
lowest rates for originating manufactured goods are those shipped
from the four western provinces, with those from the Maritimes
following closely, and the rates from Quebec and Ontario being
substantially higher. On the other hand, the rates on manufactured
goods coming into the three Prairie provinces are substantially higher

than those for Quebec, Ontario, and B.C. The Prairies thus appear to
get relatively favourable rates on manufactured goods they export but
residents pay disproportionately higher rates and thus prices on
processed imported goods. Again this is consistent both with what
was expected on theoretical grounds and with the conclusions drawn
from the aggregate data above but it runs counter to one of the main
western freight rate grievances.

The situation as regards raw material movements is mixed.
The rates on products of forests tend to be a little higher for
the three prairie provinces, both in and out. The other products
vary substantially, with some of the western figures being lower
than the Ontario and Quebec ones and others higher. Even within
the Prairies there is considerable variation. There is no obvious
tendency for rates on raw materials to be consistently lower than
those on manufactured products. But this needs to be checked
further at a greater level of disaggregation and with some
attempt to account for cost differentials.

A final step at this level of aggregation is to look at
specific province-to-province flows. Table 5 gives the revenue
per ton-mile for shipments within each of the provinces. The
rates for manufactured goods for the three prairie jurisdictions
are at or slightly below that for Ontario, and slightly above that
for Quebec. Apparently there is sufficient truck competition for
these shorter hauls of higher-valued products. Again, the charges
on forest products are a little higher relative to those for
Ontario and Quebec, with the others exhibiting great variation.

Tables 6 and 7 give the average revenue per ton-mile earned
on flows between the three Prairie provinces and Ontario and Quebec
respectively. Once more it will be noted that the rates on manufactured goods from any of the three provinces are substantially
less than those for products moving in the reverse direction. In
many cases they are less than half those on products coming in.
Even further, the fee per ton-mile is less for all three provinces
on shipments into Ontario (Quebec) than it is from Quebec (Ontario).
They also have a substantial advantage over the two central Canadian provinces when it comes to shipments into the Maritimes. In
the last two cases, though, part of the difference is undoubtedly
due to the longer average haul. Once again there is a possibility
that the degree of aggregation is too large, camouflaging the
commodity mix, and that there are substantial cost differences
involved in carrying the different types of processed products.
But as stated above, these differences would have to be substantial
to offset the figures shown in these tables.

It is possible to take the analysis to an even greater degree
of commodity disaggregation although it means reverting back to
the three geographical zones. The Waybill publication underlying
Table 1 gives freight rate data on a great number of commodity
movements among the three zones. Of these, 60 specific commodities

are reported as having moved both east to west and west to east in 1976.   Table 8 reports that only 19, or less than one third, had rates per ton-mile greater from west to east than vice versa. Even more interesting,though,is the distribution over the main commodity groups.   Nearly all of the raw materials are more expensive to move east.   In the cases of fabricated materials and end products however, the proportions are much lower. Even at this quite detailed level of disaggregation then, there is still no convincing evidence that there is a freight rate per ton-mile disadvantage facing western-based processing industries.

As a final disaggregation, unpublished data on province-by-province flows of the 69 commodities comprising the seven main groups in Tables 3-7 were obtained from the Traffic and Tariffs Branch of the CTC.   With this data, it was possible to compare rates on shipments between each of the three provinces and Quebec and Ontario.   There were seven manufactured goods that moved both ways between Alberta and Ontario, and four between Alberta and Quebec.   In every case, the rate was lower on the west-to-east haul, often significantly so.   The same was true for Saskatchewan for all five of the two-way movements.   There were 13 such pairings for Manitoba, of which only one exhibited a higher west-to-east rate.   The above conclusions apparently survive even this level of disaggregation.

The few studies that have been done on individual commodities can be consulted as yet another check on the conclusions that have emerged from the above data.   One such effort is the attempt by Gainer, Drugge and Knowles to assess the impact of transport rates on the competitive advantage of Edmonton industrial chemical firms.[27]   Their objectives were to determine whether these charges acted as a barrier to marketing primary outputs or further processed ones and whether there was a differential in rates on raw versus processed petrochemical products such as to prevent integrated operations in western Canada.   For primary products they found the rates obtained by the industry in Edmonton to be "relatively favourable."   With one exception the charges (cents/cwt) on products eastbound were significantly less than both those on the same products west-bound and the equivalent U.S. rate. For processed products of polyethylene and cellulose acetate, "... the rates obtainable by Edmonton based firms are favourable compared with west-bound Canadian rates, and are even more favourable when compared with U.S. rates." For further processing of the basic petrochemical products into final products they find that other location factors such as low-cost labour, market access and uniform pricing across the country dominate any transportation effect. At this very specific commodity level then, and for products that are among the most obvious ones for western industrialization to be based on, it must be concluded that there is no support for the thesis that discriminatory freight rates are preventing or stunting the development.

The two cases most often cited to back the contention that
freight rate structure promotes the export of raw materials
rather than finished products are rapeseed versus rapeseed products
and feedgrains versus meat products. In both cases, there is a
distortion due to the low statutory rates applicable to grain
whereas the processed products must pay a more normal, higher one.
Popular discussions of the cases, however, make it appear that these
differential charges actually result in a movement of rapeseed to
central Canada for crushing there, or a shipment of western feed
grains to eastern feedlots. In both cases, the actual market
situation is much more complex.

There is no eastward movement of rapeseed as it cannot compete with soybeans produced in Ontario and Quebec or imported
(duty free) from the U.S.[28] Instead, the grain is either purchased
locally by the crushing plants or exported via Vancouver.
Rapeseed oil and meal however are delivered to Central Canada in
competition with soyoil and soybean meal. The farm price for rapeseed then is the Vancouver export price (set by the Winnipeg
Commodity Exchange futures price which is in turn set in relation
to the market for soybean futures in Chicago) less the statutory
grain rates and handling charges. The plant price for oil and
meal on the other hand is the Ontario and Quebec price (set in
competition with the prices of soyoil and soybean meal which in
turn are set with reference to the Chicago futures market) less
normal freight and other charges. The essence of the problem, then,
is that the low statutory rates on rapeseed exports through
Vancouver are responsible for an artificially high price for
rapeseed on the Prairies. But it must be noted that even without
this distortion, the different distances shipped for rapeseed as
opposed to its products would ensure that transportation factors
weighed more heavily on the latter industry.

A removal of the statutory rates on the movement of rapeseed
to Vancouver would reduce the farm-gate price of the grain by an
equivalent amount. This would reduce input costs to western
crushing plants, allowing them either to increase their profits in
existing output or to reduce the prices of oil and meal and thereby
increase their ability to compete with soybean products in eastern
Canada. A careful study of this particular market would have to be
made before it could be determined which of the above reactions
would dominate. It is quite possible that some expansion of rape
crushing capacity in western Canada would result and, in this sense,
the claims that freight rate distortions prejudice industrial
development are likely valid.

It must be noted, however, that this gain would come at the
expense of rapeseed growers. They could offset the potential
income loss to some extent by switching to other crops, but they
would necessarily be worse off in the final analysis. Since the

production of rapeseed is concentrated in certain areas of the
Prairies the loss would not even be spread over the farm sector
generally; instead it would be borne by an identifiable, small
subset of the population. This trade-off relationship must be
kept firmly in mind, then, when changes of this sort are proposed.
The same result could be achieved by reducing the rate on the movement of finished products to a level comparable with the statutory
one, of course. But advocating this, while understandable, would
be equivalent to asking for an additional subsidy (since no one
has argued that the eastbound rates on oil and meal exceed costs)
rather than complaining about an extant distortion.

The feed grains dispute is of a similar nature.[29] Eastern
feed-lots use corn rather than grain as a basic input, so it is
not the case that the Feed Grains Assistance Act is diverting
western feed to the East instead of beef.[30] Rather, the western
meatpacker has to compete with his eastern counterpart on the
basis of landed price, recognizing that the products are not
perfect substitutes. Western feed grains are shipped east, though,
to feed hogs and poultry, a trade made possible by the subsidy
given to the movement of this grain. This market opportunity
thereby raises the farm price of feed grains beyond what it would
be under more normal rates, which in turn increases the operating
costs of western feedlots. Removal of the freight subsidy[31]
would lower these input prices by an equivalent amount, again
implying higher profits and/or lower prices for western products
in the East, and thus an expansion of their market share.

As with the rapeseed crushing dispute then, there is reason
to believe that these distortions in the freight rate structure
may be hindering the development of the meatpacking industry in
the West by an undetermined amount. But again, a removal of the
distortion implies lower incomes for those farmers producing these
products. The trade-off is largely an internal one within the
region, rather than between regions, as is sometimes alleged.

The special study commissioned to assess the impacts of the
two freight rate proposals put forth by Alberta and Manitoba came
to much the same conclusions as have been drawn from the data and
literature surveyed here.[32] The authors took a sample of important
goods-producing industries and asked what the impact would be of
replacing extant freight charges on inputs and outputs with those
implied by both the EPP and DRL cost of service schemes. The conclusion is worth quoting.[33]

> Under both EPP and DRL there is no apparent consistent
> net benefit pattern favouring any particular region. As
> a consequence, there are, in the final analysis, no sig-
> nificant regional differences. If anything, there is a
> tendency to benefit regions on the basis of the existing
> degree of concentration of particular industries which,
> in the short run, reinforces the status quo.

The results to this point do not support the main western contentions regarding the discriminatory impacts of the present freight rate system. The general incidence of rates is low on goods exported from the Prairies, suggesting they do not bear an unusually large portion of railway fixed costs. There is no obvious bias in export rates on raw versus semi-processed or processed products, except in the cases of rapeseed and feedgrains, and only here because of statutory rates that favour western farmers. Finally, charges on manufactured goods are higher on regional imports than on exports, implying relatively good access for western producers to eastern markets and a form of natural protection for industries servicing the local market. These conclusions were the ones predicted by the theoretical analysis developed at the beginning of the section and were not rejected at any of the various disaggregations employed in the discussion.

A SIMPLE STATISTICAL MODEL OF RAILWAY PRICING

In each of the above cases, the simple average revenue per ton-mile figures were used, with only casual attempts to allow for possible cost differences among commodities shipped or regions served. The above results would naturally be more convincing if the variation in freight rates due to cost factors could be separated out more rigorously. To this end an equation of the form[34]

1) $\log R = a + b \log D + c \log W + d \log N + e$

was estimated using the commodity flow data underlying Tables 3 to 7. R is the reported revenue per ton-mile for any commodity shipped from one province to another; D is the average distance travelled; W is the average weight per car; N is the number of carloads and e is the residual or error term. The regression was run for all commodity movements grouped together, and then separately for each of the classes reported in the earlier tables. Statutory grains are omitted in each instance, of course.

These variables are an admittedly crude attempt to proxy railway operating costs. Rates per ton-mile should drop as average haul increases because of terminal charges. But for longer hauls, trucking is less competitive, so the railroads might have some leeway here to increase rates above costs. Again, heavier cars should move more cheaply. But this could also be a proxy for the high-bulk, low-value traffic on which railroads have a natural monopoly. The number of cars is meant to be a proxy for the presence of any kind of specialized handling or loading facilities that might reduce terminal costs. It might have been useful to be able to account for any specialized equipment such as refrigerator cars, but the data were not available, nor would they be very meaningful with the level of aggregation employed here.

Three dummy variables were developed in an attempt to test

for the presence and direction of bias in the pricing of western products. DT in Table 9 takes a value of 1 for commodities moved into Manitoba, Saskatchewan or Alberta and 0 otherwise. DF is the same for commodities shipped from the region to other provinces, while DI represents commodities moving within the Prairies. A non-zero value for any of these dummies would mean that the freight rate per ton-mile on the product in question was significantly different from that prevailing in the rest of the country, after allowing for any cost differences due to length of haul, average car weight and number of cars.

The coefficient for length of haul is always negative and highly significant. If there is any discriminatory pricing in long-haul shipments it is swamped by the cost saving due to the spread of terminal costs over longer distances. Heavier cars also move at cheaper rates per ton-mile, so the same comment applies here. The number of carloads has a slight negative effect on average rates, if anything at all. The dummy variables are of special interest though. For all traffic grouped together, there is a statistically significant extra charge added to commodities moving into the Prairies, but none on goods exported or moving internally. This is consistent with the theoretical and empirical results obtained above.

There are some interesting variations over commodities. Agricultural and mineral products, live animals, and piggyback apparently are carried into the Prairies at rates not significantly different from those for the country as a whole, once cost factors are accounted for. Forest products and especially manufactured goods on the other hand move in at a premium rate. As expected then it is on the shipment of high-value processed products into the West that the railroads are charging relatively high rates. In terms of shipments out of the region, products of mines, piggyback and most notably manufactured goods are not priced differently from that for the country as a whole. In other words, there is no evidence that processed exports from the three prairie provinces are treated differently in any way from other similar shipments in other parts of the nation, once these three cost factors are held constant. There is typically a lower rate for agricultural and forestry products and a higher one for live animals. For internal movements the dummies for agricultural products and mining products are not different from zero. Forest products and piggyback move slightly cheaper apparently, while live animals and manufactured products attract a surcharge.

These statistical results should not be treated as anything other than the crude tests they are. There is first of all the ambiguity surrounding the appropriateness of the cost proxies used as discussed above. In addition, the independent variables have a considerable range of variation, leading one to suspect heteroskedasticity and thus inefficient estimates. But the conclusions they suggest are consistent with both the theoretical predictions and the earlier empirical efforts. Together then, these investigations imply that the western claims about the bias in the structure of freight rates are misinformed. There is a regional burden evident, but it takes the form of relatively high rates on manufactured goods brought into the region, leading to higher prices for consumers and hence lower real incomes. Neither of the general allegations about the distorting effect of rates on raw materials versus processing activities in the West appears to be valid, statutory grain rates excepted.

CONCLUSION

Two principle conclusions emerge from the above discussion. The first is that the real income generated and retained within the West from the existing resource base is significantly reduced by federal economic policies. This is most obvious in the case of energy taxes and to a much lesser extent by the tariffs and inflated freight rates on incoming goods. It is important to note here though that the loss on energy exports has only existed since 1973, that there was a net subsidy of the industry before this under the National Oil Policy, and that the current transfer will end when Canadian oil prices reach world levels. The second is that there is no apparent evidence that the industrial structure of the region is significantly adversely affected by the current mix of federal policies, railway freight rates included. The possible exceptions to this - rapeseed crushing and meat packing- contain a large element of intraregional income redistribution within them, making it difficult to judge them unambiguously. These two conclusions together, then, imply that under the more neutral policy environment that is often envisaged by western spokesmen the region would almost certainly remain a resource hinterland, albeit a wealthier one. This statement applies most directly to Alberta and least to Manitoba, since the latter province has the bulk of tariff-protected Prairie manufacturing and bears none of the energy-tax burden.

The obvious question then is what position the western provinces should take in their negotiations with the federal government. One strategy would be to demand to be left alone as far as is possible. The federal government would end its discriminatory taxation of western resource industries and turn over its regulatory powers to the provinces. They would thereby have the maximum possible latitude to nurture and structure their own economic development. This is the option favoured by Alberta for obvious reasons, but it has its adherents in Saskatchewan as well. It is, however, much more optimistic about the chances of promoting an eventual self-sustaining industrial sector than the above analysis would suggest.

An alternative would be for the West to acknowledge that it faces a natural disadvantage as regards attracting secondary industry, for the federal government to accept the legitimacy of western economic goals in this regard, and for the two to then attempt to come up with mutually satisfactory policies. The justification for such an approach could be developed along the following lines. Canadian regions, or provinces, are and always have been legitimate political entities in their own right. This is obvious and generally accepted in the case of Quebec, but it is just as valid for the other groupings as well. Accordingly, a resident of any region has the right to expect a standard of living as high and as stable as that in any other area. Some parts of the country, such as the industrial heartland of Central Canada, are naturally favoured in these respects. But others are not, meaning that the federal government has a duty to develop economic policies to help offset these natural disadvantages as far as possible. To date however, and for a variety of reasons, the federal government has been unwilling to accept this responsibility. Regional dissatisfaction in this case would be directed against the lack of any significant positive action by Ottawa.

Many of the western grievances are already in this form in fact. The belief in the right to keep the Statutory Grain Rates, or to be compensated if they are removed in the interests of increasing railway efficiency, is one example of this. Another is the demand for preferential treatment by the Export Development Agency or on western bids for federal contracts. Subsidized grain rates are viewed as the result of a basic political understanding at the time of prairie settlement, one that is as inviolable as language rights in Quebec. The other example plainly recognizes that distance creates a natural disadvantage and, in effect, asks that this be ignored.

Future western efforts would first be devoted to formulating economic development goals and demonstrating that they have the support of the provinces' populations. Then they would have to convince the federal government and the rest of the country of their right to the kinds of concessions that will be needed to overcome their natural economic disadvantages in the industrial sphere. These arguments could be based on historical or political grounds, on the infant industry thesis in the case of some Alberta sectors perhaps, or simply through exercising bargaining power.[34] In this way at least, the fact and political basis of province building[35] will be discussed and debated both within and among the various regions, something that has not occurred formally to date. Like Quebec, each region will have to decide whether the existing institutional arrangements or some variation of them are sufficient to achieve their goals. As in the Quebec case too, the other regions will at the same time have to determine whether the conditions demanded are worth it.

FOOTNOTES

1.   See for example the recent contribution by D. Usher "The English Response to the Prospect of the Separation of Quebec" Canadian Public Policy IV:1 (Winter, 1978) 57-70 and the comments by D.L. Emerson and D. Latouche immediately following.

2.   The present paper will consider the three provinces of Manitoba, Saskatchewan and Alberta only. While British Columbia is sometimes included as part of the same region, most notably at the Western Economic Opportunities Conference in 1973, many of the issues to be dealt with below affect BC somewhat differently. Discussing this province specifically in each instance would have increased the paper beyond its permissible length.

3.   In addition to the present volume see W.J. Blackman "A Western Canadian Perspective on the Economics of Confederation" Canadian Public Policy III: 4 (Autumn, 1977) 414-430, and K.H. Norrie "Natural Resources; Economic Development and Canada-US Relations: A Western Canadian Perspective" forthcoming in C.D. Howe Institute Natural Resources and Canada-US Relations. In current policy symposiums the Quebec and Western views are usually requested. One cynical inference is that this leaves the Ontario point of view as being equated with the federal one, and the Maritimes ignored completely.

4.   For a summary discussion of the western positions see Western Premiers "Capital Financing and Regional Financial Institutions", "Transportation", "Agriculture" and "Industrial Development Opportunities" (Submissions to the Western Economic Opportunity Conference, Calgary, July 24-26, 1973).

5.   This argument is developed at greater length in K.H. Norrie "Natural Resource, Economic Development..."

6.   The official western position is given in Western Premiers "Capital Financing and Regional Financial Institutions". Typical western academic statements to this effect can be found in W.J. Blackman "A Western Canadian Perspective...." or D.J. Bercuson "Canada's Burden of Unity: An Introduction" in D.J. Bercuson (ed.) Canada and the Burden of Unity (Toronto, 1977). 1-18. See also D.V. Smiley "The Political Context of Resource Development in Canada" in A. Scott (ed.) Natural Resource Revenues: A Test of Federalism (Vancouver, 1976) 61-72.

7.   K.H. Norrie "Some Comments on Prairie Economic Alienation" Canadian Public Policy II:2 (Spring, 1976) 211-224.

8.   See J.H. Dales "Introduction to the Carleton Library Edition" of W.A. Mackintosh The Economic Background of Dominion-Provincial Relations (Toronto, 1964) 6.

9.   W.A. Mackintosh The Economic Background.

10.   See T.L. Powrie "Regional Effects of the Canadian Tariff" (Unpublished paper, University of Alberta, 1967); H.M. Pinchin "The Regional Impact of the Canadian Tariff (Economic Council of Canada Background Paper, Ottawa, 1977); Ontario Treasury "Interprovincial Trade Flows, Employment, and the Tariff in Canada" (Supplementary Material to the 1977 Ontario Budget) as well as the contributions by T. Hazledine and L. Auer in the present volume.

11.   See B.W. Wilkinson and K. Norrie Effective Protection and the Return to Capital (Economic Council of Canada Special Study, 1975).

12.   M.J. Hollinshead and W. Blackman "The Cost of Confederation: An Analysis of Costs to Alberta" Part II (Independent Alberta Association, 1975).

13.   See M. Leitch "The Constitutional Position of Natural Resources" and Premier Allan Blakeney "Resources, the Constitution and Canadian Federalism" both in J. Peter Meekison (ed.) Canadian Federalism: Myth or Reality (Toronto, 1977) 170-178 and 179-187.

14.   A. Scott "Who Should Get Natural Resource Revenues?" in A. Scott (ed) Natural Resource Revenues.... 1-51.

15.   J. Helliwell "Overlapping Federal and Provincial Claims on Mineral Revenues" in M. Crommelin and A.R. Thompson (eds.) Mineral Leasing as an Instrument of Public Policy (Vancouver, 1977) 182-199.

16.   Available on request from the Economic Council of Canada, tables in unpublished mimeograph of A. Glynn.

17.   A similar calculation done for the years prior to 1973 would show a net gain for Alberta and Saskatchewan of course, since the National Oil Policy acted to raise prices in Ontario above the landed price of offshore crude.

18.   M.A. Fuss "The Demand for Energy in Canadian Manufacturing" Journal of Econometrics 5 (1977) 89-116 and M. Denny, J.D. May and C. Pinto "The demand for Energy in Canadian Manufacturing: Prologue to an Energy Policy" Canadian Journal of Economics 11, No. 2 (May, 1978) 300-313.

19.   See for example W.D. Gainer and T.L. Powrie "Public Revenue From Canadian Crude Petroleum Production" Canadian Public Policy I: 1 (Winter, 1975) 1-12 where it is argued "... that the federal share of provincial resource revenues should be the same as it would be if those revenues accrued to the private sector and were taxed accordingly". The sudden and large accrual of these revenues by Alberta has created havoc with the old equalization payments

formula. See T.J. Courchene "Equalization Payments and Energy Royalties" in A. Scott (ed.) <u>Natural Resource Revenues</u>.... 73-107 for a discussion of this.

20. Transport Research and Development Division, Department of Industry and Commerce, Government of Alberta "The Equitable Pricing Policy: A New Method of Railway Rate Making" (Edmonton, 1973).

21. Government of Manitoba "Destination Rate Principle" (no date).

22. Canadian Transport Commission <u>Waybill Analysis: Carload All-Rail Traffic</u>

23. The Commission on the Costs of Transporting Grain by Rail <u>Report Volume</u> 1 (October, 1976).

24. If the railroads were making a large profit on these rates they must be losing on some of the other ones, given the relatively low rate of return to railway operations. This would imply that the costs of these other movements were higher than the rates shown, making the implied cost differential even greater than what first appears.

25. CN and CP Rail Railway <u>Freight Rates: A Source Handbook</u>.

26. Canadian Transport Commission <u>Commodity Flow Analysis: Canadian Carload All-Rail Traffic</u>

27. W.D. Gainer, S.E. Drugge and R.A. Knowles "Economic Analysis of the Effects of Transport Rates on Products of the Industrial Chemical and Meatpacking Industry With Special Reference to Edmonton" (University of Alberta, June, 1973).

28. P.R. Perkins "An Economic Review of Western Canada's Rapeseed Processing Industry" (November, 1976) provides extensive discussion of the rapeseed case.

29. See J. Heads "Transportation Factors and the Canadian Livestock and Meat Industries" in R.M.A. Lyons and E.W. Trychniewicz (eds.) <u>Freight Rates and the Marketing of Canadian Agricultural Products</u> (Occasional Series No. 8, Department of Agricultural Economics and Farm Management, University of Manitoba, 1977) 81-94.

30. Heads ("Transportation Factors....") argues that freight rates appear to have little impact on the location of cattle production and slaughtering. Freight charges from West to East are greatest for a feeder steer plus the grain to feed it, next highest for a slaughter steer, and cheapest for sending a beef carcass and by-products. He has no explanation for the large shipments of feeder steers from Western Canada though.

31. Much of the previous subsidy has already been removed in the changes to the Feed Freight Assistance Programme that came into effect in August, 1976. Rates of assistance to Ontario and western Quebec of less than $6 per ton were removed, and subsidy rates to BC reduced by $4 per ton (Heads "Transportation Factors....").

32. P.S. Ross and Partners et.al. "Two Proposals For Rail Freight Pricing: Assessment of Their Prospective Impact" (A Report to the Federal-Provincial Committee on Western Transportation, 1974).

33. Ibid., p. 5-37.

34. See John Heads "Allegations of Rail Freight Rate Disparities in the Canadian Prairie Provinces Since the 1967 National Trans-portation Act" Transportation Research Forum 197   379-386 and T.D. Heaver and T.M. Oum "A Statistical Analysis of the Canadian Railway Rate Structure" Transportation Research Forum 197   571-578 for similar statistical exercises. The results obtained in both these studies are consistent with the ones reported here.

35. As an example, it is not at all unreasonable to demand con-cessions on freight rates in return for agreeing to hold oil and gas prices below world levels. This is especially true of the recent federal proposal to postpone an already-agreed-to price increase for oil in January, 1979 and to change the natural gas pricing agreement.

36. See J. Evenson and R. Simeon "The Roots of Discontent" (mimeo-graphed, Institute for Intergovernmental Relations, Queen's Univer-sity, May, 1978) for a discussion of province building.

TABLE 1

Average Revenue Per Ton-Mile by Rate Category and by Region, 1976
(Cents)

	Class Rates	Commodity Non-Competing	Commodity Competing	Agreed Charges	Statutory Grain
Maritimes to Maritimes	9.69	4.02	3.93	5.23	–
East to East	20.68	2.87	2.79	3.15	–
West to West	10.01	1.81	3.13	3.10	0.50
East to Maritimes	6.74	1.80	2.66	3.97	–
Maritimes to East	4.68	2.50	2.20	2.38	–
Maritimes to West	7.88	1.28	2.06	3.51	–
West to Maritimes	–	1.58	2.25	2.95	–
East to West	11.30	2.13	3.23	4.01	–
West to East	10.57	1.83	2.32	2.69	–

Source   Canadian Transport Commission Waybill Analysis:
Carload All-Rail Traffic 1976

TABLE 2

Percentage Distribution of Ton-Miles Originating in Western
Region, by Destination and Rate Group, 1976

(Per cent)

West to	Class Rates	Commodity Non-Competing	Commodity Competing	Agreed Charges	Statutory Grain
Maritimes	–	0.29	1.41	0.19	–
East	0.02	2.46	13.91	1.41	–
West	0.04	30.59	11.16	1.76	36.75
Total	0.06	33.34	26.48	3.36	36.75

Source As for Table 1.

TABLE 3

Average Revenue Per Ton-Mile by Commodity Group for Originating Traffic, 1976

(Cents)

	Statutory Grain	Products of Agriculture	Animals and Products	Products of Mines	Products of Forests	Manufacturing and Misc.	Piggy-Back
Maritimes	-	3.05	2.26	2.66	4.25	3.08	3.48
Quebec	-	3.28	2.51	2.27	2.19	3.46	3.87
Ontario	1.30	1.58	4.56	2.27	2.62	3.98	3.54
Manitoba	0.64	1.89	5.27	2.29	2.78	2.88	2.59
Saskatchewan	0.48	2.24	6.12	1.46	3.57	2.10	2.66
Alberta	0.49	1.90	4.56	1.41	2.44	2.80	2.29
BC	1.15	4.19	5.74	1.36	2.26	2.79	2.58

Source   Canadian Transport Commission Commodity Flow Analysis: Canadian Carload All-Rail Traffic 1976

TABLE 4

Average Revenue Per Ton-Mile by Commodity Group by Destination, 1976

(Cents)

	Statutory Grains	Products of Agriculture	Animals and Products	Products of Mines	Products of Forests	Manufacturing and Misc.	Piggy-back
Maritimes	1.07	1.12	4.88	2.71	2.78	3.94	5.90
Quebec	1.31	2.27	4.59	1.83	2.03	3.19	2.99
Ontario	0.50	2.98	5.84	2.20	2.10	2.80	2.61
Manitoba	0.47	2.97	4.51	2.73	2.75	3.87	2.98
Saskatchewan	–	3.33	4.27	2.16	3.16	4.09	3.82
Alberta	–	3.76	5.07	1.60	2.88	4.00	3.30
BC	0.48	2.16	2.57	1.32	2.97	2.96	3.20

Source As for Table 3.

TABLE 5

Average Revenue Per Ton-Mile by Commodity Group for Traffic Within Region, 1976

(Cents)

	Statutory Grain	Products of Agriculture	Animals and Products	Products of Mines	Products of Forests	Manufacturing and Misc.	Piggy-back
Maritimes	—	6.05	10.30	3.29	4.32	4.10	10.28
Quebec	—	6.02	4.55	3.08	2.21	3.39	6.55
Ontario	1.45	5.24	10.39	2.57	2.60	3.98	2.84
Manitoba	0.51	6.03	6.13	3.47	2.71	3.90	4.73
Saskatchewan	—	3.77	8.94	3.22	4.73	3.77	4.63
Alberta	—	4.45	6.58	2.96	3.12	3.76	4.75
BC	1.35	6.24	3.86	1.37	2.97	2.87	3.20

Source   As for Table 3.

TABLE 6

Average Revenue Per Ton-Mile by Commodity Group for Flows Between Prairies and Ontario, 1976

(Cents)

	Statutory Grains	Products of Agriculture	Animals and Products	Products of Mines	Products of Forests	Manufacturing and Misc.	Piggy-back
Ontario to Manitoba	—	4.60	4.31	2.44	4.07	4.22	3.00
Manitoba to Ontario	0.61	2.32	6.56	2.43	2.30	2.30	2.23
Ontario to Sask.	—	4.77	4.70	2.12	4.83	4.62	4.01
Sask. to Ontario	0.48	2.13	7.26	2.04	2.31	2.03	2.34
Ontario to Alberta	—	4.79	5.39	1.44	3.00	4.17	3.30
Alberta to Ontario	0.42	1.66	5.62	1.37	2.32	2.23	2.08
Quebec to Ontario	—	8.02	4.68	2.03	1.88	2.78	4.67
Maritimes to Ontario	—	2.04	1.75	2.67	2.96	2.16	2.42

Source As for Table 3

TABLE 7

Average Revenue Per Ton-Mile by Commodity Group for Flows Between Prairies and Quebec, 1976

(Cents)

	Statutory Grain	Products of Agriculture	Animals and Products	Products of Mines	Products of Forests	Manufacturing and Misc.	Piggy-back
Quebec to Manitoba	-	3.90	4.07	2.81	4.06	4.40	3.19
Manitoba to Quebec	1.50	1.52	4.72	1.30	2.11	1.81	2.21
Quebec to Sask.	-	4.32	-	1.54	3.28	3.93	4.39
Sask. to Quebec	1.27	1.03	4.89	1.83	2.33	1.59	2.01
Quebec to Alberta	-	3.87	3.61	1.19	3.07	3.93	3.56
Alberta to Quebec	1.09	1.03	4.50	1.52	2.12	1.94	2.18
Ontario to Quebec	1.32	2.90	7.47	1.75	2.49	4.05	4.67
Maritimes to Quebec	-	2.30	2.41	1.57	3.44	2.80	3.20

Source As for Table 3

TABLE 8   Norrie   233

Comparison of Average Revenue Per Ton-Mile by Detailed Commodity Group
for Goods Moving Between Eastern and Western Zones, 1976

General Group	Number of Commodities Moving Both Directions	Number for Which Rate West to East Exceeds That East to West
Live Animals	1	1
Food, Feed, Beverages and Tobacco	7	3
Crude Materials, Inedible	5	3
Fabricated Materials, Inedible	23	6
End Products, Inedible	17	3
Special	7	3
Total	60	19

Source As for Table 1.

TABLE 9

Regression Coefficients by Variable and Commodity Group From Equation 1

	Products of Agriculture	Animals and Products	Products of Mines	Products of Forests	Manufacturing and Misc.	Piggy-back	All Commodities
Constant	8.73 (7.27)	5.41 (3.65)	4.60 (8.49)	5.85 (11.38)	4.34 (5.88)	5.23 (7.99)	5.23 (17.65)
D	-0.55 (-7.41)	-0.40 (-3.03)	-0.39 (-8.79)	-0.31 (-11.69)	-0.22 (-4.28)	-0.17 (-2.72)	-0.31 (-10.22)
W	-0.75 (-3.67)	-0.38 (-1.72)	-0.14 (-1.45)	-0.62 (-6.21)	-0.50 (-5.68)	-0.76 (-4.20)	-0.48 (-12.85)
N	-0.17 (-4.17)	-0.04 (-0.53)	-0.11 (-5.69)	-0.06 (-6.35)	0.01 (0.23)	-0.07 (-3.08)	-0.05 (-4.69)
DT	0.01 (0.04)	0.29 (0.57)	-0.01 (-0.08)	0.16 (3.21)	0.22 (3.55)	-0.05 (-0.49)	0.17 (2.73)
DF	-0.42 (3.04)	0.61 (2.43)	0.08 (1.04)	-0.11 (-2.05)	-0.02 (-0.24)	-0.08 (-0.71)	-0.02 (0.28)
DI	-0.12 (-0.82)	0.17 (0.58)	0.03 (0.36)	-0.07 (-1.26)	0.15 (1.85)	-0.25 (-2.02)	-0.02 (-0.38)
R^2	0.81	0.34	0.78	0.86	0.79	0.50	0.52

Figures in brackets are t statistics. All variables except the dummies are natural logs.

Comments by H.C. Eastman, Vice-President, Research Planning,
University of Toronto

Professor Norrie has written an exceptionally clear analysis
of the three economic policies which are thought to impede the
economic growth of the Prairie Provinces. These are the tariff,
the pricing and taxation of natural resources and the structure
of freight rates. I agree with Professor Norrie's position on
these policies but will take this opportunity to make some further
remarks.

There is always a tendency to discuss the tariff as if it
affected regions rather than the income of the owners of particular
factors of production. Professor Norrie, on the other hand, stresses
how the tariff increases the demand for labour and hence either
the wages or the size of the industrial labour force chiefly in
Central Canada. The tariff also depresses the price of agricultural
land by raising the costs of agricultural production. Insofar as
the tariff raises real wages, however, these increased wages are as
beneficial to the West as they are to other parts of the country.
The regional incidence must be due to the larger proportion of
income stemming from land ownership in the West.

Any discussion of regionalism must consider the costs of
adjustment, and Professor Norrie rightly protests against the
"assumption of costless adjustment of factors." However, problems
of adjustment must be addressed within the context of time and change.
There are those who would relate Canadian tariff and freight rate
policies to costs of adjustment by virtue of the great labour
migrations from the Prairies to the industrial centres. Since the
tariff and the structure of freight rates have had an unvarying
effect on the West for the past hundred years, these labour movements
must be related to differential rates of growth in Canada, and they
would probably have occurred over time at any tariff level. Regional
attempts to link the tariff to adjustment costs founder once and
for all upon the fact that tariff removal would cause changes in
the interregional demand for factors and would, in fact, cause costs
of adjustment. These costs would involve increases in the property
income of the assets of owners of natural resources. Arguments
based on costs of adjustment are largely ideological in this context.

Professor Norrie acknowledges that there are no *a priori* rules
for a just distribution of income. Interregional distribution is
acceptable when executed on the basis of individual decisions made
when conditions have been stable and factor movements large. Tariff

and freight rate policies have not changed greatly during the past
century and the men who developed the West made their decisions
about resource ownership within the context of these policies.
Subsequent sales and purchases, many interregional, have been made
within this same context, so Prairie prices and rates of return do
not necessarily differ from those of the East. This provides a
basis for acceptable income distribution.

A major policy change would therefore result in a windfall
gain or loss for the resource owner which would have little to do
with justice. It would have as much political as economic significance.
Sudden major changes in actual or expected income, like the recent
change in the price of oil, are much harder to handle. There is a
temptation to scramble over the rents, and the pressure on established
policies is only resolved by political bargaining. The concept of
justice is ideologically powerful, but difficult to translate into
practical solutions.

Professor Norrie analyses the structure of freight rates from
two points of view, that of the railways which have to make a profit
and that of representative western spokesmen who claim that these
rates have hindered the industrial development of the West. The
search for profit should lead the railways to charge high freight
rates relative to costs for raw materials because such agricultural
and mineral products yield rents to primary factors. They have
relatively low elasticities of supply, and the rents can be transferred
from resource owner to railways in order to cover fixed costs.
Western manufacturing establishments, on the other hand, are marginal
and could not export with high freight rates. Thus, the outbound
freight rates for manufacturers are relatively close to variable
costs. The height of export freight rates for manufacturing would
be less than import rates because inbound high freight rates raise
railway revenues and the high prices are passed on to the prairie
consumer and to the import-competing prairie manufacturer.

The representative prairie spokesmen are not concerned about
the relationship of freight rates to the costs of transporting
different goods but about the effect of these rates on the location
of manufacturing, especially the further processing of western raw
materials. They believe that, in fact, freight rates are low for
raw materials relative to manufactured goods, that this inhibits
the export of finished products, encourages the export of raw materials
and induces manufacturing elsewhere. Is it possible for rational
railway pricing to inhibit Prairie development in this way? Freight
charges on raw materials could be high relative to cost compared to
manufactured goods and still be low relative to rates for manufactured

goods produced from that quantity of raw materials after taking into
account the loss of weight from processing. Thus, it would be
possible to have higher railway profits from the transportation of
raw materials than from the transportation of manufactured goods,
yet still to have locational disadvantages for western processors --
disadvantages that would only be rectified by lower freight rates
on exports of manufactured goods.

Professor Norrie shows that the structure of rates is princi-
pally determined by product competition rather than by intermodal
competition. Therefore, except for statutory rates, there is no
consistent tendency for rates on raw materials to be lower than those
on manufactured goods, which accords with his rational rate model.

Lacking information on the weight loss from the processing of
raw materials, it is impossible to reject or confirm the hypothetical
Western hypothesis. However, the freight rates on raw materials
(except under statutory rates) do not fall far below those on
manufactured goods, and it is therefore unlikely that these rates
are biased against Prairie manufacturing. This work undercuts the
traditional Prairie complaints against the structure of freight rates.
In any case, a policy dilemma follows from the fact that a readjustment
of rates to favour Western manufacturing would adversely affect non-
manufacturing interests immediately and only later, and conjecturally,
improve the position of manufacturing interests.

Professor Norrie's paper confirms that pricing, when unrelated
to costs, can generate internecine quarrels as well as inefficiency.
G.A. Elliott has deplored Canadian distributional policies because
they take a nickel out of each person's pocket and give it to his
neighbour. The redistribution is small, but its costs are high.
Professor Norrie has demonstrated that freight rate structures take
fewer nickels out of western pockets than has been widely supposed.
A greater understanding of such policy-induced distortions will lead
to more rational pricing policies and these in turn might well lead
to a tempering of interregional quarrels, reduced lobbying and greater
efficiency in both production and consumption.

PUBLIC POLICY AND CANADIAN FEDERALISM:

WHAT IS AT STAKE IN CONSTITUTIONAL CHANGE

by

Peter M. Leslie

Department of Political Studies

Queen's University

*I am grateful to Richard Simeon and James de Wilde
for comments on an earlier draft of this essay.

INTRODUCTION

Proposals for a new type of federation in Canada, or for some limited form of economic association between Canada's successor-states, are now the subject of sustained public debate.   Few participants in the debate, however, have seriously attempted to ask themselves: what relationship is there between constitutional forms and the substance of public policy?   Whose interests are at stake in constitutional change, and in what ways?   These questions are the subject of this essay.

WHY THE CONSTITUTION MATTERS, AND TO WHOM

We begin with a survey of opinion on the presumed impact, in terms of public policy, of unspecified changes in the constitution.   For this purpose we employ a six-point "impact scale" that ranks opinion according to the magnitude of anticipated policy consequences if the Canadian federation is restructured or dissolved.   For each point in the scale, we deduce what sort of interests have an apparent stake in the outcome of the constitutional issue.   A description of the points on the impact scale ensues.

Level One -- At the bottom end is the opinion that even after fundamental constitutional change, political processes would churn out very much the same policies as before.   The structural framework in which those processes are acted out is held to be irrelevant to the policy outputs.   In other words, the anticipated policy impact of redesigning the Canadian federation or of "letting Quebec go" would be negligible.

This view may be widespread.   One should beware of drawing inferences on this subject from survey data on a less specific question, but it is nonetheless significant that in January, 1977, some 22 per cent of Canadians thought that if Quebec left Confederation, the consequences for the future of the rest of the country would be "not very serious." (Fletcher, 1977, p.36). It is likely that many people think that the sparring between governments on the constitutional question reflects institu- tional rivalries and personal ambitions, and nothing else.   It is easy, even if logically unwarranted, to extend this supposi- tion and to suggest that the only things at stake in constitu- tional change are the careers and the self-esteem of those who run the machinery of government -- the politicians and bureau- crats.

Level Two -- Next on the scale is a position that still regards the policy impact of constitutional change as negligible, but takes account of possible changes in the costs incurred in running the public sector as its structure is modified.

At the political level, opinion to this effect is implicit in the demand, especially put forward by Ontario, for the "disentanglement" of federal and provincial powers. It is thought irritating and wasteful of resources that the federal and the provincial governments should both be involved in the same policy area. Bureaucrats must spend a lot of time co-ordinating their activities; inefficient programs are implemented because a subsidy is available or because one government's policy options are restricted by policies decreed elsewhere; negative by-products of one government's activities must be neutralized or undone, etc.

There is also an academic literature that treats the costs of government as a function of governmental structure, especially the allocation of functions between jurisdictions. The most elaborate exposition of this idea is contained in a recent book by Albert Breton and Anthony Scott, The Economic Constitution of Federal States (1978). Although Scott (1977, p.262) states that, " ... the permanent assignment of powers and responsibilities to the various levels of governments ... may have a most profound impact on what is actually done," there is much in the book to suggest that the impact of constitutional change will be negligible except in that it may impose or reduce costs, the incidence of which may be difficult to identify. Indeed, the book deals with the distribution of powers within federal (and other) states entirely on the basis of the "organizational costs" incurred in one or another assignment of functions to various levels of government. Interestingly, they do not rely on economies-of-scale considerations in the production of public goods. On the contrary, they reject such considerations (pp. 39-41) because they argue that economies of scale can be achieved irrespective of the size of the consuming unit. Thus, to take an example from Scott (1977), a small state can take advantage of economies of scale in providing defence services by joining a military alliance. In consequence, when economies-of-scale considerations apply, Breton and Scott take account of them by positing that organizational costs will be incurred in minimizing production costs. Organizational costs are subdivided into four categories:

-- administration: setting up the apparatus of government, obtaining information, law enforcement, etc.;

-- co-ordination, as in reaching agreements with other governments to take advantage of economies of scale, and in expending resources in negotiating compensation for spill-over effects of public and private activities from one jurisdiction to another;

-- signalling, or the costs incurred by citizens in making
their preferences known to governments; and,

-- mobility, or the costs incurred by citizens who dislike
the bundle of policies implemented within the jurisdiction
within which they live, and who respond by moving
elsewhere.

The basic proposition expounded in the book is that the assignment of functions to various levels of government in a federal
state approximates that assignment of functions which minimizes
aggregate organizational costs -- those incurred in administration, co-ordination, signalling and mobility.

Breton and Scott must make allowances for differences
between jurisdictions, either in policy outputs or in the costs
of providing public services; otherwise they could not consider
citizens' expenditures on mobility as one type of organizational
cost to be set against administration and so forth.   Apart from
this, however, the whole tenor of their argument rests on the
assumption of undifferentiated policy outputs: how many letters
to the editor, how many protest marches, and so forth -- that is,
how much signalling effort -- is required before the politicians will
supply what is wanted? How many hours meeting-time between officials will be necessary to co-ordinate the policies of different
governments, as if they were made by a central government? How
many hours of bureaucratic time are needed under this assignment
of functions compared with that one, in order to provide a
given level of service?   Asking questions such as these requires
one to discount or ignore changes in policy as the assignment of
governmental functions is (mentally) shifted around.   Except in
the case of mobility costs, only by imagining a standard set of
outputs can one make sense of the organizational-costs type of
argument.

If, then, thinking of the impact of constitutional change in
the terms presented to us by Breton and Scott, we consider whose
interests are at stake in constitutional change, we have virtually
nothing to go on.   We are led to consider an undifferentiated
public interest summed up in least-cost considerations of running
a public sector -- the costs of administration and co-ordination
being borne by taxpayers (and therefore corresponding to the
general incidence of taxation), and the costs of signalling and
mobility probably being borne disproportionately by minorities
who dislike what their governments are doing or find public
services inadequate or too expensive.   If we ask, what is at
stake in constitutional change, the answer must be, "the public
interest -- with a dollar sign."

Level Three -- At one higher level on our "impact scale" is
an opinion that is most commonly found in the speeches of
provincial politicians who favour the selective decentralization
of legislative powers, and who present the consequences of such
a move as entirely benign as far as regions other than their own

are concerned.   This is the view that argues that decentralization permits the differentiation of policy outputs, so
that in the aggregate policy is more sensitive to regional
needs and to the values, moods and preferences of provincial
electorates.   Mathematics is apparently on the side of the
decentralists in this.   Scott (1977, p.268) tells us that
it can be mathematically demonstrated that, " ... if a nation
that is divided among majority and minority parties (or interest
groups) is cut up at random into small territorial jurisdictions,
the total number of citizens who must suffer as minorities from
the policies of majorities will decline; that is, the number
of people who are in agreement with government decisions will
increase."   A negative way of making the same point (in the
Canadian context) is that if Ottawa's powers were reduced, it
would no longer find so many opportunities to impose uniform
policies across the country in the mistaken thought that they
would solve diverse problems; that no longer could Ottawa
respond to an Ontario problem with a policy which would aggravate
a different problem in New Brunswick which the federal politicians
(or bureaucrats) hadn't even heard of.

This assessment of the impact of constitutional change is
hugely important in the present Canadian context because it is
the basis of the Parti Québécois' program of sovereignty-
association.   Quebec would like, because of its distinctive
culture, (says the P.Q. and many others in Quebec, too), to do many
things of no interest to the rest of Canada, or to deal with the
standard problems of an industrial society in a distinctive way.
It is acknowledged, however, that the rest of Canada does have an
interest in maintaining economic ties, and that is the point of
economic association: thus Quebec's political independence
presents no threat to the rest of the country; the P.Q. is not
trying to break up Canada, etc.   Or listen to Premier Lougheed
(1977):

> In short, the economic centre of gravity is shifting west.   It
> will continue to do so, but I am aware - as you are - that it
> neither will nor should shift too far, if we are going to maintain
> and sustain a strong nation.   Frankly though, we can shift quite
> a way before we reach that point.   In my view, without doubt,
> such a shift is good for Canada.   As the regions strengthen, the
> country strengthens.   This is not any exclusive club for Albertans;
> everybody is welcome, each in his own way and I just urge you,
> wherever you are, whatever activity, to come aboard.

To sum up this opinion: the interests at stake in all but
the most radical forms of constitutional change, are regional in
the first instance.   But since all regions stand to benefit from
decentralization, the national interest too (as an aggregate of
regional interests) is served.

Level Four -- We now come to the opinion that recognizes
regionally differentiated consequences of constitutional change.
It is argued that a redistribution of powers, including powers

that may be used to swell the public purse (taxing powers,
ownership of resources, etc.) would shift the costs of providing
public services between provinces (regions).   In the case of
decentralization, provinces that lost revenue might not only
have to raise taxes, but might find it difficult to maintain the
same standard of services that the richer provinces provide.
Sometimes this is presented as a distinct advantage: provincial
governments would cut out wasteful expenditures on vain programs
of economic development, when the resources to be developed are
elsewhere; lavish social services and income maintenance schemes
would no longer hold back emigration from declining regions, etc.
Against these arguments, and far more commonly heard, are
considerations of equity which suggest the desirability of comparable levels of public services in all regions, without undue
levels of taxation.

Here, as is already evident, the interests at stake are
presented in regional terms, although there are also suggestions
that non-regional interests may be affected -- interests defined
by income level and occupation.

Level Five -- At the next notch on our impact scale we find
the opinion that a change in constitutional arrangements may raise
or lower the level of government services, quite apart from the
issue of regional variations in quality, and in cost, of services.
It is sometimes argued that federalism makes for "big government,"
not just in the sense that there are many bureaucrats duplicating
each others' work (if not actually undoing it), but in the sense
that two levels of government will compete with each other to
provide services, and the result will be a larger public sector
than a unitary state over the same territory would create.   So
far as I know, however plausible the argument, there is no empirical support for this view.   On the other hand, a contrary position
has been presented by Harold L. Wilensky in The Welfare State and
Equality (1975).   This book is a contribution to the literature
that looks for correlations between certain features of policy
(such as levels of state expenditure on social welfare) and other
variables.   The literature finds, in general, that policy outputs
correlate reasonably well with social characteristics like per
capita income and age of population and scarcely or not at all with
political structures (such as representativeness of institutions),
official or prevalent ideology, or type of economic system.
One of the principal conclusions of the literature is that institutions do not seem to matter very much.   Wilensky, however,
discovered that the one institutional characteristic that might
be inferred to have some significance for levels of expenditure
on social welfare is the degree of centralization of the regime.
He calculated state welfare expenditures as a percentage of gross
national product in 22 industrialized countries, and discovered that,
"Of the top nine welfare-state leaders ... six are clearly among
the nine most centralized governments ... [while] of the seven
countries ranked lowest in social security [all of them federal]

four are among the least centralized;" of the remaining three,
one was ambiguous as regards centralization, and two had high
levels of military expenditure which presumably restricted
their capacity to use state resources for welfare purposes.
(Wilensky, 1975, p.52).

Wilensky's evidence about the relationship between centralization of the regime and levels of social security services
can scarcely be taken as conclusive, but the enquiry itself
does suggest a different and rather more significant relationship between federalism and public policy than do lower points
on our impact scale. This is the first suggestion in our
discussion of the relationship between constitutional forms and
policy outputs that structural factors as such, as well as the
availability of financial resources, may have an impact on what
governments do. There is also a difference in terms of the
groups affected by constitutional forms. If "big government"
is generally more favourable to the less wealthy (because of
transfer payments and because of public services disproportionately
paid for by the middle and upper income groups) class interests
rather than, or as well as, regional ones can be seen to be impli-
cated in constitutional questions.

Level Six -- Finally, we come to the suggestion that as a
result of constitutional change, governments may aim for new or
different objectives, may abandon or trim down old ones, and/or
may become more -- or rather less -- effective in achieving
specific objectives than was formerly the case. It is not just
a question of levels of public services, but of potential changes
in the whole range of government activity. We are reminded in
the present context, that the original purpose of creating the
Canadian federation was to provide for the physical security of
the colonies in British North America, to affirm and achieve
distinctive social values ("Toryism," as Gad Horowitz would have
it, symbolized in the affirmation of the British connection;
and, in French Canada, Catholicism), and to develop the northern
half of the continent as an extension in time and space of "the
commercial empire of the St. Lawrence." (Creighton, 1935).
Whether such purposes persist, whether they are replaced or
supplemented by others, and who are the champions of such purposes,
are the questions that most fundamentally underlie the
Canadian crisis. Insofar as there is a relationship between
national purposes and constitutional structures, those purposes
and the capacity of Canadians to realize them through the agency
of government are fundamental to our present concerns with constitutional matters.

It is evident, though, that there is no undifferentiated
"national interest" in these questions. A diverse population
affirms diverse purposes. The issues at hand are quintessen-
tially political, and it is one of the defining characteristics
of a political situation that some people want to secure objec-

tives that others resist. Both groups of protagonists seek
to employ potentially coercive instruments -- the state -- to
accomplish their purposes. There is, at least in the abstract,
no way of knowing whether the groups involved are territorially
concentrated or dispersed. That is, we cannot know without
empirical enquiry whether the interests at stake in constitutional change are regional or not.

We have so far been concerned to identify various opinions
on the relationship between constitutional forms, the substance
of public policy, and the interests apparently at stake in constitutional change. We have provided an exposition of these
opinions on the basis of a rank ordering, which sees an increasingly close relationship between structural factors and policy
outputs, and which correspondingly perceives increasingly large
stakes in constitutional questions. A summary of our impact
scale in tabular form may be useful: --

PRESUMED IMPACT OF CON- STITUTION ON POLICY OUTPUTS	INTERESTS APPARENTLY AT STAKE
1. Negligible: The constitutional debate in Canada reflects in- stitutional rivalries and nothing else.	The careers of politicians and bureaucrats.
2. Negligible as far as policy outputs themselves are con- cerned, although the costs of government are affected by structural factors.	An undifferentiated "public interest"; or alternatively, taxpayers (for administration and co-ordination costs) and citizens (for signalling and mobility costs).
3. Differentiation of policy outputs between regions; the federal government no longer acts in ignorance of local needs.	Regional interests; all regions stand to benefit from decentralization; therefore, in the aggregate, the national interest.
4. Costs of providing public services may be raised/lowered in each region individually; possible variations in level or quality of services by region.	Regional interests ; standards of services may go up/down; interregional shifts in costs of services; possible impact on interregional migration.
5. Raise or lower level of public services, apart from regional variations.	Class (?)

6. Governments may aim for new or different objectives, may abandon old objectives; may become more/less effective in achieving specific purposes.

Regional (in the sense of incompatibility of regional objectives) and non-regional (i.e., interests within each region, or within some regions).

It may be objected that rather than having a scale or a rank-ordering of opinions, we have merely identified several different ways in which a constitution may affect policy and hence have an impact on the interests of various groups of people. We have; but each category absorbs the one(s) below it. For example, a person who is concerned about the constitutional question because he thinks constitutional change might lead to variations in the quality of public services in the various regions would have no difficulty in acknowledging that amendments to the constitution might well also affect the careers of politicians and bureaucrats, might raise or lower the costs of government in the aggregate, and might affect the sensitivity of government to the needs of the various regions.

What I consider of critical importance is not the logical compatibility or incompatibility of the categories, but the fact that the more one focuses on the lower end of the scale, the easier it is to lose sight of the upper end, and thus to fail to perceive what is ultimately or potentially at stake in constitutional change. In particular, the more we argue about issues such as the costs of running the apparatus of government -- important though this issue is -- the more likely it is that other issues, perhaps of an even more fundamental character, will be neglected.

For this reason the remainder of this essay deals with the selection of governmental purposes and the effectiveness of governments in achieving them on behalf of the population or identifiable interests within it. Justice can only be done this complex and demanding subject by empirical work, and a great deal of it. It will be necessary, as time permits, to survey large areas of government activity at all levels in Canada, and to try to see what impact the present federal system has had on the selection of aims and the success governments have had in carrying through with them. Each of the proposals for changing the Canadian Constitution should be examined on the same basis. Although, obviously, none of these ambitions can be realized in this essay, the essay does attempt to explore in a relatively abstract way the arguments linking constitution, public policy, and the satisfaction of specific political interests and the neglect of others; to raise some questions about what those interests are (that is, what cleavages are politically salient); and to enquire into the compatibility

of political interests, or opposition between them, when the
cleavages are regional.

CONSTITUTIONAL ROADBLOCKS TO EFFECTIVE POLICY
MAKING

The initiative in the Canadian constitutional debate
during the 1960s and 1970s has been taken by
decentralists.   They have hymned the potential achievements
of more powerful provincial governments, rather than sounding
the harsh notes of regional discord.   The other main group of
would-be constitutional reformers are those who find the
present system messy and inefficient, and would like a return
to a more classical form of federalism;   they speak of the
irritations caused by Ottawa's meddling in matters in which it
has no business.   In view of the arguments used to support
reform, public attention has been directed mainly to the issues
that appear at the lower end of our policy impact scale.   This
was not at all the case during the 1930s , when commentary on
constitutional matters focused very largely on structural
obstacles to the implementation of desired policies.

One result of the distress inflicted upon so many Canadians
by the Great Depression was an outpouring of demands for an
expansion of government activity in the fields of welfare and of
regulation of the economy.   However, the federal government's
belated response to these demands, a series of legislative
measures generally described as "Bennett's New Deal," was largely
declared *ultra vires* by the Judicial Committee of the (British)
Privy Council.   This series of court decisions made many reform-
minded persons desperately conscious of the obstacles to effective government action in certain areas under the Canadian
constitution.

Unemployment insurance and market regulation illustrate
the problem.   The establishment of an unemployment insurance
scheme was impractical at the provincial level but was nonetheless, if based on compulsory contributions to a special fund,
outside federal competence.   Neither level of government could
do what many people believed necessary.   This particular
problem was resolved by constitutional amendment in 1941.
Similarly, the establishment of compulsory marketing schemes
and output quotas for natural products was declared *ultra vires* by
the Parliament of Canada but could not be done by the provinces
because they could not control the movement of produce across
their boundaries.   The obstacles to accomplishing the aims of
the successfully impugned Natural Products Marketing Act (1934)
were partially overcome by 1949 federal legislation which
delegated certain powers to provincial marketing boards.

During the 1930s, however, these issues seemed intractable,
a fact that convinced almost a whole generation of legal

scholars and others concerned with public life that federalism was outmoded. At a minimum, they believed, Canada would have to drastically revise the division of powers enshrined in the British North America Act, producing a much more centralized sort of federalism. In short, the relationship between federalism and the substance of public policy was widely acknowledged and gave rise to animated political debate as well as to acrimonious charges levelled against the British judicial authorities who allegedly had so little understanding of Canada's needs and whose judgments accordingly made bad law.

Enquiry into the constitutional discontents of the 1930s reveals that the problems identified at that time related to legislative competence and to the uneven distribution of financial resources among the provinces. Since the onset of World War II, however, a mixture of constitutional change, legislative and administrative adaptations, and fiscal measures have served to reduce the salience of these problems. Canadians seem to have learned how to work the federal constitution which so many of them thought, during the 1930s, to be unworkable -- at least in the context of an industrialized society and an international economic order dominated by the major powers. While this has been a matter for satisfaction if not self-congratulation for many, the changes in policy-making processes within a largely unchanged Constitutional Act have not occurred without raising resentment and apprehension in several parts of the country, especially in Quebec, Alberta, and British Columbia.

If changes in the distribution of powers and even more in the working relationship between levels of government in Canada have minimized the constitutional problems that were so acutely felt during the 1930s, they have left untouched more directly political discontents. Reform-minded persons of the Depression era were struck by the near-unanimity of opinion supporting at least some of the ventures being proposed (for example, each of the nine provinces had passed legislation complementary to the federal Natural Products Marketing Act, so that this neatly dovetailed body of legislation could accomplish agreed purposes); the apparent inadaptability of the constitution was all the more obvious and galling. On the other hand, federal monetary and commercial policies designed to counter the Depression were far from neutral as between regions; they had a demonstrably adverse impact on the primary sectors of the economy and therefore on the non-industrialized regions, especially the prairies. The policies of the early 1930s were a reaffirmation, almost with a vengeance, of the national policies of the latter nineteenth century, as the analysis of the Rowell-Sirois Report (Canada, 1940) demonstrated. Those policies, with their unequal regional incidence, reflected the preferences of those segments of the Canadian political community whose resources of wealth and numbers ensured them a guiding hand over major political decisions. That is to say, policy was shaped by

pressures and constraints emanating from a particular political community.   Then as now political forces, filtered
through representative and decision-making institutions, had
and have their impact upon the chief decision-makers of the
time.   The composition of the Canadian political community,
however, has changed and decision-making processes at the
centre are increasingly subjected to constraints and impulsions
emanating from provincial governments, giving new salience to
many long-standing political disputes within the Canadian
federation, and generating new subjects of controversy.   The
relationship between these controversies and Canada's constitutional structure are explored in the next section.

POLICY AND THE CONSTITUTION: SELECTING POLICY

Consider a recently touted policy objective.   In 1973 the
premiers of four western provinces declared that the single
most potent factor holding back the industrialization of the
West was poor transportation.   Effective competition between
carriers, they thought, would improve services and would reduce
rates.   To achieve the desired competition they proposed that
the federal government take over all railway beds and operate
them as public utilities.   This done, the railbeds would
become steel-ribbon highways accessible to any licensed carrier.

There was no doubt about the legislative competence of the
federal Parliament to do this.   The project would be expensive
but if the incentives were judged compelling, the financial
resources could presumably be found.   The question boiled down
to this: did the western premiers represent a political force
powerful enough to elicit a "yes" from Ottawa?   This is the standard
form of a political question.   Indeed, whenever a proposal gets
on the political agenda, the question inevitably arises: can
an eager government get away with it?   Or alternatively: can a
reluctant government be prodded into getting on with it -- and
by whom?

Our problem is to know whether the constitution has a
bearing on the answers to these questions.   There are two major
reasons for thinking that it does.   They are:

-- the constitution selects the political community relevant
   to policy making in each subject area; and

-- it structures the key representative and decision-making
   institutions.

What is the relevant political community?

The effects of constitutional change, as discussed in this section, are similar to those flowing from a gerrymander of electoral districts.

Gerrymandering is the art of redrawing the electoral map for partisan advantage. It is a way of tampering with the system of representation; besides boosting temporarily the fortunes of a party, it makes some interests relatively more powerful while rendering others less so. In part this occurs by overrepresenting some regions or areas. More subtly, it is accomplished by creating constituencies such that seats won by the opposition are taken by overwhelming majorities, whereas government seats are typically won with narrower majorities or pluralities. One consequence is that for a given percentage of the popular vote, the governing party (the one doing the gerrymander) gets the largest possible number of seats in the legislature. Another consequence more germane to the present discussion is that a gerrymander may also affect the substance of policy because it necessarily alters the constellation of political forces in the system.

Reallocating governmental powers in a federation has effects similar to those produced by a gerrymander, though in amending a federal constitution the element of partisan advantage may be incidental. In both cases, for at least some areas of government activity, a new or modified set of political forces is brought into play. To put it another way: the constituencies relevant to policy-making processes are at least partially re-defined. But whereas with a gerrymander, this result flows from relocating territorial boundaries, in the case of a constitutional reallocation of powers it is accomplished by moving functional boundaries instead. A federal responsibility becomes provincial, or vice-versa; policy-making responds to, or is ultimately controlled by, a new electorate. In slightly broader terms -- broader, because not all political pressures are electoral -- a different political community is now the relevant one.

Take the case of the railway beds. In Canada at present it is the federal government that regulates the railways and that might (if it wished) assume ownership of some or all of their assets. Under a new constitution, however, these powers could conceivably be transferred to the provincial governments. Suppose this happened. We do not know whether the western premiers, who had found nationalization attractive if undertaken by the Government of Canada, would have sufficient incentive to take this step themselves. After all, they would have to foot the bill or to risk some form of retaliation if they expropriated

assets without "adequate" compensation. Possibly the provinces,
with governments of various ideological hue and with widely dis-
parate financial resources, would each adopt a distinctive
policy. No longer would there be (for this particular decision)
national politicians responding to or constrained by the Canadian
political community; those in charge would be provincial cabinet
ministers hoping for a renewal of their mandates from a variety
of provincial electorates.

    To generalize, one may observe that Canada contains
several political communities and that each corresponds to, or
provides the context for, a distinctive set of political processes.   Those decisions that are taken provincially implicate
primarily the various provincial political communities.   In
federal decisions, where political processes at the centre are
involved, the relevant political community is the Canadian one.
(Well, it's not quite as neat as that: governments lobby and
negotiate with each other.)   Finally, there are some decisions
that are jointly taken: policy emerges through various modes
of interaction between governments, and both the Canadian and
the several provincial political communities figure in such
decisions.

    If we posit some particular political objective, favoured
by some people and opposed by some others, we may presume that
it makes quite a difference whether that particular issue is
to be resolved through one set of political processes rather
than through another.   The most obvious reason for this is
that a minority interest in a large political community may
well be a majority interest in a small one.   For example, as
is often said, Quebec is the only part of Canada where francophones are in the majority.   This, however, is only the most
frequently mentioned case of a very common phenomenon, namely,
the regional concentration of a politically significant group-
ing.   To take other examples, fishermen and fish-processing
workers carry a political weight in Newfoundland that they do
in no other province; and the same is true of cattlemen in
Alberta, of Acadians in New Brunswick, and (perhaps) of socialists
in Saskatchewan.   None of these groupings can hope to wield
the influence in federal politics that they apparently do
within their own province.   In consequence:

(1) It is evident that some initiatives are likely to be
     undertaken only at the provincial level and within
     certain provinces.   It was this consideration that
     caused P.E. Trudeau, at the time when he described
     himself as a socialist, to reject the centralist
     constitutional preferences of the CCF and to
     argue: "Federalism must be welcomed as a valuable
     tool which permits dynamic parties to plant socialist
     governments in certain provinces, from which the seed
     of radicalism can slowly spread." (1961, p.127).

The tacit supposition here -- perhaps it was really an unexamined premise -- is that uniform action across the country is not necessary for effective implementation of policy.

(2) In cases where the realization of policy objectives requires concerted action by both levels of government, a decentralized form of federalism may discourage new governmental initiatives or cause their failure.   The same point applies, perhaps with more force, when objectives must be realized by interprovincial co-operation, without federal participation.   This is so because a federal initiative may be backed up with financial inducements, or simply have a "demonstration effect" serving to nudge the provinces into line.

-- For example, it is said that housing costs could be reduced if building codes were more uniform; greater use could be made of modular construction (prefabricated segments of houses). But the provinces would have to agree on the common standards. What uniformity there is now is provided by the national building code; it is important partly because of its application to contruction financed by the Central Mortgage and Housing Corporation, and partly because it provides a model for the provinces to emulate (or such was the fond hope of its originators.)

-- A much more serious case is that of intergovernmental fiscal transfers, particularly the equalization payments.   It has been said that these could be implemented by interprovincial agreement rather than through an Ottawa-designed and implemented program; and so they could -- technically.   But the prospect of political agreement seems remote.

-- One final example: controls on the production of milk for industrial purposes now are imposed by the Canadian Dairy Commission; if it lacked its present powers, all major milk-producing provinces would have to agree to impose controls within the province, and to allocate the desired volume of Canadian production between them.   Since special benefits would accrue to a province that refused to co-operate with the others in such a plan, such agreement would probably be difficult to achieve.

(3) Where federal powers are sufficient to permit unilateral action, policies that favour those groups that can exercise an effective voice in Ottawa will presumably be adopted. This may be to the detriment of groups that are very strong at the provincial level (though not in all

provinces).   Under a centralized constitution, then,
groups that are powerful at the centre may be able to
overwhelm objections from groups that, under a more
decentralized constitution, would be politically
untouchable.   This is so whether or not a consistent
policy is required, by the nature of the task, in all
parts of the country.

The last of these observations invites a certain cynicism.
I have suggested that some projects for governmental action are
more likely to be adopted under a centralized form of government.   Does this, stripped of its verbal varnish, simply mean
that in a large political community local interests can be
overridden with impunity?   Certainly no amount of sophistry
can alter the fact that a majority interest in a small political community may be a minority interest in a larger one.
And this may be a way of saying that political centralization
subordinates the interests of some regions to those of other
regions.   The imagery for evoking this relationship is rich
and varied: metropolis drains hinterland, centre exploits
periphery, the manufacturing and financial "heartland" coerces
the primary-producing regions into an unequal trading partnership.   In such imagery, centralization is equated with delib-
erate domination or with simple insensitivity to local and
regional interests, whether these are of an economic or cultural
nature.

Are we then simply discussing the constitutional arrangements that will enable some regions (or a single region) to
dominate the others?   Not quite.   It depends whether the
interests at stake in constitutional change are regional ones.
And when they are, it depends on whether the interests or
goals of each region tend to complement each other or are mutually incompatible.   If the latter, then any one region's gain is
another's loss, and the rationale for a free association of
provinces is destroyed.

Are the interests regional or not?

Transportation and tariffs have, for almost a century,
been regarded as policies working to the advantage of central
Canada and to the detriment of the West and the Maritimes.   The
interests at stake have been regarded as regional ones.   By
contrast, in the case of labour policy the groups most directly
involved appear to be those of occupation or class.   And similarly with social security policy: social insurance programs
and income maintenance schemes have differential impacts on
groupings defined by income, age and sex.   However, the charac-
terization of each of these policy areas as "regional" or "non-
regional" (as the case may be) may be challenged and it frequently
is.   This is not surprising as in almost every policy area, it is
very difficult to sort out the regional and the non-regional
aspects.

The western premiers' proposal to nationalize the railbeds was politically astute, even if not particularly inven-
tive, because it dealt with transportation policy in a way
that avoided controversy between the agricultural and the
non-farm interests within their own region.   The nub of
Canada's problem in rail transport is to find a way of bearing the overhead costs of the system.   The Crowsnest Pass
rates for carrying grain, established by law in 1897 and since
then maintained at that level, prevent the grain traffic from
contributing to maintenance and other fixed costs.   Rates on
some other products are kept down by competition, as in the
instance of transporting steel from Hamilton to Vancouver.
In still other cases, although the only practicable mode of
transport is by rail, high transportation costs would price
the product out of its market: then the shipper and the railways negotiate "agreed charges,"which may be as low as the
railway's marginal costs.   Thus a large part of the traffic --
grain alone accounts for about a quarter of the ton-mile total --
can carry only a small proportion of total overhead.   The railways have tried to compensate by charging higher rates per ton-
mile on goods for which there is no competing mode of transport
(such as steel to a non-port city like Calgary) and on high-
value goods for which the rates are not held down by regulation or by market considerations.   One result has been that
the transportation of industrial products to and from the
prairie region has been expensive, whereas charges for transporting raw materials and unprocessed goods have been low
(lower, in the case of grain, than in the United States).
Hence the claim that transportation policy has held back the
industrialization of the prairies and, together with the tariff,
has increased the cost of consumption goods in that region.

If this analysis is correct, then one solution would be to
eliminate the favourable rates for the products of primary
industry, including farming.   This could be done by de-
regulating the grain traffic and perhaps by provincial subsidy
for the carriage of other low-value high-bulk goods (resource
products, from which the provinces draw a royalty).   This part
of the business could then shoulder a reasonable share of the
overhead, and rates on the more highly processed goods could
drop.   If one advocated this, however, it would pit the interests of the prairie farmer against other interests within the
region*, a definition of the issue that would be clear suicide
for any prairie premier.   The solution?   To pose the problem
in regional terms by proposing public ownership of the railbeds,
which, of course, implies a large federal subsidy.   Now, let
the reader decide: is or is not transportation an area where
the relevant political cleavages are regional?   Surely it
depends on the solution envisaged, and not only the problem
itself.

---

*I am grateful to Gail Hogarth who first brought this argument to my
 attention.

Further: if in the context of the present Canadian federation, the cleavages are judged to be regional, would they still be regional in the context of a Canadian common market in which (we say for the sake of argument) central institutions have slender financial resources and perhaps also lack the constitutional power to take over the railways or even to regulate their activities? The way we conceive the problem may depend not only on what that problem is and how we think it might be solved, but also on what machinery, as established by a constitution, is available to do the job.

Labour policy and social security policy too may be described both in regional and in non-regional terms. It is quite correctly pointed out that in both policy areas class interests are at stake -- not to mention distinctions of occupation, age, education, and so forth.

Nonetheless, labour policy also inevitably reflects a culture. For example, it speaks volumes about prevalent conceptions of the social order that the official program of the Parti Québécois envisages the compulsory unionization of all employees. (Murray, 1976, p.94). The PQ also proposes collective agreements to cover entire industries, a form of industrial relations that has existed since 1968 in Quebec's construction sector. In this sector, region-wide agreements are extended by government decree to cover non-unionized workers; the agreements extended in this way are also binding on firms that are not members of the relevant employers' associations.

In the area of social security, or more broadly of bien-être social, Quebec governments have for decades insisted upon full autonomy. Only on the basis of such autonomy can Quebec devise its own institutions for providing social services and otherwise implementing policy in this field. In other words, Quebec governments, conscious that institutions inevitably embody and express a culture, have insisted that the culture reflected in Quebec institutions should be French Canadian or Québécois. As a minority, French-Canadians have been more conscious than the English-speaking people on this continent that the institutions of any society reflect a distinctive perception of social structure, of the extent and nature of social conflict, and of appropriate responses to conflict. In so doing they are likely to be typical of and unique to the culture. Indeed, it is in this sense that Quebec's particular concerns in constitutional matters are properly summed up as "cultural." The issues that involve class conflict in Ontario and Nova Scotia need not be thought to do so in Quebec in quite the same way. To ignore such differences in outlook is to demonstrate, precisely, one's insensitivity to a viewpoint properly described as regional --

though in this case, involving a regional culture rather than
a regional economic interest.

In other words, if it is a mistake to disregard
cleavages within regions, it is equally unwarranted to assume
that conflicts that seem non-regional from one cultural or
ideological standpoint will be universally so perceived. It
is an error to suppose that considerations of efficiency and
effectiveness alone can satisfactorily determine the appropriate allocation or reallocation of powers between levels of
government. It is also important to explore how people and
groups perceive their needs and how they define (if the word
is not too precise) their aspirations. It is not, I think,
adequate simply to ask how certain technical problems involved
in policy formation can be solved in accordance with a set of
values and preconceptions supplied by the observer. An
essentially political judgment is necessary to appreciate both
the regional and the non-regional element in controversial
questions.

Are regional interests compatible?

If one region is said to dominate or exploit another,
this can be so only by virtue of there being regional interests
at stake. As I have just argued, many issues do involve a
regional aspect without properly being described in exclusively
regional terms. Let us now, however, set aside these complexi-
ties and presume a regional aspect in political controversies
whose outcome is likely to be affected by constitutional
arrangements. In these cases, does enquiry into the selection
of policy objectives resolve itself into the study of regional
domination?

Obviously it does, if each issue is taken singly. But
there is no warrant to do this and on the whole, people seem
to be mainly concerned with the cumulative impact of a large
number of political decisions.

A political community exists to realize certain purposes
that its members can achieve only in common. Those purposes
may relate to material welfare; for example, they may be to
increase aggregate levels of production, to assure income
security for individuals and families, or to provide various
social services such as health care. Additionally, they may
have to do with physical security (defence, domestic peace),
or with the development and flourishing of a culture. The
definition of purposes in each of these areas will predictably
arouse controversy, as will the inevitable trade-offs between
them. The same is true of the distribution of private goods
and of deciding who will bear the costs of public services.

As we have noted, opinions on all these questions may vary by region; in some cases it may even be possible to assign a monetary value to various regionally defined interests. But whether the interests are tangible or otherwise is of no consequence: the existence of regional cleavages within a political community implies a form of bargaining between regions. In other words, we have a political process that trades off advantages and disadvantages within each aspect of governmental activity -- especially the economic -- or between economic, security-related, and cultural purposes.*

Within any state there is an understanding, constitution-ally expressed as the capacity to make laws, that such political processes will result in decisions that are binding upon all members of the political community. Naturally, this limits the individual's capacity to pursue his own interests, a paradoxical situation if one holds that political authority derives from the people and that civil society consists of a free association of individuals. One solution to the paradox has been the fiction of a social contract, according to which individuals give up some of their own freedom of action in return for the larger benefits to be derived from an ordered society: physical security, material welfare, and so forth. In federal states a "federal bargain," fictitious or otherwise, accomplishes the same purposes as an imaginary social contract: on the supposition that there is mutual benefit to be reaped from creating a political authority with the capacity to make decisions binding upon the constituent units, it provides the rationale for a free association of provinces or states for certain defined purposes.

There are *a priori* grounds that establish the potentially for mutual benefit from federation, although empirical work is necessary to know whether in any particular instance such potentiality is realized. Mutual benefit in the economic sphere may derive from any of the following:

--The establishment of an integrated economy, permitting regional specialization in production and creating economies of scale -- hence augmenting aggregate production.

--The creation of economies of scale in the provision of public services.

---

* For example, a net disadvantage in material welfare may be over-balanced by cultural gain or by greater physical security. On the other hand, a negative assessment in any one area, implying a tangible or intangible cost of the region's inclusion in the broader political community, may be compounded by disadvantages in the other areas as well: thus to a cultural "price" of political union may be added an estimated economic loss.

-- Compensating for positive or negative neighbourhood
   effects (or externalities) of economic activity.

-- The optimal allocation of resources in the society,
   especially to the production of public goods such
   as defence.

-- The implementation of effective policies of economic
   stabilization: monetary management and fiscal policy.

-- Acquiring enough economic power, and perhaps military
   strength, to bargain effectively in the international
   arena, e.g. trade negotiations.

In my opinion it is imaginable but quite unlikely that the
same range of benefits could be secured by interprovincial or
inter-state negotiation, the results of which may (in some
cases) take the form of a treaty.   This is a point of capital
importance, though we cannot afford the time to explore it now.
Suffice it to say that it is a serious intellectual and practical problem to know what powers must be exercised by some
central authority to achieve any substantial degree of economic
integration.   The choice may end up being between a political
process that is highly bureaucratic, with major decisions
taken by elites over whom there are few or only ineffective
political controls, or a political process that operates
more openly and in which governmental powers are exercised by
agencies responsible to a directly elected assembly.

The potential economic benefits of federation, or of some
other institutional solution to the problem of running an integrated economy, have been identified only in abstract terms.
Merely drawing up a list of potential benefits does not ensure
that they apply to Canada such that all regions do actually
end up better off.   On the contrary, for any one region or
province the economic benefits of federation may be outweighed
by foregone advantages that would accrue to it from (hypothetical) alternative arrangements with other political and
economic entities: the United States, the European Economic
Community, and Japan. This must remain a matter for speculation.
In addition, although defence considerations do not appear to
bulk large in determining each region's advantages/disadvantages
from Confederation, cultural concerns evidently do so.   Confederation may provide cultural advantages if Canadian values differ
in any degree from values in the United States. Moreover, Quebec
stands to gain a special advantage if, by being part of Canada,
it can endow itself with a better economic and institutional base
for withstanding the assimilationist pressures entailed by its
being in a tiny minority position on the North American continent.

Whether or not these potential advantages of federal
union are realized depends in part upon adventitious
circumstances such as the compatibility or incompatibility
of regional cultures, in part upon immutable underlying conditions (such as resource endowments by region, technological
changes that make certain resources of great strategic
importance or that render them superfluous, climatic variations,
and locational advantages of particular cities and regions),
and in part upon the design of political machinery.   The
last of these groups of factors points to one further aspect
of the constitutional question in Canada.

The Structure of Representative and Decision Making Institutions

Many people insist that the nub of Canada's constitutional
problems lies with the distribution of powers and that it is
irrelevant to start changing the design of parliamentary institutions, modifying the composition and role of the Supreme
Court, and entrenching a charter of human rights in the constitution.   This seems to me an exaggeration, since the last
two of these items have to do ultimately with the definition
of governmental powers; and the first of the three -- an
issue that hitherto has focused largely on the reform,
replacement, or abolition of the Senate -- potentially affects
the selection of the policy objectives by the Government of
Canada.   Parliamentary institutions help to shape the every-
day process of coalition-building in federal politics, and
they consequently may be expected to have a bearing on the
configuration of political forces within the system.

If regional interests are incompatible, no restructuring of policy-making processes can prevent a dominant-
subordinate relationship from arising between regions.   On
the other hand, where the interests are in principle compatible, a region may still think that it is not obtaining its
fair share of the benefits of federal political union.
Indeed, representative and decision making institutions may
be such that the region is consistently outvoted or its
interests disregarded in the policy-making process.   The
feeling of being politically slighted or even overwhelmed
is widespread in Canada today, particularly in the West.
That is why the constitutional debate rightly concerns not
only the extent and allocation of governmental powers and
their distribution between jurisdictions, but the structure
of political institutions at the centre: Supreme Court,
electoral law, upper chamber, and regulatory agencies.

CONCLUSION

If we ask, what is at stake in constitutional change,
a part of the answer necessarily refers to symbolic and
emotive concerns.   People do care a great deal what community they belong to.   The individual's self-esteem and
indeed the very idea of "self" are commonly affected by one's

identification with a collectivity or a whole network of
social entities -- family, locality and nation. For those
who feel most keenly the broadest of such attachments, the
political options facing Canadians today reflect the emotional
question: "What is my country?"

There is another dimension, however, to the choice between
various political options, a dimension related to the performance of the functions of government. It is the latter
concern that is the focus of this essay.

The argument presented here has attempted to show that
changes in governmental powers -- their scope, and their distribution between jurisdictions -- is likely to have an impact
on the substance of policy decisions. The same is true of
changes in representative and decision-making institutions.
Public debate, and some academic literature, has tended to
minimize the impact of such structural factors both on political processes and the outputs that emerge from them.
The argument presented here does not refute this position,
but it does present what I hope is a plausible case to the
contrary. To the extent that the issue can be resolved at
all, only careful examination case by case of the relationship between federalism and public policy in Canada can do
it.

One issue that is bound to remain in dispute is whether
the interests at stake are primarily regional. Although
federalism is frequently described as a form of government
that reduces conflict between regions since it permits
diversity in policy and keeps some potentially disruptive
issues off the federal political agenda, it also may have
a contrary effect -- that of exaggerating the regional character of some public issues. Issues that, in a unitary state,
would not be thought of in regional terms may appear as
disputes involving the regions. In this way provincial/
state governments may be pitted against each other and against
the centre.

No academic enquiry will significantly affect the way
that public opinion defines political issues. Nevertheless,
the right sort of work carefully conducted, may help in the
resolution of political conflicts. If dissatisfaction
arises because the central government is incapable of doing
what is necessary to operate an integrated economy, then
decentralization will only exacerbate the problem. It
might be much better to adapt political institutions at the
centre in order to render the federal political authorities
more susceptible to political pressure from the neglected
regions. Conversely, if basic regional interests are at
stake and cannot effectively be accommodated within the
federal political arena, decentralization may be called for.

In that case, the question arises whether the more powerful
state/provincial governments will act in a way to prevent
the achievement of purposes regarded, in other regions, as
essential to their welfare.   In Canadian terms, this thought
boils down to the consideration that some provinces must
rely upon the federal government to underwrite the risks
inherent in having a resource-based economy, which is subject
to wide, externally induced and unpredictable fluctuations.
They are, or may become, dependent upon the fiscal transfers
and the public services provided by the federal government;
they pay some of the costs of national policies, and they
need compensation in return.   If the compensation cannot be
provided by a weakened federal government, or by interprovincial agreement, then the rationale for a free association
of provinces within the Canadian federation disappears.

REFERENCES

BRETON, Albert, and SCOTT, Anthony (1978), The Economic Constitution of Federal States (Toronto: University of Toronto Press).

CANADA (1940), Report of the Royal Commission on Dominion-Provincial Relations ("The Rowell-Sirois Report"), Book I.

CREIGHTON, Donald C. (1935), The Commercial Empire of the St. Lawrence (Toronto: Macmillan).

FLETCHER, Frederick J. (1977), "Public Attitudes and Alternative Futures," in Must Canada Fail? (Richard Simeon, ed.) pp. 28-41 (Montreal: McGill-Queen's University Press).

LOUGHEED, Peter (1977) "Address by Premier Peter Lougheed at the Progressive Conservative Conference on March 26, 1977 -- MacDonald Hotel (Edmonton)."

MURRAY, Vera (1976), Le Parti québécois: de la fondation à la prise du pouvoir (Montreal: Hurtubise HMH).

SCOTT, Anthony (1977), "An Economic Approach to the Federal Structure," in Options: Proceedings of the Conference on the Future of the Canadian Federation, pp. 257-280 (Toronto: "Published by the University of Toronto").

TRUDEAU, Pierre Elliott (1961), "The Practice and Theory of Federalism," in Social Purpose for Canada, edited by Michael Oliver, cited in Pierre E. Trudeau Federalism and the French Canadians (Toronto: Macmillan, 1968), pp. 124-50.

WILENSKY, Harold L. (1975), The Welfare State and Equality (Berkeley: University of California Press).

Comments by B. Bonin, Assistant Deputy Minister,
Ministry of Intergovernmental Affairs, Quebec.

What Peter Leslie calls *Impact Level One* consists of the belief
that changes in the constitutional arrangement will not have serious
consequences. The opinion of those who are convinced that the changes
in question would have few consequences is apparently that "the
structural framework in which these processes are acted out is
irrelevant to the policy outputs." I find such a view difficult to
accept. If I correctly understand the meaning that should be given
to it, we must therefore conclude that the policy output is absolutely
independent, for example, of a government's composition. It should
not be difficult to find examples disproving this viewpoint, and I
believe it would be wise to assume that constitutional changes would
likely produce changes in the type of policies. The question then
becomes: what changes?

Impact Level Two in Peter Leslie's classification involves the
cost of governments. In a federal system, therefore, particular
attention is naturally given to overlapping jurisdictions or intervention. It would be quite appropriate, in fact, to clarify this
issue in the framework of Canadian federalism, with a view to reducing
the costs of government. Moreover, even those federalist systems
widely thought to be based on a clearer division of tasks do not
appear to have avoided overlapping jurisdictions. Switzerland is
one example. A survey was recently conducted on this question following a motion presented in 1972. In the introduction to the report,
Répartition des tâches entre la Confédération et les Cantons: principes
de l'Etat actuel, which followed this survey in 1977, we find the
following passage:

The present distribution of tasks between the Confederation
and the Cantons is characterized by an extraordinarily high degree
of overlapping in federal and canton responsibilities. We are
hard pressed to find another federated state in which the powers
of the central government and those of the federated states are
so greatly confused. This appears to be the result of two major
causes. First, the federal level prefers to proceed by small
steps; consequently, the jurisdictional rules adopted by the
Confederation are often drafted in a detailed way. Second, the
federal jurisdictions were established on the basis of varied
principles. Over the decades, these rules have proliferated to
the point that there now remains practically no field to which
the Confederation does not have access. The Canton jurisdictions
have simultaneously become "residual" jurisdictions which are
always more difficult to define, and the Cantons therefore have
less and less opportunity to exert their own authority.
(Unofficial translation)

It would be difficult to claim that the federal system automatically leads to a greater extension by governments into the activity of a society than a single-tier system (*Level Five* in Peter Leslie's classification): many other factors besides the political system itself must be taken into consideration. But any change that could help to make governments more responsible (the term *accountability* is perhaps preferable because it appears to carry less of a value judgement) can only be an improvement. If, through a different arrangement, we can obtain the same services at a lower cost, society can't help but benefit. Moreover, we must not lose sight of the fact that often what is called the "demand for government services" originates with politicians and civil servants who convince each other that the people need a given service and are actually demanding it. In other words, the supply of services may sometimes create its own demand.

Impact Levels Three and Four in Peter Leslie's classification are based on the conviction that "if Ottawa's powers were reduced, it would no longer find so many opportunities to impose uniform policies across the country in the mistaken thought that they would solve diverse problems." Thus, the question here is that of regional variations in the quality and cost of services.

This variation would not necessarily be harmful, and in reading current literature we quickly reach the conclusion that this ability of the central government to "impose uniform policies across the country" could well be, in large part, the origin of Canada's present problems. First, when Ottawa takes this stance, it is in effect deciding which concept of the quality of life will prevail in Canada's various regions. Second, once adopted, this reasoning will not tolerate many hitches. On the one hand, a large number of analysts and politicians will contest that the federal government is automatically better informed than the other levels to make this decision, while on the other hand, it appears to be difficult to reconcile this central decision with the intensity that is generally associated with Canadian regionalism. If this regionalism is in fact as deeply rooted in Canada as now believed, it must signify not only different capacities of different regions to provide a minimum level of services to the population, but also different tastes in different regions with respect to the "basket" of government goods and services desired.

Furthermore, federal policies uniformly applied across the country do not have the same effects in all regions: because original conditions vary, these policies may help the strong regions and harm the others, or at least prove insufficient to alter the major trends.

On the sole basis of work conducted by university economists
or the Economic Council of Canada, it appears that Canada's trade
policy has had, at best, barely favourable effects, and at worst,
highly ambiguous effects on Quebec's economy; that transportation
policy has sometimes served Quebec's interests well (air transportation), and sometimes poorly (rail transportation and particularly
shipping); that energy policy was at first unfavourable to Quebec's
interests, then more favourable; that agricultural policy has in
some cases reaped substantial profits for Quebec farmers (dairy
policy); that immigration policy has not had a very considerable
economic impact but has raised cultural problems in Quebec; that
some aspects of manpower policy cannot have very marked effects
because the French-speaking population is not very mobile outside
Quebec and would have difficulty in becoming mobile under any circumstances; etc.

Once Ottawa had considered all these sometimes contradictory
effects and found that regional disparities still had not decreased
as much as hoped, it resorted to DREE interventions. These interventions were then held up as a benefit of confederation even if,
according to an Economic Council of Canada report, they were too
limited to have a significant impact in Quebec on either the unemployment rate or income disparities.

We, in turn, have analysed the impact of federal policies on
Quebec's economy in a greater number of fields. Inclusion of a
greater number of policies in the analysis does not basically modify
the diagnosis to which I have just made allusion; they may even
reinforce it because the most favourable general conclusion that
could probably be advanced would be that the effects of various
federal policies end up counterbalancing each other. It is therefore
appropriate to question more seriously the various impacts of so-
called national policies on Canada's various regions.

In another line of thinking, Peter Leslie mentions the mutual
economic advantages that are generally attributed to a federation
and which he doubts could be obtained through a treaty or interprovincial negotiations: 1) establishment of an integrated economy;
2) economies of scale in the provision of public services; 3) the
compensation of "spillover effects"; 4) optimum distribution of
resources in a society, particularly for the production of public
goods such as defense; 5) effective stabilization policies; 6) the
establishment of sufficient bargaining power at the international
level.

Only further work would reveal to what extent these advantages are important. The question of whether they could not be obtained otherwise is an empirical one that would be difficult to answer *a priori*. But it already appears that the importance of these economic advantages should not be exaggerated, although they may indeed exist. First, an integrated economic territory can exist without the presence of a federal government and, in return, the existence of a federal government in Canada has not made the present Canadian common market immune from numerous imperfections. Moreover, although economies of scale in the provision of public services are even greater when the services provided are uniform throughout the entire country, this creates other types of problems which may run counter to regional interests. In any case, the governments provide little of the type of compensation on which the third advantage is based, and the true public goods referred to in the fourth are not very numerous. Finally, we expect to be able to rely on efficient stabilization policies. The results of the Lacroix and Rabeau report again appear to warn against exaggerating this aspect; these two authors demonstrate quite clearly that stabilization policies have experienced their share of problems in Canada despite the federal system and perhaps even in part because of this federal system (distribution of powers).

A large number of authors have stressed that the advantages of federalism are found outside the economic sphere. They may very well be correct.

ALTERNATIVE ELECTORAL SYSTEMS

by

William P. Irvine

Department of Political Studies

Queen's University

Many features of the Canadian political and constitutional system rest to a large extent on inheritance and tradition. One of the salutary effects of the November 1976 election in Quebec has been to force Canadians to take a second look at these institutions to see if any better justification is possible or to see if modifications might be desirable. In an imperfect world with people neither impartial nor ignorant of their own interests, political institutions raise as many questions of engineering as they do of morals. There is no uniquely and universally desirable constitutional division of power, method of court appointment, or electoral system. Rather, we must decide what we want to accomplish and marshall the best available knowledge as to how to bring about these ends.

In the past few years, all Canadians have felt a sharpening of the tension among three forces which Richard Simeon has characterized as "country-building, province-building, and Quebec nation-building." (Simeon, 1978). As the labels imply, these are thrusts, at both the mass and elite levels, aimed at extending the range of decision-making authority of federal or provincial governments. Each force has an affective component as well, with the last two forces distinguished by the intensity of that component. Though all provinces have special interests and grievances about their capacity to deal with these areas of interest, Quebec can add to this an especially strong sense of self-identity and self-assertion as an entity distinct from its neighbours.

Country-building, province-building and Quebec nation-building are tendencies that have coexisted throughout Canadian history, but have varied in relative force. Most recently, country-building was the dominant force after the Second World War. It began somewhat hesitantly during the Depression but found its major impetus in the mobilization of wealth, manpower and resources for combat. Though most of the war-time apparatus was dismantled after 1945, the initial momentum persisted for some fifteen years. A fear of post-war economic dislocation, coupled with a highly talented Ottawa civil service committed to Keynesian economic management and proud of its war-time accomplishments, sustained this thrust. At the popular level, total war always seems to generate support for new social organization and Canada after 1945 was no exception. That and the world-wide economic boom provided mass support for country-building, support that, to some extent, cut across cultural and regional divisions.

We now know that this was not an inexorable self-sustaining process. Province-building and Quebec nation-building tendencies were submerged but not eliminated during the 1950s. They have come to dominate the 1960s and 1970s under leaders whose education and major formative experiences came in the country-building decade.

It is clear that these forces are not yet spent and that the
1980s will probably afford them greater institutional recognition. Legal authority over matters such as communications,
immigration and economic development will devolve to provinces
on either an exclusive or a shared basis. Provinces may obtain
a greater role in the formation of central government policy as
well.

What will happen to the centre in Canadian politics is not
now predictable. Theoretically, one could do away entirely with
an independent central power. Canada could become a confederation
in the strict sense with matters settled though multilateral
negotiation. It is not necessarily the case that such a change
would produce major redirections of Canadian policy. What is
clear is that such a development would seriously violate many of
the beliefs, assumptions and interests of the Canadian people -
the same set of beliefs, assumptions and interests that have
influenced and been influenced by the country-building process in
the past. Among these are self-definitions as heirs of a country
stretching from sea to sea, a liberalism implying equal standing
before government, whether one stands as a consumer of services
or as a voter, and an egalitarianism designed to make the liberalism more effective. (Irvine, 1977). Many of these beliefs and
assumptions are spillovers of American political culture. As such,
they affect English-speakers more than French-speakers, but the
latter are certainly not immune to the moral claims implied in
liberalism and egalitarianism. Policies now justified on these
moral grounds could possibly be shown to be consistent with
self-interest. On the basis of liberalism, we believe that
Canadians must have a choice of cultural offerings insofar as
these are publicly provided. Specifically, we believe that
people ought to be able to choose the language of education for
their children and the language and "height of brow" of media
offerings. Though Quebec has now violated what would be defined
as liberal educational policy, the leaders of the Parti Québécois
themselves see this as a transitional measure. It is entirely
possible that a separate Quebec would discover that its self-
interest required it to maximize the facility of its population
in the use of English - even to the point of broadening access to
schools in which English was the language of instruction. Similarly, in the richer provinces in Canada, being taxed to provide
equalization payments is now justified in terms of a basic egalitarianism. It is quite probable that it could be justified in
terms of self-interest. The enhanced standard of living made
possible in poorer provinces by equalization payments makes them
better consumers of products than the richer provinces.

While such possibilities exist, one doubts that self-interest
can justify as many things to as many people as can now be based

on a diffuse moral sense of community. However this may be, it
is clear that the violation of these sensibilities would produce
an intolerable short-run situation. In this short run, the
response is likely to be punitive rather than self-interested.
There will, as a result, be no basis for mutually beneficial
policies or communitarian policies, and every likelihood of
mutually destructive tendencies. For this reason, as well as for
the dynamic quality generated by the coexistence of contrary social
tendencies, it seems appropriate to try to rebuild central institutions and to attempt to reassert this particular thrust. It is
still possible to establish the authority of a central government
based directly on popular support, albeit one operating within
narrower jurisdictional limits. Whether this rebuilding would be
helped or hindered by a reform of the Canadian electoral system
and consequent changes in the party system is the question to be
asked in this paper.

    The central government is a system of interacting parts.
Still, it is both possible and analytically useful to distinguish
between the input and output sides of this system. The growth of
central authority requires development on both sides: there must
be a growth both in the legitimacy and in the responsiveness of
the central government. Legitimacy is a function of group representation, procedural quality, institutional resources, and
capacity to manage conflict. A government will be supported, that
is, will be seen as legitimate, to the extent that social groups
feel that they are represented in it. Government can also benefit
if it is linked to the popular will by fair and understandable
mechanisms. Conversely, government will have less appeal where
the link seems capricious or based on irrelevant considerations.
A voting system that appeared to favour Mr. Brown over Mr. White
because it discouraged voters from looking past the top of the
ballot would be an example. By institutional resources, I mean
the capacity to mobilize, channel and commit social forces directly.
(Huntington, 1965, pp. 8-11). Representational capacity assumes
that all social forces are at some remove from government which,
in a passive way, affords access to some or all interests. A
government with institutional capacity has direct social roots,
through a political party, and benefits from support that is
diffuse - not linked to specific actions of government. It also
benefits to the extent that politically active elites work through
the party that is commited to government rather than through social
organizations committed only to their own self-interest. Finally,
a government's authority is enhanced when its functioning is such
as to cut across and blur major social divisions in the society.
It is diminished if the governmental system contains incentives
to mobilize social differences.

    On the output side, governmental responsiveness is a function

of two things: the capacity of the government to make and change
policy and to do so in a way satisfactory to contending social
interests; and the opportunities afforded by government to individuals and groups for the redress of policy choices and administrative discretion where these are perceived as unsatisfactory.
Given the systematic interrelationships, responsiveness in these
two senses may be expected to enhance legitimacy, and legitimacy
makes it easier for a government to mobilize the resources needed
to produce satisfactory response.

On reflection, one realizes that these goods are not all
mutually consistent, at least at the extremes. Institutionalization
implies the capacity to schedule and manage the distribution of one's
attention. Within a limited time frame, at least, this means that
some interests will be ignored and there is always the danger that
these could be completely ignored. A highly institutionalized
government may, by virtue of its very strength, be limited in its
capacity for representation and responsiveness. Similar reasoning
suggests that a government could be so successful in blurring social
forces that it leaves itself both directionless and devoid of the
capacity to mobilize social support.

Other problems arise when one tries to engineer an increase
in governmental authority. As we shall see shortly, the literature
on electoral systems links different methods of casting and counting votes with all of these aspects of authority. Any particular
electoral system will be linked positively in some respects,
negatively with others. When we come to evaluate the evidence in
the fourth section of this paper, it will be clear that many
supposed effects are either weak or nonexistent. It will also be
apparent that other things impinge on the working of government
with sufficient force to nullify effects from the electoral system.

I am now working on a more detailed analysis of the relationship between types of electoral systems and the kinds of "goods"
and "bads" that might be consequent on each. In this paper, I
want to offer a very much abbreviated version of the larger work.
I will consider only four electoral systems, and four broad classes
of values: representativeness, party-building, policy-making capacity and capacity for redress. After a brief description of the
four electoral systems in the next section of this paper, the
third section will offer a design of a new electoral system for
federal elections in Canada. The next section will argue that
this design is preferable to the alternatives over the range of
values considered. As will be clear, this does not mean that it
is superior on each value, but that it involves a set of trade-offs
that is preferable to the sets associated with the alternatives.
In the longer work, I argue that this desirability remains even if
one considers more electoral systems and more values, but I will
not lengthen this paper by offering the grounds for this assertion.

As a final preliminary point, we should note that the link between an electoral system and government authority is provided by the fact that we live in a system of cabinet government, that cabinets are products of political parties, and that parties are conceived as organizations primarily interested in maximizing electoral success subject to certain policy constraints. In a formal sense, Canada is a parliamentary democracy and the authority of a parliament seems quite independent of the electoral system. Certainly all interests having a territorial base do find representation in parliament and would do so under all electoral systems. But parliament neither initiates nor disposes of public policy; that is done by cabinets and government parties. It is the authority that these can muster that is most relevant in exploring ways of rebuilding the central government. Given that cabinets and parties respond to electoral considerations, the electoral system seems a fruitful point of intervention. This paper seeks to discover the most promising form for that intervention.

TYPES OF ELECTORAL SYSTEM

Countries whose governments derive from British traditions generally have plurality electoral systems, though there have been experiments with other systems for local government and the English themselves have never felt that the Irish were to be trusted to operate a plurality electoral system. In any case, that is now the form used in Canada for federal and provincial elections. Elections take place in constituencies where a number of candidates seek to win a single seat in parliament. This seat is allocated to that candidate winning the largest number of votes. There is no requirement that that number exceed any specified percentage.

Elections in the Republic of Ireland and for the Australian Senate proceed according to a system of single transferable votes (to be referred to hereafter as STV). Three to five (rarely more) people are returned to parliament from each constituency. The number of candidates is quite large as major parties will nominate as many candidates as there are seats available for the constituency. Voters do not mark a cross for a single candidate, but indicate their relative preferences among candidates by marking a 1, 2, 3... etc. opposite the name of each candidate. To determine the winners under such a system, returning officers must establish a quota. There are a variety of formulae for doing this, but one is established by the country's electoral law. A common quota is the number of votes cast divided by one more than the number of seats to be filled in that constituency. First preferences are then tabulated. Any candidate receiving more than the quota is declared elected and his surplus votes (his actual vote minus the quota) are redistributed according to the next available preference indicated. If there are more seats to be filled, the candidate with the fewest first preferences is dropped and his vote is reallocated according to the next available preferences indicated. This process goes on until all seats are filled.

A list electoral system also requires large constituencies. Indeed, in Israel and the Netherlands, the whole country forms one constituency. Constituencies return several members to parliament and parties nominate lists of candidates for each constituency. The number on the list usually equals the number of seats to be filled from that constituency. The list system probably has the most variants. In one form, the voter casts a single vote for a list. In other cases, he can indicate his relative preference among the candidates on a single list by rank-ordering them. In other cases, the voter can create a new list by writing down a rank-ordered set of candidates of his own. (This must be drawn from people already on the ballot.) Depending on the variant chosen, counting rules become more complicated. In the simplest case of a single vote for a party list, the number of votes is totalled for each party. Seats may be allocated by calculating a quota and using highest remainders or by a "highest average" method which involves successive application of a set of divisors. Without going into details, each party can count on receiving a number of seats closely corresponding to its proportion of the constituency vote and will fill those seats starting with the top of its constituency list.

The electoral system of the Federal Republic of Germany is a compromise between the plurality system and the list system and involves electing two types of parliamentarian: some who represent constituencies and others elected "at large." The proposal in the next section is a modification of this system, so I shall not take the time to describe it further here. I should stress, however, that what is described in the next section is not the West German electoral system.

A NEW ELECTORAL SYSTEM FOR CANADA

Future federal parliaments could be composed of two types of members: those representing constituencies as in the current system, and those who would represent provinces. The former would be elected as at present; the latter would be selected from lists of candidates prepared by the political parties for each province. The allocation of list seats to parties would be such that the overall composition of the parliament would reflect as closely as mathematically possible the distribution of votes among parties in each province. In developing the following example of how such a system might be constructed and might work, the total size of the parliament and the balance between constituency and provincial representatives has been selected arbitrarily. These parameters do affect representativeness, but could be varied within substantial margins without too much loss. They also affect other values not considered in this paper: the cost of paying and pensioning MPs and the disappearance of an MP's seat.

There are practical difficulties in adapting the German system to Canada's small provinces or territories. If the decision were to allocate one-third of the seats proportionately and two-thirds as at present, very poor proportionality could be achieved in the Atlantic provinces or in the north. Prince Edward Island would have only one at large seat, Newfoundland only two, and the Yukon/Northwest Territories might have no at large seat. One could keep all the current constituencies and increase the size of the House of Commons by one-third to one-half, but this would create an unwieldy parliament without really improving proportionality at the provincial level. A possible compromise might be to increase the size of the House of Commons by one-quarter to 354 and reduce the number of directly electing constituencies by one-third to 188, thus increasing constituency size by 50%. This would still not allow proportionality for the North, though residents might be permitted to vote for the Alberta lists. The effect on other provinces would be as shown in Table 1.

Table 1

Distribution of Seats among Provinces for
a Mixed Proportionality Electoral System

Province	Current	New Direct	New List	Threshold
Newfoundland	7	5	4	.10
Prince Edward Island	4	3	2	.17
New Brunswick	10	7	5	.08
Nova Scotia	11	7	7	.07
Quebec	75	50	44	.013
Ontario	95	63	56	.011
Manitoba	14	9	9	.05
Saskatchewan	14	9	9	.05
Alberta	21	14	12	.04
British Columbia	28	19	16	.03
North	3	2	2	.20
TOTAL	282	188	166	

The representation thresholds would be quite different from province to province. In Prince Edward Island, a party would have to have support from slightly more than one-sixth of the electorate to be assured of representation (though, of course, it might hope to get representation with something around 40% of the vote in one constituency). In Ontario and Quebec, by contrast,representation could be assured by virtually any serious group. The inequalities in thresholds could be reduced if it were possible to have an "Atlantic Provinces list" or a "Prairie plus North list." Drawing up such lists would produce consider-able intraparty tension in allocating top places to different provinces. However, the tension might not be any more formidable (or unmanageable) than would be faced by the Ontario parties in allocating top spots among claimants from Toronto, the Niagara peninsula, or eastern or northern Ontario.

This proposed system has many similarities to the present one. As now, political parties would nominate candidates in each consti-tuency they wished to contest. They would, in addition, establish provincial lists of candidates ranking these candidates from one to however many provincial representatives are allocated to that province. Each party would have a Quebec list of 44 names, a British Columbia list of 16, a Nova Scotia list of 7, and so on. The same people could appear as constituency candidates and prov-incial candidates.

For the voter, nothing would be changed except that his consti-tuency would be larger. As at present, he would enter the voting booth with a ballot containing the names of all who wished to represent his constituency and who could qualify as candidates. Those nominated by recognized parties would have their affiliation indicated on the ballot. Voters would make a single cross opposite the name of the candidate they supported and deposit their ballot in the ballot box.

The candidate preferred by the largest number of voters in his constituency would be declared elected. Again, this represents no change from current practice. However, the votes for each party's constituency candidates would be totalled for each province. This is regularly done now, both by election night commentators and by the Chief Electoral Officer in his official report of election results.

Provincial representatives would be declared elected in such a way as to make the proportion of the total provincial seats won by any party approximate the proportion of provincial votes won by that party. To see how this could be done, let us suppose that the 1974 election had been fought under our proposal for the House of Commons used in our example. Let us also suppose that all voters had cast their ballots the same way they did in 1974 and that the success rate for each party in the constituencies was the same as at that election. Consider now the following examples.

In 1974, the Liberal Party obtained 54% of the vote and 81% of the constituencies in Quebec. In our example, Quebec had 50 constituencies. With the same success rate, the Liberals would have captured 40 constituencies in our re-run of the 1974 election. Since Quebec would have a total of 94 members, the vote for the Liberal party would make it eligible for 51 members. Since it had already elected 40, the first 11 names on its provincial list would also be declared elected. If any person had already been declared elected for a constituency, allocation of the provincial seat would go down the list to a name not already elected.

The Progressive Conservative Party obtained 21% of the vote in Quebec in 1974 and would, under our proposal, be entitled to 20 members from Quebec. At the same success rate in the constituencies as in 1974, only about 2 Progressive Conservative candidates would win direct election. Therefore, the first 18 names on the Progressive Conservative list for Quebec would be declared elected (again, skipping over any person already declared elected). The New Democratic Party would be eligible for 7 Quebec members. Having elected none at the constituency level, the first seven names on their Quebec list would be returned to Parliament. The Social Credit Party obtained 17% of the vote in Quebec in 1974 and so would be entitled to 16 members. Eight Social Credit candidates might have captured constituencies, and the first eight names on their provincial list would also be elected as provincial representatives, provided those people were not already elected in constituencies.

How would our proposal work in Alberta? With the same assumptions made in the discussion for Quebec, and excluding the five percent of the vote which neither captured a seat nor concentrated on a single party, we get the following results. The Progressive Conservative Party would be entitled to 16 of the 26 seats in Alberta, the Liberal Party to 7 and the NDP to 3. If the PCs had swept all 14 constituencies, they would get two members from their list. The top 7 on the Liberal list and the top 3 on the NDP list would be elected. Note that some balances between constituency and provincial representation could not have accommodated the 1974 Alberta result. Were we to opt for one-third list seats and two-thirds constituency seats, Alberta would have 17 direct seats and 9 provincial seats. With the Progressive Conservative Party sweeping all 17 seats, and only nine to allocate, the Liberals would get 7 and the NDP 2. While a departure from strict proportionality, it would not be as serious as could have occurred under a plurality system.

WOULD WE BE ANY BETTER OFF?

STV, list systems and the West German hybrid are all proportional representation systems. Though they differ somewhat
in how well they achieve proportionality, they may be considered
as belonging to a single class when contrasted with plurality
electoral systems on the values of representativeness and of
policy-making capacity. With respect to capacity for redress,
the hybrid might be grouped with the plurality system in a single
class in contrast to STV and list electoral systems. In affecting parties as institutions, STV and plurality electoral systems
are similar in weakening parties and may be contrasted with the
list and hybrid systems which tend to strengthen parties and,
within them, organizational leadership.

With respect to representativeness, proportional systems
produce party caucuses that reflect, in size and geographical
distribution, the electorate of the party. The plurality electoral system does not. It translates votes into seats in a
capricious way, and in a way that exacerbates the divisions in the
country. This emerges quite clearly if we examine the results of
the last three elections as set out in Table 2. The inconsisten-
cies of the system are evident where in different places, years,
or as between different parties, the same proportion of seats can
be won with very different proportions of the vote, or similar
proportions of vote are rewarded with quite different proportions
of seats. (For related studies, see Rae (1967), Cairns (1968) and
Johnston and Ballantyne (1977).)

Apart from these issues, we find large blocs of voters in
each province robbed of any representation at all. Even if we
disregard as very unusual the case of Prince Edward Island in
1968, when 45% of the voters supported Liberal candidates without
electing a single one of them, we still find one-fifth of British
Columbia voters in that year supporting the Progressive Conservative Party without being able to elect a single Progressive
Conservative Member of Parliament. Similarly, the 1972 and 1974
elections gave many the impression that Albertans had unanimously
rejected the Liberal government. In fact, one-quarter of Albertans
had supported that government, but that support was concealed by
the electoral system. In recent elections, the New Democratic Party
has failed to elect a member from Alberta, Quebec, New Brunswick,
Prince Edward Island and Newfoundland yet there exist sizeable
numbers of New Democrats in each of those provinces. In Nova Scotia
in 1974, the New Democratic Party did discover the secret of electing an eastern member. It paid them to give up some of the support
enjoyed in the preceeding election in order to better concentrate
the remainder. This is not the only instance where a party's vote
has gone down, but its share of seats has increased. The Progressive Party has benefited from the same phenomenon in Saskatchewan.

Table 2

The Distribution of Votes and Seats among Parties
in Recent Canadian Elections, 1968 - 1974

Year and Province	Liberal		Progressive Conservative		New Democratic		Social Credit	
	%Votes	%Seats	%Votes	%Seats	%Votes	%Seats	%Votes	%Seats
1968								
Nfld	43	14	53	86	4	0		
PEI	45	0	52	100	3	0		
NS	38	9	55	91	7	0		
NB	44	50	50	50	5	0	1	0
Quebec	54	76	21	5	8	0	16	19
Ontario	47	73	32	19	21	8		
Manitoba	42	38	31	38	25	24		
Sask	27	15	37	38	36	46		
Alberta	36	21	50	79	9	0		
BC	42	70	19	0	33	30		
1972								
Nfld	45	43	49	57	5	0		
PEI	40	25	52	75	8	0		
NS	34	9	53	91	12	0		
NB	43	50	45	50	6	0	6	0
Quebec	49	76	17	3	6	0	24	21
Ontario	38	41	39	45	22	13		
Manitoba	31	15	42	62	26	23	1	0
Sask	25	8	37	54	36	38		
Alberta	25	0	58	100	13	0	5	0
BC	29	17	33	35	35	48	3	0
1974								
Nfld	47	57	44	43	10	0		
PEI	46	25	49	75	5	0		
NS	41	18	48	73	11	9		
NB	47	60	33	30	9	0	3	0
Quebec	54	81	21	4	7	0	17	15
Ontario	45	62	35	28	19	10		
Manitoba	27	15	48	69	24	15	1	0
Sask	31	23	36	61	32	15	1	0
Alberta	25	0	61	100	9	0	3	0
BC	33	35	42	56	23	9	1	0

With very few and very minor exceptions, our electoral system unduly rewards the party that is dominant in any province. It thus makes provinces appear more unanimous than they really are. Quebec voters are <u>not</u> solidly behind the Liberal Party: one in two votes for other parties. This reality is concealed at the parliamentary level where the Liberals gain more than three seats in every four. A similar effect has been observed for Alberta. These are only the most dramatic effects. The leading party in popular votes gets a bonus in parliamentary seats in all provinces. Thus, political parties have an incentive to concentrate campaigns on their areas of strength, further reinforcing their image as captives of one or two regions.

There is no general pattern in the way the electoral system treats the less popular parties in each province. In some cases, the second most popular party is the most seriously disadvantaged. Liberals in Nova Scotia and Prince Edward Island could testify to this on the basis of recent experience. So too could Progressive Conservatives in Quebec. In both 1968 and 1974 that party received the second highest popular vote in Quebec. In both of those years, it only received about one-quarter as many seats as the less popular Social Credit Party.

In the Canadian context, the working of the plurality system offends not only against fairness in an abstract way but also sharpens regional cleavages and alienation. It makes the West and Quebec seem single-minded in support of one political party. When the Liberals form the government, the West is only weakly represented and Quebecers play leading roles. However this situation might satisfy Quebecers in the short run, they can have no long-term confidence in the normal democratic process. They know that, if the Progressive Conservatives were to form a government, the likely con- sequence would not be a change of the French-Canadians <u>in</u> govern- ment but an exclusion of French-Canadians <u>from</u> government. Under a more proportional electoral system, such as the one suggested, national parties would have support in all provinces. Even if new provincialist parties were to arise, taking advantage of the lower initial barriers to entry in a proportional electoral system, it is hard to believe that the present national parties would lose all their support in some province or other.

While defenders of the present electoral system might concede that a change would enhance representativeness in party caucuses and so increase legitimacy, they would probably insist that a more proportional electoral system would render Canada ungovernable. By returning parliaments in which there was no majority party, the capacity of government to make and to change policy would be weak- ened and so, ultimately, would be the acceptability of the whole governmental system - in a word, legitimacy. They fear that a representative parliament would be subject to deadlock and delay:

unable to agree on a cabinet to support, unable to continue that support for four years, unable to pass laws or budgets wherever these were opposed by significant segments of the community. In the Canadian context, it could also be argued that a government that was more representative in both a territorial and a partisan sense would be unable to effectively defend the interests of the federal government vis-a-vis the provinces.

The evidence that would permit us to comment on these propositions is sadly lacking, since there are many specific factors that make it difficult to apply European experience and there has been little systematic study of the nine years of Canadian minority government since 1957. On the one hand, this means that we should not make too much of the instances that are regularly cited as showing the weakness of proportional electoral systems: Italy and Germany before the Fascist takeovers, IVth Republic France or Italy immediately after World War II. In all of those examples, there was at least one (sometimes more) major party committed to the overthrow of, or very radical change in, the political system. In the German and Italian cases, there was a limited history of democratic government as well. None of these conditions obtain in Canada, nor are they forseeable. Similarly, in the 1960-69 period, Canada had lower inflation than most Western European countries, and government absorbed less of the GDP in 1971/72 than it did in most West European countries. However, Canada had much higher unemployment in the same period and a higher rate of expansion of the public economy than most European countries over the 1960-74 period. Especially when we recall that the 1960-69 period includes seven years of minority government, we cannot claim that the present electoral system is necessary to desirable economic performance. Indeed, the most relevant difference between Canada and Western Europe in this context is the relative weight of social democratic parties. (See Tufte (1978) and work there cited.)

It would be all the more difficult if new parties were also to arise. While there is no reason to believe that these would sweep away the present parties at precisely the moment when votes for those parties come to have some weight, it is possible that some strongly regionalist parties might emerge. If a nationalist party from Quebec were both large, and so extreme in its demands that it could not be included in a governing coalition, the Canadian situation would be even worse than at present. On the other hand, if such a party were willing to bargain, Quebec would find itself with a wider range of coalition options than it now has. A similar analysis could be made for a "Prairie" party.

Moreover, if there is a basis for a large (more than 1/3 of the electorate for example) new party in some province, the most that our present electoral system could do is to delay its full emergence for an election or two. Any new party with committed support, at both the mass and elite levels, could eventually turn a plurality system to its own advantage. The rise of the Parti Québécois provides eloquent testimony.

The suggested trade-off between representativeness and decisiveness is thus far from established. Minority governments can occur under the present electoral rules. In any case, the evidence of their weak policy-making capacity is hardly overwhelming. Moreover, to the extent that majority governments are artificially generated by the electoral system, any advantage they might have in policy-making permits them to go beyond the limits of social consensus and generates opposition to the whole system. Decisiveness easily shades into blundering wrong-headedness. As between the values of representational capacity and policy-making capacity, strong evidence on the former, and ambiguity with respect to the latter suggests that one should opt for the system offering representation: a proportional electoral system. But which of the three should it be? To make this decision, we look at two other values: party building, and procedural quality.

Party-building contrasts the STV system with those proportional systems requiring party lists. In the absence of a list, the voter becomes decisive in determining who is to be elected, and his choice is not only between party representatives as in the plurality system but also among representatives of the same party. Party is weakened, therefore, because its own candidates are encouraged to compete against each other. While this competition can be benign or even positive in its consequences if it takes the form of constituency service or patronage, it can be unfortunate if it encourages candidates to depart from the party line in articulating local interests. In a five-man STV constituency in Saskatchewan, there would probably be two guaranteed PC seats and a third marginal one. There would, however, be five PC candidates and one could expect that each would vie with the others in opposition to the national party's language policy or even, perhaps, to its natural resources policy. The incentive is quite the opposite in a list system, at least insofar as the national leadership determines the ranking on the list. Since the top ranks are the crucial ones, the proper strategy for the aspiring politician is to mirror as closely as possible the policy line of those who establish the list.

Party-building also means that each party not only elects candidates in regions where it is now weak, but that it can offer political careers to candidates in those regions. The Progressive Conservative Party has always had good candidates in Quebec; it has less often had the same good candidate at two successive elections. Given the operation of the plurality electoral system, this is hardly surprising. However, an STV system would not be much better. At present levels of support, Liberals could only be assured of one seat for every five-man constituency on the Prairies. The same

would hold for the PCs in five-man Quebec constituencies. In
each case, there would be five Liberals or five Progressive Conservatives competing for that seat. Even if they could, by some
pact, all agree to abide by the party line, chance variation in
vote magnitudes would interrupt political careers. It would
certainly make it very difficult for a party leader to recruit a
prestigious spokesman in Quebec or the Prairies with promises of
a political career. This is precisely what could be offered under
a list system for achieving proportionality. A party leader could
offer the top list positions to those whom he expects to represent
the party to some regional or linguistic group and vice versa.
Those playing these broad linkage roles could be insulated from
specifically local constituency concerns and from idiosyncrasies
in local level election returns.

As between the two proportional systems using lists, the
hybrid system has the greater capacity for redress simply because
it does not use lists exclusively. In the example given, just
over half would hold their seats directly on suffrance of a local
electorate. The ratio could be made higher by changing the balance
between direct and list seats. This personal responsibility gives
individuals and groups someone to turn to for assistance. No
doubt the quality of that assistance depends much on the personality
of the candidate. No plurality voting system can insure this kind
of responsiveness, particularly in safe seats. However, the norms
of parliamentary life may compensate for, if they do not reinforce,
the parliamentarian's degree of self-interest in being attentive
to local needs. Moreover, any mixed system would contain fewer
parliamentarians with job security than any list system. In this
sense, the hybrid system marshalls more incentive for acting to
seek redress of local grievances than would a straight list system.

CONCLUSION

The above analysis contains an implicit hierarchy of values
and has proceeded largely by pair-wise comparisons - a voting system
known to produce paradoxical results. Another analyst might offer
an extended discussion of STV which, even on the above discussion,
obviously has more substantial capacity for redress of local grievances. Some might prefer this to party-building. Insofar as
constituencies under STV return no more than five members, the
barriers to entry would also be higher than in other PR systems.
The NDP would likely elect no more candidates in the Atlantic region
than it does currently, and would have little or no success in Quebec or Alberta. The system would not, however, be more likely to
produce majority government (whose value, let it be recalled, is
not established). It would, instead, produce two more evenly matched
minority parties and might complicate policy-making.

Insofar as one conceives the analysis of electoral systems as a policy recommendation to governments or advisory panels, it would be desirable to be able to make an overall comparison of all electoral systems. One would like to be able to weight the values at issue and to discount these by the probability that any given system does contribute to realizing that value, given existing and probable future distributions of preferences. Political science is not (not yet?) at a point to enable us to do this. My own reading of the evidence, with implicit weights and discount factors, suggests that a hybrid plurality/proportionality system (such as the one described in section III) would end up with the highest score on the ideal balance sheet.

REFERENCES

Cairns, Alan C. (1968), "The Electoral System and the Party
    System in Canada, 1921-1965", Canadian Journal of Political
    Science, Vol. I, pp. 55-80

Huntington, Samuel P. (1965), Political Order in Changing Societies
    (New Haven: Yale University Press)

Irvine, William P. (1977), "Liberté, Egalité, Efficacité: Respeci-
    fying the Federal Role" in Richard Simeon (ed.) Must Canada
    Fail? (Montreal and London: McGill-Queen's Press)

Johnston, Richard and Ballantyne, Janet (1977), "Geography and
    the Electoral System", Canadian Journal of Political Science,
    Vol. X, pp. 857-866

Rae, Douglas (1967), The Political Consequences of Electoral Laws
    (New Haven: Yale University Press)

Simeon, Richard (1978), The Contemporary Canadian Political Crisis
    and Possible Directions for Change (mimeo, Queen's University)

Tufte, Edward R. (1978), Political Control of the Economy (Princeton,
    N.J.: Princeton University Press)

Comments by K.Z. Paltiel, Department of Political Science, Carleton University

In his oral remarks Professor Irvine correctly stresses the problem of parties and their declining role in our political system, matters which receive less attention in his written paper. In his formal presentation Professor Irvine argues that our faulty electoral system is one of the principal reasons for the current crisis facing the central institutions of the government of Canada. The "first past the post" territorial electoral system, as Alan Cairns pointed out more than a decade ago, seriously misrepresents the will of the Canadian people in the way it translates votes into seats; it inflates the strength of the largest party, exaggerates the representation of parties with strong regional bases and penalizes parties with broad but diffuse pan-Canadian support. This benefits regionally-oriented third parties and penalizes the Liberals in the Prairie provinces and the Progressive-Conservatives in Quebec.

The results, Irvine says, are a crisis of authority in the central governing institutions and growing popular frustration arising from the failure of governing parties to respond with policies capable of conciliating contending social forces. A more representative electoral system, in his view, would enhance the legitimacy of the Federal Government and pave the way for more satisfactory public policies. This could be achieved by adopting an electoral system that would more truly reflect rather than distort Canadian opinion.

For a variety of reasons Irvine rejects the Single Transferable Vote scheme practised in Ireland and Australia as well as the Netherlands. Irvine proposes that Canada adopt a variant of the West German hybrid plurality--constituency *cum* list system. This would entail fewer territorial constituencies in each province whose Members of Parliament would be chosen by the present voting system plus a number of seats-at-large for each province which would be allocated amongst the parties according to their proportion of the total vote in the election of the constituency members; the seats-at-large would be distributed so that the total number of seats received by each party would not exceed their proportion of the total vote cast.

My comments on this proposal fall into two categories:

(a) the soundness of the details of the proposal;
(b) a critique of Irvine's claims that his scheme will cure the defects of the current electoral system.

1. Irvine's scheme does not eliminate the possibilities of gerry-mandering; indeed, it puts a premium on such practices. How and by whom will the new constituency boundaries be drawn? The present system of distribution already contains grave distortions and biases--a constituency's population may vary by 25% above or below the provincial quotient. The biases favour rural areas and areas of declining population; the greater the number of seats to be chosen territorially, the greater the bias will be and the greater the temptation to bias.

2. Who will nominate and determine the position of candidates to be chosen from the "list" as opposed to those nominated in the constituencies? Will this not set up a two or three-class system of candidates composed of those nominated only by the local constit-uency organizations, those whose names appear only on the provincial "list," and the "stars" who appear both in a constituency and high on the list? At one point Irvine speaks of the provincial party organizations choosing the "list" candidate, at another he speaks of the national leader performing this function. If it is to be the party, which will it be? The provincial party organization, the provincial-wing of the federal party, or a central party cabal? All the evidence from existing list systems indicates that the real political struggle in such regimes is over one's location on the party list, and real political power rests with those who are authorized to do the choosing and placing of the candidates. In what way will this contentious process, which is bound to undermine local party organizations, enhance or revivify the parties? Will it not rather encourage the trend towards centralization and the atrophy of party infrastructure?

3. Under Irvine's proposal a candidate rejected by constituency voters could nevertheless be declared "elected" provided that his name also appeared in a high position on a "list." Thus party leaders could frustrate the will of the electorate. Furthermore, a candidate who had received a smaller number of direct votes in a constituency could be sent to Parliament over another who was endorsed elsewhere by a greater number of voters but whose name had appeared on a list which would not be compensated.

4. In the light of the foregoing, if proportionality is the goal, then why not opt for a straightforward list system on a provincial basis, or a system of multi-member constituencies chosen through a proportional or preferential system? This multi-member system would avoid the contradictory anomalies of Irvine's version of the West German hybrid.

Irvine rightly dwells on the weakness of parties in Canada, on their subsistence as mere electoral instruments, on their failure as "representative" bodies and on the implications of this failure for policy responsiveness and legitimacy. But will his scheme cure these weaknesses?

1. A large number of Quebec Liberals in the House of Commons since the turn of the century has not produced policy outputs over time or promoted administrative structures with adequate French-Canadian representation, moves which, according to some, could have allayed the current discontent in Quebec. Likewise, there is still discontent in the Maritimes where party representation has been, over time, more or less proportional to popular support. Why, therefore, should a "mechanically" achieved greater representation of Liberals from the West or Conservatives from Quebec assure different policy outcomes in Ottawa? Policy outcomes are influenced by interest groups and a variety of other forces, such as the leadership selection process, which lie outside the electoral process.

2. Nothing in the proposal before us would alter the internal structuring of our parties. Indeed, the bias towards the centre and the party leader which has been strengthened by recent changes in the Canada Elections Act concerning the recognition of parties, the placing of the party name on the ballot and party financing would be further enhanced by giving the leadership control of the proposed "lists" of candidates. A concern for parties, which is ostensibly the goal of this proposal, should at least indicate how the rank-and-file and middle-range leadership can participate in the candidate selection process. The recent proceedings in Ottawa Centre, Rosedale and other Toronto Liberal Party nomination "contests," that is to say, the displacement of locally-chosen candidates by hand-picked nominees parachuted from the central party organizations, would be given legitimate sanction by the creation of a hybrid "list" system.

3. The Irvine proposal as presently constituted, when coupled with the laws concerning the "recognition" of parties, would simply reinforce the existing, institutionalised and incumbent parties as a group. It would further impede the appearance of independents and grossly inhibit the emergence of "new parties." In this way our party system would be rendered less representative and less responsive to regional, sectional and social demands. Since the end of the First World War, it has been the rebellion of the regions as expressed by "new" and "third" parties which has prompted most of the innovation within our political system. Only in the face of the threat from these maverick groups have our established parties begun

to face up to pressing regional and social demands. Professor
Irvine's proposal appears to thwart the future emergence of such
yeasty and innovation-producing groups. As such it appears to me
to be counter-productive in its attempt to restore "country-building"
processes.

ECONOMIC STABILIZATION AND THE REGIONS:

THE DILEMMA IN CANADA

by

Y. Rabeau and R. Lacroix

Department of Economics

University of Montreal

PREFACE

Canada is now going through one of the most crucial periods in its history. The most serious economic crisis since the Great Depression has occurred at the same time as the most dangerous political crisis in Canadian history. Confederation is being questioned more each day, and while Quebec is the most direct critic, many other provinces are having considerable doubts about the distribution of power and jurisdictions as well as about the federal government's past use of the powers it has held or gradually accumulated.

The problem of regional economic disparities is a prime factor in these doubts. The poorest provinces ask, for example, why regional differences in unemployment and income have remained high. It is felt that income redistribution policies between regions and individuals through various forms of transfer payments have merely redistributed demand among the regions without redistributing employment. This would explain why some provinces are living increasingly off federal transfers and why this situation is accepted by the rich provinces, since these transfers allow the recipients to purchase products from the rich provinces. *Past economic policies have not allowed the poor provinces to become self-developing. To survive, they must rely on an uninterrupted flow of outside transfers. We must, therefore, question policies based solely on redistribution of demand as a means of reducing, and eventually eliminating, regional disparities.*

It is in this perspective that this study on regional economic stabilization must be viewed.

INTRODUCTION

While we have no intention of reopening the debate between Keynesians and monetarists, we agree with the neo-Keynesians that, while stabilization of the economy is definitely a difficult and delicate operation, it is, nonetheless, possible. While all economists now admit that "fine tuning" is not possible, the same cannot be said of the reduction of cyclical effects through appropriate budget policies.

This introduction will examine the two facets of budget policy -- expenditure and revenue -- in an attempt to provide a detailed profile of the characteristics a spending or tax program should have for maximum effectiveness as a stabilization instrument in a homogeneous economic context and in Canada's particular geopolitical context.

1   Public Spending

Through its direct effect on aggregate demand, a change in goverment expenditure is the form of intervention with the greatest and quickest impact on the level of economic activity and employment. However, to remain a true stabilization instrument, this type of spending must, above all, be flexible enough to increase or decrease substantially over relatively short periods of time. Unfortunately, a large proportion of public spending is easily increased, but not so easily curtailed.

In fact, it can even be argued that some expenditures, long considered non-recurrent, have created expectations such that it has become practically impossible to reduce them, unless we accept serious social tensions. If we therefore wish to prevent special government spending programs with contracyclical purposes from further increasing the relative size of government, we must first ensure that they are *non-recurrent*.

Moreover, if we wish to concentrate the impact of this spending within a short period, it must be implemented with an absolute minimum of delay. Finally, although it may appear paradoxical at first glance, this spending must not be inflationary. Recession does not equally affect all sectors of the economy and we must prevent the recovery policy from creating inflationary pressures in some sectors.

2   Fiscal Policy

Three major categories of taxes provide most of the government's revenue, and are generally considered as potential stabilization instruments.

Personal Income Tax   Various studies indicate that the marginal propensity to consume for additional income from temporary variations in personal income tax is lower than the marginal propensity to

consume for permanent income. Moreover, we must remember that at
the trough of a serious recession, consumers may worry about
temporary cash-flow problems that a lay-off would cause, and are,
therefore, more inclined to save all temporary income. Thus, in
view of the considerable uncertainty existing over the impact on
consumption of a variation in personal income tax, its utilization
as a stabilization instrument appears very imprudent, at least
during recessions.

Corporate Income Tax   The effect on the economy of a change
in corporate taxes -- modification of taxes on profits, variation
of investment credits, changes to various depreciation formulas --
appears to be even more uncertain that that of a change in personal
income tax. Michael K. Evans (1969) best summed up the various
opinions on the issue: "It would (...) seem that the corporate
income tax rate should be decided more on equity grounds or as a
means of balancing the budget than as a method of regulating
GNP."

Indirect Taxes   Except for the jurisdictional problems that
may arise in Canada, the use of indirect taxes as a stabilization
instrument may be of some worth in particular situations. The
impact of a temporary variation in the sales tax, for example,
is double: it first leads to a change in the real income of
individuals and then, over time, shifts their consumption pattern.
This measure may also be selectively applied to only certain
categories of goods whose national output content is high. While
a sales tax cut is recommended in periods of recession and, particularly, of stagflation (since it stimulates demand while temporarily
reducing inflationary pressure), any increase in the sales tax in
a period of inflation is unadvisable since it pushes even higher.

3 The Particular Case of Canada

The preceding discussion of the effectiveness of stabilization
instruments is based on the assumption that they are applied to
homogeneous and particularly punctiform economies. However, the
Canadian geopolitical reality differs greatly from this ideal world.
Each major region has its own climate, its own resource and factor
endowment, and its own commercial relations that cause it to react
in a particular way to the business cycle.

A recent study by the Economic Council of Canada found, for
example, that "an increase of 2 percentage points in the Canadian
unemployment rate is typically accompanied by an increase of
roughly 3.7 points in the Atlantic Region, 2.6 points in Quebec,
1.3 points in Ontario, 1.7 points in the Prairie Region, and 1.9
points in British Columbia.[1]

---

1 Economic Council of Canada, *Living Together*, p.49.

This casts doubt on the effectiveness of stabilization policies that are applied at the same time and to the same extent in all regions of the country. It has long been claimed in Canada that we cannot regionalize economic policies but only structural policies. In other words, stabilization is carried out at the national level, while development can be conducted on a regional basis.

Yet, the differentiation in the utilization of stabilization instruments by region raises major problems if we use public spending. However, in Canada account must be made for the distribution of jurisdictions: we will see later that those expenditures most likely to be used for stabilization purposes fall, in large part, under provincial or municipal jurisdiction, while the responsibility for stabilization and the means for financing it form part of the federal jurisdiction.

1   LEVELS OF GOVERNMENT AND STABILIZATION INSTRUMENTS

An analysis of the past growth of revenue and expenditure at the various levels of Canadian government from 1950 to the present, will reveal which level of government has the most effective stabilization tools.

This overview will also make it possible to evaluate the fiscal performance of these governments by determining in particular whether they actually used the various stabilization instruments at their disposition.

1.1   The Federal Government's Instruments

Our analysis reveals that approximately 96 per cent of all federal government expenditures are not suitable for stabilization purposes.

The tests that we conducted indicate that spending on goods and services by the federal government (23.1 per cent of total expenditure in 1975) is, in large part, recurrent. Transfer payments to individuals (30.9 per cent of total expenditure) and interest payments on public debt (10.3 per cent) are also recurrent. Finally, transfers by the central government to other levels of government (21.3 per cent) can be considered to serve primarily to finance current expenditures and are, therefore, unsuited to stabilization. As a result, the federal administration's ability to stabilize the economy through its expenditures appears to be very limited.

Among the non-recurrent expenditures, only those for gross fixed capital formation (GFCF) could be used for stabilization purposes by the federal government. However, these expenditures represent only a very small share (3.1 per cent) of the federal government's budget and a minor proportion (slightly over 15 per cent) of total public GFCF in Canada. The federal government GFCF represents practically a negligible proportion of GNP and its fiscal lever effect would thus be very limited.

Consequently, the federal government's ability to intervene is based more on income than on expenditure. We have seen that the utilization of taxation as a means of stabilization is not necessarily very effective. Households and businessmen do not automatically spend a temporary increase in their disposable income and, even if they do, this often occurs too long afterwards to be effective. Thus, the federal government is faced with a dilemma in terms of the management of its stabilization policies in Canada. It has the extensive financial resources but its means of intervention are among the least effective for stabilization.

A short summary of the difficulties the federal government has experienced since 1950 in the use of public expenditure for stabilization purposes will provide a clearer picture of Ottawa's dilemma:

-- With respect to fixed capital formation expenditures, the distribution of jurisdictions in Canada does not particularly favour increased federal intervention. Even when it did succeed in moving into this spending sector, the federal government was unable to inject amounts of any significance on an annual basis.

-- In any case, it proved difficult to control the growth of federal spending because of its highly recurrent nature. In 1968, despite a promise to exert tight control over spending in an attempt to stop inflation, federal government expenditure continued to grow at 11 per cent, while the growth of GNP did not exceed 9 per cent.

-- To stabilize the economy, the central government is reduced to using expenditures that, by their very nature, are unsuited to this purpose. In particular, it has often used transfer payments to individuals and provinces.

-- On occasion, the federal government has resorted to the spending power of lower government levels to stimulate the economy through expenditure. In 1970, for example, it financed provincial and municipal spending on infrastructure, whose multiplier effect is known to be large.

-- The federal government has attempted to circumvent its fiscal dilemma at the start of the 1971 expansion by launching special job-creation programs -- Opportunities For Youth, Local Initiatives Program -- that have rapidly become recurrent. In May 1972, Opportunities For Youth was renewed while gross national demand was growing at a rate of 11 per cent annually. Similarly, in the following year when the Canadian economy reached a peak of expansion, Opportunities For Youth and Local Initiatives Programs were renewed. These expenditures eventually helped to increase the government's size in relation to GNP and thus no longer met the basic criteria for stabilization expenditures.

1.2 The Provincial and Municipal Governments' Instruments

In the case of the provinces, if we accept the findings of our research on recurrent expenditures that part of the spending on goods and services other than wages is sufficiently flexible to be used for stabilization, this could supplement the part of gross fixed capital formation (GFCF) suited to contracyclical use.

Since GFCF already accounts for slightly over 7 per cent of the provincial budgets, the amount of provincial government expenditure that could be applied to stabilization can be estimated at over 10 per cent. Therefore, the provinces clearly have greater spending flexibility than the federal government (approximately 4 per cent). If, for example, the provinces made a 25 per cent increase in their non-recurrent expenditures, approximately 1 billion dollars would be injected into the Canadian economy on the basis of 1977 data. A similar increase by the federal government in the same year would only have produced an injection of about $400 million. Moreover, as shown by a special study that we conducted for Quebec, the labour content of provincial spending is likely to be greater than that of federal spending.

Municipal governments, as immediate providers of services, devoted 74 per cent of their 1975 budget to the purchase of goods and services. Of this amount, 20 per cent went to the purchase of goods and services other than civil servants' wages. Their GFCF expenditures represented 17.2 per cent of total expenditure and almost 40 per cent of total public GFCF in Canada. We believe that the pattern of municipal GFCF over time could be changed if the provinces decided to co-ordinate this spending and use part of it for stabilization. For example, if we assume that 30 per cent of municipal spending could be accelerated or delayed relative to the cycle, approximately $825 million, based on 1977 data, would thus be available for stabilization.

We have now found about $2 billion that could be used for stabilization purposes at the lower levels of government, while the federal government's power of intervention would be only about $400 million. It should be stressed here that capital expenditures exclude investments by parapublic corporations, part of the education sector and the hospital sector.

Finally, a survey of federal spending in Quebec indicates that the proportion likely to be used for stabilization purposes is relatively smaller than in the other provinces. Federal expenditure on goods and services averages only 15 per cent of total government expenditure in Quebec, compared with 27 per cent at the national level. When wages are excluded, this proportion rises to over 20 per cent, but still remains far below the national

average of approximately 35 per cent. The average share of federal
GFCF spending, even after a clear upward trend in the 1960s, still
remains clearly below the 15 per cent level observed nationally.
Ottawa's spending flexibility, already very limited in all Canadian
provinces, is even more severely restricted in Quebec.

1.3   The Performance of the Federal Government

Now that we have identified the types of expenditure or
revenue at all three levels of government that could effectively
be used for stabilizing the economy, we must determine whether
they were actually used and achieved good results over the period
analysed,1950-75. Table 1.1 summarizes our conclusions.

It is evident from our analysis that the orientation of the
federal government's fiscal policy has not always met the needs
of the Canadian economy. The 1960 and 1969 anti-inflation measures
are the most conspicuous major errors.

The 1959-61 period was dominated by fear of the appearance
of inflationary pressures in Canada. This crusade against inflation
had adverse effects on the entire Canadian economy, since the cycle
had already begun to slow in 1960 and the inflation rate had fallen
from 2.6 per cent in 1958 to 1.2 per cent in 1959. The already
adverse effects of this policy at the national level were even
greater in Quebec. While the unemployment rate exceeded 9 per cent
in 1960 and 1961, the inflation rate did not exceed 1 per cent for
this period. The obvious conclusion is that a national policy that
is harmful throughout Canada has even more serious consequences in
a region where the participation rate is below the national average
and the effects of the recession (in terms of the magnitude and
length) are generally greater than at the national level.

The same error was repeated in 1969 when the federal government
began a new crusade against inflation through three successive tax
hikes. At the time, Quebec was experiencing a serious slowdown of
investment and the federal policies thus exacerbated the particular
problems of the Quebec economy.

The lack of adaptation between federal fiscal policy and
Quebec's stabilization needs consequently arose not only from the
lack of a regionalized stabilization policy, but also particularly
from its poor orientation at the macroeconomic level. In fact,
the periods when federal government action was particularly harmful
for Quebec also correspond to those when the stabilization policy
was clearly misdirected for the nation as a whole.

The existence of a regional stabilization mechanism would have
made it possible, in the first place, to better adapt the federal
government's policy to Quebec's needs. When the policy was not
sufficiently expansionist, a regionalization mechanism would have
ensured an injection of sufficient fiscal stimulants to allow Quebec
to operate closer to its potential or to benefit more rapidly from
the effects of a recovery.

Table 1.1

Effectiveness of Various Fiscal Policies
in Terms of Stabilization[1]

	Federal					Provincial				
	(1)	(2)	(3)	(4)	(5)	(1)	(2)	(3)	(4)	(5)
A. Expenditures										
Wages	TR	NO	Occasionally (EG: 1969)	NE	D	TR	NO	NO	NE	D
Other Goods and Services	AR	Periodically	NO	PE	D (1952-65) N (1966-71) D (1972-76)	AR	Periodically	NO	PE	D (1952-65) S (1966-71) N (1972-76)
Transfers to Individuals	AR	NO	YES	PE[2]	S	AR	NO	YES	PE	S
Equipment Subsidies	TPR	NO	NO	NE	N	TPR	NO	NO	NE	N
GFCF[3]	PR	YES	Periodically	PE	S (1952-65) D (1966-71) N (1972-76)	PR	YES	Periodically	TE	D (1952-71) N (1972-76)
B. Revenue[4]										
1. Autonomous										
Direct Taxes								–		
Personal	–	YES	YES	PE	S	–	YES	YES	PE	S
On Profits	–	YES	YES	NE	S	–	YES	YES	NE	S
Indirect Taxes	–	YES	YES	AE	S	–	YES	YES	E	S
2. Current Transfers from Other Levels of Public Administration	–	–	–	–		PR	YES	NO	NE	N

1 Column 1 indicates whether the category of expenditure considered is: highly recurrent (TR), fairly recurrent (AR), fairly non-recurrent (PR) or very non-recurrent (TPR). This classification is based on the results of recurrence tests. The second column indicates whether the instrument (expenditure or income) can be utilized for purposes of stabilization. Column 3 asks the question, "Was this instrument regularly used for purposes of stabilization?" Column 4 indicates whether the instrument can be used for stabilization purposes effectively (E), fairly effectively (PE), not very effectively (PE) or ineffectively (NE). Finally, the last column summarizes the effect of using this instrument in the past on the economy; there are three possibilities here: the instrument may have a stabilizing or contracyclical effect (S), destabilizing or procyclical (D), or neutral or undetermined (N).

2 The handling of transfers to individuals in a discretionary way cannot be effective for purposes of stabilization because of the tendency of these modifications to become permanent. On the other hand, we do not deny that *as an automatic stabilizer* these expenditures play a very effective role at the federal level.

3 The only case in which the municipal sector in co-ordination with the provincial sector was able to use its spending for stabilization is that of GFCF. As indicated in the text, however, this type of expenditure has an undetermined behaviour at the *national* level.

4 In view of our analysis, the recurrence test is useless for revenue (the test was conducted, however, for transfers to the provinces from the federal government, since this is a federal expenditure).

Secondly, a body responsible for the regionalization of tax policy would have been able to inform federal authorities and draw their attention to the economic situation in Quebec -- and the other provinces -- at the moment when the latter intended to introduce restrictive measures. Such an agency could also have warned of the disastrous consequences of the federal anti-inflation policies on a regional economy where no true inflationary pressures existed and where the participation rate was already well below the national average.

Such intervention would have been able to modify the orientation of Canadian policy or at least reduce an anti-inflation policy's adverse effects if it had still been applied by Ottawa.

Our analysis also shows that, while the federal government did not technically regionalize its fiscal policy, it nonetheless showed a real concern for regional disparity problems in the management of its fiscal policy. But the means of intervention proposed to compensate for these disparities -- for example, the declared intention of using DREE programs to lessen the harmful effects of the national policy at the regional level -- did not make it possible to regionalize the effects of the stabilization policy.

1.4   The Quebec Government's Performance

Our analysis also reveals that the Quebec government never used the major fiscal lever at its disposition to support the federal stabilization policies or, in some cases, to lessen the adverse effects of these federal policies. The provincial authorities have, upon occasion, mentioned the possibility of using their taxing power to stabilize the regional economy but have never actually done so. The orientation of Quebec's fiscal policy since the early 1950s has often been procyclical and sometimes has even reinforced the harmful effects of the federal policy. In 1969, for example, when the province reached the trough of a recession and the federal government began its crusade against inflation, the Quebec government took no step to stimulate its economy and even exerted a slightly deflationary action through a cut in its budget deficit.

However, the 1975 recession constitutes an interesting experience for Quebec because it allows us to complete our conclusions on the postwar fiscal policies. This experience indicates first, that regionalized fiscal policy could effectively help to stabilize the economy of a province such as Quebec; second, that the utilization of expenditure on public infrastructure, while effective in stabilizing the economy, raises the problem of bottlenecks whose inflationary effects may be aggravated by provincial labour legislation.

When Canada was experiencing one of the most severe postwar recessions, the moderately expansionist fiscal policy of the federal government in 1975 was combined with a strong growth of public

infrastructure spending in Quebec. While the gap between unemployment rates in Quebec and the rest of Canada widens during a
recession -- in direct proportion to the seriousness of the
recession -- this large increase in public spending resulted in
the participation rate disparity registered in 1974 remaining steady
in 1975. The growth rate of employment in Quebec in 1975 was
roughly the same as that in the rest of Canada. This fairly
exceptional behaviour of the cycle in Quebec tends to illustrate
to what extent a regional stabilization policy can be effective.

We must remember, however, that this was not the result of
policy co-ordination between the three levels of government, but
rather coincidence. In previous years, the three levels of government had begun various public infrastructure projects that, by 1975,
had strongly stimulated activity in the construction sector and,
indirectly, in the entire Quebec economy.

Unfortunately, the infrastructure expenditures for the Olympic
Games created considerable inflationary pressures. The fact that
the project imposed delivery of the infrastructure by a precise
date, plus the characteristics of the decree system used in the
Quebec construction industry, created a twofold monopoly situation
in this sector. One buyer -- the organizing committee and, therefore, indirectly, the provincial government -- and one supplier --
the construction unions -- confronted each other over the renewal
of a collective agreement that, through the decree system, would
apply to all workers in the sector for a period of three years,
extending well beyond the closing of the Olympic site.

In 1976-77 these escalating construction costs began to hit
the Quebec economy -- the growth of these costs has been partially
responsible for the slowing of investment in Quebec since 1975.
Moreover, the extensive borrowing that the Quebec government was
forced to undertake in 1975-76 to finance the Olympic games reduced
the province's borrowing power at a time when the Quebec economy
still needed fiscal stimulus.

1.5 A Few Important Principles

Quebec's experience in 1975 reveals a few principles that should
be followed in managing a regionalized fiscal policy:

-- Close co-ordination between the three levels of government is
  essential in the utilization of GFCF expenditures in order to
  avoid bottlenecks in certain subsectors of the construction
  industry.

-- The use of an infrastructure spending policy as a means of
  stabilization would require changes to provincial labour laws;
  a change to mechanisms such as the Construction Decree System
  appears essential in order to apply a stabilization policy
  through GFCF. For example, the use of *ad hoc* contracts for

particular projects with construction workers allocated to this project could be one way during a recession of avoiding excessive pressure on wages in the construction sector;

-- When provincial and municipal capital expenditures increase, the provincial government should have access to a special source of financing so as not to affect its normal flexibility in financial markets following the stabilization measures.

-- Finally, a major increase in public infrastructure expenditures for purposes of regional economic stabilization raises the problem of the social return on public investment projects. There can be no justification for stabilizing the economy with projects that do not contribute to the development of the economy's productive capacity. We cannot afford to stabilize the regional economy at any price by digging holes as suggested by Keynes. What is needed is a cost/benefit analysis conducted on a continuing basis by the three levels of government so as to develop a series of projects that could be undertaken during periods of economic slowdown.

2   ECONOMIC STABILIZATION AND REGIONAL DISPARITIES

Doubt has long been expressed over the effectiveness of stabilization intervention at the regional level even if public spending, apparently the most effective instrument, were used. In particular, it has been argued that the flight of funds would be too large for an increase in public expenditure during a recession to have a significant effect on regional employment.

However, studies of interregional flows in Canada in recent years have tended to disprove these doubts over the efficiency of regional stabilization policies. It has been demonstrated, in particular, that the results of a regional stabilization policy are highly dependent on the nature of the expenditure injected into a regional economy. If, for example, we increase transfer payments to households rather than public GFCF, the regional multipliers drop significantly.

Moreover, government expenditures in any given region generally have a larger multiplier effect when the labour content is high and the required supplies, equipment, materials, etc. are, for the most part, locally made. A special chapter attempts to evaluate the relative effectiveness of the different government levels in stabilizing the economy and to determine what type of intervention is most effective for each individual government.

2.1   Relative Effectiveness of Various Budget Measures

We have attempted to evaluate, through an input-output table based on 1977 labour market data, the amount of expenditures (or tax cuts) that government should inject into the Quebec economy to reduce the provincial unemployment rate by one percentage point during the fiscal stimulus's first period of economic impact.

The effectiveness of a fiscal measure was measured in man-years of employment created by the treasury expenditures, with account taken of the fiscal receipts generated by direct and indirect purchases of goods and services.

The reduction by one percentage point of the 1977 unemployment rate in Quebec would have required the creation of 37,000 jobs. We, therefore, computed the amount of public funds that would have had to be injected into the economy to create this number of jobs during the first initial impact period. The results are presented in *Table 2.1*.

These show that expenditure on goods and services is more effective than that on GFCF in creating jobs in the initial period. Except for the federal government, the amount of expenditure on goods and services required to reduce the unemployment rate by one percentage point is less than the amount of GFCF required. The former is a more effective stimulant, primarily because of the very low import content and the important role of wages in these expenditures. It should be noted, however, that this type of expenditure, with a high wage content, does not meet our criteria of non-recurrence and would thus contribute over the long run to an increase in the government's share of the economy.

Expenditures on goods and services are most effective at the provincial level in stimulating employment, followed by the municipal, and finally the federal, levels. The net cost to the provincial treasury over the initial period would be 88 per cent of the original cost, so that the 37,000 jobs would have cost the province $700 million. To obtain the same impact on employment, municipalities as a whole would have had to spend some $300 million more. The federal government in turn would have had to spend almost double the expenditures incurred by the provincial government to obtain the same impact on employment.

The ranking obtained for the effectiveness of *fixed capital formation expenditures* by levels of government remains the same. However, the differences between the amounts that must be spent by the various levels are substantially smaller. To create the same number of jobs, the federal and municipal administrations would have had to spend $214 million and $37 million more, respectively, than the provincial government. We can thus say that municipal spending is, for all practical purposes, as effective as provincial spending in stimulating the economy. The advanced technology of federal fixed assets results in a 22 per cent import content of the amount injected, while the same coefficient is about 16 per cent for provincial and municipal administrations. This, essentially, is why the federal government must spend more to obtain the same result.

Finally, we must note that the net cost of the expenditure of the federal government, taking into account the receipts generated in Quebec and the other provinces and the ensuing drop in transfer

Table 2.1

Fiscal Measures Required to Create 37,000 Jobs (Man-Years) in Quebec

(Based on 1977 Data)

Nature of the Measure	Amount to be injected ($ millions)	Income created by the injection ($ millions) Wages	Other	Total	Expressed as a percentage of the initial injection	Final receipts ($ millions) Fed.	Prov.	Net cost to the treasury[1] ($ millions) Fed.	Prov.
1. Injection (Expenditure)									
A. Current Expenditures									
Federal	1,370	507	822	1,329	35	192		978 (71%)	
Quebec	787.2	433	314.9	747.9	5.9		87		700 (88%)
Municipal	1,088	511.3	446	957.3	9.1		123		
B. Gross Fixed Capital Formation									
Federal	1,370	561.7	438	999.7	21.7	278		891 (65%)	
Quebec	1,156	566.4	358.3	924.7	17.2		130		1,026 (88%)
Municipal	1,193	584.6	381.8	966.4	15.6				
2. Tax Cut (transferred to households)									
Hypothesis A: Additional savings by households on temporary income -- 10 per cent	1,522	342.5	452.1	794.6	27.2	188	171	1,134 (74%)	1,351 (87%)
Hypothesis B: Additional savings by households on temporary income -- 50 per cent	2,740							2,352 (85%)	2,549 (93%)

1 Takes into account the reduction in unemployment insurance and equalization payments.

payments, is less than the net cost to the provincial government,
despite the fact that the federal expenditures are less effective,
in the Keynesian sense, in creating jobs. This fact leads some
people to suggest *a combination of expenditures at all three levels
of government*, so as to minimize the net combined cost for treasuries
involved. For example, if we assume that the capital expenditures
are made entirely by the provincial government (or even in part by
municipalities), and that the central government assumes 50 per
cent of the financing of these projects, the net cost of the
fiscal measure over the first period would be about $890 million
for the federal and provincial treasuries involved, a saving of
$135 million over the net cost of the provincial government acting
alone.

The results of our analysis indicate that a *tax cut* is clearly
less effective than an increase in public spending. Under the
most favourable assumption -- that a tax cut would be spent in the
same way as the households generally spend transfer payments --
the required tax cut is just as large as the injection of federal
public expenditure required to create 37,000 jobs. This result
is explained by the high import content of household expenditures:
over 27 per cent terminates in other provinces or countries. If
we assume that, *ceteris paribus*, consumers save an extra 10 per
cent of their temporary income, the tax cut required to obtain the
same result rises from $1.3 billion to $1.52 billion. Finally,
if we assume that consumers save 50 per cent of their temporary
income from the tax cut -- not an unrealistic hypothesis -- the
necessary injection would then be $2.5 billion, or more than double
the federal expenditure necessary to obtain the same result.

Finally, the problems raised by consumer behaviour following
the temporary drop in taxes serve as a reminder that the management
of a regional stabilization policy should ideally take into account
the interregional effects and be applied in the perspective of
general equilibrium at the national level. If we wish, for example,
to stimulate Quebec's economy without immediately exerting additional
pressures on the Ontario economy, a tax cut obviously will not be
the appropriate instrument to achieve this. Flights of funds to
Ontario in the initial period could climb to more than a third of
the fiscal stimulus, and would thus be capable of creating
inflationary pressure in that province. On the other hand, an
injection of public funds would limit a larger share of the effects
to the designated province and flights would only occur in precise
sectors and, even then, generally outside Canada.

2.2   The Causes of Unemployment Disparities in Quebec

Of the various regional disparities, we have retained the
unemployment rate for two reasons. First, it is the most important
aspect of the economic stabilization problem and the one felt most
by the population of the underprivileged regions. Moreover, the
unemployment disparity is one cause of a large disparity in income,
which, in turn, determines a large number of other disparities.

Two traits characterize Quebec's unemployment compared with Ontario's or Canada's: the unemployment rate is always higher in Quebec than Ontario and the spread between the two rates varies over the business cycle. The persistent disparity in unemployment rates between the two neighbouring provinces is the result of two factors:

-- a difference in the seasonal unemployment rate;

-- and a gap that could be qualified as "structural," due in part to rigidities in wage determination (often found only in Quebec), and to an obvious lack of mobility in Quebec's labour force.

The authors generally agree that the difference in the seasonal unemployment rate accounts for half a percentage point out of the three-point disparity in aggregate unemployment between Quebec and Ontario.

In turn, wage flexibility is largely offset by particular labour market conditions occurring only in Quebec. In fact, various regulations are unique to Quebec. Of particular interest are the decree system for collective agreements that affects an average of over 200,000 employees, labour relations in the construction industry, terms of application of the minimum wage act and a collective bargaining system in the public and parapublic sectors unlike any other in Canada. All these unique regulations in Quebec have combined simultaneously or at various moments to reduce the efficiency of the labour market and prevent wages from reflecting real labour market conditions in the province.

It should also be remembered that Quebec, like other regions of Canada, is evolving within a country -- a continent, even -- in which some factors prevent wages from truly reflecting regional labour market and productivity conditions. Some examples are the wage policy of the federal government, Crown corporations and major national and U.S. firms that often provide practically identical working conditions for all employees regardless of their region of employment. In this same vein, we could also mention union demands for wage parity across the country and, in some cases, between Canada and the United States.

Faced with this relative wage rigidity between regions, we can now count only on worker mobility to lessen regional unemployment disparities. But here the second unique aspect enters the picture: Quebec's population is still 61 per cent unilingual francophone, and the province, therefore, has a culture, religion, and even history that are different from those of the majority in the rest of Canada. It follows that the personal cost of mobility within Canada for most Québecois is considerably higher than for other Canadians. To this add a very generous federal unemployment insurance policy that further reduces the benefits of moving to find work, especially when the unemployed worker lives in a region of high unemployment.

We thus find that two sets of phenomena combine to explain the persistence of higher unemployment in Quebec than in Ontario.

Aside from this disparity between unemployment rates in Quebec and Ontario, which can be considered as a constant, we find that the sensitivity of the unemployment rate to changes in aggregate demand is greater in Quebec than in Ontario. For a region such as Quebec, whose participation rate is traditionally below the national average, an expansionist policy based on the national average of economic indicators will not generally provide sufficient stimulus in periods of sluggishness. In periods of inflationary pressures, a restrictive federal policy may, on the other hand, take effect too soon for Quebec or may apply too much braking power.

2.3 Unemployment Disparities and Economic Policies

Reduction of these disparities in the unemployment rate between Quebec and Ontario could arise from an increase in the efficiency of the labour market through elimination of obstacles to adjustments of relative wages and from an increase in incentives for mobility. This solution would require, however, that the federal and provincial governments take regional conditions into account when drawing up their wage policies.

It would also be necessary to convince unions to give up their demands for wage parity. By facilitating the adjustment of relative wages, these measures would reduce the problem of regional unemployment disparities. In addition, the federal government should increase the benefits of mobility by cutting back unemployment insurance benefits and sharply boosting mobility bonuses.

But even if the different levels of government gradually adjusted their wage policies to take greater account of regional conditions, the strict application of the above-mentioned policies is highly unlikely for political reasons.

Of greater importance, however, is the fact that any solution dependent on labour force mobility to solve the problem of regional unemployment disparities between Quebec, Ontario, and the rest of Canada has always been, and will always remain, unacceptable to the Quebec elite, and perhaps the Quebec people as a whole. Any significant emigration of francophones from Quebec not only reduces the province's political weight in Confederation, but also threatens the survival of Quebec's culture.

The other theoretically possible solutions are based on a different approach, consisting of economic policies designed to create jobs mainly in areas with a high concentration of unemployed workers.

A set of restructuring and development policies for the
Quebec economy, as well as policies aimed at increasing the skill
of Quebec's labour force by promoting faster growth of productivity,
would undoubtedly boost the equilibrium level of employment in
this province under prevailing wage conditions. While generally
considered as medium- and long-term policies, these could very well
be partially tied to stabilization policies in a different context.

Furthermore, stabilization policies that would stimulate
aggregate demand to varying degrees in different regions could,
among other things, help to reduce disparities in the natural
unemployment rate. These policies would have two beneficial effects:
the first short-term, resulting from a better adjustment between
the particular economic situation in Quebec and the stabilization
policy aimed at maintaining the economy as close as possible to
full employment; the second longer-term, a reduction of disparities
in the unemployment rate through the gradual reduction of interregional differences in productivity.

As previously noted, these differences in productivity are a
source of unemployment disparities because of a strong trend toward
wage parity. How can a regionally differentiated stimulation of
demand affect differences in productivity? The assimilation of
technical progress through the activity of producing and increases
in the quality of labour are two important factors in the growth
of productivity. The rate of assimilation of technical progress
depends in large part on the rate of renewal and growth of capital
stock, which is a function of aggregate demand conditions. Thus,
a particularly strong and persistent stimulation of demand in
regions with high unemployment should eventually lead to a considerable improvement in productivity and finally in the equilibrium
employment level of these regions.

However, these policies would not have a truly lasting effect
on employment through productivity unless wages in the underprivileged regions continued to rise at a slower rate than in other
regions, despite the fact that the unemployment rate had abandoned
past trends. This danger is even greater since workers and unions
would have become accustomed to high rates of unemployment and
would, therefore, view the sudden drop in unemployment rates as
the ideal situation to push for higher wages. Concerted action by
the major social partners is therefore essential to the success
of such a policy.

2.4   The Canadian Dilemma

In the postwar period, the federal government has traditionally
assumed responsibility for stabilization in Canada. The provinces,
in turn, have generally refused to intervene in this field, arguing
that they had no access to the central bank and thus had neither
the means nor the financial instruments to stabilize their economies.
In addition, they also cited the problem of flights of funds to
other regions.

Consequently, interventions by the provinces to stabilize their economies have been limited to a few precise cases.

2.4.1 The Responsibility for Stabilization

A set of arguments could be advanced to show that *in a federal system* the primary responsibility for stabilization must fall to the central government.

-- Even if regional segments of demand are stimulated in such a way that interregional flights are minimized, there will still be significant "overflow" effects on other regions. However, the federal government is the only administrative level capable of recuperating part of these flights through its fiscal policy.

-- One of Canada's main problems is the disparities in unemployment rates. While some regions are, for all practical purposes, in a full employment situation, others (all those east of Ontario) continue to register very high unemployment rates. The rate of output must, therefore, be held down or, perhaps, even decreased in low-unemployment regions while it is accelerated in high-unemployment areas. However, since regions are interrelated, the stimulation of demand in high unemployment regions should be accompanied by a more restrictive tax policy in low-unemployment regions to avoid overheating and inflation. In our opinion, only a responsible central government, by citing the national objective of its intervention, could apply such a policy.

-- Finally a stabilization policy requires that the government responsible be capable of carrying a considerable budget deficit over a long period of time. Under present circumstances, this obligation would pose major problems if the provinces had the main responsibility for stabilization, mainly because they do not have use of the monetary instrument.

It would thus be an illusion to think that, in a federal system, one or more regions could take on the *primary* and *main* responsibility for stabilization of their own economy.

In view of this, a new organization of Canada's stabilization policies would absolutely require that we distinguish between the technical capacity for stabilizing intervention by provincial governments, and their ability to finance these interventions, including the consequences of such financing on the provinces.

We must, therefore, draw up an arrangement for stabilization policy that makes maximum use of the provinces' existing technical capacity for intervention, that retains the federal government's co-ordinating role and that prevents provincial interventions from having indirectly negative effects on the economies of other provinces.

2.4.2 The Provinces' Fiscal Lever

A detailed examination of public expenditures in Canada
(Table 1.1) and Quebec has clearly indicated to us that non-
recurrent expenditures on GFCF are made primarily by provincial
and municipal administrations. The classification used in the
national accounts was retained for this first section.

To obtain an even clearer picture of the influence of provincial governments, we must go beyond the national accounts and
attempt to retrace the various investments that depend in one way
or another on the provincial government. This exercise was carried
out for Quebec and the results appear in *Table 2.2*.

The proportion of total investment excluding housing made,
authorized or subsidized by the Quebec government, has been over
40 per cent for the last eight years. If we then add investments
made by municipalities, the government share exceeds 45 per cent
of total investment in Quebec. Thus, the Quebec government's
powers under the present constitution give it quite considerable
influence over the cyclical behaviour of the regional economy,
since it can exert a certain measure of control over at least
45 per cent of the investment made within its jurisdiction.
Appropriate planning of direct or indirect public investment would
allow the Quebec government to take contracyclical action within
the province. If we assume, for example, that approximately 10 per
cent of the total investment can be delayed or speeded up for contracyclical purposes, approximately one-half billion dollars in
investment could be utilized for stabilization purposes on the
basis of 1978-79 data. On an annual basis, according to the calculations aready performed (Section 2.1) this amount could reduce the
unemployment rate by 0.5 to 1 per cent, if we take into account the
effects of respending over the year in which the funds are first
spent.

In view of this appreciable impact, the Quebec government (nor any
of the other provinces in all probability) cannot feign an inability
to exert contracyclical influence on its own economy through normal
budget operations.

It should be remembered, however, that the analysis of the
last fifteen years' experience tends to indicate that this influence
has generally been neglected. In fact, we have demonstrated that
the Quebec government has generally amplified the harmful effects
of federal fiscal policies in Quebec (particularly during the 1960
and 1970 recessions). Ottawa's stabilization policy, therefore,
does not deserve all the blame for aggravating the economic fluctuations in Quebec.

Table 2.2

Investments Made Directly or Indirectly by
the Quebec Government

			1971	1972	1973	1974	1975
			($ millions)				
I	(a)	Government Investment[1]	466.3	491.4	527.4	628.0	752.5
	(b)	Subsidies for Investment[2]	205.7	212.8	206.6	265.0	228.7
	(c)	Authorized Investment[3]	328.2	446.1	617.9	661.2	888.3
	(d)	Hydro-Quebec and James Bay Energy Corporation	388.0	450.0	550.7	616.0	1,142.0
	(e)	Olympic Facilities					910.
			1,388.2	1,600.3	1,902.6	2,170.2	3,921.5
II	GFCF of Local Administrations		461.	448.	522.	598.	603.
III	Private Residential Construction		892.	1,006.	1,223.	1,555.	1,695.
IV	Total GFCF		4,145.	4,823.	5,846.	7,424.	9,013.
			(Per cent)				
Government GFCF/Total GFCF			33.5	33.2	32.5	29.2	43.5
Government GFCF/(Total GFCF-Residential Construction)			42.7	41.9	41.1	37.0	53.6
Government GFCF/(Total GFCF-Municipal GFCF)			37.7	30.0	35.7	31.8	46.6

1 Includes some purchases of existing assets; the amount is generally very small.

2 The amount invested could exceed the subsidy; part of this difference appears in line (c). The synchronization between investment and the year of subsidization can also vary slightly from year to year.

3 Same remark as 2 above, respecting the synchronization of investment.

Source   Quebec budgets;
         Quebec accounts and expenditures, Department of Industry, Trade and Commerce.

2.4.3 The Provinces' Financial Constraints

The year 1975 constitutes, as we have already stated, an interesting and exemplary experience. The increase of almost 40 per cent in investment made, subsidized or authorized by the provincial government, combined with the investment related to the Olympic games, has allowed Quebec to soften the effects of the North American recession: the disparity observed in Quebec's and Canada's 1973 and 1974 unemployment rates remained constant in 1975, although the Canadian economy was suffering a severe economic slowdown.

Although pure coincidence, the 1975 figures also illustrate the problems encountered by a provincial government single-handedly financing a contracyclical program. The Quebec government's relative ease in obtaining an additional $1 billion beyond its normal financing needs proves that the financing flexibility of provincial governments is not as limited as previously believed. It was shown that a provincial government can markedly increase its borrowing on foreign markets at specific points in time, such as during the worst of a recession.

On the other hand, these same 1975 figures demonstrate that, in view of the particular nature of cycles in the Canadian and, particularly,the Quebec economy, a provincial government cannot use its own financial means to provide prolonged economic support over the usual full duration of a recession. The experience of the last two decades appears, in effect, to indicate that recessions in Canada last at least three years, and it can be argued that recessions in Quebec last even slightly longer. Stabilization policies, particularly in Quebec, should, therefore, be based on stimulation of demand over several years.

It was found that the exceptional borrowing required for the preparation of the Olympic games forced the Quebec government to impose fairly harsh restrictions in order to respect the conditions imposed by money-lenders. These restrictions produced a sharp decline in the growth of investment made, subsidized or authorized by the Quebec government, at the same time as a continuing period of contraction in the private sector.

The provinces must, therefore, have access to a source of financing other than traditional financial markets if they are to exert a significant stabilizing action on their own economy, and we have already seen that only the federal government has the financial and monetary instruments capable of supporting such policies.

3   A NEW ORGANIZATION OF STABILIZATION POLICY

Our analysis of the problem of stabilization in Canada and the disparities between regions leads us to propose a new organization of economic policy under which stabilization policy would become an important means of redistributing the nation's wealth and of modifying the economic structure of certain provinces over the medium and long terms.

We thus recommend a regionalization of stabilization policy in Canada. Before discussing the technical details of this regionalization, we should examine the question of interregional transfers involved in any regionalized stabilization policy financed by the federal government.

The federal government already oversees considerable transfers of wealth between Canada's regions. In addition, transfer payments between regions under the present system are not immediately evident because they pass through many channels: equalization; family allowance; old age allowance; unemployment insurance; DREE subsidies; other departmental subsidies; etc. Our proposal does not actually intend to increase transfers from one region to another, but rather to increase their economic effectiveness.

Under our proposal, transfer payments made for purposes of stabilization would also be designed to restructure the regional economies. Over the medium term, these stabilization policies would lead to a reduction or even a complete disappearance of some other transfers.

The major change in Canadian economic policy proposed here could, eventually, increase significantly the efficiency of the national system of redistributing wealth. Transfer payments to regions with lower productivity should, therefore, not increase significantly over present levels, but should become more effective by using new channels.

3.1   Creation of a Stabilization Fund

Our study of Canadian stabilization policy has revealed two points:

-- The federal government controls the supply of money and possesses the independent financial resources that allow it to underwrite stabilization policies;

-- The provincial governments do not have access to the central bank and the independent share of their income is much smaller than Ottawa's, particularly when we take into account the conditional transfers of tax points for personal income tax.

We believe this situation could be used for stabilization. Utilization of the fiscal lever available to the provinces for purposes of stabilization based on federal financing would make it possible to sidestep the problems faced by the central authorities in the area of stabilization instruments, as well as to meet the need for a regionalized stabilization policy in Canada.

The *Stabilization Fund* that would be made available to the provincial governments to finance their capital formation expenditures for purposes of stabilization would be entirely financed by the federal government.

Use of the fund by the provinces would be tied to certain procedures. The provinces would decide the nature of the capital formation expenditures on the basis of certain regulations, imposed particularly on interregional flows. The capital expenditures would be made by the provinces and any corporation, agency, or other level of administration responsible to the provinces. The amounts distributed to the provinces through the fund would constitute a transfer payment and would not, therefore, require any repayment.

Access to the Fund by the provinces would be controlled by a method related to economic indicators and calculations of the impact of capital expenditures on employment and output. This mechanism, therefore, assumes that the provinces and central government would keep close tabs on the growth of the economy and would make predictions on turning points in the economy as well as the duration and magnitude of recessions.

These forecasts should be made through an independent federal-provincial committee of politicians. Once this diagnosis is drawn up, the federal government, through arrangement with the provinces, would set objectives for the stabilization policy in terms of economic indicators such as the creation of a certain number of jobs in Canada and their regionaldistribution. Following this, the capital expenditures required in each region would be computed.

The formula for transfer payments to the provinces should be relatively simple, but a certain number of adjustments in the rules of accessibility to this fund would be unavoidable. For example, if a province had a particularly high fiscal burden -- the present case in Quebec -- a relatively larger amount of spending would be necessary to obtain the same results. Under these conditions, the amount transferred could not possibly achieve the predetermined objective for job creation, so the province involved would have to make up the difference. The province would thus have to accept this "price" or reduce its fiscal burden to the national average level.

Furthermore, the provinces would generally be free to supplement the moneys received from the stabilization fund in order to boost the target for job creation, particularly at low points in the recession. They would thus be able to decide whether an

additional injection of capital spending would create excessive
inflationary pressure in their own economy.

Subsidy payments to the provinces to finance capital expenditures for stabilization raise questions concerning the social return
on these investments and the co-ordination of stabilization policies
with medium- and long-term structural policies. Obviously, the
fund should not finance just any public infrastructure expenditure.
Without conducting a precise calculation of cost-benefit analysis,
we can reasonably expect the provinces and central government to
agree on a fairly exhaustive list of "eligible" projects for the
fund. Some notable examples are:

-- the construction of transportation facilities;

-- the development of infrastructures for industrial purposes;

-- the part of capital expenditures paid by the state for
   reconversion of an industrial sector;

-- anti-pollution equipment; and

-- the construction of infrastructures helping to produce
   energy.

It would be particularly necessary to give priority to
expenditures promoting the development of the potential output of
a regional economy and forming part of a provincial or federal
industrial strategy.

Among the particular advantages that we see in the establishment of such a fund are:

-- The proposed mechanism should minimize typical delays in
   making problems known and getting decisions made. In effect,
   the fund would have its own "spending power" based on rules
   drawn up and passed by Parliament.

-- The participation of provincial governments in setting
   stabilization targets and disseminating enlightened information
   on the economic situation of each region, should considerably
   reduce the problem of harmful fiscal policies at the national
   and regional levels.

-- The federal government could also increase the automatic
   stabilization properties of its present means of intervention,
   such as reductions in taxes on profits reinvested during
   periods of slow economic growth.

The federal government would finance the stabilization fund in
its entirety from its budget. When preparing its budget, Ottawa
would receive an estimate of transfers for the current year. The
fund would also have a credit margin guaranteed with the chartered

banks, which would allow it to make all transfers to provinces in the shortest time possible. Any use of this credit margin would be immediately repaid by the federal treasury through either a supplementary budget or the following budget.

Finally, there is no indication that the creation of this fund would increase the size of the federal government. It should especially be remembered that the effects of the stabilization policies would reduce other transfer payments. It was found, for example, that a drop of one point in the 1975 unemployment rate in Quebec would have reduced federal treasury payouts by $154 million.

3.2   Some Implications of the Creation of the Stabilization Fund

The stabilization fund would give the provinces indirect access to the central bank since the financing of the fund would be integrated with the federal government's budget operations.

The creation of the fund would lead to an extensive reorganization of Ottawa's main expenditure items. As the fund itself should not result in an increase in the relative size of the central government, we can expect the federal government to transfer some budget items to the fund, while others would gradually disappear over the medium- or long term. This would be the case for:

-- the Department of Urban Affairs;

-- the various expenditures for job creation;

-- all expenditures duplicating provincial budgets, such as the manpower training programs and some social programs; and

-- the Department of Regional Economic Expansion.

This last budget item suggests another major implication of the creation of this fund: Ottawa and the provinces would be forced to agree upon a national economic strategy.

The creation and particularly the operation of the fund, would require the provinces to agree among themselves and with the federal government on how to co-ordinate their efforts.

CONCLUSION

Some federal transfers to the poorest provinces are now used to increase household demand or finance the current expenditures of the provincial governments.

However, transfers to households involve flights of funds to other provinces, particularly Ontario, and have no restructuring effect. The status quo favours the wealthiest provinces over the long term and undoubtedly explains why they agree without too much complaint to participate in this process of regional redistribution of wealth.

Since the stabilization fund would also have restructuring effects over the medium- and long term, it would help to reduce the comparative advantage now enjoyed by Ontario. In addition, since transfers are aimed at financing capital formation expenditures, flights of funds to other provinces would be fewer.

We admit that a federal-provincial consensus on such a stabilization and restructuring system for the Canadian economy would be hard to obtain, but it is a question of recognizing that this may be the price that must be paid to keep Canada together and to achieve a considerable reduction of regional disparities over the medium- and long terms.

Comments by P. Fortin, Department of Economics,
University of Laval, Quebec

The final conclusions of the Rabeau-Lacroix study are that
national stabilization policy since the middle fifties has lamentably
failed to achieve a state of non-inflationary full-employment in
Canada (and its regions), and, furthermore, that structural policies
to reduce regional disparities have not altered the differential
pattern at all. It is difficult not to concur with this judgment.

Their study attributes these failures to the fact that, more
often than not, the wrong instruments have pursued the wrong targets.

Targets

Concerning stabilization targets they mention a number of years
in which national policy was restrictive when it should have been
expansionary (1960, 1969, 1977) or was expansionary when it should
have been restrictive (1965, 1974). Again, I agree with their
judgment in all examples. However, I suspect that the reason for
this is that we share the same views on the relative importance of
the social costs of unemployment and inflation. Perhaps the federal
government, or even the Canadian public, thinks otherwise. If so,
the question of what the socially desirable objectives of stabilization
policy in Canada should be must be faced squarely. I am somewhat
disappointed by the brief mention they make of this issue, but I
understand their limitations in terms of space and time.

My own perception of the matter is that Canadian governments
have recently been retreating from the goal of full employment for
two main reasons:

(1) The social costs of unemployment have been downplayed.
Nowadays, all unemployment is viewed either as voluntary, or structural,
or demographic, or individually affordable given our generous unemployment insurance program and the rise of the multiple-earner family.
This view is plainly wrong and socially dangerous. To be sure, their
has been some increase in voluntary, structural and demographic
unemployment since the middle 60's, but at least 30% of unemployment
in Canada at this moment is still cyclical in nature and could have
been wiped out by non-inflationary expansionary policies in the last
2 years. Moreover, even if individual jobless persons are compensated,
society cannot be compensated for its unused productive resources
which now cost in excess of $15 billion a year in Canada as a whole.

(2)   Other objectives have overridden the pursuit of full employment.

(i)   Since 1975, just as in 1960 and in 1969, the federal government has launched a sterile crusade against inflation, forgetting at once the lesson of history and the results of two decades of hard economic research which have shown that inflation is very insensitive to high doses of unemployment, especially in a country like Canada which is so open to foreign influences.

(ii)   Attempts to compress the share of the public sector in the aggregate economy have induced sharp reductions in the rate of growth of public expenditure in the last four years. This may be desirable from a structural point of view, but it has compounded the problem of unemployment, especially in view of the government's reluctance to cut taxes as an antidote. It has brought us back to a recessionary vicious circle ā la Herbert Hoover or ā la R.B. Bennett, despite the fact that the public sector deficit as a fraction of GNP has already been much higher at other times in both Canada and the U.S.

(iii)   The maintenance of a stable or rising Canadian dollar up to the end of 1976, despite the important downward pressures on the currency already noticeable in 1974 through the extremely restrictive monetary policy of 1975-76, is also an indication that the government had chosen a cold-shower, unemployment-creating policy in 1975 rather than an employment-creating, currency-depreciation policy like the one it was finally forced to adopt in 1977-78.

I think it is time to restate clearly what the targets of stabilization policy should be in this country and how the available policy instruments should be assigned to the various targets. It is disgraceful that the Canadian discussion of macro objectives should have fallen to so low a level in this decade. My own suggestions are fourfold (following Mundell):

(1)   Stabilize the exchange rate with the help of monetary policy so that we import foreign inflation on average, except when severe problems appear in the balance of payments (then depreciate or appreciate the currency).

(2)   Reduce the unemployment rate in Canada to the 5.75-6% non-inflationary level with the help of federal fiscal policy. Experiment with tax-based incomes policy as President Carter is now doing to check whether lower unemployment rates could not be reached without accelerating inflation.

(3)   Reduce the unemployment rate to about 7-7.5% in Quebec with the help of provincial fiscal policy.

(4)   Reduce non-cyclical unemployment by providing seasonal employment alternatives, checking down accelerations in the minimum wage, reforming the UI program, adopting a more careful wage policy in the public sector and fighting against discrimination, protection and exclusion practices in the labor market.

Instruments

Rabeau and Lacroix also argue that the wrong stabilization policy instruments have been used. I am again in general agreement with their claim, although not totally with the specifics of what they say.

Their argument here is (1) that neither the federal nor the provincial governments have ever displayed any systematic preoccupation with the economic fluctuations specific to the regions; (2) that, despite its financial ability to incur large deficits, the federal government has been restrained in the stabilization field (i) by its fear lest any substantial decrease in its share of the income tax induce the provinces to steal this fat fiscal revenue source, and (ii) by the poor short-term efficiency of its policy tools; and (3) that, despite the high efficiency of their stabilization instruments, and their direct or indirect control over a third of aggregate capital expenditure, the provinces have been reluctant to realize budget deficits of the size needed in times of prolonged recession because the cost of borrowing is higher for them than for the central government.

The propositions that the regional business cycles in Canada are varied enough to warrant specific regional policy measures and that the provincial governments, if only because of their size and location, should be the main source of these measures,are not open to question. The longer the provinces postpone their systematic involvement in stabilization policy and continue to hold the federal government responsible for any slack or excess pressure in the economy, the longer Canadians will have to wait for an adequate anti-cyclical steering of overall economic policy and support the related welfare loss.

The federal government's fear of losing its income tax revenue to the provinces is justifiable. However, it would be good for this country to see more of this growth revenue in the hands of provincial and local governments. What we have now is a system of intergovernmental transfers which finances 25% of provincial expenditure and 50% of local expenditure. This system and most notably conditional transfers breed fiscal irresponsibility.

Rabeau and Lacroix also insist on the poor efficiency of taxes, current expenditure on goods and services and transfers as tools of economic stabilization. Temporary tax cuts or temporary surtaxes are said to generate low income and employment multipliers. Transfer and current expenditure programs are branded as recurrent expenditure which are quite inflexible in the short run. Therefore, they argue, stabilization policy should rely essentially on capital expenditure, which is the only instrument with both short-run flexibility and high income and employment multipliers.

I agree that capital expenditure should be one most important anti-cyclical tool, given only that it is harmonized with allocative efficiency. However, I find the authors' willingness to reduce stabilization policy to the exclusive manipulation of that instrument somewhat misleading. First, I think they have overestimated the rigidity of the expenditure budget and underestimated the efficiency of tax cuts. Second, it is the overall budget that has an impact on the economy. Governments include in any budget many temporary and permanent measures for all sorts of allocative and redistributional purposes, including decisions on capital expenditure. It would be strange to witness a situation in which only the latter would adjust to the needs of economic stabilization. Why not decide to advance or postpone temporary or permanent changes in taxes and current expenditure programs in addition to capital expenditure? For instance, why should we not have seen a postponement of current expenditure cuts and a rapid and permanent decrease in tax rates in the high and rising unemployment period from 1975-1978? In other words, I feel that their negative judgment on the empirical efficiency of tax cuts or raises is premature. And I submit that all policy measures, be they temporary as a capital expenditure or permanent as a change in a transfer program, should be scrutinized concerning the cyclical appropriateness of their timing.

Therefore, I believe it is true that the low percentage of capital expenditure in the federal budget reduces its stabilization efficiency, but I would refrain from exaggerating the situation in that respect. On the other hand, I side very much with Rabeau and Lacroix when they claim that the direct or indirect control by the provinces of more than a third of total capital expenditure is a definite proof of the immense potential of that level of government in the field of economic stabilization.

The problem that they raise here, however, is that of the high borrowing costs faced by the provinces, compared with the federal government, and the concomitant reluctance with which they plunge into important cumulative deficits in times of prolonged recession. I would have liked the authors to give a numerical estimate of the federal-provincial borrowing cost differentials and to check if, indeed, the disincentive to borrow provincially is real. I shall now do this for them. There are two things to note when considering the provinces' higher borrowing costs. First, they cannot borrow as easily as Ottawa on the short side of the financial market, which is generally less costly. This is largely due to the deep involvement of the banking system in the establishment of monetary policy and, notably, to the secondary reserve requirement imposed on chartered banks which provides the federal government with a captive market for 75% of its treasury bills. This reserve requirement is useless and should be wiped out. Second, the market charges higher interest rates to the provinces than to Ottawa for any bond issue with similar characteristics because it attaches a lower risk to federal bonds. This is due to the size of the federal government and to its pervasive involvement in the market through the central bank. These two factors account for various federal-provincial average interest rate differentials on the public debt across time and across provinces. In 1977 the Quebec-Ottawa differential was about 1.2%. What we need in principle is a scheme which will equalize federal and provincial borrowing costs at the margin, especially in times of recession.

But do interest differentials *per se* constitute a genuine disincentive for the provinces to incur deficits in slack periods? I have never seen any empirical evidence on this issue and, acknowledgeably, it would be hard to come by. One thing that we know is that since 1975 the cumulative budget deficit of the Quebec government has been of the order of 3.3 billions of 1978 dollars, which has been enough not only to maintain the full-employment (7.5%) budget surplus unchanged but even to decrease it somewhat. The Quebec budget has been gradually stabilizing every year since 1975, except in 1977. I think the importance of the recession would have required a quarter-billion-dollar additional deficit each year since 1975, which, at a 1.5% marginal borrowing cost differential, would have meant a permanent $15 million dollar interest flow annually. Budget surpluses in future overfull-employment years could provide partial compensation for this. A federal-provincial interest equalization scheme might contribute to this stabilizing effort. Once again, I am not sure that provinces borrow less during recessions because of interest costs.

What I do know, however, is that if it is not more costly at the margin for them **to** borrow than for Ottawa, they will at least lose this excuse for not getting more actively involved in stabilization policy. Of course, one would also like to examine any equalization proposal on efficiency grounds.

Proposal

My remarks contain an implicit judgment on the authors' proposal for a Stabilization Fund. The Fund would transfer cyclical funds at no cost from the low-cost borrower and inefficient stabilizer - the federal government - to the high-cost borrower and efficient stabilizers - the provinces. The money would help finance capital expenditure projects contained in a list of admissable projects. The transfers would be generated from a reduction in other, "structural" transfer programs and/or from suppression of the DREE, the SDUA, the myriad of federal job creation programs, etc. They would involve no new additional transfers to the depressed regions from the have provinces. It is hoped that this scheme would help enhance the national and regional performance of stabilization policy and eventually make a substantial contribution to solving the structural disparities as well, presumably through the upgrading of manpower and equipment in the low income regions arising from a lower average unemployment rate there, and through the minimization of interregional import leakages brought about by the intensive use of the capital expenditure tool.

Rabeau and Lacroix's proposal is technically consistent with their premises. As I have said, I find that their emphasis on capital expenditure is pushed too far and their paper establishes no clear relationship between the size of the disincentive arising from higher borrowing cost at the provincial level and the size of the transfer scheme proposed. In fact, the authors are too modest to put any figures on the cost of their proposal to the federal government. But beyond that, if only a change in the nature, not in the size, of the transfers from rich regions to poor regions over a complete business cycle is involved, I see little net income and employment gains made by the poor regions in the long run, since there would be no incentives for higher federal or provincial deficits on the average. From a cyclical point of view, the proposal is equivalent to a switch from federal transfers to households to provincial capital information, and the balanced-budget multiplier of such a move is very low, something of the order of one-third of the usual government expenditure multiplier. Viewed upside down, this means that only a huge transfer scheme should bring an appreciable impact on the regional economies.

Furthermore, I doubt very much that the proposal of a
stabilization fund will ever achieve political acceptability. The
even more modest suggestion of Raynauld in 1971 involved only loans,
not transfers, from Ottawa to the provinces. After a small trial
in the early 70's it was scrapped outright by the federal government.
There are three points to make here. First, it is extremely unlikely
that Ottawa would abandon some types of expenditure it now controls
in favour of additional transfers to the provinces, the use of which
it would not control. Second, if Ottawa ever wants to put any
condition on the use of funds, there will be still more intergovernmental battles, the likes of which we have seen too often in
this country, and the Fund will never be born. And third, the very
operation of the Fund, the choice of cyclical indicators and of
their differential regional target values, and the examination of
the economic outlook would, at best, be exercises that would breed
repeated conflicts between Ottawa and the provinces and amongst the
provinces themselves.

Summary

I conclude the following:

(1) The problem of stabilization policy in Canada at this
moment is primarily one of ends and only secondarily one of assigning
means to ends. I have tried to offer a few suggestions in this
respect.

(2) Rabeau and Lacroix are basically right to give very low
grades to the performance of stabilization policy in Canada in the
last 20 years and to stress the need for a regional focus. But I
find they have done some overselling of the propositions (1) that
the federal budget cannot stabilize the national economy efficiently
and (2) that the provincial budgets are severely constrained by
borrowing costs in slack periods.

(3) The idea of a Stabilization Fund is most commendable,
but its emphasis on capital expenditure is perhaps exaggerated; its
link with higher provincial borrowing costs is not made clear enough;
and its impact on the efficiency of regional stabilization policy
is likely to be smaller than is claimed by Lacroix and Rabeau.
Furthermore, I don't believe it is politically expedient for it to
be implemented in the near future. I would personally prefer a
federal provincial interest equalization scheme which would minimize
the interfacing of the two levels of government and maximize the
freedom of the provinces to spend where they want, with no federal
interference, and the possibility for the provincial electorates to

judge their governments for their own stabilization efficiency.

The authors should be congratulated for the high quality of their study. I must thank them for the opportunity they have given me to go behind and beyond.

REGIONAL IMPACT OF SELECTED
NON-EXPENDITURES DECISIONS OF
THE FEDERAL GOVERNMENT OF CANADA

by

Fernand Martin

Department of Economics
University of Montreal

in collaboration with

A.R. Moroz

PART I

INTRODUCTION

Purpose of the Study

Balanced regional development would undoubtedly contribute to moderating strains within the Canadian Confederation, and unbalanced development to increasing them. It is against that background that this study was undertaken. The empirical research which it contains was done for the purpose of justifying the following proposition: non-expenditures or "pure decisions" are as potent for regional development (or lack of it) as expenditures decisions such as fiscal and monetary stabilization policies, provincial equalization payments, transport subsidies, exchange rate manipulations, etc. In other words, we plan to demonstrate that from a regional point of view "pure decisions" are in many cases an acceptable if not a preferable alternative to expenditures policies.

Non-expenditure policies or "pure decisions" are those federal government decisions which correspond to those policies that are not primarily implemented through its expenditures and/ or changes in its fiscal or monetary operations. Specifically, they do not involve direct changes in the federal government fiscal aggregates; however, some expenditures might be incidental to their implementation. Pure decisions fall into three categories: (1) regulatory activities, including the setting of rates of the outputs of utilities, (2) international trade agreements and tariffs, and (3) the location of federal government footloose activities, i.e., situations where federal government activities such as its own administration activities could, without appreciable loss of efficiency, be located elsewhere than in Ottawa; similarly (under equivalent efficiency provisions), activities such as federal government purchases of goods and services.

Our proposition on the importance of pure decisions has two interesting implications:

1   The real cost of an explicit change in the fiscal aggregates of the federal government may not be the lost production of some other fiscal or monetary operation, but the loss of output which would result from the best alternative "pure decision."

2   Some regional absolute or comparative advantages (disadvantages) can be created by the stroke of a pen. A region's performance can be conditioned as much by "pure decisions" made by the federal

government as it is by the quality of the local
natural and human resources and/or by the access
to financial resources, etc.

A third major aspect of this proposition is that the resource
cost, as well as the consequence of an expenditure action on
the performance of other key variables in the economy, is not
the same for a "pure decision" action as it is for most fiscal
or monetary manipulations.

The above implications are only acceptable if we empirically
demonstrate that the impact of a "pure decision" is spatially
biased and that the regional impact can be considerable.
Furthermore, the empirical work must support the proposition that
regional consequences of the pursuit of a national objective differ
considerably when a non-expenditure, as opposed to an expenditure
policy, is utilized.

Canada's Past Experience with Pure Decisions

Non-expenditure policies are not a contemporary phenomenon.
In the period of National Policies, which roughly stretches from
1867 to 1940, pure decisions were the cornerstone of the federal
government's intervention in the economy. Three "basic national
decisions"[1] characterize this period of Canadian economic history:
Prairie Settlement; an All-Canadian Transportation System; and
Industrialization by Protective Tariffs. While the last one is
entirely a "pure" decision, the workings of the transportation
system, at least with respect to rail rates, involved and still
involves a large dose of "arbitrary decision and regulation by the
state."

During the next twenty years, non-expenditure policies were
displaced by changes in fiscal aggregates as the prime instruments
of the federal government's policy arsenal. Known as the "Keynesian
Period," the stabilization of the national economy by the use of
macro-economic instruments became the major concern of the federal
government. However, in the early sixties, the emerging regional
disparities began to be more acutely felt and this led to a national
commitment to the alleviation of spatial inequalities. The
Keynesian doctrine remained as the basic rationale for policy
actions, and the federal government resorted to Equalization
Payments and an assortment of other regional development funds and
agencies for needy regions. This culminated in 1969 with the
establishment of the Department of Regional Economic Expansion (DREE).
By the beginning of the sixties, Canada had entered an era of
"Regional Awareness."

---

1 Mackintosh, 1967, p. 9ff.

"Regional Awareness" policies were first exclusively of the government expenditures type. Later, through DREE's mediation activities directed at other federal government departments (e.g., Transport), attempts were made to secure "pure" decisions favouring certain regions. Thus, by this time, the potential of "pure" decisions as a policy instrument had been rediscovered. The federal government had to have recourse to these measures partly to offset some of the adverse side effects, not only of the original national policies but also of the national stabilization policies.

The juxtaposition of regional goals with national goals, all this in a Keynesian policy framework, makes for very strange bedfellows, mainly because the mode of intervention to achieve regional goals has gradually moved from a state of compatibility with Keynesian policies (where regional goals were encouraged only by Equalization Payments and Shared Programs) to a state of near incompatibility where federal intervention is now directed at modifying the regional economic structure directly. In other words, when the "new" awareness of regional disparities was taken care of only with methods to ameliorate directly the per capita disposable income (e.g., through Equalization Payments), there was no fundamental incompatibility with Keynesian philosophy and, more importantly, with the pursuit of the original national goals. However, it gradually became apparent that trying to increase regional income directly by intergovernmental transfer payments had limited possibilities, and, more importantly, that it was very different in nature from an alternative set of regional policies attempting to buttress the ability of each region to create employment and high income on the spot. Indeed, in a federal country, there is a great difference between government policies that are oriented towards reducing regional income disparities and those that are directed towards reducing the regional differences in the ability of each region to embark on self-propelled development.[2] Simply reducing income disparities (when this is the only goal of regional policy) can be adequately dealt with by transfer payments (to alleviate short-run sufferings), financing emigration from depressed areas, and other similar measures. However, converting depressed areas

---

2   Many people refuse to recognize job creation within a region as a legitimate goal; they prefer national efficiency and thus prefer to encourage interregional migration of factors of production as the regulating mechanism. On the other hand, those who favour job creation on the spot prefer to speak about the ability to engage in self-propelled development on the part of the region. This removes part of the stigma attached to the policy of creating jobs for jobs' sake, without taking into account the quality of those jobs, or the "cost" of creating them.

into prosperous economic regions[3] requires large structural changes which enhance or artificially create regional comparative advantages or eliminate the barriers to these advantages. It is the hypothesis of this paper that "pure decisions" offer an attractive and viable substitute to expenditure-oriented policies, and while non-expenditure policies do not eliminate the potential of tax rebates, transfer payments and decentralization of federal activities, they do provide a greater probability of success with less cost to the federal government, other regions, and the national economy.

To test the plausibility of this hypothesis, we use two examples: the Canada-United States Automotive Agreement and the impact on the flour and breakfast cereals industry of the regulation of railway freight rates in Canada. Despite their widely differing social importance, we believe that both examples support our thesis in a most convincing manner.

---

3 There are sociological, cultural and political reasons why development should occur in each region while not resorting to wholesale outmigration or transfer payments.

PART II

THE CANADA-UNITED STATES AUTOMOTIVE AGREEMENT

Introduction

The Automotive Agreement is a trade agreement made between the United States and Canada in 1965 which enabled automobile producers in Canada to import, free of duty, motor vehicles, parts and accessories as long as they satisfied certain conditions concerning the ratio of motor vehicle production to sales in Canada and the proportion of domestic value added in Canadian automobile assembly. The federal government also demanded and received "letters of intent" from the automotive assembly industry which pertained to the level of domestic value added in Canada. While these "letters of intent" are not part of the Agreement signed by the two governments, they constitute an important part of the arrangement.

Previous researchers (Beigie, Alexander and Wilton) have shown that great benefits have accrued to the Canadian economy. Our present study indicates that these benefits continued after 1971, the date with which the above investigators concluded their work. On the other hand, it now seems clear that the Automotive Agreement has increased the sensitivity of the Canadian economy to the U.S. business cycle.

The demonstration of our thesis outlined in Part I requires that we measure the net impact of the automobile agreement, first on the national economy (for a longer period than previous researchers), and then that we regionalize these results. We study the period from the inception of the Automotive Agreement in 1965 up to and including 1976.

The Net Impact of the Automotive
Agreement at the National Level

The net impact of the Automotive Agreement is the difference between "what has happened to the Canadian economy and what reasonably could have happened in the absence of such an Agreement." This rewriting of history is, of course, a difficult job, but it is not completely arbitrary since we use a coherent general equilibrium econometric model developed by the Economic Council of Canada, CANDIDE Model 1.2M.[1] This model permits quantitative assessment of

---

1   We would like to thank Bobbi Cain and Tom Schweitzer of the CANDIDE Group, and Professor D.A. Wilton of Guelph University, for their valuable help and comments. However, the views expressed here are those of the authors, and not necessarily those of these individuals or the Economic Council. The following presentation is brief. Further discussion of the model and of the modeling of the Agreement in CANDIDE 1.2M as well as discussion concerning our differences with Wilton (1976) are available on request in A.R. Moroz, *The Auto Pact Study: Progress Report; The National Impact*; mimeo., June 1978, Economic Council of Canada.

the impact of structural changes, as well as of changes in fiscal policy, interest rates, the foreign exchange rate, etc.

In rewriting history in this way we follow what has become standard procedure in work of this type. First, we develop a "reference or control simulation." This is a set of tables which gives the model's estimates, for the period 1965 to 1976, of all important variables that are useful in describing the Canadian economy, ie. the gross national product, the consumer price index, the unemployment rate, etc. Then we develop alternative simulations, or scenarios, in which the influence of the automobile agreement has been removed. We choose several alternatives according to what government policies might have been followed in the absence of the automobile agreement, such as fiscal and exchange rate policies. We include as one possibility a policy of "no policy," or "passive government." Each of these alternative simulations is also a set of tables. Each set gives the model's estimates, again for 1965 to 1976, of what happens to all important economic variables under the chosen government policy. The difference between the control solution tables and the alternative scenario tables is the model's estimates of the effects of the automobile agreement on the economy. More precisely, it is the estimate of the effect of the automobile agreement relative to whatever government policy might have replaced it.

In choosing alternative scenarios we have tried to pick several plausible variants of the course of government policy and economic history that might have occurred in the absence of the Automotive Agreement. The choice of these scenarios must follow certain criteria, or we may end up being grossly unfaithful to history. For instance, we have ruled out other industrial policies that would have directly modified the Canadian industrial structure, because since 1965 the Canadian government has not (except) in the Automotive Assembly Industry) been willing to change appreciably such a structure. Thus, there remains the realm of fiscal, monetary (interest rate), and exchange rate policies, or combinations of these. The main guiding criterion we used to produce the policies underlying the alternative scenarios was their effect on the annual level of the unemployment rate. We assumed that the rate of unemployment that has actually prevailed since the Automotive Agreement is one that the government would have tried to match even in the absence of an agreement, and we designed our alternative scenarios with this in mind. However, it soon became apparent that a rigid adherence to this criterion led, when ordinary fiscal policies were used, to unacceptable effects on other variables such as the balance of payments, the government deficit, etc. We therefore allowed a little more unemployment than in the control solution in order to achieve more acceptable results in terms of other variables.[*]

However, in our various scenarios the unemployment rate did play the role of a trigger setting in motion the government's intervention.

The fiscal policies that we have utilized for our alternative scenarios consist mainly of variations in personal income taxes and general federal sales taxes on consumer items, without involving, as Wilton (1976, p. 96) did, federal fiscal policies that would try, in a massive way, to influence *directly* private business investments. Our main reason for this choice is that the efficiency of fiscal policy designed to directly influence private investment has not been satisfactorily demonstrated.[2] In general, the effects of corporation tax rate changes, investment tax credits, etc.,[3] are more uncertain than those involving personal income tax rates. Those who advocate influencing investment decisions through fiscal policies (or monetary policies) make the doubtful assumption that at any time and, more importantly, *anywhere* in Canada there exists an inexhaustible reservoir of worthwhile private projects at current interest rates.

A number of alternative strategies or scenarios were simulated, of which three are reported below. These are:

(1)   Alternative Strategy No. 4, which consisted of reducing the personal income tax by one percentage point from 1969 through 1976, and the federal sales tax by 2 percentage points from 1968 through 1976.

(2)   Alternative Strategy No. 6, which combined the fiscal policy in Strategy No. 4 with an exchange rate policy of setting the U.S.-Canadian exchange at its 1968 level for the entire simulation period, equivalent to a devaluation of 5 per cent over the period as a whole. This was done to ameliorate

---

*For the technically minded, we note that we used the concept of a disutility function as a guide to the formulation and acceptability of the alternative policy strategies. The arguments are real GNP, federal government deficit, current trade balance, basic current and capital account balance, unemployment rate, and the consumer price index. Details are available on request in a mimeo. by A. Moroz, "The Formulation of Alternative Strategies and some Results." Economic Council of Canada.

2   "Dans l'état actuel des connaissances, on doit considérer comme inefficace, une politique cherchant à affecter directement un investissement suivé" (Lacrois et Rabeau, 1978, p. 10, Chapter I.)

3   *Ibid.*, p. 9, Chapter I.

foreign deficits occurring under Strategy 4.

(3)   A "passive government" scenario, which assumed no change in the federal government's discretionary actions. This allows a measure of the maximum net possible impact that can be hypothesized for the Automotive Agreement. Strategies 4 and 6, in (1) and (2) above, assume that, had the Automotive Agreement not been concluded, the federal government would not have let the Canadian economy deteriorate as much as pictured by the "passive" or "*status quo*" scenario. But this eventuality, although very plausible, is not a certainty, especially if we examine the attitude of the government towards the present performance of the Canadian economy.

Table 1 shows the impact of the Automotive Agreement on Canada as a whole under the above alternative scenarios. Seven indicators (shown in Table 1) cover the main features of the impact on the simulated Canadian economy.

Consider first the passive government scenario. Although unrealistic in our view, this scenario is a useful benchmark. Real gross domestic product is annually about $ 1 1/4 billion less in the nine years from 1968 to 1976, on average, as a result of eliminating the automobile agreement. There is also a 2 per cent annual loss in real wages. Unemployment goes up by nearly a percentage point in this nine-year period, though the rate of inflation rises less than half a percentage point per year. There is a serious deficit in government and foreign accounts.

Strategy 4, involving income and sales tax cuts, improves matters somewhat over the passive government scenario. It succeeds in generating nearly half as much gross domestic product, real wages, and employment as the automobile agreement. But the government and foreign account deficits are substantially worse than under the agreement. The performance on inflation is better, however, with the consumer price index rising less than half a percentage point per year.

Strategy 6 uses devaluation to try to offset the foreign account deficit problems associated with Strategy 4. This is partially successful, and in addition real gross domestic product and employment are improved in comparison with Strategy 4. They are still, however, not as good as under the automobile agreement, while the rate of inflation is worse, as are the other indicators.

Overall, the Automotive Agreement scenario is clearly superior to the three alternatives discussed. Indeed, it proved

Table 1

Impact of Various Policy Actions on Specefic Indicators

Indicators or Targets	Control Automotive Agreement (What actually happened)	SCENARIOS Non-Automative Agreement: Replaced By		
		Alternative Strategy No. 4 (Income Tax and General Federal Sales Tax Reductions)	Alternative Strategy No. 6 (Strategy No. 4 plus Devaluation)	Nothing (Passive Government)
(a) Real RDP (1968-76 average)	66.34	65.62	65.89	65.09
		(Billions of 1961 dollars)		
(b) Unemployment Rate (1968-76 average)	6.03	6.47	6.26	6.83
		(Percentage)		
(c) Rate of Change of CPI (1968-76 average)	6.72	6.05	6.90	6.24
(d) Federal Government Deficit (1968-76 average)	-0.42	-1.67	-1.08	-1.12
		(Billions of current dollars)		
(e) Current Trade Balance (1968-76 average)	-1.29	-2.03	-1.50	-1.60
(f) Basic Current and Capital Account Balance (1968-76 average)	0.47	-1.02	-0.10	-0.82
		(Thousands of 1961 dollars)		
(g) Average Personal Real Wages, Salaries, and Supplementary Income and Military Pay (1968-76 average)	4.97	4.90	4.89	4.86

impossible to find a scenario that, from the overall Canadian point of view as measured by variables such as employment, inflation performance, real wages, size of deficits, etc., was as good as the automobile agreement. A number of other strategies were simulated, involving larger and different types of tax cuts. We have not retained them for formal comparison because of the relatively large increases in both government and balance-of-payments deficits that they led to. For instance, we tried what might be called the "big bang" scenario.[4] The results translated themselves into a larger level of real GNP for 1974-76 as compared to the Automotive Agreement; however, the government deficit is larger by 140 per cent in 1976 in the simulations and the deficit of the basic external balance would have required large corrective measures.[5]

In sum, a direct intervention in the economic structure of a country seems to be, from certain angles, a better way to stimulate the national economy, especially when the differences in federal government deficits are taken into account. The benefits of the Automotive Agreement include a larger level of real output, a higher level of real wages, a better external account, and less burden on the federal government. The cost is a slightly higher rate of increase in prices and, from detailed simulation evidence not presented here, a greater dependency of the internal economy on short-run U.S. economic conditions.

In terms of relationships with the rest of the world, the higher average real wage can be considered as part of the cost, and it is clear that this and the structural rearrangment of this relationship with the United States are important considerations. In our regional analysis this point will reappear, especially in the case of Quebec.

Finally, from the point of view of our research proposal, one important building block has been secured: we now know that pure decisions are significant, at least at the national level, i.e. the Automotive Agreement (a "pure" decision) has been revealed as a potent and plausible alternative expenditure policy.

---

4   In this strategy the income tax is cut to 15 per cent; the general federal sales tax on consumption expenditures is reduced to 9 per cent; the general federal sales tax on building materials and supplies is slashed to 5 per cent for the 1968-76 period.

5   The deficit on the external account increases approximately by $3 billion in each of the last three years of the simulations and by approximately $1.4 billion in the years 1971 to 1973.

The Impact of the Automotive Agreement
at the Regional Level

We have established in the preceding section that a "pure" decision like the Automotive Agreement can be as potent at the national level as rival expenditure policies and that, furthermore, the Automotive Agreement has two main characteristics:

(i)   Compared to the "passive" or *status quo* scenario, its net impact is very large.

(ii)   It is often superior to other more interventionist (comparable with the "passive" scenario) and desirable strategies.

Does this potency also apply at the regional level? To answer this question we have regionalized the national results obtained in section I at the level of the provinces. To expedite the matter we have computed the net impact only with respect to real domestic products.[6] For each province and for selected years, we have subtracted from the RDP obtained for the Automotive Agreement (control solution) the various RDPs obtained through simulating three scenarios: the "passive" or *status quo*, Strategy No. 4, and Strategy No. 6. Another feature of our methodology is that our results can be provided not only by province, but by economic sector at varying levels of disaggregation (e.g., 31 manufacturing industries) so that more information is furnished for the detailed analysis of these provincial impacts. The method of regionalizing the national data (obtained in section I) makes use of the Inter-provincial Trade Matrix Data which is part of the 1966 Interprovin-cial Input/Output model constructed by Statistics Canada.[7]

Analysis of the Results

Using data provided by the third panel of Table 2, one realizes that the potency of the Automotive Agreement scenario is great when it is compared to the "passive" scenario, and that, furthermore, this potency differs drastically among provinces. The annual average impact on Canada for the years selected is over a billion dollars. Nearly 90 per cent of this billion goes to Ontario, and correspondingly

---

6   Resources permitted regionalization for only six years. Comparison of the results for these years for Canada with those shown for RDP for all nine years in Table 1 indicates that Table 2 is, if anything, somewhat conservative in its implications concerning the order of magnitude of the regional distributional effects of the Automobile Agreement.

7   Our procedure is described in greater detail in A. Moroz, "Regionalization Methods for Automotive Agreement Study", mimeo., Economic Council of Canada.

Table 2

Increase or Decrease in Real Domestic Product Attributable to the Automotive Agreement, by Region, under Three Alternative Views about What Might Have Replaced it, in Selected Years

(Millions of 1961 dollars)

	Year	New-foundland	Prince Edward Island	Nova Scotia	New Brunswick	Quebec	Ontario	Manitoba	Sask-atchewan	Alberta	British Columbia	Canada
Alternative Strategy No. 4	1968	1.54	0.62	7.83	7.27	85.55	684.95	12.94	7.51	21.34	19.73	849.28
	1971	-1.67	0.19	2.22	4.46	47.10	846.94	7.62	-0.74	7.05	-2.09	911.08
	1973	-3.07	0.19	0.26	4.49	39.61	1,007.95	7.59	-1.18	5.95	-7.20	1,054.59
	1974	-14.59	-2.11	-27.54	-16.97	-227.33	142.05	-31.24	-32.32	-64.97	-93.88	-368.90
	1975	-10.29	-1.47	-18.95	-10.22	-149.09	369.59	-18.84	-22.48	-41.36	-66.15	30.74
	1976	-9.49	-1.23	-13.84	-5.46	-88.16	859.38	-12.43	-21.50	-31.75	-56.30	619.22
Average of Selected Years		-6.26	-0.64	-8.34	-2.74	-48.72	651.81	-5.73	-11.79	-17.29	-22.88	516.00
Alternative Strategy No. 6	1968	1.54	0.62	7.83	7.27	85.55	684.95	12.94	7.51	21.34	19.73	849.28
	1971	-6.63	-0.62	-7.56	-3.05	-67.42	615.99	-7.74	-16.15	-21.39	-36.63	448.60
	1973	-9.32	-0.63	-10.42	-3.24	-106.68	711.31	-11.27	-21.05	-25.95	-41.26	481.49
	1974	-16.44	-2.21	-31.02	-18.16	-309.67	-21.22	-40.25	-46.25	-75.61	-99.15	-659.75
	1975	-11.82	-1.57	-20.31	-10.85	-208.09	235.07	-26.45	-33.17	-51.43	-68.44	-197.06
	1976	-8.66	-0.87	-9.99	-1.90	-100.46	818.34	-12.93	-26.69	-26.92	-42.05	567.87
Average		-8.56	-0.88	-12.03	-4.99	-117.80	507.41	-14.28	-22.63	-29.99	-44.63	251.77
Passive Government	1968	3.06	0.93	11.01	9.85	116.71	749.09	17.44	11.51	30.29	31.28	981.17
	1971	5.76	2.05	18.94	18.07	209.62	1,137.32	33.13	24.07	56.91	62.01	1,567.88
	1973	1.79	1.58	11.44	13.67	151.02	1,186.23	25.43	16.71	40.54	37.04	1,485.45
	1974	-7.24	-0.11	-10.89	-3.20	-62.81	420.99	-4.93	-6.17	-13.51	-29.80	59.42
	1975	-3.41	0.46	-3.37	2.87	4.04	620.77	5.42	2.05	6.44	-5.54	629.73
	1976	-0.02	1.25	7.11	12.03	115.94	1,198.21	21.00	12.52	33.98	26.47	1,428.49
Average		-0.01	1.03	5.71	8.88	89.09	885.44	16.24	10.12	25.78	20.24	1,025.36

little to Quebec[8] and the other provinces. On the other hand, a
comparison of the Automotive Agreement with Strategies 4 and 6 shows
even more inequality in the distribution of the effects of the
Automotive Agreement among the provinces. The automotive agreement
continues to have a positive effect in Ontario for every year except
1974. But it is a different story for Quebec, where the automobile
agreement is less valuable than Strategy number 4 would have been
for the years beginning in 1974, and then Strategy number 6 for the
years starting in 1971. The overall effect for all years considered
is an actual loss of real domestic product in Quebec when the effects
of the automobile agreement are compared with Strategies 4 and 6
rather than with "passive" government policy. The same is true for
every province other than Quebec and Ontario.

Another way to demonstrate the point that a "pure" decision
such as the Automotive Agreement affects regions differently is to
analyse the share of each province in the Canadian net impact of
the Automotive Agreement (when compared to alternative strategies).
By and large, whatever the scenario, the net Canadian impact is
concentrated in Ontario. In the case of the net impact *vis à vis*
the "passive" government scenario, the share of the net Canadian
impact accruing to Ontario is (for selected years): 76 per cent,
72 per cent, 80 per cent, 149 per cent, 98 per cent, 80 per cent;
while Quebec's share is, respectively: 12 per cent, 13 per cent,
10 per cent, negative, 0.6 per cent, 8 per cent. An interesting
year is 1974 when all provinces are worse off than under the "passive"
scenario, except for Ontario which still manages to gain, obviously
partly at the expense of the other provinces. But 1974 is an
exceptional year, so that over the entire period every province
(except Newfoundland for some years) wins. Consequently, if we refer
to the "passive" scenario, the Automotive Agreement is *not*, at the
level of the provinces, a zero sum game: everybody wins.

When we envisage other plausible scenarios (No. 4 and No. 6),
the picture is less clear, and the superiority of the Automotive
Agreement in terms of increased output, employment, etc. is
accompanied by pronounced regional effects. For Ontario, the
Automotive Agreement is still preferable, whatever the alternative
scenario envisaged, except for 1974 with respect to Strategy No. 6.
Furthermore, its share of the Canadian gains, or more appropriately
the ratios of its net gains over total Canadian net gains (in the
case of Strategy No. 6) are as follows: 81 per cent, 137 per cent,
148 per cent, negative, positive gains, while Canada loses, and 139
per cent. This means that the Automotive Agreement is always

---

8   The ratio for each year of the net impact of the Automotive
     Agreement over the RDP of Ontario is, for the six years studied:
     3.2 per cent, 4.4 per cent, 3.9 per cent, 1.3 per cent, 1.9 per
     cent and 3.1 per cent. For Quebec the corresponding ratios are:
     0.84 per cent, 1.35 per cent, 0.84 per cent, negative, insignificant,
     and 0.57 per cent.

(except for 1974) more potent for Ontario than Strategy No. 6, and that for 1971, 1973, 1975 and 1976, the advantages for Ontario are greater than Canadian gains. This means that the potency of the Automotive Agreement is often compromised by a decided slip in potency for the other provinces when it is compared to Strategy No. 6.

From what precedes, it seems that the Automotive Agreement is necessarily a preferable scenario for Ontario and a much less desirable scenario for the other provinces, notably Quebec. But the matter is much more complicated than we have seen so far. In this respect five remarks are in order:

(1) Only two scenarios are absolutely certain: the Automotive Agreement and the "passive" or *status quo* scenario. Although Strategy No. 6 seems preferable for Quebec, because of uncertainty, it might still have been the choice of Quebec in 1965, because even for Quebec the Automotive Agreement is preferable to the *status quo*.

(2) The provincial results we have presented account for changes only in RDP. If other indicators are taken into consideration, the overall judgment might be different. We have shown in section I that Strategy No. 6 is inferior to the Automotive Agreement in many respects, notably as regards the level of unemployment. Since Quebec's unemployment level is usually higher than the Canadian level, that would have modified the value of this strategy for Quebec.

(3) Let us not forget that, except for 1974 and 1975, the Automotive Agreement (in RDP terms) is, at the Canadian level, superior to all other scenarios. Consequently, there is an overall surplus that could be (and probably was) redistributed to the other regions, which, because of distance or because of the characteristics of their own industrial structures, found (in some specific years only) the Automotive Agreement inferior to some other plausible strategies. In other words, to the extent that Ontario has been made richer by the Auto Pact, it has also contributed to the various transfer payments of the federal government to other regions.

(4) The implication of these results is not that "pure" decisions with characteristics similar to the Automotive Agreement should not be implemented, but that a whole arsenal of such "decisions" should be put to work in different regions because of their local and Canadian success.

(5) Finally, readers should bear in mind that our results come from the workings of two black boxes: CANDIDE 1.2M and Statistics Canada's Interprovincial Trade Data. To the extent that

these "boxes" produce imperfect results, especially because of the
length of the period studied, one must interpret our results
cautiously. Yet, we maintain that our results are of a better
quality than "guesstimates" or other partial evaluations. We do
not, however, pursue this line of inquiry because the purpose of
this study is not to judge, *ex post facto*, whether the Automotive
Agreement has been a "good" or a "bad" thing for Quebec. We wish
simply to show that at the regional level:

(i)   "pure" decisions of the federal government are
       sometimes equivalent, if not superior, to fiscal,
       monetary or foreign exchange policies; for example,
       the case of Ontario.

(ii)   but that simultaneously, that same "pure" decision
       might be inferior in some ways to alternative (and
       equivalent at the Canadian level) fiscal, monetary
       and foreign exchange policies for other regions;
       for example, Quebec after 1971.

PART III

THE ROLE OF RAIL RATES
IN THE LOCATION OF ECONOMIC ACTIVITY

The purpose of this part of our study is to stress the importance of major policy decisions in the field of railway transportation. These decisions either encourage or constrain regional economic development by making transportation costs an incentive (or a disincentive) for business firms to locate in certain regions. These decisions range from approving certain accounting practices (used to determine the variable costs that constitute both the floor below which railway rates must not go and the reference rate which can be increased up to 1.5 times), to authorizing the setting of rates according to what the traffic will bear (again up to 1.5 times the variable costs), to meeting competition and setting statutory rates such as the Crow's Nest Pass rate on grains and grain products.

These are "pure" federal government decisions because there are other **railway** pricing philosophies[1] which could significantly alter the rates being charged. These decisions also have important implications for the existence of regional comparative advantages. In this respect, Blackman (1977) contends that the western provinces are exploited:[2] "it is in reality a combination of geography and a transport system consisting of rail, trucks, and pipeline which makes this continued exploitation possible" (Blackman (1977) p. 45).

The upshot, according to Blackman and other writers, is that the Western region cannot industrialize except for a few activities not subject to returns to scale, these activities being able to survive within the region because of the protection of freight rates given to the local producers.

If the West has to increase its sales of finished goods in the central Canadian markets in order to industrialize, then railway freight rates will prohibit industrial expansion for one or both of the following reasons:

(1) Distance;

---

1 See, for instance, K.I. Wahn, *Transportation and Industrial Development in Manitoba*, May 1973; or, The Government of Alberta, *The Equitable Pricing Policy, A New Method of Railway Rate Making* (1973).

2 See Blackman (1977), p. 414, for his definition of the concept of "exploitation".

(2)   Discriminating rail rates, i.e., rail rates that
      discriminate:

    (a)   between raw materials and finished products;

    (b)   among shippers of the same product either
         according to direction of shipments, distance,
         or according to volumes of shipments.

The case of distance does not necessarily imply any "foul play"
on the part of the "pure decisions" of the federal government
because the federal government does not always have to suppress
distance in a country as large as Canada.[3]

An interesting case for us is the discrimination practice of
the railways. For instance, abstracting from space, western
industrialization would be rendered difficult if the federal
government decisions condoned railway rates (or forced railways
to charge rates, i.e., Crow's Nest Pass rates) that would be unduly
low on raw materials produced by the western provinces and very
high on western-central region shipments of the corresponding
finished products.[4]   Such a policy would condemn resource regions
to remain resource regions indefinitely with little hope of
industrialization based on local resources.[5]   The solution to
this problem is, of course, for the western region to become a
market; in order to become a market, however, it is necessary to
industrialize. The western region is consequently faced with a
chicken and egg problem. At least, this is the position of the

---

3   Consequently, it seems that Blackman (1977, pp. 415-16) has no
    ground to cite the case of "davit style lamppost" because it is
    obvious that, if both the market and the raw material (steel)
    are in central Canada, you cannot be competitive by incurring large
    freight costs even without rail rate discrimination, unless you
    provide exceptionally cheap labour and/or capital. However, there
    is one argument which could conceivably lead to a cry of "foul
    play" and that involves the West's perceiving one of the objectives
    or reasons for Confederation to be the elimination of distance
    as a factor in the location of economic activity. Specifically
    this argument would require the assertion that confederation in-
    cludes the formation of a spaceless economy in Canada.

4   Neglecting cases involving large weight-losing production processes,
    etc. The case is reinforced if the production process requires
    intermediate inputs available only in central Canada.

5   A famous case is the one of *Rapeseed Oil* (Heaver and Nelson, 1977,
    p. 260).

representatives of the western provinces.[6] As a follow-up to the
Western Economic Opportunities Conference (held in 1973) where
these claims were made, the federal government financed a series
of studies to investigate these claims.[7] For instance, the MPS
(1975) study was made "to determine whether the cost of transport
for inbound and outbound commodities for the same 'average plant'
located in the Prairie provinces and in central Canada would
significantly influence industrial development" (Heaver and Nelson,
1977, p. 56). Not unexpectedly, the MPS (1975) study found that
industries trying to serve the Canadian national market in a central
Canada location incur less transportation costs, the only reason
for this conclusion (according to Heaver and Nelson (1977, pp. 56-
57)) being the distance factor.[8] If this is so, there is no room
for "pure government" decisions having themselves, i.e., besides
the distance factor, an impact on the location of plants through
the freight rate structure. Consequently, in order to evaluate the
possible impact of "pure" government decisions in freight rate matters
we must distinguish among the total effects of freight rates, a
distance effect and a rate of discrimination effect. This involves
calculating the Effective Protective Rate (EPR) received by

6   See: "Freight rates exert an impact upon the location of economic
     activity because of weight and volume changes which occur during
     manufacturing or processing of raw materials into products. Rates
     thus usually encourage the concentration of industry at large
     population centres in Central Canada, or in a foreign country,
     instead of where the raw materials are located." (Government of
     Alberta, 1973, p. 10.)

7   Two of them have received some publicity:

     (i)   P.S. Ross and Partners, *et al: Two Proposals for Rail
           Freight Pricing: Assessment of Their Prospective Impact.*
           A report to the Federal-Provincial Committee on Western
           Transportation, 1974.

     (ii) MPS Associates Ltd.: *Transport and Regional Development*
           in the Prairies. A report for the Federal Ministry of
           Transport, Vols. I and II, December 1975 (but released only
           in the Fall of 1976). This study is more extensive than
           ours. It consists of thirteen theoretical case studies
           in food products industries, metal products industries,
           and miscellaneous industries.

8   Apparently in this study, rate discrimination bears the name of
     "so-called rate anomalies" and has been either eliminated as a
     factor or averaged out! See Heaver and Nelson (1977), p. 57.

central Canada producers[9] in two variants (for the same industry).

    (i)   The EPR received on account of actual freight rates; and

   (ii)   The EPR received on account of theoretical freight rates that would approximate the real full costs of moving different types of merchandise.

The difference between the two results measures the impact of "pure" government decisions in freight rate matters. The formula of the EPR in a simple case[10] is:

$$EPR = \frac{[T_a \cdot F_a + T_b \cdot F_b + T_c \cdot F_c] - [T_x \cdot F_x + T_y \cdot F_y + T_z \cdot F_z]}{\text{Value added per unit of volume, the composite output}}$$

where T_a, T_b, T_c are the various tonnages of output that must be transported to central Canada; F_a, F_b, F_c are the corresponding freight costs that must be incurred. Freight costs are the product of freight rates multiplied by distance. In our calculations we used Regina as the typical location in the Prairies, and Toronto as the typical location for central Canada. Similarly, T_x, T_y, T_z represent the necessary inputs that must be imported from the Prairie region, and F_x, F_y, F_z, their corresponding freight costs. The unit of volume of composite output was one hundred pounds, comprising all the usual outputs in weights corresponding to their relative importance (in weight) in Canadian production.

    Our main hypotheses are:

    (1)   Every producing region must produce the different outputs in the fixed proportion (in tonnages) given by the Canadian production structure of the industry.

---

9   It measures the percentage increase in value added per unit of composite output of central Canada (or Ontario) producers made possible by freight rates. There is a vast literature on the subject. For instance, see: Waters II, W.G., "Transport Costs, Tariffs and the Pattern of Industrial Protection," *American Economic Review*, December 1970; Finger, J.M., and Yeats, A.J., "Effective Protection by Transportation Costs and Tariffs," *Quarterly Journal of Economics*, vol. 90, February 1976; Reisnsch, A.E., *The Protective Effects of Domestic Rail Structures*, M.A. Thesis, Calgary, 1977.

10 A simple case is where all inputs are available in the Prairie region (if production is in the Prairie region) -- and most of the inputs must be imported from the Prairie region if production is in central Canada.

(2)   The same returns to scale are available and used everywhere.

(3)   In the calculations of real full cost rates, we assume that the cost of transporting different commodities is solely related to the type of equipment used (type of freight car used).[11]

(4)   That the total costs of providing freight services correspond to the total freight revenues of the railways.

This approach is different from others in the following way:

(a)   We are *not* evaluating the viability of western region production.

(b)   Our method of pricing railway services does not involve (as the Alberta and Manitoba schemes do) federal government subsidies to balance the operating budgets of the railways. However, it does involve some redistribution of the freight costs among some commodities where the elasticity of demand for railway services does not intervene in any way.

(c)   Our study will not answer the question "is there a *general* rate discrimination against the Western region?" But if many cases (not yet studied) fall in the pattern of the results we obtained for SIC 105, our answer would be: "discrimination may not be "general" but it exists where it hurts, i.e., particularly in manufactured products linked to local resources, where the west is supposed to have a comparative advantage.

Ideally we should investigate all the industries in order to furnish the total amount of damages or benefits experienced by the Prairie region due to the freight rate structure designed under federal government rate-making rules. Lack of time and funds prevent this but it is not crucial to us since our purpose is simply to prove that federal government pure decisions, i.e., rate-making rules, have a regional impact. We will demonstrate our point by studying SIC 105 (Flour and Breakfast Cereal Products), an industry already studied by MPS Associates Ltd. Comparisons of results will then be possible.

---

11   A similar approach is used by the Government of Alberta (1973), p.22. Other experts consulted also agree that for a rough and ready estimate of operating costs such an approach can be used.

The Case of Flour and Breakfast Cereals -- SIC 105

Grains that are grown mainly in the Prairie region are the main input of this industry.[12] The outputs are mainly flour, breakfast cereals and feeds. In 1967, Ontario produced 36.7 per cent of the Canadian output of flour, 87.3 per cent of Canadian breakfast cereal output, or 45.4 per cent of the combined outputs. In 1974, Ontario produced 54 per cent of the combined Canadian outputs (in value terms). In 1974, it satisfied 90 per cent of its own needs for flour and breakfast cereals, while this proportion was 77 per cent in 1967. On the other hand, although the Prairies have the raw materials, they provided little of Ontario's needs for the finished products; not below 3.5 per cent in 1974 and probably 10 per cent in 1967, while Ontario satisfied the needs of the Prairies to the extent of 22.7 per cent in 1967 (mainly in breakfast cereals) and 23.6 per cent in both flour and breakfast cereals.[13]

There are many reasons for this activity being in central Canada (urban external economies, propensity of U.S. firms to locate in Ontario, etc.). However, two reasons might be the protection offered by distance to central Canada producers and the structure of freight rates. As we have said before, this is measured by the EPR. The necessary data to compute the EPR are as follows.[14]

In 1974, 67.4 per cent of Canadian output (measured in weights) of the Flour and Breakfast Cereal Products Industry (SIC 105) is in the form of flour, 3.8 per cent in breakfast cereals (32 per cent of them cooked and 68 per cent of them uncooked), and 28.8 per cent in the form of feeds. The inputs are 94 per cent in the form of grains, oil cakes and meals, and 6 per cent in the form of corn, peas, vitamins, cattle and dairy products, sugar boxes, etc. For our calculations, we hypothesize that, as far as Ontario producers are concerned, grains must be imported from the Prairies and the other inputs are available locally at no transportation costs.

---

12 Although some Ontario wheat is now available. Since we will work with the assumption that wheat is only available in the Prairie region, our results underestimate the true competitive position of the Ontario producers if they use some local wheat.

13 The data sources to make these calculations are Statistics Canada, Cat. Nos. 31-504 and 31-522.

14 Based on Statistics Canada, Cat. No. 32-228.

The nominal rates for shipment from Regina to Toronto charged by the railways on July 1, 1974 are:[15]

$1.29 per hundred pounds of grains and wheat flour

$2.25 per hundred pounds of cooked cereal preparations of grains and wheat flour

$1.29 per hundred pounds of uncooked grains and wheat flour

$0.584 per hundred pounds for feeds.

However, shippers can reduce the freight rate of shipping wheat and other grains to $0.584 if they use boats to carry the grains from Thunder Bay to Toronto.[16] It is assumed that shippers do so; it is also assumed that the feed travels by boat, and uncooked breakfast cereals move by rail.

The value added per one hundred pounds of output is established as $2.4438. The results are as follows:

$$EPR = \frac{[.86946 + 0.16819 + 0.03333 + 0.02736]-[.54896 + 0]}{2.4438} = 22.5\%$$

The total amount of effective protection from western producers received by Ontario producers is thus $18.5 million.[17] This must

---

15   The sources consulted were: Canadian Freight Association (Ottawa); Redma et Associés (Montreal); B.G. Baker, freight rate officer, CN Rail (Montreal); *Waybill Analysis 1974*; the MPS Associates Ltd. 1975 study; Mr. B. Hopkins, Canadian Livestock Association (Montreal). It should be noted that the rail rates for wheat and other grains to be exclusively used in the production of feed were approximately 54 cents; however, this is the result of the pricing policy of the railways to compete against boat rates for this particular demand for wheat.

16   Wheat flour or flour is not shipped by boat due to the high cost of handling, loading, unloading and sanitation. Prior to March 3, 1973, a shipper could save approximately five cents for every one hundred pounds off the rail charge for moving grains and grain products by using the rail and lake system; however, this was discontinued after this date.

17   Statistics Canada Cat. No. 32-228, Table 1, establishes at 84,102,000 the value added by Ontario producers of industry SIC 105. Multiplying this amount by EPR (i.e., 22 per cent) = 18.5 million.

be compared with their profits estimated at $12.6 million.[18]
This means that without freight rate protection some Ontario
producers would have to reorganize or relocate their production
activities.

The effective protection is, consequently, rather important;
however, this is for the most part due to the availability of an
alternative mode of transportation for wheat and other grains from
Thunder Bay to Toronto. In an "all rail" system the effective
protection is only 3.8 per cent, and this protection is exclusively
the result of the higher rate for prepared breakfast cereals and,
more importantly, the availability of some of the inputs in both
regions. It is evident that the Crow's Nest Pass rate system
reduces drastically the cost of distance between Regina and Thunder
Bay, and it seems that the railway's pricing policy almost elimi-
nates distance as a location factor between the West and central
Canada locations, when only the central Canada market is considered.

The effective protection, however, exists because of the
availability of boats for moving wheat and feeds but not wheat
flour and unprepared breakfast cereals. It is interesting to note
that the boats in the Great Lakes system are subsidized and, with
no charge for using the Welland Canal, it is suggestive that a
"pure decision" is contributing to this protection and, furthermore,
that a pure decision with regard to lake transportation contributes
to eliminating distance as a locational constraint for the eastern
producers.

This issue is further complicated by the pricing policy of
the railways for the movement of wheat and wheat products from
Thunder Bay to Toronto. While it seems that there is no apparent
favouritism for finished products as opposed to inputs when costs
are considered as opposed to rates, part of this protection, offered
by the availability of boats, is due to the railway rates from
Thunder Bay to Toronto being set significantly above the costs.
Our full cost rates[19] are calculated as follows:

---

18 There is no statistical source furnishing this information.
    However, the MPS Associates Ltd. study (1975) uses (p. 32, Table
    3-2) an average of 14.5 per cent to estimate the ratio of net
    profit before tax over value added for a typical flour and
    breakfast cereal producer. We used this percentage to arrive
    at $12.6 million of overall profits.

19 Our "full-costs" rate is based, among other things, on the same
    reasoning put forward in the case of an efficient rate structure
    as proposed in *Living Together*, pp. 199-200. Besides, rates
    are presented only for the purpose of regional analysis and are
    not alone a sufficient reason to suggest a change of the actual
    ones. Many other factors must be taken into consideration when
    rates are changed.

(a)   The cost of moving commodities depends upon the cost of the equipment in which it moves

(b)   Making an index (according to cost per car and the numbers of these different types of cars) for the eight types of cars used in Canada and applying it to the average cost of moving a ton-mile in 1975 (1.565 cents) and transforming that into rates per one hundred pounds per ton-mile we have the following rates:

Boxcar	= .08776¢ per 100 lbs. carried a mile
Flatcar	= .0553 ¢ per 100 lbs. carried a mile
Gondola car	= .0585 ¢ per 100 lbs. carried a mile
Hopper car	= .0715 ¢ per 100 lbs. carried a mile
Ore car	= .0683 ¢ per 100 lbs. carried a mile
Refrigerator car	= .1235 ¢ per 100 lbs. carried a mile
Stockbar	= .08776¢ per 100 lbs. carried a mile
Tank car	= .0845 ¢ per 100 lbs. carried a mile
Average car	= .0783 ¢ per 100 lbs. carried a mile

Wheat, grains and feed are assumed to travel in hopper cars, while breakfast cereals move in boxcars. On the basis of this, the full cost rate scheme, the effective protection for eastern producers is dramatically reduced to 4.8 per cent, as our estimate of the variable cost of moving grain and grain products (except prepared breakfast cereals) from Thunder Bay to Toronto is 57.2¢ per 100 lbs. This full cost rate rises to 70.2¢ if only boxcars are used; however, it is evident that the ability of the railways to set prices above their true full costs, which in turn are determined by accounting practices allowed by the government, results in an incentive to locate the processing plants in Ontario.

In short, pure decisions play an important role in the maintenance of effective protection. For the movement of these goods from the West to Thunder Bay, pure decisions reduce to almost nothing the differential effect of distance. Yet from Thunder Bay to Toronto, a number of pure decisions, as well as economic factors, result in a significant degree of protection for the central producers. By charging $1.09 per 100 lbs. for grains and grain products for this latter journey, grain shippers have an incentive to move these inputs by boat. Consequently, the EPR enjoyed by Ontario producers has two causes:

(1)   Rail rates discrimination "from Thunder Bay to Toronto,"

(2)   The presence of an alternative mode of
      transport, whose competitive position
      is partly due to two federal government
      decisions-subsidization of the Canadian
      Great Lakes Fleet, and disregard of the
      cost of the Welland Canal.

PART IV

CONCLUSIONS

The results of this study should not be too surprising. Intuitively, under *ceteris paribus* conditions, in an economy as diversified as Canada and with widely separated regions, "pure" government decisions are overwhelmingly more potent on a regional basis than general expenditure policies. This is because they directly modify the industrial structure of a particular region, or, as in the case of discriminating rail rates, they directly modify the comparative advantages of regions, while federal fiscal and monetary policies (which at the moment are not regionalized) have only a diffused and runabout influence on local economic structures.

One explanation for this is that "pure" decisions can be better tailored to meet local conditions; furthermore, the transmission of local effects is short-circuited.

In the filed of regional policy, it is much more effective to work directly on the economic structure or on the comparative advantages, and results are more assured through "pure" federal government non-expenditure decisions then through fiscal and monetary policies which, as Lacroix and Rabeau put it, have at the national level a highly uncertain effect on private investments. *A fortiori* (and the empirical testimonies we have offered in this study point in this direction), this statement should be true at the regional level.

Comments by M. Walker, Research and Editorial Director,
The Fraser Institute, Vancouver, B.C.

     In his first sentence, Professor Martin asserts, "Balanced
regional development would undoubtedly contribute to moderating
strains within the Canadian Confederation." If this balanced
development is achieved through national policy intervention, it will
not necessarily have such a soothing effect. Although development
potential varies from region to region, leading one to expect
unbalanced development to be the norm, Economics tells us that
the equilibrium situation within a free market area will eventually involve equal per capita incomes. When people are left to their
own devices, the natural process of adjustment tends towards balance.
If we take this assertion as a bench mark, it does not imply that
GPPs will be equal for every province. It only tells us that
differences must be compensated for by non-measureable income effects.

     Every region comes equipped with an endowment of government
policy, some regional and some national, whose objectives are often
unfortunately at odds with the natural process of adjustment. Sometimes these policies involve territorial or population objectives
which could never be attained if the market were allowed to operate
freely. Thus, optimum development of the Maritimes and Quebec may
involve out-migration and a consequent weakening of the local power
base of their respective regional governments. The more highly developed recipient regions, on the other hand, must deal with the
increased social pressures created by rapid population growth. Neither
scenario is particularly attractive, and one solution has been for
the "have-provinces" to bolster the "have-nots," in effect, to short
circuit the natural adjustment process. Unfortunately such deals,
insofar as they favour the faster growth regions and only seldom
enjoy the unanimous consent of all the provinces, tend to prevent
balanced development. They only exacerbate the development gap and
put even greater pressure on the inter-regional transfer process.

     In this brief digression from Professor Martin's paper, I have
attempted to provide a bench mark - that a free market situation
should naturally induce regional balance - and to indicate that
government intervention may not facilitate balanced growth but
frustrate it. Turning now to the paper, I should like to comment
on three things in particular: on Professor Martin's taxonomic
distinction between pure decisions and expenditure decisions, on
his econometric evaluation of the Auto Pact, and on some of the
wider implications of the kinds of solutions that political economists promote.

In terms of their economic effects, there is very little difference between pure decisions and expenditure decisions. Moreover, this suggested taxonomy confuses the real isssues and cuts across policy categories instead of delineating them. The economic development of Quebec would obviously be hurt if one of its clothing manufacturers were put out of business by foreign competition. According to Professor Martin, the Federal Government can intervene and make either a pure decision, which would involve a quota, an embargo or some other non-tariff barrier, or an expenditure decision, which would entail an explicit subsidy to the firm and an increase in either the deficit or the general tax rates.

From an accounting point of view, the differences between these two choices are more apparent than real. The effect of the quota is simply to tax clothes buyers and give the proceeds to clothes manufactureres. The pure decision differs from the expenditure decision only to the extent that its tax and transfer do not go through the government's fiscal framework.

There are, of course, real differences. First, the quota benefits all clothing manufacturers, not just the endangered Quebec firm, and therefore costs more than a comparable expenditure decision. Secondly, this wide-ranging redistribution would probably cut across acceptable lines of tax equity. Finally, these two policies differ in the extent to which their costs are defineable. The actual cost and regional redistribution resulting from a pure decision is difficult to calculate, while the cost of a tax expenditure transfer is obvious and the inter-regional deal involved is explicit. Obviously, these two policies are not equally amenable to econometric simulation.

The third sort of pure decision mentioned by Professor Martin relates to the regional location of federal activities. Such expenditures do provide some "on the spot" stimulation, but federal agencies operating in lower income provinces often impose a higher wage sector with which local employers cannot compete. The introduction of this high income sub-sector interferes with local economic activity and, relative to the bench mark mentioned earlier, has a similar effect on migration. Thus, location decisions have many negative spill-overs on activity and cannot be regarded as costless.

With regard to Professor Martin's econometric evaluation of the Auto Pact, it is worthwhile to note that models are very much like sausages -- you like them much more before you know how they are made. I am especially sceptical about models which try to assess structural change. How does one really go about simulating the non-existence of the Auto Pact? It seems especially silly to assume that a reaction function with the unemployment rate as argument and tax rates as output could possibly reflect all of the changes that the elimination of the Auto Pact would bring.

The Auto Pact has induced a regional redistribution of income from provinces which have no auto production to those which have. This is a redistribution relative to free trade in autos. If we wish to compare the Auto Pact to some tax expenditure pattern, then we have to know precisely what these income flows are in the case of the Auto Pact. The only way to calculate them is to use the free trade bench mark. I would conclude that the most interesting and important consequences of Professor Martin's simulation are not measureable within the confines of Candide.

Finally, I should like to look at some of the practical impli- cations of the solutions we political economists have been suggesting. Professor Martin suggests that pure decisions are superior to expend- iture decisions. I do not think the analyses in his paper prove this point, but the choice between these two sorts of policy gener- ates two major concerns.

First of all, we should be concerned with the visibility diff- erences between them. Since tax and expenditure policies are trans- parent as to incidence and first round effect, the "deals" struck dur- ing inter-regional bargaining are much more obvious. The other crucial difference between these two policies involves the extent to which they are each capable of serving the public interest. Cab- inet government can make reasonably sound tax and expenditure decisions within the confines of a fiscal framework because the natural checks and balances of the adversary system ensure that different interests are represented. While such competition does not ensure that the best choice will always prevail, it does at least ensure some expos- ure to rival viewpoints. More importantly, Cabinet can be held responsible for its decisions because the effects of its policy are identifiable.

New regulations emerging from pure decisions do not generate this natural adversarial response unless the individuals affected have a concentrated interest. Moreover, the costs of these regulations are often hidden, which makes it difficult to assess their effective- ness. One could certainly question whether the recent regulatory changes related to foreign trade and agriculture are in the best public interest.

In closing, I would like to thank Professor Martin for his stimulating paper. I am sure you will find it useful in your delib- erations.

THE EVOLUTION OF CANADIAN FEDERALISM

1867-1976

by

R. Durocher

Department of History

University of Montreal

The Parti Québécois victory on November 15, 1976 launched one of the most serious challenges that Canada has faced since 1867. How has Canada reached the stage where a provincial government representing more than one-fourth of the country's population holds as its stated objective the achievement of independence? This is a fundamental question for Canadians because the very existence of the country is threatened.

No one can doubt the seriousness of the crisis, even if the final outcome is still very uncertain and may remain so for a few years. The problem will not disappear on its own; even if the Quebec government loses its referendum for a mandate to negotiate sovereignty with association, the Parti Québécois would not disappear any more than the nationalists who run it and constitute its main driving force. Any possible succeeding government, even if it accepted the federal framework, could not break with Quebec's autonomous tradition, and would thus have to implement numerous reforms, involving difficult negotiations.

The present crisis is all the more serious because it has been mounting for some time, while some groups have chosen to deny its existence completely or at least play it down. Thirteen years ago, the Royal Commission on Bilingualism and Biculturalism wrote:

> Le Canada traverse actuellement, sans toujours
> en être conscient, la crise majeure de son
> histoire, cette crise a sa source dans le Québec:
> il n'est pas nécessaire de mener une enquête
> approfondie pour le savoir (...) Quoique
> provinciale au départ, la crise devient canadienne
> à cause de l'importance numérique et stratégique
> du Québec, et parce qu'elle suscite ailleurs, ce
> qui est inévitable, des réactions en chaine.

Well before 1965, this crisis had taken roots in the history of the country. It is a fact that the mythical vision many Canadians have of their history hardly helps them to understand the present. To begin with, Canada's history did not start with Confederation, nor even with the conquest in 1760, but with Champlain in the early 17th century. Furthermore, the relations between French and English Canadians have not always been peaceful: there was the military conquest in 1760, the 1837-38 rebellions, numerous ethnic conflicts, the conscription crises and, within Quebec itself, a situation in which the majority was dominated by the minority. Finally, Canada has not always enjoyed an unalterable and sacred constitutional framework. From 1760 to 1867, it underwent five constitutional arrangements: the Royal Proclamation of 1763, the Quebec Act of 1774, the Constitutional Act of 1791, the Act of Union of 1840 and, finally, the British North America Act, which is deeply marked by the achievements and shortcomings of the preceding constitutions.

After studying the factors that led to the new constitution of 1867, we will analyse the nature of the B.N.A. Act. In the history of Canada's federalism, three major turning points stand out; to simplify things we will label them with three dates: 1896, 1939 and 1960. During this historical review, we will see how each period has solved the inherent problems of federalism such as power-sharing between the various levels of government, financing of the federation, the role of constitutional amendments and the judicial interpretation of constitutional change.

Canada's immensity and diversity have ruled out all but a federal political structure. Each province and each of the major regions in the country has its own particular physiognomy and has made specific contributions to the development of Canadian federalism. The political situation, the interaction of institutions and politicians the economic situation, structural changes in the economy and changing relationships between the social classes in their fight for power are all elements that should be analysed to gain a thorough understanding of federalism.

In my paper, several of these dimensions will only be touched upon because of limitations of time and space. There is, however, one dimension that is paramount and that is Quebec's special role in the evolution of Canadian federalism. My reading of history has led me to believe that the most difficult problem facing the federal system is to reconcile Quebec's nationalism with Canadian national unity.

Canada is threatened with disintegration essentially because it has been unable to solve the Quebec problem. In the framework of federalism, Quebec has behaved as a province and a region in much the same way as the others. But Quebec has always been aware, with varying intensity depending on the period and the situation, that it constituted a distinct society and has intended to remain so. This national conscience has marked its relations with federalism and influenced the evolution of federalism.

History may help us to better understand the present national crisis since, as the political scientist Lucian W. Pye writes:

> All political systems are deeply wedded to a particular place and time. The importance of the individuality of every policy means that its history is of enduring significance. Political systems cannot seek to advance by merely denying their past. Somehow or other they must seek to come to terms with what they once represented even as they take on new forms and new content.

I THE CAUSES OF CONFEDERATION

In the 1860s, the small English colonies in North America were forced to federate in order to survive in the face of an American colossus ten times more populous and infinitely richer and more dynamic, as was demonstrated by its canal and railway building and its settling of the West.

In 1861, when the U.S. Civil War broke out, the tensions between the United States and Great Britain, which recognized the Confederate States, proliferated. British North America, which shared a border with the United States and was a British colony, could not remain indifferent, since the colonies would serve as the battleground if a conflict broke out between the two major powers, as had occurred in 1775 and 1812.

Numerous incidents between Britain and the United States, as well as border incidents between the English colonies and the United States, caused Canadians much concern over the defence of their territory, as well as over their economic future since, as a retaliatory measure, the U.S. announced in 1865 that it would end the Reciprocity Treaty the following year.

The U.S. threat was all the more serious to British North America because London had begun in the 1840s to profoundly change its imperial policy. Beginning in 1846, the home country gradually abandoned the preferential trade system that protected Canada and began to move towards free trade. Since Britain refused to protect its colonies, they had to protect themselves through high tariffs applied even to English products. London gave in to Canadian protectionist policy and granted extensive internal autonomy to its colonies. In return, however, it planned to let the colonies assume responsibility for their own defence. The small British colonies, not having the necessary resources to defend themselves against their only possible enemy, the United States, were forced to consider a military as well as an economic union.

These external causes alone were not sufficient to explain the constitutional change in 1867, nor the specific terms that accompanied this change. They did, however, coincide with a set of economic and political problems that would force anglophones and francophones to accept this federal compromise.

The British western territories, a vast land extending from the Great Lakes to the Arctic and Pacific Oceans, were administered by the Hudson's Bay Company. In the mid-19th century, Americans were making a strong push towards the West and settlers were hungry for fertile land. The Hudson's Bay Company constituted a very weak obstacle to this drive.

As London did not wish to take on too much colonial responsibility, it attempted to persuade Canada to act as the owner of this territory. Canada beat around the bush because it was experiencing economic difficulties and particularly because French-Canadians in Lower Canada would not accept annexation of the West. They felt it would upset the unstable and artificial balance that had emerged from the union of the two Canadas.

For several Fathers of Confederation, for Great Britain, for the English-Canadian bourgeoisie, annexation of the West would be an important justification for Confederation. In turn, Confederation would be a necessary condition for annexation of the West.

Canada undertook a large railway-building program in an attempt to compete with the U.S. and found itself in serious difficulties in the 1860s. The only alternative to bankruptcy appeared to be further and deeper commitment to the railway venture by uniting the Maritimes, Canada and the West: it was hoped that the railway could be made profitable by a larger market. However, this required a political union of the various colonies.

Finally, in 1850 and 1860, United Canada suffered chronic political instability that could only be overcome through a new political structure. The Union had been imposed on French-Canadians and it was hoped that, being in a minority, they would begin to assimilate as had the Louisianans before them. But it quickly became apparent that the new system could not function without their participation. Consequently, the legislative union became a *de facto* federal system.

In return for French-Canadian acceptance of the new system which placed them in a minority, it was necessary to grant some degree of cultural autonomy in the areas of language, religion, law and education. They were even given some economic powers such as the control of some appointed offices, and of land and agricultural policy in Canada East. Thus, a *de facto* federal system gradually emerged, symbolized by bicephalous departments: Baldwin-LaFontaine, Hinks-Morin, Macdonald-Cartier, etc. Several departments were doubled, with one responsible for each section, which resulted in some duplication of the public service.

The system was generally as expensive as it was inefficient and tempers simmered among the majority of citizens in Canada-West, who denounced the French domination. Between 1861 and 1864, there were two elections and preparations were made to call a third that would have continued the impasse created by the constitutional status quo. The only solution was to transform the *de facto* federation into a true federation that would be both a union and separation of the colonies.

London wholeheartedly supported the project. It exerted strong pressure on Nova Scotia and New Brunswick to join the new union to be negotiated between the colonies from 1864 to 1867.

The long political crisis created by the imposed union of the two Canadas was solved under the pressure of powerful external and internal factors and by a long process of negotiation.

II   THE BRITISH NORTH AMERICA ACT

From 1864 to 1867, the politicians who drew up the Constitution agreed on two basic points, that the union of the colonies would be of a federal type and that the federalism would be centralized. Most would have preferred a legislative union but because of the Maritimes and Quebec they had to accept the federal idea. On the other hand, the conservative French-Canadian leaders did not oppose the idea of centralization because, in their view, it did not threaten the rights of their nationality, which fell under the jurisdiction of the provincial government in which they held a majority. They stressed that in the federal system the central government would only deal with general issues, in which questions of "race" and religion would not be included. Finally, the federal model most familiar to the "Fathers" was that found in the United States. After witnessing the United States Civil War, they believed that the U.S. Constitution was too decentralized and thus wished to avoid repeating this error.

The result of their efforts was an Act passed by the British Parliament under the name of the British North America Act, which has no official French translation and provides no formula for amending the Act. The B.N.A. Act is a lifeless and pragmatic document written in a heavy legal style whose text is as interesting and as complex as an insurance contract. We will now examine how the Constitution divides powers between the two levels of government and provides for the protection of minority rights.

In 1867, the powers granted to the provinces were those closely related to the social and cultural organization of the various communities, such as property and civil rights, health and social security, Crown Land, municipalities and local works, the administration of justice and education. At a time when governments intervened very little in these sectors and when the sums required to provide these services were fairly small, the powers granted exclusively to the provinces by Section 92 of the B.N.A. Act were believed to be secondary.

Section 91 of the act gave the central government exclusive power in particular over trade and commerce, currency, credit and banks, the post office, Indians, defence and criminal law.

While these powers are important, the centralizing characteristic of the union emerges in a set of provisions scattered throughout the Act. The preamble to Section 91 gives Ottawa the right to legislate "with a view to peace, public order, and the good administration of Canada, on any issue not falling into the categories of subjects that this Act grants exclusively to the provincial legislators" (unofficial translation). In other words, the federal government obtains the residual powers that may eventually become very important. This clause also allows it to legislate in all fields in emergency cases.

Agriculture and immigration are recognized as joint responsibilities, but in cases of conflict between the federal and provincial levels, the federal point of view automatically predominates. The federal government has the right to disallow any provincial legislation, and in 1867 there was no limit set to this right of disallowance. The Lieutenant-Governor, who must sign all provincial acts to make them official, is a public servant appointed by Ottawa. The federal government may exert its authority "over those works which although entirely located in the province will be declared prior to or after their realization by the Parliament of Canada to be to the general advantage of Canada or to the advantage of two or more provinces" (unoffical translation). In a federal system, in principle at least, the Senate must defend the provinces, but Senators, as well as judges of the Supreme Court that the federal government created in 1875, are appointed by Ottawa. All this clearly demonstrates the centralizing character of the 1867 system. Macdonald himself admitted that the system granted "all the advantages of a legislative union." This judgment was later confirmed by K.C. Wheare in a classic study of federalism which presented the Canadian situation in 1867 as an example of quasi-federalism.

On the financial level, the same federal predominance prevailed. In effect, the federal government had the right to carry out "the levying of duties by all modes or systems of taxation," while the provinces were allowed "direct contributions in the province with a view to obtaining revenue for provincial purposes" (unofficial translations). The provincial governments had such limited revenue that the bulk of their financing came from Ottawa in 1867, and this placed them in a state of dependency.

The 1867 Constitution effectively made the provincial governments nothing but overgrown municipal administrations. Not only was Macdonald pleased with this situation, but he also believed that it was only temporary since, as he confided to a friend, these local governments would disappear within a generation and Canada would become a legislative union. This fully confirmed the apprehensions of French-Canadian opponents to the Confederation project, but we will see, however, the system evolved in an entirely different direction.

The Constitution provided very few guarantees for the protection of minority rights. Section 93 was totally ineffective in protecting the schooling rights of Catholics outside Quebec and Section 133 was clearly insufficient to ensure that federal institutions would be bilingual. The only minority truly protected was the Protestant minority in Quebec, but it was not because of the Constitution that this group was able to develop without any harassment by the majority. Rather, it was primarily because this minority relied on the Canadian majority and wielded enormous economic power.

III   THE EMERGENCE OF THE PROVINCES

From 1867 to 1896, the new central government proved to be

extremely active. In only a few years, it succeeded in extending
the territories of the new Dominion through annexation of the West
and the admission of British Columbia and Prince Edward Island into
the federation. It undertook the construction of the Intercolonial
Railway and massively subsidized construction of the Canadian Pacific.
It instituted a protectionist tariff policy that it publicized under
the wisely-chosen name of National Policy.

However, the dream of John A. Macdonald and most of the Fathers
of Confederation of erecting an increasingly centralized state was
severely put to the test. During these first 30 years, the provinces
succeeded in asserting their individuality and the central government
was consequently forced to cool its centralizing ambitions.

The immensity and diversity of the new country made a decentralized federalism necessary. This was all the more true since the
former colonies, now united by Confederation, had solid autonomous
traditions and did not have any strong loyalty to this new Dominion
of Canada. The ethnic and religious tensions that divided the country
made its unification even more difficult. The unfavourable economic
situation from 1873 to 1896 increased the provinces' discontent with
Ottawa because it could not meet their financial demands. Thus, the
provinces were highly unsatisfied with the agreements reached in 1867
which left them few resources.

This evolution towards a more decentralized federalism was
confirmed and supported by the Privy Council in London which served
as a final court of appeal for constitutional matters. The Privy
Council, through its rulings, supported the autonomist views of the
provincial leaders and, undoubtedly, of their electorate which
identified more easily with their province than with the central
government.

From the first federal elections in 1867, Nova Scotia vigorously
expressed its opposition to the new system which had eliminated the
autonomy the province had formerly enjoyed. Of its 18 elected members,
17 were opposed to Confederation. London's veto and an increase in
the subsidies allocated to this province were necessary to prevent
its secession. Despite all this, in 1886, Nova Scotians elected the
Fielding government and again threatened to separate from Canada,
which they held responsible for their economic difficulties.

The situation in the West was hardly any easier for the central
government. Manitoba and British Columbia were unhappy with the
stagnation that afflicted them and with Ottawa's rail policy, which

slowed their development. In addition to the West's economic difficulties, there was the problem of the Métis and the Indians, a large number of whom, under the leadership of Louis Riel, would twice take up arms against Ottawa.

These two rebellions had repercussions on relationships between French and English Canadians and placed the federal government in a difficult situation. In the same way, the issue of schools in New Brunswick and, later, in Manitoba, clearly demonstrated that federalism could not provide a miracle solution to ethnic problems. The federal government was forced by the majority to avoid effective intervention in these conflicts. This indirectly promoted provincial autonomy and also weakened Ottawa's prestige, at least in the eyes of French-Canadians in Quebec and the other provinces. Consequently, francophones in Quebec began to turn more towards their provincial government.

And to top it all off, even the richest and most influential province in the country was vigorously opposed to Ottawa's centralizing views. From 1867 to 1896, Ontario was unquestionably the leader in the fight for provincial autonomy. From 1868, the Liberals, who were in the opposition, denounced the centralizing manoeuvres of the federal Conservatives. Of course they were in favour of Confederation, but they emphasized that federalism was both a union and a separation. One of the basic reasons that prompted Ontario to support Confederation was the desire to control its local affairs and avoid what was termed the "French Domination." Moreover, since Ontario was the richest province, it was relatively independent of Ottawa even in difficult times. Ontarians were aware that as the federal government extended its powers and increased its expenditures, they would be required to pay more for the other, less fortunate provinces. When the province was led by the Liberal, Oliver Mowatt, from 1872 to 1896, he repeatedly and successfully contested federal moves either before his loyal electorate or before the highest court of the Empire, the Privy Council in London.

As the B.N.A. Act was particularly ambiguous, the courts were called upon to play an important role in the area of interpretation. In a series of rulings, particularly from 1883 to 1896, the Privy Council gave an interpretation very favourable to those who supported provincial autonomy. The Court opposed the idea that the provinces were subordinate to the federal government in the fields that were granted to them in the Constitution. The judges wrote in 1883: "Dans les limites des sujets précités (article 92) la législature locale exerce un pouvoir sourverain, et possède la même autorité que le parlement ou le parlement du Dominion aurait, dans des circonstances analogues."

This theory of provinces sovereign in their spheres of jurisdiction would come, through the force of events, to limit the federal government's right of disallowal and even seriously limit the general character of the preamble to Section 91 which authorized the federal government to legislate for peace, order and good administration. The Privy Council believed that it was necessary to strictly limit the powers of the federal government, particularly when dealing with residual powers or when the federal government cited the national scope of certain local problems. Stated in the words of the Council, this "would destroy in practice the autonomy of the provinces." Along the same lines the Court recognized that the Lieutenant-Governor directly represented the Crown in the provinces and was not a simple public servant of Ottawa. This meant that the provincial parliaments were not simple municipal councils.

In 1896, the Constitution still read the same, but the interpretation given to it had considerably modified the balance of power between the federal and provincial governments. The provincial governments alone, or in a coalition, as occurred at the first interprovincial conference in 1887 called by Premiers Mowatt and Mercier, succeeded, with the support of their electorate and the Privy Council, in ensuring a certain jurisdictional autonomy.

From the financial point of view, they were still largely dependent on Ottawa since, in 1896, 43.1 per cent of their revenue came from federal subsidies. When the provinces could not obtain an increase in the federal subsidies, they gradually resorted to various forms of direct taxes: personal and corporate income tax and inheritance tax. These taxes represented 9.6 per cent of their revenue, while the sums coming from licences and the public field represented 47.3 per cent.

IV   CO-ORDINATED FEDERALISM 1896-1939

Laurier's arrival in power in 1896 coincided with a phase of economic prosperity in Canada. The federal government was successful in furthering the National Policy: settlement of the West, railway building and protectionism.

Despite the conflicts dividing French- and English-Canadians over the school rights of minorities and imperialism, Laurier succeeded in maintaining a certain degree of harmony.

The provinces, particularly Quebec, Ontario and British Columbia, entered into what was called the second industrial revolution. The natural resources of the forest, hydraulic energy and mines became increasingly important for the provinces. Provincial revenues rose by more than 400 per cent from 1896 to 1913. However, with the rapid increase in population, growing urbanization and the necessity to develop their resources and provide public services, the provinces wanted more subsidies from Ottawa.

In 1902, the provincial premiers met and were successful in petitioning Ottawa to increase its subsidies to the provinces. In 1906, they succeeded in convincing Laurier to be flexible and he called a federal-provincial conference. He agreed to increase federal subsidies by approximately one-third and to adjust them after each census. Laurier hoped this revision would be final. In 1913, the provinces again took the offensive, this time against the new Borden government, but without success. The provinces wanted the federal government to redistribute to the provinces each year 10 per cent of customs and excise receipts.

Even the increased federal subsidies represented no more than 28.6 per cent of the provinces' revenue in 1913. As sums drawn from the public field and the sale of permits and licences represented 50 per cent of provincial revenue, the provinces had to rely increasingly on their direct taxes which represented 20.7 per cent. The provinces' expenditures represented approximately 50 per cent of federal spending and played an increasingly important role in the development of their territory and the organization of society.

The war which broke out in 1914 slowed the development of the provinces. To meet the emergency situation, the federal government passed the War Measures Act giving it greater powers. It had to intervene heavily to mobilize the population and the economy for the war effort.

To finance the enormous expenditure incurred by the war, the federal government, in addition to resorting to borrowing and inflation, had to use all its fiscal powers. In 1916, for the first time, it levied a tax on corporations and in 1917, on personal income. In both cases, Ottawa was almost apologetic for its actions and implied that after the war it would withdraw from these two fields previously held solely by the provinces. The federal government also wished to control borrowing by the provinces but, faced with protests from Quebec and Ontario, abandoned this idea.

Following the war, however, needs became so large that the federal government refused to repeal the two major direct taxes. Nonetheless, it provided assistance in the form of loans to the poorest provinces. It used conditional subsidies for programs in the fields of health (venereal diseases) and education (technical courses). This financing technique, which plays such an important role in present-day federalism, had been used for the first time in 1912 in the area of agriculture and had not triggered any opposition.

The federal government made spectacular progress during the war: Canada's economic potential grew considerably and the country gained a presence on the international scene. But it was also saddled with a very heavy debt and was deeply divided along ethnic, social and regional lines.

The provinces also had enormous needs to fill and were very critical of Ottawa. Consequently, the conservative federal government became increasingly unpopular.

The 1920s were marked by the federal government's loss of momentum. Because of the war effort and the bankruptcy of the railways, public debt rose by a factor of seven from 1913 to 1920. The central government wished to return to an orthodox finance policy of reducing the debt, cutting taxes and balancing the budget, and so adopted a careful attitude. The only major social measure during the period was the establishment of old age pensions in 1927. The government promised to pay 50 per cent of the cost of pensions paid to the elderly in provinces that agreed to participate in the program. Some provinces objected to this federal intrusion into an area of provincial jurisdiction. Quebec was the last province to give in, in 1936. This policy clearly discriminated against those provinces not participating, since they paid taxes for a service their citizens did not receive, but was a particularly effective technique.

However, the development of industries based on the provinces' natural resources and the growing importance of the automobile allowed the provinces to play a major economic role. They had to make considerable investment in infrastructure, and increased industrialization brought on accelerated urbanization and created new social needs: education, health, etc., that exceeded the municipalities' abilities and forced the provinces to shoulder greater responsibility.

Parallel to these new responsibilities, the provinces found

new sources of income. Receipts from the major direct taxes grew
with the new prosperity, particularly since the federal government
exhibited extreme moderation in these sectors. The sale of alcohol
and automobile licences brought in large sums. Moreover, the
provinces added taxes on consumption to their fiscal panoply:
amusement tax, gasoline tax, tobacco tax and sales tax.

In the 1920s, the provinces had truly taken the initiative,
and it was the golden age of provincial autonomy. They exerted a
motivating influence on the economy, where the federal government
had previously played this same role. In addition, they displaced
municipalities in sectors such as education and social policy.

However, this type of development created problems of inequality
between regions. Since the Maritimes and the Prairies were unable
to benefit to the extent that Quebec, Ontario and British Columbia
did, the federal government was forced to assist these underprivileged
regions. Following the report of the Duncan Commission, it increased
subsidies to the Maritimes and subsidized the railways to lower
transportation costs. In 1930, it transferred to the Prairie Provinces
the administration of their natural resources and provided financial
compensation for the revenue they were unable to draw from these
resources.

The economic crisis of the 1930s vividly exposed some of the
latent problems of Canadian federalism and launched a move to question
the very basis of the Constitution.

At the start of the crisis the federal government limited itself to traditional measures: monetary policy and tariffs. But as
unemployment increased and municipal and provincial finances were
overburdened, it intervened to bring assistance to the unemployed
through agreements with the provinces. An effort was made to launch
public works programs, colonization programs, direct aid, the establishment of work camps, etc. These measures were insufficient and
anarchic. Discontent among the population ran deep when the Bennett
government, inspired by Roosevelt's example, launched its own New
Deal in 1935. This was a series of **social** and economic measures:
limitation of the work week, limitation of working hours, marketing
boards, etc. The liberals objected, pointing out that these measures
were unconstitutional; they were, in fact, disallowed by the Privy
Council.

Once in power, the liberals were faced with the same problems.

In 1937 they instituted the Rowell Commission to study the situation and suggest means for getting out of the impasse. However, Quebec and Ontario joined forces to block any profound changes to the federal system.

During this time, the situation continued to worsen and the federal government had to bail out the Prairie Provinces, which were on the brink of bankruptcy, and provide aid to the Maritimes.

The crisis hit the provinces unequally: the major industrialized provinces were better able to withstand the crisis. This did not, however, prevent them from asking the federal government to help the unemployed, provided of course, it did not invade provincial jurisdictions.

The years of misery traumatized many people and in English Canada in particular, there was growing criticism of provincial autonomy as a barrier to social justice and a threat to the nation's survival. The time had come for the central government to assume its national role.

Although the premiers of Quebec and Ontario successfully convinced Prime Minister Bennett in 1930 that the BNA Act constituted a pact between the provinces and that nothing in the Westminster Statute could infringe upon the roles of the provinces, this situation did not last long. The theory of the confederative pact was studied and rejected by many. It was discovered that the spirit and the letter of the BNA Act, constantly cited by Quebec and Ontario, were in fact centralizing. It was the Privy Council that had altered the Constitution. This centralizing current of thought was a consequence of the crisis and helped pave the way for the future.

The federal government made every possible effort to broaden its powers: it obtained authority over radio, created the Bank of Canada, implemented centralization of the major ports and sought ways to overcome opposition from Quebec and Ontario, which had managed to maintain their predominance and the constitutional status quo.

The Second World War helped to settle the economic crisis and gave the federal government the opportunity and means to work a basic change in federalism.

V THE NEW NATIONAL POLICY, 1939-1960

Canada's entry into the war gave the federal government the opportunity to take over all the levers of power. The War Measures Act became a surrogate Canadian Constitution.

Although there was no doubt that Canada would become fully involved in the war on the Allied side, King promised that the participation of Canadians would be voluntary because he wished to avoid a conscription crisis such as that which had deeply split the country in 1917. It was this double-edged commitment and his political ability that allowed him to get rid of Maurice Duplessis in 1939, obtain the massive support of Canadians in the federal election in 1940, and undermine the leadership of the provincialist Premier of Ontario, Mitchell Hepburn.

In 1940, the Rowell-Sirois Commission submitted its report, which remains to this day one of the most remarkable analyses of Canadian federalism. The Commission proposed that the federal government institute and administer a program of unemployment insurance and cover the full cost of old age pensions. It recommended that the central government have a monopoly on personal and corporate income tax and on inheritance tax. In return, the federal government would take on the provinces' debts and pay to the provinces an annual unconditional subsidy determined on the basis of the so-called "national standard." In addition, it recommended that the practice of delegating powers from one level of government to another be implemented as dictated by needs and circumstances. The Commission believed that by adopting these proposals, the taxation powers of each government would be clearly spelled out, the provincial governments would have a stable income and Canadians in all provinces would enjoy comparable services.

The following year, the federal government convened a federal-provincial conference to study this report. Ontario, Alberta and British Columbia vigourously opposed the project, while Premier Godbout did show a willingness to discuss the subject. The conference ended abruptly and apparently in failure. In fact, however, it constituted a victory for King. He had obtained the agreement of all provinces to mobilize all of Canada's resources for the war effort. Thus in 1942, he signed with each of the provinces an agreement for the duration of the war, through which the federal government would be the only government to levy personal and corporate income taxes in return for an unconditional subsidy. Moreover, after 1940, he had obtained the agreement of all provinces to amend the Constitution in order to implement unemployment insurance.

As the war effort gained momentum, King was forced to do an about-face on the issue of Conscription. Francophone Quebecois were massively against this measure. The liberal regime of Gobout in Quebec was undermined, and he personally fell victim to the policy of the Ottawa liberals. The reaction of the Quebec francophones was autonomist, so that once again the political expression of their nationalism took the route of defending provincial autonomy. The Bloc Populaire as well as the Union Nationale denounced the Godbout government's allegiance to Ottawa and criticized it in particular for accepting the Constitutional amendment creating unemployment insurance, and for signing the 1942 tax agreements. They promised that if elected, they would fight Ottawa's centralizing policies tooth and nail.

During this time, not only did the war effort in Ottawa continue, but preparations were also made in the midst of combat for the post-war policy. This was a lesson that had been learned from the First World War. It was essential to plan for reconversion of the economy and avoid the social crises and economic depression experienced by Canadians in the 1930s. The growth of the CCF served as a reminder of this necessity. The central government was surrounded by experts and was convinced intellectually and politically of the absolute necessity of retaining exclusive control over major direct taxes and major social legislation.

At the 1944-45 session, the federal government passed several bills of great significance, particularly: a National Housing Act, a Family Allowance Act, and one announcing the creation of a Health and Welfare Department. All these measures dealt with sectors that could be considered as provincial jurisdiction.

The federal-provincial conference on reconversion (August 6-7, 1945 and April 29-May 3, 1946) provided the opportunity for the federal government to unveil its complete program for the post-war period. Ottawa intended to retain an almost total monopoly over the direct major taxes (personal income tax, corporate tax and inheritance tax). In return, the provinces would receive an unconditional subsidy of $12.00 per capita that would be adjusted in terms of the GNP. It also proposed a shared-cost program, gradually leading through stages to a full program of health insurance. The federal government temporarily granted the conditional subsidies dealing with eight sectors in health. It alone shouldered the cost of old age pensions for all citizens over 70 years of age and it also agreed to pay 50 per cent of the pensions granted to needy citizens from 65 to 69 years of age. It took responsibility for providing social assistance to all unemployed workers capable of working. In the natural resources sector, in addition to intensifying its efforts to develop agriculture, forestry, industry and mining (these sectors already fell under its jurisdiction), Ottawa established shared-cost programs and offered conditional subsidies to the provinces to include them in its development effort.

These federal proposals constituted an impressive program based on a Keynesian vision of the economy which gave it a remarkable coherence. The program had been carefully prepared over many years by large numbers of experts. The day after the war ended, the federal government found itself in a strong position: Canada enjoyed considerable prestige on the international scene; English Canada had gained a greater awareness of its unity and identity; and the federal government was motivated by a profound determination.

The federal program raised fundamental questions over the functioning of federalism as it had developed up to 1939. Ottawa planned to carry out this reform which gave it overwhelming power, without resorting to constitutional amendments or the courts. The government believed its spending power and the support of the population were sufficient to push through the new, extremely centralizing, national policy.

The war had perhaps caused the central government to forget certain basic realities in the country: its immensity, its diversity, its provincialist tradition that was still alive even though it had been contested in the 1930s and temporarily shelved during the 1939-1945 war period. And then there was Quebec, led by Duplessis with the support of a population that felt oppressed and dominated during these years, and whose nationalist desire had been frustrated.

Ontario, Alberta, Nova Scotia and Quebec formally opposed the proposals. In addition to finding the proposed subsidy insufficient to meet their enormous needs, the provincial governments felt they were in a better position to define the needs of their population and provide an effective response; they were unable to do this because of the crisis and the war which deprived them of the necessary financial means. Furthermore, the autonomist provinces demanded a

return to the spirit of federalism, which signified for them the
respect of powersharing, as it had been defined and interpreted by
the Privy Council from 1883 to 1937, and fiscal autonomy for the
provinces. While the most articulate adversary was George Drew,
Premier of Ontario, the most dangerous opponent was undoubtedly
Maurice Duplessis. He was steadfastly opposed to the federal project. To begin with, social policy fell under provincial jurisdiction, as upheld in 1937 when the Privy Council in London disallowed Bennett's New Deal. Second, Duplessis insisted that provincial
autonomy without fiscal autonomy was meaningless. He would never
allow Quebec to be placed in trusteeship.

The federal government, however, was not to be stopped so
easily. Following the conference, which ended in failure, it began
to negotiate with the provinces individually. All, except Ontario
and Quebec, signed an agreement for the 1947-52 period. In 1952,
Ontario relented, leaving Quebec completely isolated in its opposition
to the new national policy.

While it did not gain a monopoly over taxes, Ottawa nonetheless
gained the upper hand and succeeded in completely reversing the
situation prevailing before the war. "In 1939, federal government
expenditures constituted 38 per cent of all government expenditure,
while provincial and municipal spending accounted for 62 per cent.
In 1952, this proportion was completely reversed, to 66.7 per cent
for the federal government and 33.3 per cent for the other governments.
Moreover, Ottawa's share of total revenue reached 67 per cent."
(M. Lamontagne - unofficial translation)

In this way, Ottawa succeeded in gradually implementing --
if not imposing -- a large part of its program. When an agreement
on health insurance proved impossible, it offered conditional subsidies for programs in the health sector. In 1957, a shared-cost
hospital insurance program was launched. Ottawa succeeded in gaining
support for an amendment to the Constitution, giving it authority
over old age pensions, and also established a shared-cost program
for needy individuals between 65 and 69 years of age. In 1957, the
federal government began providing assistance to welfare recipients
capable of working, and also participated in several shared-cost
programs in the natural resources and transportation sectors.

During these years, the federal government implemented a policy
of Canadianizing institutions. In 1949, it single-handedly abolished

appeals to the Privy Council in London, thus making the Supreme Court the final court of appeal. Similarly, it obtained from Westminster an amendment allowing it to modify, without consulting the provinces, what could be called the federal constitution. In 1950, Ottawa unsuccessfully attempted to obtain a provincial consensus to fully repatriate the constitution and work out an amending formula. In 1952, a Canadian was appointed governor-general.

During the same period, the federal government began to adopt cultural policies to complement its economic and social policies. The creation in 1949 of the Royal Commission on Literature, the Arts and Sciences, headed by Vincent Massey, marked the beginning of this new orientation. The federal government had in fact already created a place for itself in the cultural life of the country through a certain number of institutions: the National Archives, National Gallery, CBC, CNR, National Film Board, etc. The Commission's task was to analyse the operation of these institutions and "recommend the most effective means of administering them in the national interest." The Commission was also asked to suggest means by which Canada could participate fully in international cultural organizations. Finally, it was to analyse how the federal government and its agencies could assist the various nationwide volunteer groups dealing with cultural life.

After revealing the dangers threatening cultural life in Canada (Americanization, materialism, lack of funds, etc.), the Commission concluded that it was the duty of a national government to assist individuals and groups in their cultural development. Arts and literature "are also the basis of our national unity." The Commission was confident that it would be possible to promote the development of true Canadianism and safeguard the nation's integrity. Although some concern was expressed over respecting provincial autonomy in the area of education, the Commission could not overlook the fundamental role played by universities and research, which extended beyond provincial borders. After making a distinction between academic and general education, it recommended that the federal government come to the rescue of universities and researchers. The Commission also recommended an increase in the budgets of existing federal cultural agencies.

Beginning in 1951, the government agreed to provide assistance to universities by providing an unconditional subsidy of $0.50 per capita, while in 1957, the Canada Council was founded.

Quebec, under Duplessis' leadership, headed the opposition to this new national policy. With an unbelievable obstinacy, Duplessis held out despite the fact his actions deprived the province of millions of dollars each year that could have been obtained by accepting Ottawa's tax agreements and conditional subsidies. Donald Smiley estimates that in 1959-60, Quebec lost $82,031,000 or $15.60 per capita as a direct result of its opposition to Ottawa.

In turn, it opposed repatriation of the Constitution and the amending formula that was worked out in 1950. In 1951, it agreed to an amendment on old age pensions but obtained recognition of provincial legislative priority that would prove very useful to Lesage when Quebec created its own pension plan. In 1952, after accepting the federal subsidy to universities for one year, Quebec reversed its stance and touched off a major controversy. P.E. Trudeau himself was a defender of provincial autonomy in the area of education. In 1953, he set up a Royal Commission on the constitutional problems that would help to crystallize and reinforce opposition to the new federalism It was also at the urging of the Chairman of this Commission, Judge T. Tremblay, who was a personal friend of Duplessis, that Duplessis decided in 1953 to levy a provincial income tax. Prime Minister Saint-Laurent realized that the conflict over fiscal autonomy had spilled out of government offices into the streets. Until a compromise could be reached between Quebec City and Ottawa, Quebec residents would be subjected to double taxation, and the electorate would have to decide which government was in the wrong. In a famous speech in Valleyfield on September 26, Duplessis explained in simple terms why he was fighting so tenaciously. After first stressing the importance of revenue to ensure Quebec's development, he explained why Quebec should never accept the substitution of grants for taxation powers essential to responsible governments. Continuing, he explained that in addition to this reason , which was valid for all governments, Quebec was a province unlike the others. After recalling the poor treatment of French-speaking Canadians outside Quebec, he declared that "the best means of obtaining justice is through a government in which we are a majority. Do you think that we would have justice in a government in which we were a minority?" Although the new federal policy might suit English Canada, Duplessis believed it was unacceptable for Quebec, and added:

> We will never accept it. Why should we accept
> it? We would be replacing ropes with handcuffs.
> To accept it would be to replace a strong and
> lively future for our province with a federal
> oxygen tent. To accept it would be to replace
> our right of ownership, our control of our life
> in all fields with the title and function of a
> pensioner.

Shortly after, negotiations began between Saint-Laurent and
Duplessis. The latter had to withdraw from his income tax bill the
untenable assertion that the province had priority in the field of
direct taxes; he also had to cut the reduction that taxpayers could
obtain from the federal government from 15 to 10 per cent. Despite
all this, Duplessis still won a very large political victory and was
solidly supported by public opinion in Quebec. In 1957, the new
fiscal accords ended financial discrimination against provinces
not agreeing to hand over their major direct taxes. Not only did
Ottawa have to show more generosity towards all provinces, but a
method of equalization was also drawn up which constituted a major
step forward for Canadian federalism.

To his very death, Duplessis remained firmly opposed to federal
subsidies to universities. In 1959-60, the Diefenbaker government
negotiated the first "opting-out" **agreement with** Duplessis' successors.
The Quebec government obtained another corporate income tax point for
subsidies to universities.

Despite all the numerous, justified criticisms that could be
levelled at Duplessis and his regime, he won a fairly important
victory on the constitutional level. He was a particularly clever
politician, capable of communicating his message to the people. He
forced the liberal opposition that had attacked his autonomist views
to sit up and take notice.

It is certain, and I insist on this point, that Duplessis alone
certainly could never have succeeded. The issue of autonomy involves
deep-seated aspects of Quebec's history and is based on solid founda-
tions which also explain the Quiet Revolution, the veto of the Victoria
Charter and the rise to power of the Parti Québécois.

Nor is there any doubt that although federal dominance was
lessened, this was also due to the actions of the other provinces and
other regions of the country as well as to the political and economic
situation in the world in the 1950s.

Ottawa realized that its Keynesian policy had not worked as
planned. The overall policies of the federal government had a negative
impact on some regions, some economic sectors and some social groups.
The stabilization policy demanded a great deal of courage among
politicians as well as close co-ordination between the various levels
of government in the area of public investment. By the end of the
1950s, rising unemployment and inflation had harmed the credibility
of the federal policy. The growing role of natural resources and the

weight of American interests gave new strategic importance to the
provinces. Furthermore, in order to adjust its economic policy,
Ottawa increasingly required co-operation from the provinces.

VI   FROM COOPERATION TO CONFRONTATION, 1960-76

It is in this context that the Quiet Revolution began in
Quebec. Under Jean Lesage, the liberals continued Duplessis' autonomist policy. In contrast, however, the liberals decided to make major
reforms to the economic, social and cultural sectors. The government
became the favoured instrument for giving Quebec's people some control
over their development and their province. The liberals surrounded
themselves with many competent civil servants. The reforms undertaken
became a large burden, especially since the province had to make up
for lost time. Taxes increased, the public debt rose and an effort
was made to obtain the maximum funds available from Ottawa. In the
area of federal-provincial relations, the liberals abandoned the
doctrinaire and legalistic attitude of Duplessis in favour of a
pragmatic approach. Quebec attempted to move into all sectors that
fell under provincial jurisdiction and also showed interest in sectors
that had been neglected, such as immigration and international relations.
It even asked the federal government to consult the provinces before
making decisions in areas under its jurisdiction but which might have
repercussions on the provinces. The Quebec government, with facts
and figures to back it up, pointed out that the issues coming under
provincial jurisdiction should receive priority. The liberals accepted,
with reservations, the conditional subsidies in almost all fields and
participated in cost-sharing programs. They actively participated
in federal-provincial conferences and an ever-increasing number of
committees. After 1960, they even revived the long-abandoned tradition
of interprovincial conferences.

The impact of the Quiet Revolution was all the greater because
it was originally well-received in the rest of Canada and coincided
on several levels with similar movements in other provinces except,
of course, with respect to its nationalist dimension.

The various federal governments between 1960 and 1968 were not
in a strong position as had been the governments of King and Saint-
Laurent. Under Diefenbaker, the provinces considerably improved their
position in the fiscal field and the federal government, through its
lack of leadership, left increasing numbers of initiatives up to the
provinces. Pearson's arrival bore some promise for Quebec at least.
Through political necessity, but also through temperament, Pearson
was ready to negotiate a "new deal" between French and English Canadians

But Pearson, who had been in Ottawa for many years, still believed in the ideals of the new national policy. He was ready to make concessions to Quebec but wanted the federal government to stay closely in touch with the people. He therefore promised the establishment of a health insurance plan, showed interest in the Canada Pension Plan, created a municipal borrowing fund, instituted loans to students, extended family allowance to those 16 and 17 year-olds still in school, etc. He attempted to mobilize the population around the war against poverty and regional disparities.

During this period, Quebec was unquestionably in a position to exert its power in all traditional sectors as well as in the grey areas. Also, as a result primarily of the "opting-out" formula negotiated in 1964, it enjoyed much greater fiscal flexibility than the other provinces. However, the impression persists that the federal government continued to enter more and more sectors. Co-operative federalism had evolved into competitive federalism. Nor had Pearson lost sight of certain major "national objectives" such as a Canadian flag, repatriation of the Constitution and development of an amending formula.

In 1963-64, a spectacular break-through appeared to occur with the opting-out formula and the Quebec pension plan. In return, Lesage appeared to be ready to accept the Fulton-Favreau formula. But the nationalist movement was growing in strength and Lesage was forced to step back.

English Canada began to worry about events in Quebec and had difficulty understanding the accelerated and turbulent growth. There was concern over the special status that Quebec was in the process of obtaining, over the Quebec people's ambitions, their nationalism, and the first bombs exploding.

In 1965, the three doves, Marchand, Pelletier and Trudeau, entered the federal arena...to save federalism. Ottawa slowly took hold of itself, refuted the two-nations formula, the associated states proposal, and special status. Opting-out was severely criticized, and it was time to apply the brakes. Quebec would be treated like the other provinces, even if this required granting the other provinces certain privileges granted to Quebec. Obviously, the other provinces had no objection.

The rise to power of the Union Nationale under Daniel Johnson, who had just published the manifesto, Equality or Independence, failed to solve a thing. He called for a new constitution based on

the principle of two nations and wanted a greater share of direct
taxes for Quebec, which Ottawa refused to accept. Quebec's international presence and de Gaulle's cry of "Vive le Québec libre"
hardened positions on both sides.

Trudeau's ascendancy in 1968 singularly aggravated the debate.
In some circles he was seen as a saviour who could put Quebec in its
place.

Trudeau's credo in power could be briefly summarized as follows:
on the constitutional level, Quebec must be a province like the others
and the federal government is the government of all Canadians,
including those who live in Quebec; Canada needs a strong central
government that is in direct contact with its population; what Canada
needs is a bilingualism and biculturalism policy; we must fight, if
not expose, Quebec's nationalism on its homeground. All these symbolic
battles, all the intrusions and manipulations of both governments
over the past ten years which provoked a polarisation between federalists
and independentists in Quebec culminated in the October Crisis.

After ruling out revision of the constitution, the federal
government decided instead to bend. But it had made careful preparations, as demonstrated by the series of white papers published
between 1968 and 1970. Three years of work and negotiations culminated
in the 1971 Victoria Charter proposals. Even staunch federalists
such as Claude Castonguay and Robert Bourassa could not agree to
this Charter despite acceptance by all the other provinces. One must
carefully read the opening statement by Robert Bourassa in Victoria
on June 14 to understand why Quebec was so insistent on the decentralized
federalism. Claude Castonguay carried the argument even further in a
speech on June 7, 1972:

> In Quebec in 1972, nationalism is an example of
> realism, of sentiment, of course, but of reason as
> well. It simply demonstrates that groups of men,
> those who make up governments among others, assume
> a continuity between ways of living, a way of speaking
> and rational planning of the techniques and resources
> available. When we in Quebec plead for coherent
> policies, we also defend the coherence of our society
> and culture. We defend the right to our own
> priorities, the right to do things in our own way,
> the right to combine our values and our tasks,
> particularly in the fields that affect us most or
> which are basic to achieving the social rights for
> our collective future (...)

> I have already said, and I repeat, that I am
> convinced that the coherence required to govern
> Quebec is not incompatible with that required
> to govern Canada. Provided, however, that we
> agree that Quebec constitutes a social and
> cultural reality distinct from the rest of
> Canada, a reality that needs a sufficient
> framework for its development in terms of
> political and power structures to ensure for
> Quebec's citizens the maintenance of a dynamic
> and vigorous society and also the satisfaction
> of their basic needs. (unofficial translation)

From 1971 to 1975, the constitutional issues stagnated.
However, the Quebec government slowly succeeded in explaining its
point of view to premiers of the other provinces, particularly during
the interprovincial conferences. In 1975, the federal government
again took up the fight for repatriation. In November, after
individual consultation with the premiers, the federal government
suggested a few amendments to the Victoria Charter which tended to
lessen Quebec's opposition on linguistic guarantees. Following this,
in 1976, Trudeau defined his position: repatriation first, then
discussion on the distribution of powers; he even mentioned the
possibility of acting unilaterally if the provinces could not agree.
The Bourassa government declared its staunch opposition and discreetly
obtained the support of several provincial premiers. From August 18
to 20, the provincial premiers met at Banff, and Premier Lougheed
announced that his government would officially ask that Alberta be
given a right of veto, along with Ontario and Quebec, in the amending
formula. The provincial premiers met again on October 1 and 2 in
Toronto and succeeded in reaching a certain consensus on several
points, as can be seen in a letter from Premier Lougheed to Prime
Minister Trudeau on October 14:

> All provinces agreed with the objective of
> patriation. They also agreed that patriation
> should not be undertaken without a consensus
> being developed on an expansion of the role
> of the provinces and/or jurisdiction in the
> following areas: culture, communications,
> Supreme Court of Canada, spending power, senate
> representation and regional disparities.

No unanimous decision was reached on the amending formula.
British Columbia wanted to be considered as a distinct region and
have the right of veto, as did Quebec and Ontario. Alberta, in turn,

wanted the veto on ownership of natural resources. Finally, Premier Lougheed mentioned the points where a consensus existed among the provinces: they wish to play a larger role in immigration; they agree on linguistic rights; they wish to see the provinces' taxation rights reinforced for their natural resources; the power of proclamation must be limited; the new constitution must provide for at least one conference of the eleven first ministers each year; the creation of a new province must occur through constitutional amendment. Finally, Premier Lougheed mentioned other points (cultural affairs, communications, Supreme Court, spending power, Senate, regional disparities and equalization) which did not have unanimous approval but still were the subject of some agreement.

The direction of the letter is very clear: 1) the provinces wish to discuss the distribution of power and repatriation at the same time; 2) the new constitution must respect provincial autonomy. In part, this repeats the demands made by Quebec over several years and extensively reverses or opposes the constitutional strategy developed since 1968 by the federal government.

This bourgeoning consensus among the provinces is not coincidental. Since the end of the 1950s, the provinces have recouped many initiatives. Provincial and municipal public spending have grown spectacularly when compared to Ottawa's (see Appendix 1).

The increased strategic importance of natural resources, particularly of oil, has provoked a serious crisis involving Ottawa and two of the Western provinces.

Federalism, at first co-operative, then competitive, has resulted in acute problems. The conditional subsidies entail many disadvantages, and the cost-sharing programs have become so expensive and restrictive for the federal government that it has attempted to withdraw from them, despite the protests of the provinces. The overlapping of federal and provincial programs constitutes a source of waste and frustration.

The provinces are generally discontented with the federal government's economic management and want more control over their development. They are convinced that they know better the needs of their population than politicians in Ottawa. The provinces have finally accepted equalization and the importance of reducing regional disparities. They have learned to collaborate with each other: interprovincial conferences, regional conferences in the West and the Maritimes. The provinces' desire for autonomy is based on a deep-rooted regionalism that is a basic fact of federal Canada and that was far too often neglected in the 1940s and 1950s.

As Canada's provinces and regions have matured, so has Quebec. The balance of power in Quebec has changed profoundly since 1968, and the emergence of the Parti Québécois has given a voice to those Quebecers who wish to manage their own affairs. A growing number of them are rejecting dependence, collective welfare and perpetual guerilla warfare with Ottawa. The real bargaining between Quebec and Canada will soon begin.

Comments by S. Ryerson, Department of History,
University of Quebec at Montreal

Lester Pearson stated in 1964 that Quebec is, in a sense, the homeland of a people. Surely it is just this peculiar dynamic of two nation-communities evolving within the structure of one state, of regionalisms evolving within the framework of empire, that has led to our present impasse of conflict, deadlock and frustration. My reservations regarding Professor Durocher's survey should perhaps be directed against a more general tendency, common amongst historiographers, to view historical events as if they were reduceable to stages in a totally self-contained and self-propelling unilinear development. This predisposition has led Durocher to overlook an important relationship between property and power.

Current democratic theory, except for some analyses of interest groups, takes little account of business enterprise. Government must consider the needs and preferences of large corporations no less than the wishes of its citizens, yet corporations wield greater political clout than ordinary men on the street. As Lindblom says:

> It has been a curious feature of democratic thought that it has not faced up to the private corporation as a peculiar organization in an ostensible democracy. Disproportionately powerful, the large corporation fits oddly into democratic theory and vision.[1]

Indeed, it does not fit, but its role in our current crisis must be viewed within the context of our colonial past.

In their paper on "The Roots of Discontent," Professors Evenson and Simeon stress the importance of specifying what our current crisis is not. Professor Durocher seems to share their belief that the fundamental social and economic order of Canadian society is not at issue. He views the current unrest as a political crisis in which government institutions and mechanisms are under attack. This is probably true to the extent that most things pass through the filter of government, but that filter is not the totality of the social organism. I would suggest that "the roots of discontent" are more easily scrutinized in the interweaving of socio-economic inequality and ethnic cleavage.

Lord Durham had little doubt that French Canadians would eventually abandon their nationalistic yearnings and begin to mingle

---

1 Charles Lindblom, Politics and Markets: The World's Political Economic Systems (New York, Basic, 1977), p.356.

with the English, if only to better themselves economically. Those
who were unable, or unwilling, to fraternize in this way would be
reduced to labourers in the employ of English capitalists. Thus,
many French Canadians were doomed to occupy inferior positions and
to be dependent upon the English for employment. There is both a
sting and a warning in the following statement by Durham.

> The evils of poverty and dependence would
> merely be aggravated in a tenfold degree
> by a spirit of jealous and resentful
> nationality, which should separate the
> working class of the community from the
> possessors of wealth and employers of
> labour.[2]

This statement anticipates the October Crisis by focusing on the
three areas of property, private business and labour in which the
basic structure of inequality between the two nation-communities of
British America was so blatantly expressed. The resulting ethnic
cleavage has encumbered the evolution of federal state structures
and contributed in no small measure to the current crisis in their
development.

Durocher concludes that "the real negotiations between Quebec
and Canada are about to begin," and that "the new Quebec Government
is now actively participating in the elaboration of what might become
a new federalism." If a truly new and satisfactory federal structure
is to emerge from these negotiations, they will have to encompass,
what I would call, the basic equivocation of 1867. On the one hand,
Canada professes to be an equal partnership of peoples; on the other
hand, the assumptions underlying this structure of equality appear
to be triple-mortgaged, not only by our constitutional insufficiencies
and the reality of our social, economic and ethnic situation, but by
the underlying fact that these impediments are intimately related to
an industrial revolution that began in the workshops of Britain, the
country that defeated France in the Seven Years War and annexed Canada.
Thus, the Conquest and the Industrial Revolution are themselves equal
partners in a pattern of equivocation that has become intolerably
frustrating because of its pretensions to be something that it is not.

If the sixth man in the Cross Kidnapping is identified as a
police *provocateur* we may have to reassess the October Crisis as an
act of desperation designed, not to snuff out the flames of separation,
but to head off the possibility of a restructuring of Confederation
which would overcome the equivocation of 1867, pay off our historical

---

2   Sir C.P. Lucas (ed.), Lord Durham's Report on the Affairs of British
    North America, Vol.I: Text of the Report (Oxford at the Clarendon
    Press, 1912), p.293.

triple mortgage and establish our two nation-communities on a truly
equal footing. This is a disquieting scenario because of its
implications for American investment and for the structure of private
business and property; we note that some sixty corporations control
sixty-two per cent of the industrial output of Quebec. However, this
is part of the anatomy of the social and economic structure of Canada.
We must take into account the physiology and,especially, the pathology
of this structure as we begin to deal with our present crisis.

LIST OF PARTICIPANTS

Mr. A. Alexandroff
Queen's University
Kingston

Mr. George Anderson
Federal Provincial
 Relations Office
Ottawa

Professor H. Bakvis
Queen's University
Kingston

M. Claude Beauchamp
Le Soleil
Québec

Monsieur Gérard Bélanger
C. D. Howe Research Institute
Montréal

Professor D. Blake
University of British Columbia
Vancouver, B.C.

Mr. D. Brown
Queen's University
Kingston

Monsieur Jean Chapdelaine
Ministère des Affaires
 intergouvernementales
Québec

Mme. Solange Chaput-Rolland
Task Force on Canadian Unity
Ottawa

Professor A. Corry
Queen's University
Kingston

Professor T. Courchene
University of Western Ontario
London, Ontario

Monsieur Léon Courville
Ecole des Hautes Etudes
 Commerciales
Montréal

Professor J. de Wilde
Queen's University
Kingston

Mr. Joel Diena
Statistics Canada
Ottawa

Mr. J. Evenson
Queen's University
Kingston

Monsieur Pierre Fréchette
Université du Québec
 à Montréal
Montréal

J. F. Gautrin
Expansion Economic Region
Ottawa

Mr. John Gray
The Citizen
Ottawa

Professor H. Guindon
Concordia University
Montréal

Mr. Richard Gwynn
The Toronto Star
Ottawa

Dr. Michael Jenkin
Science Council of Canada
Ottawa

Mr. William Johnson
The Toronto Globe and Mail
Québec

Mr. Kalmen Kaplansky
International Labour Office
Ottawa

Monsieur Pierre Lamonde
Office de planification
 et de développement
 du Québec
Québec

Monsieur Réjean Landry
Université Laval
Québec

M. R. J. Lévesque
Director
Economic Council of Canada
Ottawa

Professor Richard Lipsey
Queen's University
Kingston

Professor John Meisel
Dept. of Political Studies
Queen's University
Kingston

Mrs. S. Ostry
Chairman
Economic Council of Canada
Ottawa

Ms. C. Pestineau
C. D. Howe Research Institute
Montréal

Mr. D. Slater
Director
Economic Council of Canada
Ottawa

Professor D. Soberman
Queen's University
Kingston

Monsieur Pierre Tremblay
Le Droit
Ottawa

Professor J. Whyte
Queen's University
Kingston

LIST OF AUTHORS

Mr. L. Auer
Economic Council of Canada
Ottawa

M. R. Durocher
Universite de Montréal
Montréal

Mr. T. Hazledine
Economic Council of Canada
Ottawa

Mr. W. P. Irvine
Queen's University
Kingston

M. R. Lacroix
Université de Montréal
Montréal

Mr. P. Leslie
Queen's University
Kingston

M. F. Martin
Université de Montréal
Montréal

Mr. B. MacDonald
Economic Council of Canada
Ottawa

Mr. K. Norrie
University of Alberta
Edmonton

M. Y. Rabeau
Université de Montréal
Montréal

Mr. G. Rawlyk
Queen's University
Kingston

Mr. R. Simeon
Queen's University
Kingston

LIST OF DISCUSSANTS

Mr. R. Boadway
Queen's University
Kingston

M. B. Bonin
Ministères des Affaires
  intergouvernementales
Québec

Dr. V. Corbo
Concordia University
Montréal

Mr. H. C. Eastman
University of Toronto
Toronto

M. P. Fortin
Université de Montréal
Montréal

Mr. P. Gunther
Task Force on Canadian Unity
Ottawa

Mr. K. Z. Paltiel
Carleton University
Ottawa

Mr. D. Perry
Canadian Tax Foundation
Toronto

Mr. S. Roberts
Canada-West Foundation
Calgary

Mr. S. Ryerson
Université du Québec à
  Montréal
Montréal

Professor D. Usher
Queen's University
Kingston

Mr. M. A. Walker
The Fraser Institute
Vancouver

STAFF

B. Guitard
Economic Council of Canada
Ottawa

E. Nyberg
Economic Council of Canada
Ottawa

K. Mills
Economic Council of Canada
Ottawa

N. Swan
Economic Council of Canada
Ottawa

A. Moroz
Economic Council of Canada
Ottawa

M. Vastel
Economic Council of Canada
Ottawa

H. Bradley
Carleton University
Editorial Service
Ottawa